Psychology and the Aging Revolution

Psychology and the Aging Revolution

How We Adapt to Longer Life

Edited by
Sara Honn Qualls and Norman Abeles

American Psychological Association
Washington, DC

Published by
American Psychological Association
750 First Street, NE
Washington, DC 20002

Copies may be ordered from
APA Order Department
P.O. Box 92984
Washington, DC 20090-2984

In the U.K., Europe, Africa, and the Middle East, copies may be ordered from
American Psychological Association
3 Henrietta Street
Covent Garden, London
WC2E 8LU England

Typeset in Goudy by EPS Group Inc., Easton, MD

Printer: United Book Press, Baltimore, MD
Cover Designer: NiDesign, Baltimore, MD
Production Editor: Kristine Enderle

The opinions and statements published are the responsibility of the authors, and such opinions and statements do not necessarily represent the policies of the APA.

Library of Congress Cataloging-in-Publication Data
Psychology and the aging revolution : how we adapt to longer life / edited by Sara Honn Qualls, Norman Abeles.—1st ed.
        p. cm.
    Includes bibliographical references and index.
    ISBN 1-55798-707-6 (alk. paper)
        1. Aging—Psychological aspects.   2. Aging.   3. Aged—Psychology.
    I. Qualls, Sara Honn.   II. Abeles, Norman.

    BF724.55.A35 P794 2000
    155.67—dc21

                                                                                00-036265

British Library Cataloguing-in-Publication Data
A CIP record is available from the British Library.

Printed in the United States of America
First Edition

CONTENTS

CONTRIBUTORS

Norman Abeles, PhD, Department of Psychology, Michigan State University, East Lansing

Marilyn S. Albert, PhD, Department of Psychiatry, Massachusetts General Hospital, Boston

James E. Birren, PhD, UCLA Center on Aging, Los Angeles

Neil Charness, PhD, Department of Psychology, Florida State University, Tallahassee

Margaret Gatz, PhD, Department of Psychology, University of Southern California, Los Angeles

Thomas E. Joiner, Jr., PhD, Department of Psychology, Florida State University, Tallahassee

Alfred W. Kaszniak, PhD, Department of Psychology, University of Arizona, Tucson

Bob G. Knight, PhD, Andrus Gerontology Center, University of Southern California, Los Angeles

Jennifer G. La Guardia, MA, Department of Clinical and Social Sciences in Psychology, University of Rochester, Rochester, NY

Robert W. Levenson, PhD, Department of Psychology, University of California, Berkeley

Leah L. Light, PhD, Pitzer College, Claremont, CA

Karen A. Matthews, PhD, Department of Psychiatry, University of Pittsburgh, Pittsburgh, PA

Mary C. Newman, PhD, National Center for Neurogenic Communication Disorders, University of Arizona, Tucson

John C. Norcross, PhD, Department of Psychology, University of Scranton, Scranton, PA

Sara Honn Qualls, PhD, Psychology Department, University of Colorado, Colorado Springs

Karen S. Rook, PhD, Department of Psychology and Social Behavior, University of California, Irvine

Richard M. Ryan, PhD, Department of Psychology, University of Rochester, Rochester, NY

Ilene C. Siegler, PhD, MPH, Department of Psychiatry and Behavioral Sciences, Behavioral Medicine Research Center, Duke University Medical Center, Durham, NC

ACKNOWLEDGMENTS

The editors developed this book from the presentations at the miniconvention "Psychology and the Aging Revolution" at the 105th Annual Convention of the American Psychological Association (APA) in 1997. Two groups contributed substantially to the development of that miniconvention, and we wish to express our appreciation to them for their influence on this volume as well. A small working group was selected from a larger advisory group to assist in implementing the group's many suggestions. The following members of the working group contributed substantially to the structure and content of the miniconvention and, hence, this book: Laura Carstensen, Margaret Gatz, Alfred W. Kaszniak, M. Powell Lawton, and Timothy Salthouse. This group structured the many creative ideas generated by the advisory group (although only a portion of them could be developed in this project). The following served in the advisory group: Laura Carstensen, John Cavanaugh, Susan G. Cooley, Royda Crose, Irene Deitch, Michael Duffy, Barry Edelstein, John Feather, Dolores Gallagher-Thompson, Margaret Gatz, Alfred W. Kaszniak, M. Powell Lawton, Peter Lichtenberg, Mary Mittelman, Timothy A. Salthouse, John Santos, K. Warner Schaie, Michael A. Smyer, George Stricker, George P. Taylor, Linda Teri, Larry W. Thompson, Susan Krauss Whitbourne, Jack G. Wiggins, Paul Wohlford, Rose Zacks, and Steven H. Zarit.

The aim of this book is to continue the dialogue launched in those symposia. Authors are primarily drawn from the presenters, with a few exceptions. However, all of those who contributed to the miniconvention must be acknowledged for adding their spark to the discussions of theory, research, and practice. Finally, the APA has shared the expertise of excellent editors, including Judy Nemes and Kristine Enderle, whose contributions are substantial.

Psychology and the Aging Revolution

1

PSYCHOLOGY AND THE AGING REVOLUTION

SARA HONN QUALLS AND NORMAN ABELES

Is there really such a thing as an *aging revolution*? Consider the facts. At the turn of the century, life expectancy was around 47 years. Children born today can expect to live about 76 years. The fastest growing age group is the oldest-old (over 85 years), and the number of centenarians is increasing particularly rapidly. There were only 37,000 people over age 100 in 1990, but by 2050 an unbelievable 834,000 people over age 100 will be alive (Krach & Velkoff, 1999).

How is this demographic *aging revolution* changing the fabric of society and of individual lives? Every domain of human life is affected. For example, the role of work in the human life span has already changed. Adults now experience a *"third age,"* after retirement, during which they can expect to have 20–30 years for meaningful activities (see chap. 2 of this volume). The average retirement age in the United States is around 63.5 years and is dropping. Economic pressures are pushing for later retirement (e.g., eligibility for full Social Security benefits will be age 67 instead of 65 in the near future), but delays even to age 70 would still leave a rapidly growing postretirement population.

Societal concerns about the economic costs of an aging society have gained widespread media attention, whereas productive uses of the third age are rarely elaborated. Of special concern is escalating health care costs, although some analyses suggest that the aging population may not be driving those increases. For example, the Alliance for Aging Research recently (1998) published a brochure titled *Seven Deadly Myths: Uncovering the Facts About the High Cost of the Last Year of Life*, which examines the notion that the growth in the number of older people in this country has been the major cause of increases in health care costs. The brochure points out that, to the contrary, researchers have found that general price inflation, rather than inflation specific to health expenditures, was the principal detriment of rising health care costs. Indeed, the Alliance for Aging Research contends that an aging society is less of an economic factor than previously presumed, yet we can assume that the debate about social and economic impacts of the aging revolution will continue.

Far less media attention has been granted to the positive potentials of the aging revolution. What contributions can this booming population of older adults make to society? Key to imaging the possibilities is a clear perception of older adults' capabilities. Psychologists are playing a integral role in defining how functional capacities change with advancing age and how aging may foster positive characteristics (e.g., wisdom and emotional maturity) that may be useful. The common perception that aging is a period of inevitable decline, significant chronic illness, and loss of meaningful roles is simply wrong. Although the balance of gains and losses may tip in favor of losses, older adults clearly engage in proactive strategies for shaping their lives in meaningful ways (Baltes & Baltes, 1990).

Even the commonly held presumption that all of us will age within a context of serious chronic illness is now being brought into question. Within two decades scientific advances are expected to dramatically decrease the rate of serious illness in older adults. In his book, *The Road to 2015*, Peterson (1994) suggested that by 2015 we will have found a cure for cancer and will have artificial organs made from human tissue for all except the brain and the central nervous system. He also noted that scientists are very close to claiming the use of genetically engineered drugs to prevent paralysis due to spinal cord injury such that by 2020 there will be few, if any, cases of paraplegia or quadriplegia. Data from the National Long-Term Care Survey already indicate a decline in the rates of serious illness in older adults, with the most significant declines occurring for the oldest-old (Manton, Corder, & Stallard, 1993). If this trend is sustained, it may have a significant impact on health care costs, quality of life, and the meaning of aging.

Psychology must and will play a meaningful role in describing and explaining age changes in psychological and social functioning. Interventions (preventative as well as treatment) to improve quality of life will rely heavily on what psychologists learn about neuropsychology, cognition, and emotion, among other topics. Future projections suggest that low-technology preventative and supportive interventions, such as those initiated by psychologists, will play a significant role in improving quality of life (Cohen, 1994).

How has the field of psychology responded to the aging revolution thus far? Organizational responses and scientific advances are both visibly affecting society's views of aging. Within the American Psychological Association (APA), 1997 was an important year, because its president, Norman Abeles, focused his initiatives on aging (Abeles, 1997). Two task forces were appointed. One produced a brochure (*What Practitioners Should Know About Working With Older Adults*; Abeles et al., 1998) designed to give psychologists and other health care providers appropriate information to guide their work with older adults. (This brochure was later published in the October 1998 issue of *Professional Psychology*.) The second task force produced *Guidelines for the Evaluation of Dementia and Age-Related Cognitive Decline* (APA Presidential Task Force on the Assessment of Age-Consistent Memory Decline and Dementia, 1998). In addition, the Committee on Aging was established by the Council of Representatives to oversee aging-related activities within APA. Its broad agenda includes scientific issues, practice concerns, policy matters, educational concerns, and public interest matters. In response to the need to recognize the special skills needed by practitioners who work with older adults, clinical geropsychology was approved as a clinical proficiency by the APA Council of Representatives, and groups are working to develop mechanisms for practitioners to acquire proficiency certification.

Psychology's scholarly response to the aging revolution has been even stronger over a period of many decades. Every subdiscipline within psychology has examined how aging changes basic human processes (e.g., cognition, emotion, social relationships). The chapters that follow describe some of the most exciting theoretical, empirical, and applied scholarship that will contribute to the understanding of aging.

Scholars engaged in cutting-edge work within seven domains of psychology were invited to contribute to this volume, which highlights psychology's response to the aging revolution. Within the various subdisciplines are contributions from major figures in geropsychology as well as leaders in the subdiscipline whose work holds exciting opportunities to look at aging through different theoretical lenses than have typically been used in geropsychology.

The book begins with a provocative essay on the meaning of an extended life span. James E. Birren raises important questions about how society needs to alter its view of aging, given the common experience of life into the 80s and beyond. How can, and should, we use this "gift of long life" to maximize its value for older adults and society? What will psychology contribute to social efforts to benefit from the aging revolution? Scholars are addressing these questions in all subdisciplines of psychology.

The book proceeds to explore research on three basic psychological processes: neuropsychological functioning, memory, and emotion. Next, two domains of psychological functioning that take on particular importance in later life—social relationships and health—are explored. One domain of problematic functioning, depression, is examined in some depth because of the many myths that purport its high prevalence among older adults. Finally, one applied area of psychology—psychotherapy—is examined for its contributions.

Neuropsychology and related fields in neuroscience represent one of the hotbeds of scholarship in psychology generally and within aging in particular. Coming from different theoretical traditions, neuropsychological research and cognitive aging research have experienced a dynamic interplay that has enriched both fields. Nowhere is this more evident than in the investigation of age-related changes in cognition and memory. The process of distinguishing between normal aging and effects of diseases that commonly occur in old age (e.g., dementia) has propelled theory and research in both neuropsychology and cognitive aging. Two outstanding neuropsychologists (Marilyn S. Albert and Alfred W. Kaszniak; along with his colleague Mary C. Newman) who have contributed heavily to these fields describe the interplay between them in chapters 3 and 4.

Research on memory represents one of the most prolific streams of investigation in the psychology of aging. Perhaps memory has received so much attention because memory problems represent a commonly feared component of normal aging and one of the most feared diseases associated with age: dementia. Or, perhaps it is the rapidly growing sophistication of empirical research techniques that have propelled the field forward so rapidly. The research literature on this topic is complex, making it difficult to state generalizations about the effects of age on memory. Leah L. Light (chap. 5) elegantly details the main lines of research in memory and aging, culminating in a summary of what is and is not known and of what frameworks appear to be most fruitful for organizing the complex data. On a different tack, Neil Charness (chap. 6) describes a program of research that addresses the exciting question of how people adapt to cognitive deterioration through alternative-skill acquisition. Given our knowledge that many cognitive skills deteriorate with advanced age, compensatory mechanisms are of great importance to older adults. Charness uses chess as a model of a highly complex skill that can grow with advancing age through the use of alternative cognitive skills that reduce reliance on cognitive efficiency.

Emotion is another particularly exciting area in psychology, and the field of aging has contributed significantly to a life span perspective on emotional functioning. Robert W. Levenson (chap. 7) describes key findings about the relationship between age and emotion. Taking a developmental perspective on the entire life span, Levenson examines emerging emotional capacities from childhood through later life. Emotion represents a basic psychological function that may continue to grow and mature throughout the life span, bringing emerging capacities in old age that our families and society need to use.

Although aging is often viewed primarily as a time of social loss, scholars specializing in social relationships offer other theoretical perspectives on how social relationships function for older adults. Richard M. Ryan and Jennifer G. La Guardia (chap. 8) consider how developmental changes across the life span, including aging, are expected to influence social motivations and subsequent social behavior. Karen S. Rook (chap. 9) examines motivational and other variables that influence adaptation to undesired and unpredictable social losses that often accompany old age. The authors of both chapters push current theoretical frameworks to consider how aging challenges the ability of the theories to examine human behavior.

Health is another domain of human functioning that dramatically affects, and is affected by, aging. Many chronic illnesses are increasingly probable with advancing age (e.g., cardiovascular disease, dementia) yet are certainly not synonymous with aging. What characterizes people who are most at risk? What can people do to prevent, manage, or cope with disease well? What is "excellent health" in advanced old age? Ilene C. Siegler (chap. 10) and Karen A. Matthews (chap. 11) respond to the challenge of differentiating the core questions, methods, and contributions of two fields that address health and aging. Behavioral medicine and health psychology have developed as independent fields whose research is intricately interrelated. How are the fields shaping each other? What can both fields contribute to scholarship on adult development and aging? Siegler and Matthews take readers on a tour of another exciting research area that is changing views about aging.

One of the persistent myths about aging is that most older adults experience clinical depression. Recent epidemiological studies have firmly dispelled those myths and moved us to focus on who is at risk for depression and why. Thomas E. Joiner (chap. 12) takes a broad view of the entire field of depression research to categorize risk factors for depression, a source of suffering and impairment across age groups. He raises interesting questions about how cognitive, interpersonal, and personality characteristics can place a person at risk for depression. Margaret Gatz (chap. 13) focuses on how depression may be distinctive in later life. Are the risk factors for depression the same in older and younger adults? Do the same mechanisms work to cause depression at all stages of the life span? What interventions are known to prevent and treat depression in older adults?

Psychotherapy is a rapidly evolving field that is witnessing dramatic changes in its financial and organizational contexts. Two scholars of psychotherapy, John C. Norcross and Bob G. Knight, collaborated to identify several major shifts in the way psychotherapy is practiced (chap. 14). For example, under the spector of managed care psychotherapists are forced to rely on brief-intervention models. Furthermore, despite the proliferation of new therapies that are tested in increasingly rigorous clinical trials, most practitioners describe themselves as either eclectic or integrative psychotherapists. How do these changes in the field affect the future of psychotherapy research and practice? How have the broader changes in the field affected the practice of psychotherapy with older adults? As we anticipate the aging of the baby boom generation that brings to old age a greater readiness to use psychological services, these issues will require increasing scrutiny by scholars and practitioners alike.

In summary, this book offers an opportunity to peek into the future. How will society handle the aging revolution? Certainly with great reliance on the research and practice of psychologists. The contributors to this volume point the field in important new directions to address some of the most fascinating problems and possibilities that will accrue from the *aging revolution*.

REFERENCES

Abeles, N. (1997). President's report. *American Psychologist, 53*, 154–157.

Abeles, N., Cooley, S., Deitch, I. M., Harper, M. S., Hinrichsen, G., Lopez, M. A., & Molinari V. (1998). *What practitioners should know about working with older adults* [Brochure]. Washington, DC: American Psychological Association.

Alliance for Aging Research. (1998). *Seven deadly myths: Uncovering the facts about the high cost of the last year of life* [Brochure]. Washington, DC: Author.

American Psychological Association Presidential Task Force on the Assessment of Age-Consistent Memory Decline and Dementia. (1998, February). *Guidelines for the evaluation of dementia and age-related cognitive decline*. Washington, DC: American Psychological Association Council of Representatives.

Baltes, P. B., & Baltes, M. M. (1990). *Successful aging: Perspective from the behavioral sciences*. New York: Cambridge University Press.

Cohen, G. (1994). Journalistic elder abuse: It's time to get rid of fictions. Get down to the facts. *The Gerontologists, 34*, 399–401.

Krach, C. A., & Velkoff, V. A. (1999). *Current population reports: Series P23-199RV, Centenarians of the United States*. Washington, DC: U.S. Government Printing Office.

Manton, K. G., Corder, L. S., & Stallard, E. (1993). Estimates of changes in chronic disability and institutional incidence and prevalence rates in the U.S. elderly population from the 1982, 1984, and 1989 National Long Term Care Survey. *Journal of Gerontology: Social Sciences, 48,* S153–S166.

Peterson, J. L. (1994). *The road to 2015: Profiles of the future.* Corte Madera, CA: Waite Group Press.

2

USING THE GIFT OF LONG LIFE: PSYCHOLOGICAL IMPLICATIONS OF THE AGE REVOLUTION

JAMES E. BIRREN

Aging may be the most complex topic mankind is facing in the 21st century. There are important emerging implications for biology, the social sciences, psychology, and philosophy (Binstock & George, 1996; Birren & Schaie, 1996; McFadden, 1996; Schneider & Rowe, 1996). What we refer to as *aging* is a product of a dynamic ecological relationship among heredity, environment, and behavior that has given us a longer and active life (Birren, 1996).

THE GIFT OF LONG LIFE

Never before in recorded history has the average length of life increased as much as it did in the 20th century. In 1900 the average life expectancy was 47 years. The average family disintegrated before the last child left home through the death of one of the parents. Orphans were common, and special institutions—orphanages—were set up to care for them. As the end of the century the life expectancy at birth for men was about 73 years; for women it was 80 years. Parents now can live together long years beyond the empty-nest phase.

In 1900, *retirement* was a word in the dictionary, but it had little practical reality. The average worker died harnessed to a job. If a person retires at age 60 today he or she can easily have 30 years ahead of him or her, a gift of years few of our grandparents saw or had the opportunity of contemplating. In addition to living longer, we are working shorter. One of the shifts in the population has been the drift of older workers away from the labor force. This is adding further years to retirement or other uses for the gift of long life. The *New York Times Magazine* special issue on aging (March 9, 1997) stated that the number of working men over age 65 dropped from 46% in 1950 to 16% in 1993. The number of women dropped from 10% participation to 8%. Obviously, most people over 65 are not working as long as they used to.

The changes in the age structure of society are equally as dramatic as the expanding life expectancy of individuals. People are living longer, having fewer children, and having shorter work lives, and that is changing the society that we have known. The age pyramid of society is turning upside down. This has produced a situation in which the institutional assumptions about the society in which we live are much out of date. Matilda Riley, a senior sociologist at the National Institute on Aging, and her colleagues, called this *institutional lag effects* (Riley, Kahn, & Foner, 1994).

Manton and Stallard (1994) analyzed data on medical demography and reported evidence that life expectancy is being extended not only in the earlier years of life but also in the later years. According to Manton and Stallard, at age 85 we have an additional 6.1 years of life expectancy, with 4.4 years of active life expectancy. In the 1980s the increase was 1.1 years for life expectancy and 1.3 for active life expectancy. In other words, our active life appears to be expanding slightly more at age 85 than our life expectancy. We have more active years to consider as well as more years.

Surprisingly, Manton and Stallard's (1994) data revealed that there was a 2-year greater active-life increase for the people who were highly educated compared to people who had low levels of education. At age 85, in the period 1982–1989, highly educated men had 7.3 years of life expectancy, whereas men with lower levels of education had 4.8 years. At age 85, highly educated women had 10.3 years of life expectancy, and women with less education had 5.6 years. Clearly, educated men and women have longer life expectancies. Thus, the gift of a long and active life favors educated people.

We are all living longer, and educated people are living longer still. The dynamic factors associated with education require study. It isn't likely that a greater number of years of schooling gives extended biological immunity or that the correlates of education and higher income level explain it all. It is likely that the decision styles that develop with higher education maximize both the conservation and uses of personal resources. Highly educated people seek information, discuss it, consult experts, and initiate action (Birren, 1994). On the personal agendas of educated people in particular should be consideration of the question, How do I want to invest my gift of long life?

USING THE GIFT OF LONG LIFE

Psychologists as scientists and professionals should study not only the dynamics of extended life expectancy, but also the issue of how the gift of long life may be used. The English social demographer Peter Laslett (1989) developed the concept of the new "third age" in the population to refer to the emerging new phase of life. We may indeed be facing a new age.

As individuals we likely have out-of-date models of what later life is like and can be like. Our images of old age are often carryovers from our models of grandparents and parents, who lived shorter lives, in different eras, with different demands. Young people often project onto older people more negative views and expectations than do elderly people themselves. The use of the term *greedy geezer* exemplifies this tendency, when in fact surveys show that there are large sums of money and caretaking resources transferred from the retired to the young, from grandparents to grandchildren. The potentials for productive aging surrounding us are large and are just beginning to be recognized (Bass & Caro, 1996).

The entertainment industry continues to portray out-of-date images of elderly people and their lives. It is still focused on the young as it has been in the past, and the mature audience is overlooked. The older audiences get the hand-me-up films and television programs developed for the young market and tend to adopt stereotyped views of old age and its potentials.

How to use our gift of long life is a question facing everyone in developed countries in the 21st century. As individuals we can live out our lives according to some carried-forward model of later life developed from characteristics of people we have known from past generations. However, we can also explore the issue of how we want to use the gift of long life we are facing. How we invest our time, energy, and concerns is as important as balancing our investment portfolios to accumulate money for the retirement years (Birren & Feldman, 1997). In our life portfolios we have creative options of reinvesting the time freed from work and other obligations into further education, friendships, public service, the study of art and music, and recreation. These may add to our physical and mental health and certainly to the pleasure of living long. Adjusting our life portfolios to accommodate our gift of long life is a 21st-century necessity if we are to use well the years we have been given.

LAG EFFECTS

G. S. Hall, an early psychologist and founder of the American Psychological Association, anticipated some of the changes in society. In his 1922 book, he said:

> The time is ripe for some kind of a senescence league of national dimensions which should, of course, establish relations with all existing associations of the old but should slowly develop a somewhat elaborate organization of its own, with committees on finance, on the literature of senescence, including its psychology, physiology, and hygiene, etc. If such an organization under any name were founded, it should certainly have an organ or journal of its own that should be the medium of correspondence, keeping its members informed to date upon all matters of interest or profit to them, perhaps keeping tab on instances of extreme longevity or unusual conservation of energy, with possibly a junior department eventually for youngsters of fifty. (p. 194)

This prophecy was realized in recent years with the spectacular rise of the American Association of Retired Persons' (AARP's) membership to more than 30 million and the similar increase in the readership of its publication *Modern Maturity*, which is now the most widely read magazine in the United States, with more readers than either *TV Guide* or *Reader's Digest*.

It is not my intent here to explore psychology's theoretical legacies that may have lag effects in providing society with the data about human development and aging. We need in other contexts to think about and discuss the contributions and roadblocks introduced by excesses of gestalt psychology, psychoanalysis, behaviorism, cognitive psychology, and other historical orientations that rarely considered the organization of behavior over the life span and certainly not the uses of the gift of long life.

EXPLORING THE MATURE MARKET

Despite the growth of the mature market in numbers and wealth, advertisers have shown a strong lag effect by not approaching the mature market with a high degree of enthusiasm and skill. In his 1999 *New York Times Magazine* article, Jerry Femina wrote, "advertisers know that an older consumer will buy any product that is marketed to a younger consumer. But no self-respecting young person will buy a product aimed at an elderly person," (p. 74). This is a bit overstated, because few people over 50 are lining up to get a pearl in their nose, a tattoo, or the latest rap music.

However, there is an element of truth in the statement, a truth that needs to be explored. If young people get their own things in their own way, why can't older adults as well?

Marketing survey questions are directed at what consumers are likely to spend money for and what kind of advertising will put them into a state of pleasant anticipatory euphoria in which wallets or purses are opened. Exploring the organization of the mature market brings with it some surprises. For me, it came about through interactions with a group of five master's-degree candidates in the School of Management at the University of California, Los Angeles. They had been given a grant to conduct a group project to support the analysis of surveys of the mature market. I served as their outside advisor on the psychology of aging. Available to them were 33 large market segmentation studies, about half of which used demographic characteristics such as age, sex, income, and education as variables. The other half introduced social and psychological concepts, such as life experience and values, that might predict consumer behavior.

In general, the studies identified about five categories of people who make up the mature market. For example, some of the descriptors of the subgroups were the "upbeat enjoyers," the "insecure," the "threatened actives," and the "financial positives." Other descriptors were the "explorers," the "adapters," and the "martyrs." The adapters, for example, were thought to be preoccupied with adjusting to changes in health, money, work, and family life. They were trying to hold onto what they had, whereas the explorers were trying to expand their lives through foreign travel, education, reading, and physical activities. It is interesting that the psychology of personality heavily uses terminology appropriate to the adapters, such as *coping* and *defense mechanisms*, rather than terms of expansion relevant to the explorers. In their meta-analysis of the marketing surveys the students identified what a psychologist was not at all surprised to see: that education was a variable related to the explorers, or "grower" segment of the population. The explorers want to add some new dimensions to life. Perhaps they should be called the "experimental aging," because they actively experiment with life.

One of the features of the mature population is the large number—perhaps a quarter—who believe that the best years of their lives are now and yet to come. They consider themselves lucky. A smaller group is threatened by life in the later years and is just trying to hold on. This analysis, together with other studies, has shown that there are in the population both explorers who are expanding their lives and, at the same time, there are the "retreaters," who are threatened by life, and many others in between, such as conservers and those in need of assistance. Any notion that old age is a single population or a narrowly defined stage of life has to be regarded as a past simplification, reflecting a lag effect of society and a lack of sufficient research in the behavioral sciences. Later life brings with it the probability that an older explorer can open new territories for living in the later years. Personality traits may remain relatively stable with age, but what we do with our personalities, and how we manage our predispositions, can develop with age.

Ethel Percy Andrus founded the AARP after she retired as a high school principal in Los Angeles. In England the novelist Mary Wesley published her first book after age 70 and became a best-selling author. Such persons are late late-life bloomers, and although they may be exceptions they do provide examples of the fact that the course of adult life is not a universal smooth downhill slide or the daily dwindles.

PATTERNS OF LATE-LIFE CHANGE

The topic of patterns of terminal decline is now being dealt with by psychologists who are trying to characterize the patterns of the last years of individuals' lives in longitudinal studies. There are those people who, after living to be 100 or more, step out of life in a brief period of declining function that is not painful, resented, or generative of fear. The proportion of the very old population who step out of life in a quick and easy move is not well known, but if the young population can use a wishful futurity to project themselves into a more tolerable tomorrow, why can't older adults use the probability that they will take a short step out of late life with painless ease and contentment about a long life fully explored and lived?

Young people associate later life with disability and death. The idea of death threatens the dreams of youth. Getting through today when one is young often rests on a confidence that tomorrow will bring greater personal recognition, achievements, and love. Faith in the future is a great mechanism for getting out of a poor or bad today into a better tomorrow. What is not realized is that although the probabilities of death increase with age, they do not represent a smooth declining process for individuals. Late-life dwindles is not a universal model. The existence of late-life bloomers suggests that whereas the Gompertz curve portrays the increasing probability of dying with age, it does not portray the variety of individual courses of life. Some centenarians can maintain full lives and live alone by choice (Perls & Silver, 1999).

WHAT SCIENCE IS TELLING US ABOUT AGING

The gift of long life has come so quickly in the 20th century that societies, institutions, and individuals are surprised. It has come about so quickly that evolution cannot have operated in humankind's favor. It has to have resulted from things that humankind has done to help itself (Rowe & Kahn, 1998). Higher standards of living have minimized seasonal dietary deficiencies, and science has reduced dramatically the direct and indirect effects of infectious diseases. Exercise and food are now accepted as influences on our health. The work of Clive McKay at Cornell University has been known for more than 50 years and shows that underfeeding rats greatly increases their life expectancy. Later, we learned that underfeeding rats delays the onset of diseases to which rats usually succumb. The latter point was not followed up quickly. The scientific question now is, "What is the general mechanism underlying the process?" Oxidants are being implicated. These reactive free radicals are released in the processing of large amounts of food and can damage cellular molecules, including the DNA. Advances in research on oxidative damage led Balin and Vilenchik (1996) to conclude that "observations suggest that a combination of agents, such as selected radioprotectors, which could decrease oxidative stress and increase DNA repair efficiency, might reduce the rate of aging and the risk of common chronic disease synergistically" (p. 246). Here is a basis of an optimistic belief that diseases associated with aging can be further reduced in their consequences and that our general rate of biological aging can be slowed. That leaves the prospect for still further extensions of our life expectancies and more years to invest and explore interesting and productive pursuits (Bass & Caro, 1996).

We have learned from life span identical-twin studies that both heredity and environments play important roles in aging (Pedersen, 1996). Psychology, as a profession and a science, has only begun to scratch the surface of aging as a dynamic ecological process that will continue to change. It is in need of new organizing concepts, metaphors, and new questions whose answers will enable us to understand the organization of behavior and its potentials for facilitating longer and more productive lives. There seems to be little doubt that as psychologists we will have many important things to say about the potential uses of the gift of long life and the dynamics of educated decision making leading to the creation of lives that are most favorable to life satisfaction, contentment, and productivity for self and society.

SUMMARY

The phenomenon we refer to as *aging* appears to be the product of a dynamic ecological relationship among factors of heredity, behavior, and environment. Changes in these relationships have resulted in the gift of long life in the 20th century. We cannot rely on simplistic ideas that aging is all hereditary, all environmental, or all behavioral. It is a dynamic interaction. An important feature of how long and how well we live is our education. It affects our capacity to maximize our personal resources by influencing our daily life decisions. Educated people are more effective agents in determining how long they live and how well they live.

The gift of long life is real and large in the 21st century. We are living longer and more actively. With people living longer and having fewer children, the age pyramid is turning upside down. What used to be the most populous part of society, children, will soon be the smallest. What used to be the smallest part, the population over 65, is becoming the largest.

Every institution in our society—from churches to universities, from entertainment to health services, from department stores to recreation—will be affected by the change in age structure. All professions will experience change as the growing population of elderly people is increasingly served. A broad spectrum of new careers and businesses will emerge as the wants and needs of a mature population are served. Psychology has many important and expanding functions to serve in a maturing society, including exploring the uses of the gift of long life (Beaudreau, Knight, & Greve, 1999).

Psychology appears to be going through a transition from a period in which the components of behavior were the focus of research and teaching careers. The question "How is behavior organized?" is being broadened to the bigger question of "How does behavior become organized and change over the life span?" It seems likely that general psychology and the components of behavior will increasingly be taught in the context of child and adult development and aging.

Pressures are increasing that will encourage the development of psychological measurements to distinguish age-related disease effects from long-term functional adaptations and behavior patterns and risk factors for disabilities. Guidance and therapy for older adults will proceed on an increasingly sophisticated knowledge base using research findings from longitudinal studies and from both neuropsychology and social psychology and our neighbors in other sciences.

A broad spectrum of new careers will emerge as we serve an older society. There is little reason to resist the changes, because they will broaden psychology as a science and as a profession and increase the depth of knowledge and skills psychology can bring to serve an older society. The chapters that follow in this book, from the APA miniconvention on aging, provide windows through which new perspectives on the psychology of adult development and aging can be viewed and clues sought for using to advantage our gift of long life.

REFERENCES

Balin, A. K., & Vilenchik, M. M. (1996). Oxidative damage. In J. Birren (Ed.), *Encyclopedia of gerontology* (pp. 233–246). San Diego, CA: Academic Press.

Bass, S. A., & Caro, F. G. (1996). Theoretical perspectives on productive aging. In W. H. Crown (Ed.), *Handbook on employment and the elderly* (pp. 262–275). Westport, CT: Greenwood Press.

Beaudreau, S. A., Knight, J. A., & Greve, K. W. (1999, August). *Job trends and the future of geropsychology*. Paper presented at the 107th Annual Convention of the American Psychological Association, Boston.

Binstock, R. H., & George, L. K. (Eds.). (1996). *Handbook of aging and the social sciences*. San Diego, CA: Academic Press.

Birren, J. E. (1994). Consumer decision-making and age: Maintaining resources and independence. Boettner Lecture. Philadelphia: Boettner Center of Financial Gerontology, University of Pennsylvania.

Birren, J. E. (Ed.). (1996). *Encyclopedia of gerontology* (2 vols.). San Diego, CA: Academic Press.

Birren, J. E., & Feldman, L. (1997). *Where to go from here*. New York: Simon & Schuster.

Birren, J. E., & Schaie, K. W. (Eds.). (1996). *Handbook of the psychology of aging*. San Diego, CA: Academic Press.

Femina, J. D. (1999, March 9). When will Madison Avenue get it. *New York Times Magazine*, pp. 74–75.

Hall, G. S. (1922). *Senescence*. New York: D. Appleton.

Laslett, P. (1989). *A fresh map of age: The emergence of the third age*. London: Weidenfeld & Nicolson.

Manton, K. G., & Stallard, E. (1994). Medical demography, interaction of disability dynamics and mortality. In L. G. Martin & S. H. Preston (Eds.), *Demography of aging* (pp. 217–278). Washington, DC: National Academy Press.

McFadden, S. H. (1996). Religion, spirituality and aging. In J. E. Birren & K. W. Schaie (Eds.), *Handbook of the psychology of aging* (pp. 162–177). San Diego, CA: Academic Press.

New York Times Magazine. (1997, March 9). The age boom [special issue].

Pedersen, N. L. (1996). Gerontological behavioral genetics. In J. E. Birren & K. W. Schaie (Eds.), *Handbook of the psychology of aging* (pp. 59–77). San Diego, CA: Academic Press.

Perls, T. T., & Silver, M. H. (1999). *Living to 100*. New York: Basic Books.

Riley, M. W., Kahn, R. L., & Foner, A. (Eds.). (1994). *Age and structural lag*. New York: Wiley.

Rowe, J. W., & Kahn, R. L. (1998). *Successful aging*. New York: Pantheon.

Schneider, E. L., & Rowe, J. W. (Eds.). (1996). *Handbook of the biology of aging*. San Diego, CA: Academic Press.

I

NEUROPSYCHOLOGY AND COGNITIVE AGING

PART I: NEUROPSYCHOLOGY AND COGNITIVE AGING

The benefits of an inherently comparative (animal) science that links psychological functioning to biological processes are immense. Nevertheless, we are constantly challenged by clinical cases that are more complex than our theories presume. Both chapters in this section link biological, clinical, and cognitive research efforts to advance our state of knowledge. Should the majority of our research efforts and research funding be devoted to interdisciplinary undertakings, or should we recognize that there may be value in more clearly differentiated inquiries? Alfred W. Kaszniak and Mary C. Newman note the heuristic potential for neuropsychological models of cognitive aging and cite the right-hemisphere hypothesis and the frontal-system hypotheses as examples of current theorizing that involve neurobiologic, neuropsychological, and novel experimental cognitive research efforts. Marilyn S. Albert describes changes in brain structure in early Alzheimer's disease as a likely explanation for memory problems in older adults and discusses the interaction between our knowledge of cognitive aging and our understanding of the basic components of the memory system.

Neuroscience is one of the fastest growing areas in our discipline. Even the popular press frequently highlights the exciting findings from neuroscience (e.g., *Time* and *Newsweek* and TV news magazines regularly describe research on brain–behavior relationships). What are the implications for the structure of our discipline with the rapid emergence of neuroscience in the area of training, the emergence of a significant number of new scientific journals, and the development of numerous neuroscience organizations? Will this field force or reshape the disciplines as we regularly cross traditional disciplinary lines to move our investigations forward?

The dialogue between neuropsychology and cognitive aging research has been rich and productive. Well-established findings about cognitive decline with age are now being re-examined using new measures and new understandings of the role of specific brain structures. Such findings have shaped dramatically the theories used to explain age-related deterioration in cognition and memory. These chapters highlight some of the key points of interaction between the fields, offering evidence of the tremendous benefit of dialogue between disciplines. The demographic explosion of the aging revolution may have met its match in the scientific explosion that happens when neuropsychology and cognitive aging inform each other.

—

3

NEUROPSYCHOLOGY AND COGNITIVE AGING: WHAT HAVE WE TAUGHT EACH OTHER?

MARILYN S. ALBERT

In 1957, Scoville and Milner described a patient who had undergone surgery for treatment of epilepsy. Brain tissue was removed from a selected region in both hemispheres of the patient's brain (the medial temporal lobe) to remove damaged tissue that was the primary source of his seizures (Scoville & Milner, 1957). The extensive neuropsychological evaluation of this patient (patient H. M.) convincingly demonstrates that the ability to acquire new memories was a distinct mental ability that was separable from other perceptual and cognitive functions (Corkin, 1984; Milner, 1972; Milner, Corkin, & Teuber, 1968).

These neuropsychological studies revealed that patient H. M. had a normal IQ and retained his premorbid personality but experienced a profound deficit in retaining memory for day-to-day events. Moreover, even though H. M. had severe difficulty in learning and retaining new infor-

The preparation of this chapter was supported in part by funds from Grant P01-AG04953 from the National Institute on Aging and by a grant from the Dana Foundation.

mation, the knowledge of his early life was largely intact; he could learn some new skills about which he was consciously unaware, and his immediate attention span (i.e., the ability to retain very small amounts of information, such as 6 or 7 numbers, for a very brief period of time, such as 30 seconds) was relatively preserved.

It is fair to say that this series of studies regarding H. M. galvanized the neuropsychological world, because it demonstrated that the memory system was complex and could be parcellated into different functions that appeared to be served by different aspects of brain function. During the past 30 years, most of the major aspects of memory function have been elucidated, and there has been considerable progress in understanding the underlying brain mechanisms responsible for them.

TYPES OF MEMORY IDENTIFIED BY NEUROPSYCHOLOGY

Most models of memory function hypothesize that memory consists of a series of specific yet interactive stores (e.g., Tulving, 1972; Waugh & Norman, 1965). Figure 3.1 presents an outline of the way in which these aspects of memory, which are described below, are thought to be related to one another.

Sensory memory, or *registration*, represents the earliest stage of information processing. It is modality specific (i.e., visual, auditory, tactile), highly unstable, and characterized by rapid decay. The component of the memory system referred to as *primary* or *immediate memory* permits one to hold spans of auditory and visual information for relatively long periods of time by active rehearsal. The ability to concentrate on, rehearse, and recall a span of digits, words, or visual features is perhaps the best example of this capacity. Any disruption to the rehearsal process results in the information being lost from immediate memory. Experiments by L. Petersen and Petersen (1959) demonstrated that normal individuals forget a significant proportion of new information in less than 1 minute when distractions are present. The amount of information that immediate memory can store is limited to about 5 to 7 items, as mentioned earlier. There is no consensus

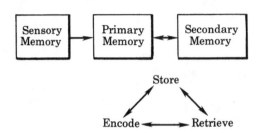

Figure 3.1. Theoretical model of types of memory processes.

among neuropsychologists and memory researchers as to whether immediate memory should be considered a form of memory at all. Primary, or immediate memory, as described here, may rely more on attention skills. Thus, Spitz (1972), among others, has argued that digit span forward is actually a measure of attention rather than of memory.

To be retained over a long period of time, information from immediate memory must be assembled into multimodal units so it can be placed in storage. Storage of information by the memory system appears to take place differentially. As early as 1949, Hebb postulated that two processes were necessary for the brain to retain information. The first process, analogous to what we have termed *recent memory*, requires the continual reverberation of a neural circuit. The second process, equivalent to *secondary memory*, requires an actual structural change in the neural pattern of the central nervous system.

Over the past few years, accumulating evidence has suggested that memory functions are composed of at least two distinct types of memory: explicit memory and implicit memory. *Explicit memory* pertains to information that is acquired because a person makes a conscious effort to learn and retain it; *implicit memory* pertains to information that is acquired without a conscious effort to learn it. Implicit memory therefore is said to refer to "knowing how," or "procedural," or "habit" (Cohen & Squire, 1980; Hirsh, 1974; Ryle, 1949) memory; implicit memory is accessible primarily through the performance of a task or by engaging in the skill in which the knowledge is embedded (Squire, 1986).

Recently, an additional aspect of memory function has been hypothesized: *working memory* (e.g., Baddeley, 1992). This appears to be a system for the transient storage and processing of information. It is most easily examined in memory tasks that require deliberate processing of information that requires online integration.

APPLICATION OF MEMORY STUDIES TO PROBLEMS OF AGING

This understanding of the various aspects of memory and neurobiology has enabled researchers to clarify the types of memory changes that occur with age and to compare them with the ways in which memory changes in the age-related diseases that have substantial effects on memory, such as Alzheimer's disease (AD). These studies indicate that there is a considerable difference between the nature of the memory changes in aging and in AD and the underlying neurobiology responsible for those changes. In the remainder of this chapter I focus on the changes in secondary memory seen in healthy individuals across the age range, compare them with the secondary-memory changes that characterize the early stages of AD, and describe what is known about their neurobiologic correlates.

AGE-RELATED CHANGES IN MEMORY

There are substantial changes with age in explicit secondary memory, in contrast to the minimal age changes in sensory and primary memory (see Craik [1977] and Poon [1985] for a review). The age at which changes in secondary memory occur depends on the methods that are used to test the memory store. Difficult explicit-memory tasks (e.g., delayed recall) demonstrate statistically significant differences by individuals in their 50s, compared to younger individuals (Albert, Duffy, & Naeser, 1987). Age decrements are greater on recall tasks than on recognition tasks. This is true whether words or pictures are used. Cueing during encoding or retrieval also alters the appearance of an age decline. Cueing at both encoding and retrieval produces the smallest age differences, whereas no cueing at either stage of the task maximizes age differences (Craik, Byrd, & Swanson, 1987). However, even with cued recall and recognition, there are often declines. Rabinowitz (1986) reported a 33% age-related decrement in cued recall and an 11% age-related decrement in recognition, when comparing young and old individuals (mean ages 19 years vs. 68 years).

Figure 3.2 shows the performance of individuals across the age range on delayed recall of two lengthy paragraphs. Each individual was read two lengthy paragraphs. Immediately after hearing each one, and then again after 20 minutes, he or she was asked to state what he or she could recall of the paragraphs.

A close examination of these data indicates that the older individuals did not more rapidly forget what they learned but rather that they took

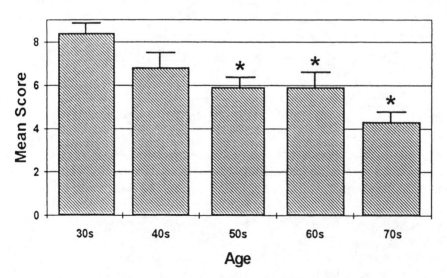

Figure 3.2. Delayed-recall performance of individuals 30–80 years old. The individuals were asked to report what they remembered of two lengthy paragraphs after a 20-minute delay.

longer to learn the new information. For example, if one compares the difference between immediate and delayed recall over the life span, one will find no statistically significant age differences (R. Petersen, Smith, Kokmen, Ivnik, & Tangalos, 1992). Thus, if one allows older individuals to learn material well (i.e., to the point where few errors are made), one will find that these individuals do not forget what they have learned more rapidly than young individuals do (see Figure 3.3). However, if older individuals are not given the ability to learn material to the same level of proficiency as younger individuals, after a delay less information will be retained by the average older person (Salthouse, 1994).

However, there is considerable variability among older individuals on tasks of this sort. There are many healthy older individuals who have test scores that overlap those of people many years younger than themselves (e.g., about one third of healthy 70-year-old humans have delayed-recall scores that overlap those of 30-year-olds [equated for education]).

Similar findings have emerged from studies of monkeys. Because free recall cannot be easily tested in monkeys, considerable effort has gone into developing a memory task that uses recognition but determines the quantity of information aging monkeys can retain across varying delay intervals. The *delayed nonmatching to sample* (DNMS) task is the most widely used method for assessing recognition memory in the nonhuman primate (Bachevalier & Mishkin, 1989; Mahut, Zola-Morgan, & Moss, 1982; Mishkin, 1978; Murray & Mishkin, 1984, 1986; Zola-Morgan & Squire, 1984). This task relies on a two-alternative forced-choice paradigm in which the monkey is required to discriminate which of two objects was recently presented.

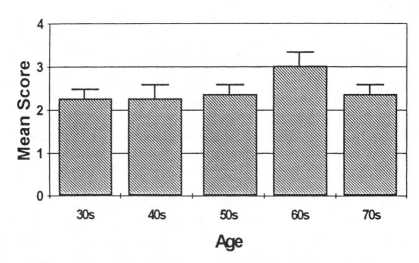

Figure 3.3. Differences between immediate- and delayed-recall performance in individuals 30–80 years of age. The individuals were asked to report what they remembered of two lengthy paragraphs after a 20-minute delay.

By using the DNMS task, many researchers have shown that aged monkeys are impaired at learning the nonmatching principle but are at best only mildly impaired across the delay conditions of the test (Arnsten & Goldman-Rakic, 1990; Bachevalier et al., 1991; Moss, Rosene, & Peters, 1988; Presty et al., 1987; Rapp & Amaral, 1989). Thus, like humans, the old monkeys take longer to learn something new but do not appear to forget this information more rapidly over lengthening delays than younger monkeys.

Another task, the *delayed recognition span test* (DRST; Moss, 1983; Rehbein, 1983), has demonstrated similar findings. This test requires a monkey to identify a novel stimulus from an increasing array of previously presented stimuli. The task has been administered to monkeys with two types of conditions: a spatial version and an object version. In both conditions the monkey first sees a board with 18 portions (food wells) and a stimulus object on one position. A second stimulus is added, while the board is obscured from view, and the animal is required to point to the new stimulus. On the first trial of the spatial version, the animal's task is to indicate which of two disks is occupying the new position on the board (i.e., a nonmatching-to-position task). On the first trial of the object version, the animal's task is to indicate which of two objects on the board is the new one (i.e., in essence, a nonmatching-to-sample task). However, because new disks/objects are then added in series to the previous ones on the board, the task becomes increasingly difficult. For example, young adult monkeys often achieve a span of five or greater before committing an error.

Middle-aged monkeys (16–23 years) are impaired on the spatial version of the DRST but not on the color version (see Figure 3.4; Moss, Killiany, Lai, & Herndon, 1997). This finding is similar to the declines in performance on delayed recall seen in middle-aged humans. Aged monkeys (24–32 years) are impaired relative to young adults (4–6 years) under both conditions of the task. This suggests that the performance of monkeys on the spatial version of the DRST may be functionally equivalent to the performance of humans on difficult delayed-recall tasks. In addition, the difference between performance on the DNMS and the spatial conditions of the DRST appears to be similar to what one sees between recall and recognition paradigms in aging humans.

Like aging humans, there is also considerable variability in the performance of aging monkeys. Among the oldest animals there are subjects who perform within the range of younger animals, even though the mean performance of the group declines significantly. For example, on the DNMS task, the number of trials to criterion ranges from 50 to 220, and the number of errors ranges from 29 to 60. Among the older monkeys the number of trials to criterion ranges from 200 to 516 and the number of errors ranges from 50 to 115.

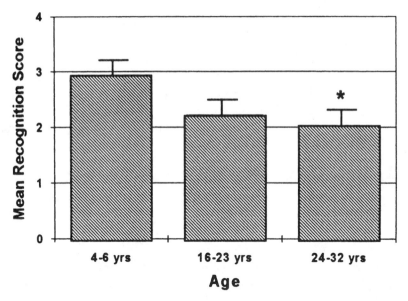

Figure 3.4. Spatial delayed recognition span scores by young adult monkeys (aged 4–6 years), middle-age monkeys (aged 16–23 years), and elderly monkeys (aged 24–32 years).

AGE-RELATED CHANGES IN BRAIN STRUCTURE AND FUNCTION

There is substantial evidence that, as people age, they show significant increases in cerebrospinal fluid and decreases in brain tissue (Stafford, Albert, Naeser, Sandor, & Garvey, 1988; Zatz, Jernigan, & Ahumada, 1982); that is, there is increasing atrophy with age. This alteration becomes statistically significant when people reach their 70s (Stafford et al., 1988).

However, recent studies in humans suggest that the decrease in brain tissue observed is primarily the result of decreases in white matter with age ($p < .001$). Decreases in gray matter are only marginally statistically significant; approximately 48% of brain tissue consists of gray matter among both 30-year-olds and 70-year-olds (Guttmann et al., 1998). These findings are consistent with recent data from humans (Haug, 1984; Leuba & Garey, 1989; Terry, DeTeresa, & Hansen, 1987), indicating that, with advancing age, neuronal loss in the cortex is either not significant or not as extensive as earlier reports (i.e., reports prior to 1984) had suggested (Anderson, Hubbard, Coghill, & Slidders, 1983; Brody, 1955, 1970; Colon, 1972; Henderson, Tomlinson, & Gibson, 1980; Shefer, 1973).

There are comparable data from monkeys. A recent study of magnetic resonance imaging scans (MRIs) in young and old monkeys demonstrates significant decreases in white matter volume with age but minimal decreases in gray matter volume (Rosene, Lai, & Killiany, 2000). Neuronal counts of numerous brain regions in young and old monkeys also demonstrate minimal neuronal cortical loss with age, including the striate cortex (Vincent, Peters, & Tigges, 1989), motor cortex (Tigges, Herndon, & Peters, 1992), frontal cortex (Peters, Leahu, Moss, & McNally, 1994), and the entorhinal cortex (Amaral, 1993). (It should be noted that these findings do not exclude focal changes with age in small areas of gray matter, such as selected areas of cortex or small subcortical nuclei, as discussed further below.)

Data from monkeys and humans also indicate that neuronal loss is highly selective within the hippocampal formation. For example, the subiculum shows a significant age-related loss in humans and a similar trend in monkeys; however, the CA1, CA2, and CA3 fields show no evidence of an age-related neuronal loss (Amaral, 1993; Rosene, 1993; West, Coleman, Flood, & Troncoso, 1994).

A recent positron emission tomography (PET) study also suggests that the hippocampal formation is more highly functional with age than previously thought (Schacter, Savage, Alpert, Rauch, & Albert, 1996). In Schacter et al.'s (1996) study, young and elderly participants attempted to learn two types of word lists. The testing conditions were such that high levels of recall were achieved with one set of word lists, and low levels of recall were achieved with the other. Analyses of the PET data from both the younger and older adults revealed blood flow increases in the hippocampal formation in comparisons in which the high-recall condition was emphasized; bilateral blood flow increases were seen in the high-recall-minus-baseline comparison, and right unilateral increases were seen in the high-recall-minus-low-recall comparison. The pattern of blood flow increases were similar in both the young and older participants, in both z score units and location of change. This suggests that the features of recollection indexed by hippocampal activity operates in a similar manner in old and young individuals. Schacter et al.'s study, however, also demonstrates differences in brain activities between young and older individuals. These differences were evident in comparisons emphasizing the low-recall condition. Most striking was the difference between the groups in the low-recall-minus-baseline comparison, which produced blood flow increases bilaterally in the anterior frontal lobe (centering on Area 10) for young participants but not for older ones. By contrast, the older participants demonstrated unilateral blood flow increases in the right posterior frontal lobe (centering on Area 4/6) and the right motor area (centering on Area 4/6). These differences in frontal activation between the young and older adults may reflect differences in retrieval strategies when older individuals are attempting to recall information that is not well learned (and may thus reflect differences in "working memory" with age). It seems unlikely, on the basis of the reports of preserved neuronal populations in the cortex cited above, that these frontal-activation differences between young and old are the result of substantial cortical neuronal loss. Age-related alterations in subcortical nuclei that project to the cortex seem to be the more likely explanation for these findings, because there is substantial neuronal loss in selected subcortical regions involved in neurotransmitter systems important for memory function, such as the basal forebrain and the locus coeruleus (e.g., Chan-Palay & Asan, 1989). For example, in humans and monkeys there is approximately a 50% neuronal loss with age in the basal forebrain and a 35%–40% loss in the locus coeruleus and dorsal raphe (Kemper, 1993). This compares with an approximate loss of 5% in CA1 of the hippocampus. Although neuronal loss appears to be minimal in the hippocampus with age, recent reports suggest alterations in specific receptor types (e.g., N-methyl-D-aspartate [NMDA] receptors) that may plan a role in memory function (Gazzaley, Siegal, Kordower, Mufson, & Morrison, 1996).

In addition, there is an age-related decrease in dopaminergic binding sites in the caudate nucleus (Severson, Marcusson, Winblad, & Finch, 1982) and the substantia nigra and a loss of neurons in the substantia nigra of about 6% per year (McGeer, McGeer, & Susuki, 1977). This loss of dopamine is thought to be responsible for many neurological symptoms that increase in frequency with age, such as decreased armswing and increased rigidity (Odenheimer et al., 1994). Changes in dopamine levels may also cause age-related changes in cognitive flexibility. This is suggested by the fact that patients with Parkinson's disease (a disorder associated with a loss of cells in the substantia nigra and a severe decline in dopamine levels) have cognitive deficits that have variably been described as "mental inflexibility" (Lees & Smith, 1983), a disorder of the "shifting attitude" (Cools, van den Bercken, Horstink, van Spaendonck, & Berger, 1984), an "instability of cognitive set" (Flowers & Robertson, 1985), and difficulty with "set formation, maintenance and shifting" (Taylor, Saint-Cyr, & Lang, 1987). An age-related functional loss of dopamine has been demonstrated in monkeys (Arnsten, Cai, Steere, & Goldman-Rakic, 1994), making it possible to study this hypothesis in nonhuman primates.

MEMORY CHANGES IN EARLY AD

The alterations in memory associated with early AD differ in important ways from those associated with age-related changes in memory. Difficulty with the acquisition of new information is generally the first and most salient symptom to emerge in patients with AD. When clinical neuropsychological tests are used to evaluate memory in AD patients, it is clear that recall and recognition performance are impaired in both the verbal and nonverbal domains (Storandt & Hill, 1989; Wilson, Bacon, Fox, & Kaszniak, 1983).

Experimental studies have examined AD patients to determine

whether the manner in which information is lost over brief delays is unique in any way to this patient group. The results of these studies suggest that a comparison of immediate and delayed recall performance may be a useful diagnostic measure for identifying patients with AD.

The first such study was conducted by Moss, Albert, Butters, and Payne (1986). They compared patients with AD to a group of patients with amnesia who had alcoholic Korsakoff's syndrome (KS), to a group of patients with dementia and Huntington's disease (HD), and to a group of normal control patients (NC). All of the participants were administered the DRST, the task mentioned above with respect to studies of memory in monkeys. The recognition portion of the task is entirely comparable to that used with monkeys. Disks are used, on which are placed a variety of stimuli (words, colors, faces, patterns, etc.). During the recognition portion of the task, the disks are placed on a board one at a time (there are 16 disks in all). As each disk is added, the board is hidden from view. The individual is then asked to point to the disk that was added during the delay interval. To do this, the individual must keep track of an increasingly long series of disks. The disks are then added one at a time, until the person makes an error. This yields a delayed recognition span for each of the stimuli sets. All of the patient groups were impaired in their recognition performance with respect to the control group, but there was overlap among the patient groups. There was no significant difference among the three patient groups in their ability to recognize new spatial, color, pattern, or facial stimuli; patients with HD performed significantly better than the other two groups when verbal stimuli were used.

However, when the DRST was given to humans, a recall portion was added to the verbal recognition span paradigm that is unique. Fifteen seconds and 2 minutes after completion of the last verbal recognition trial, the patients were asked to recall the words that had been on the disks. In this condition, the AD patients differed considerably from the other patients. They recall significantly fewer words over this brief delay interval (2 minutes) than either HD or KS patients. Although all three patient groups were equally impaired relative to normal control patients at the 15-second interval, patients with AD recalled significantly fewer words than either the HD or KS groups at the 2-minute interval; in fact, only the AD group performed significantly worse at the longer interval compared to the shorter interval (see Figure 3.5). It is notable that by the end of the 2-minute interval, 11 of the 12 patients in the AD group could recall fewer than 3 of the 16 words presented repeatedly during recognition testing. Of these 11 patients 7 were unable to recall any of the 16 words at the longer interval. Whereas the KS, HD, and NC participants lost an average of 10%–15% of verbal information between the 15-second and 2-minute delay intervals, patients with AD lost an average of 75% of the material. This pattern of recall performance demonstrated for the first time that

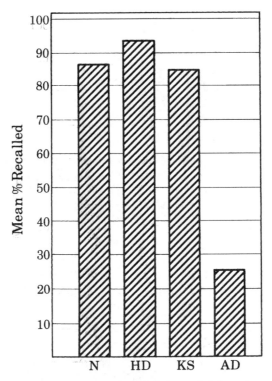

Figure 3.5. The difference between immediate and delayed recall on the verbal recall portion of the delayed recognition span test. The groups compared are normal control patients (N), patients with Huntington's disease (HD), patients with alcoholic Korsakoff's syndrome (KS), and patients with Alzheimer's disease (AD).

patients with AD lose more information over a brief delay than other patients with amnesic or dementing disorders.

A similar pattern of results has since been reported by numerous other investigators (e.g., Butters, Salmon, Heindel, & Granholm, 1988; Hart, Kwentus, Harkins, & Taylor, 1988; Tierney, Nores, Snow, Reid Fisher, & Zorzitto, 1994; Welsh, Butters, Hughes, Mohs, & Heyman, 1991). Hart et al.'s (1988) findings are particularly notable. Hart et al. administered a continuous-recognition task to AD and control patients and equated both groups of participants for retention 90 seconds after the task was completed. They then retested the participants at 10 minutes, 2 hours, and 48 hours after completion of the task. The AD patients showed a greater loss of information than the control patients between the 90-second interval and the 10-minute interval but not between the 10-minute and 2-hour interval or between the 10-minute and 48 hour-interval, suggesting that intervals of 10 minutes or less may be optimal for differentiating AD patients from other patient groups and from control patients.

Since these findings were first reported, additional patient groups have

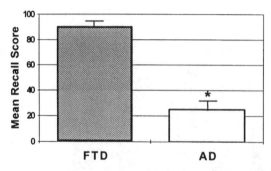

Figure 3.6. The difference between immediate and delayed recall on the verbal recall portion of the delayed recognition span test. The groups compared are patients with frontotemporal dementia (FTD) and patients with Alzheimer's disease (AD).

been compared with AD patients on tasks of this nature. They, likewise, appear to recall more information after a delay than patients with AD. Milberg and Albert (1989) compared the performance of AD patients with that of progressive supranuclear palsy (PSP) patients. The two groups were equated for overall level of impairment on the basis of the Mattis Dementia Rating Scale (Mattis, 1976) and were equivalent in number of years of education. There was no difference between the patient groups on most of the tasks administered (e.g., Vocabulary, Digit Span Forward, Similarities, Block Design). There was, however, a striking difference between the groups on both of the memory tasks. The AD patients were significantly impaired in comparison to the PSP patients on tests of both verbal and nonverbal memory.

A comparison of patients with AD and patients with frontotemporal dementia (FTD; Moss & Albert, 1988) also demonstrated the severe recall deficits of the AD patients. Here again, patients with AD and patients with FTD, equated for overall level of cognitive impairment, were administered the DRST. As in the earlier study (Moss et al., 1986), the difference in total recall between the 15-second interval and the 2-minute delay interval (i.e., the savings score) differentiated the groups (see Figure 3.6). The retention of the FTD patients over this delay interval approaches normality, whereas the AD patients lost a substantial amount of information.

In general, these findings suggest that the nature and severity of the AD patients' memory disturbance, in relation to delays spanning the first 10 minutes after encoding, is likely to be the result of a unique pattern of neuropathological dysfunction, neurochemical dysfunction, or both.

CHANGES IN BRAIN STRUCTURE IN EARLY AD

The most likely explanation for the abnormalities in memory that characterize the early stage of AD pertains to the damage to the hippocampal formation seen in these patients (Ball, 1977; Hyman, Van Hoesen, Damasio, & Barnes, 1984). In the hippocampal formation, neuronal loss and abnormal formations with the cells (e.g., neurofibrillary tangles and neuritic plaques) are seen primarily in the entorhinal cortex and subiculum, the primary pathways that convey information into and out of the hippocampus. It has been suggested that abnormalities in these regions produce a functional isolation of the hippocampus (Hyman, Van Hoesen, Damasio, & Barnes, 1984; Hyman, Van Hoesen, Kromer, & Damasio, 1986). These findings suggest that neuropathological damage to medial temporal lobe structures may be responsible for the marked short-term memory impairment evident in the early stages of AD. These results were first observed in patients with end-stage disease; however, they have recently been extended to patients with very mild disease (Gomez-Isla et al., 1996). Most striking is the fact that the entorhinal cortex has neuronal loss of approximately 60% and 40% in Layers 2 and 4, respectively. The normal control group examined in this investigation spanned the ages of 60 to 90. They were carefully screened to exclude individuals with AD and demonstrated no significant neuronal loss in Layers 2 and 4 of the entorhinal cortex. Because this region is known to be critically important for the acquisition and retention of new information (Zola-Morgan, Squire, & Ramos, 1994), abnormalities in these regions are likely to be responsible for the severe anterograde memory loss evident early in the course of AD. Taken together with the findings described above—that there is significant age-related neuronal loss in the subiculum of the hippocampal formation, but no significant age-related change in the CA1, CA2, and CA3 regions of the hippocampus—these data suggest that a comparison of activation patterns in the subfields of the hippocampal formation (e.g., with newer functional MRI techniques) may differentiate patients in the very earliest stages of AD from those with age-related changes in memory.

CONCLUSION

It appears that there has been an extremely beneficial interaction between the progress made in understanding the basic components of the memory system and their neurobiologic substrates and studies of cognitive aging, particularly as they pertain to changes in memory related to age and age-related disease. The conceptual framework provided by neuropsychologists and cognitive neuroscientists has enabled investigators involved in cognitive aging to identify the sometimes subtle differences between different types of memory change, suggesting that the memory changes that occur with age differ in important and significant ways from those seen in the early stages of AD and that selected, and differing, alterations in the brain are responsible for them. Understanding the nature of these cognitive changes and the brain alterations associated with them is the first step in developing methods of changing them.

REFERENCES

Albert, M., Duffy, F., & Naeser, M. (1987). Non-linear changes in cognition with age and neurophysiological correlates. *Canadian Journal of Psychology, 41*, 141–157.

Amaral, D. (1993). Morphological analyses of the brain of behaviorally characterized aged nonhuman primates. *Neurobiology of Aging, 14*, 671–672.

Anderson, J. M., Hubbard, B. M., Coghill, G. R., & Slidders, W. (1983). The effect of advanced old age on the neurone content of the cerebral cortex: Observations with an automatic image analyser point counting method. *Journal of Neurological Science, 58*, 233–244.

Arnsten, A., Cai, J., Steere, J., & Goldman-Rakic, P. (1994). Dopamine D2 receptor mechanisms in the cognitive performance of young adult and aged monkeys. *Psychopharmacology, 116*, 143–151.

Arnsten, A., & Goldman-Rakic, P. (1990). Analysis of alpha-2 adrenergic agonist effects on the delayed non-matching-to-sample performance of aged rhesus monkeys. *Neurobiology of Aging, 11*, 583–590.

Bachevalier, J., Landis, L., Walker, M., Brickson, M., Mishkin, M., Price, D., & Cork, L. (1991). Aged monkeys exhibit behavioral deficits indicative of widespread cerebral dysfunction. *Neurobiology of Aging, 12*, 99–111.

Bachevalier J., & Mishkin, M. (1989). Mnemonic and neuropathological effects of occluding the posterior cerebral artery in *macaca mulatta*. *Neuropsychologia, 27*, 83–105.

Baddeley, A. (1992, January). Working memory. *Science, 255*, 556–559.

Ball, M. H. (1977). Neuronal loss, neurofibrillary tangles and granulovacuolar degeneration in the hippocampus with aging and dementia. *Acta Neuropathologica, 37*, 11–18.

Brody, H. (1955). Organization of cerebral cortex III: A study of aging in the human cerebral cortex. *Journal of Comparative Neurology, 102*, 511–556.

Brody, H. (1970). Structural changes in the aging nervous system. *Interdisaplinary Topics in Gerontology, 7*, 9–21.

Butters, N., Salmon, D., Heindel, W., & Granholm, E. (1988). Episodic, semantic and procedural memory: Some comparisons of Alzheimer's and Huntington's disease patients. In R. D. Terry (Ed.), *Aging and the brain* (pp. 63–87). New York: Raven Press.

Chan-Palay, V., & Asan, E. (1989). Quantitation of catecholamine neurons in the locus ceruleus in human brains of normal young and older adults in depression. *Journal of Comparative Neurology, 287*, 357–372.

Cohen, N., & Squire, L. (1980, October). Preserved learning and retention of pattern analyzing skill in amnesia: Dissociation of knowing how and knowing that. *Science, 210,* 207–210.

Colon, E. J. (1972). The elderly brain: A quantitative analysis of the cerebral cortex in two cases. *Psychiatria, Neurologic, Neurochirurgia, 75,* 261–270.

Cools, A., van den Bercken, J., Horstink, M., van Spaendonck, K., & Berger, H. (1984). Cognitive and motor shifting aptitude disorder in Parkinson's disease. *Journal of Neurology, Neurosurgery and Psychology, 47,* 443–453.

Corkin, S. (1984). Lasting consequences of bilateral medial temporal lobectomy: Clinical course and experimental findings in H.M. *Seminars in Neurology, 4,* 249–259.

Craik, F. I. M. (1977). Age differences in human memory. In J. E. Birren & K. W. Schaie (Eds.), *Handbook of the psychology of aging* (pp. 384–420). New York: Van Nostrand Reinhold.

Craik, F., Byrd, M., & Swanson, J. (1987). Patterns of memory loss in three elderly samples. *Psychology and Aging, 2,* 79–86.

Flowers, K., & Robertson, C. (1985). The effect of Parkinson's disease on the ability to maintain mental set. *Journal of Neurology, Neurosurgery and Psychology, 48,* 517–529.

Gazzaley, A., Siegal, S., Kordower, J., Mufson, E., & Morrison, J. (1996). Circuit-specific alterations of N-methyl–D-aspartate receptor subunit I in the dentate gyrus of aged monkeys. *Proceedings of the National Academy of Sciences, 93,* 3121–3125.

Gomez-Isla, T., Price, J., McKeel, D., Morris, J., Growdon, J., & Hyman, B. (1996). Profound loss of layer 11 entorhinal cortex neurons occurs in very mild Alzheimer's disease. *Journal of Neuroscience, 16,* 4491–4500.

Guttmann, C., Jolesz, F., Kikinis, R., Killiany, R., Moss, M., Sandor, T., & Albert, M. (1998). White matter and gray matter differences with age. *Neurology, 50,* 972–978.

Hart, R. P., Kwentus, J. A., Harkins, S. W., & Taylor, J. R. (1988). Rate of forgetting in mild Alzheimer's type dementia. *Brain and Cognition, 7,* 31–38.

Haug, H. (1984). Macroscopic and microscopic morphometry of the human brain and cortex: A survey in the light of new results. *Brain Pathology, 1,* 123–149.

Hebb, D. (1949). *The organization of behavior: A neuropsychology theory.* New York: Wiley.

Henderson, G., Tomlinson, B., & Gibson, P. (1980). Cell counts in human cerebral cortex in normal adults throughout life, using an image analysing computer. *Journal of Neurological Science, 46,* 113–136.

Hirsh, R. (1974). The hippocampus and contextual retrieval of information from memory: A theory. *Behavioral Biology, 12,* 421–444.

Hyman, B. T., VanHoesen, G. W., Damasio, A. R., & Barnes, C. L. (1984). Alzheimer's disease: Cell specific pathology isolates the hippocampal formation. *Science, 225,* 1168–1170.

Hyman, B., Van Hoesen, G., Kromer, L., & Damasio, A. (1984). Perforant pathway changes and the memory impairment of Alzheimer's disease. *Annals of Neurology, 20,* 472–481.

Kemper, T. (1993). The relationship of cerebral cortical changes to nuclei in the brainstem. *Neurobiology of Aging, 14,* 659–660.

Lees, A., & Smith, E. (1983). Cognitive deficits in the early stages of Parkinson's disease. *Brain, 106,* 257–270.

Leuba, G., & Garey, L. (1989). Comparison of neuronal and glial numerical density in primary and secondary visual cortex. *Experimental Brain Research, 77,* 31–38.

Mahut, H., Zola-Morgan, S., & Moss, M. (1982). Hippocampal resections impair associative learning and recognition memory in the monkey. *Journal of Neuroscience, 2,* 1214–1229.

Mattis, S. (1976). Mental status examination for organic mental syndrome in the elderly patient. In L. Bellak & T. B. Karasu (Eds.), *Geriatric psychiatry* (pp. 71–121). New York: Grune & Stratton.

McGeer, P., McGeer, E., & Susuki, J. (1977). Aging and extrapyramidal function. *Archives of Neurology, 34,* 33–35.

Milberg, W., & Albert, M. (1989). Cognitive differences between patients with PSP and Alzheimer's disease. *Journal of Clinical and Experimental Neuropsychology, 11,* 605–614.

Milner, B., Corkin, S., & Teuber, H.-L. (1968). Further analysis of the hippocampal amnesic syndrome: 14 year follow-up study of H. M. *Neuropsychologia, 6,* 215–234.

Milner, B. (1972). Disorders of learning and memory after temporal lobe lesions in man. *Clinical Neurosurgery, 19,* 421–446.

Mishkin, M. (1978). Memory in monkeys severely impaired by combined but not separate removal of amygdala and hippocampus. *Nature, 273,* 297–298.

Moss, M. (1983). Assessment of memory in amnesic and dementia patients: Adaptation of behavioral tests used with non-human primates. *International Neuropsychology Society Bulletin, 5,* 15.

Moss, M., & Albert, M. (1988). Alzheimer's disease and other dementing disorders. In M. Albert & M. Moss (Eds.), Geriatric *neuropsychology* (pp. 145–178). New York: Guilford Press.

Moss, M. B., Albert, M. S., Butters, N., & Payne, M. (1986). Differential patterns of memory loss among patients with Alzheimer's disease, Huntington's disease and alcoholic Korsakoff's syndrome. *Archives of Neurology, 43,* 239–246.

Moss, M., Killiany, R., Lai, Z., & Herndon, J. (1997). *Recognition memory span in aged monkeys. Neurobiology of Aging, 18,* 13–19.

Moss, M., Rosene, D., & Peters, A. (1988). Effects of aging on visual recognition memory in the rhesus monkey. *Neurobiology of Aging, 9,* 495–502.

Murray, E., & Mishkin, M. (1984). Severe tactual as well as visual memory deficits follow combined removal of the amygdala and hippocampus in monkeys. *Journal of Neuroscience, 4,* 2565–2580.

Murray, E., & Mishkin, M. (1986). Visual recognition in monkeys following rhinal cortical ablations combined with either amygdalectomy or hippocampectomy. *Journal of Neuroscience, 6,* 1991–2003.

Odenheimer, G., Funkenstein, H., Beckett, L., Chown, M., Pilgrim, D., Evans, D., & Albert, M. (1994). Comparison of neurologic changes in successfully aging persons vs the total aging population. *Archives of Neurology, 51,* 573–580.

Peters, A., Leahu, D., Moss, M., & McNally, K. (1994). The effects of aging on Area 46 of the cortex of the rhesus monkey. *Cerebral Cortex, 6,* 621–635.

Petersen, L., & Petersen, M. (1959). Short term retention of individual items. *Journal of Experimental Psychology, 91,* 341–343.

Petersen, R., Smith, G., Kokmen, E., Ivnik, R., & Tangalos, E. (1992). Memory function in normal aging. *Neurology, 42,* 396–401.

Poon, L. W. (1985). Differences in human memory with aging: Nature, causes, and clinical implications. In J. E. Birren & K. W. Schaie (Eds.), *Handbook of the psychology of aging.* New York: Van Nostrand Reinhold.

Presty, S., Bachevalier, J., Walker, L., Struble, R., Price, D., Mishkin, M., & Cork, L. (1987). Age differences in recognition memory of the rhesus monkey (*macaca mulatta*). *Neurobiology of Aging, 8,* 435–440.

Rabinowitz, J. (1986). Priming in episodic memory. *Journal of Gerontology, 41,* 204–213.

Rapp, P., & Amaral, D. (1989). Evidence for task-dependent memory dysfunction in the aged monkey. *Journal of Neuroscience, 9,* 3568–3576.

Rehbein, L. (1983). Long-term effects of early hippocampectomy in the monkey. Doctoral Dissertation, Northeastern University.

Rosene, D. (1993). Comparing age-related changes in the basal forebrain and hippocampus of the rhesus monkey. *Neurobiology of Aging, 14,* 669–670.

Rosene, D., Lai, Z., & Killiany, R. (2000). *Age-related loss of white matter with preservation of gray matter in the forebrain of the rhesus monkey: An MRI study.* Manuscript submitted for publication.

Ryle, G. (1949). *The concept of mind.* London: Hitchinson.

Salthouse, T. (1994). Aging associations: Influence of speed on adult age differences in associative learning. *Journal of Experimental Psychology: Learning, Memory, and Cognition, 20,* 1486–1503.

Schacter, D. L., Savage, C. R., Alpert, N. M., Rauch, S., & Albert, M. (1996). The role of hippocampus and frontal cortex in age-related memory changes: A PET study. *NeuroReport, 7,* 1165–1169.

Scoville, W., & Milner, B. (1957). Loss of recent memory after bilateral hippocampal lesions. *Neurological Psychiatry, 20,* 11–21.

Severson, J., Marcusson, J., Winblad, B., & Finch, C. (1982). Age-correlated loss of dopaminergic binding sites in human basal ganglia. *Journal of Neurochemistry, 39,* 1623–1631.

Shefer, V. (1973). Absolute number of neurons and thickness of the cerebral cortex during aging, senile and vascular dementia, and Pick's and Alzheimer's diseases. *Neuroscience Behavorial Physiology, 6,* 319–324.

Spitz H. (1972). Note on immediate memory for digits: Invariance over the years. *Psychological Bulletin, 78,* 183–185.

Squire L. (1986, June). Mechanisms of memory. *Science, 232*, 1612–1619.

Stafford, J. L., Albert, M. S., Naeser, M. H., Sandor, T., & Garvey, A. (1988). Age-related differences in CT scan measurements. *Archives of Neurology, 45*, 409–419.

Storandt, M., & Hill, R. D. (1989). Very mild senile dementia of the Alzheimer type II: Psychometric test performance. *Archives of Neurology, 46*, 383–386.

Taylor, A., Saint-Cyr, J., & Lang, A. (1987). Parkinson's disease: Cognitive changes in relation to treatment response. *Brain, 110*, 35–51.

Terry, R. D., DeTeresa, R., & Hansen, L. A. (1987). Neocortical cell counts in normal human adult aging. *Annals of Neurology, 21*, 530–539.

Tierney, M., Nores, A., Snow, W., Reid Fisher, R., & Zorzitto, M. (1994). Utility of the Rey Auditory Verbal Learning Test in the differentiation of normal aging from Alzheimer's and Parkinson's disease. *Psychological Assessment, 6*, 129–134.

Tigges, J., Herndon, J., & Peters, A. (1992). Neuronal population of Area 4 during life span of rhesus monkeys. *Neurobiology of Aging, 11*, 201–208.

Tulving, E. (1972). Episodic and semantic memory. In E. Tulving & W. Donaldson (Eds.), *Organization of memory* (pp. 381–403). New York: Academic Press.

Vincent, S., Peters, A., & Tigges, J. (1989). Effects of aging on neurons within Area 17 of rhesus monkey cerebral cortex. *Anatomical Record, 223*, 329–341.

Waugh, N., & Norman, D. (1965). Primary memory. *Psychological Review, 72*, 89–104.

Welsh, K., Butters, N., Hughes, J., Mohs, R., & Heyman, A. (1991). Detection of abnormal memory decline in mild cases of Alzheimer's disease using CERAD neuropsychological measures. *Archives of Neurology, 48*, 289–291.

West, M., Coleman, P., Flood, D., & Troncoso, J. (1994). Differences in the pattern of hippocampal neuronal loss in normal ageing and Alzheimer's disease. *The Lancet, 344*, 769–772.

Wilson, R., Bacon, L., Fox, P., & Kaszniak, A. (1983). Primary memory and secondary memory in dementia of the Alzheimer type. *Journal of Clinical Neuropsychology, 5*, 337–344.

Zatz, L., Jernigan, T., & Ahumada, A. (1982). Changes in computed cranial tomography with aging: Intracranial fluid volume. *American Journal of Neuroradiology, 3*, 1–11.

Zola-Morgan, S., & Squire, L. (1984). Preserved learning in monkeys with medial temporal lesions: Sparing of motor and cognitive skills. *Journal of Neuroscience, 4*, 1072–1085.

Zola-Morgan, S., Squire, L., & Ramos, S. (1994). Severity of memory impairment in monkeys as a function of locus an extent of damage within the medial temporal lobe memory system. *Hippocampus, 4*, 483–495.

4

TOWARD A NEUROPSYCHOLOGY OF COGNITIVE AGING

ALFRED W. KASZNIAK AND MARY C. NEWMAN

Since the 1980s, there has been a dramatic increase in research concerned with neurobiologic and neuropsychologic aspects of both healthy older age and age-associated neurological illness (Nussbaum, 1997). In the present chapter we review the ways in which neuropsychological research and theory have influenced cognitive aging research and practice. The chapter is divided into five sections. First, a brief review is provided of parallels between neuropsychological deficits following focal brain damage and cognitive changes seen in normal aging. The second section examines how such parallels led several theorists to hypothesize a specific neuropsychological model of cognitive aging (i.e., the *right-hemisphere hypothesis*). Neuropsychologic, neurobiologic, and experimental cognitive investigations designed to test the various implications of this model are selectively reviewed. The third section focuses on an alternative neuropsychological model of cognitive aging (i.e., the *frontal-system hypothesis*) and its sup-

This work was supported by the University of Arizona Cognitive Neuroscience Center and funded through grants from the McDonnell–Pew and Flinn Foundations, National Multipurpose Research and Training Center Grant DC-01409, and the National Institute on Deafness and Other Communication Disorders, which funds a postdoctoral fellowship for Mary C. Newman.

porting evidence. In examining the body of cognitive aging research that has been motivated by this model, particular emphasis is placed on studies of working memory, organizational control processes in recall, temporal order memory, fact versus source memory, explicit versus implicit memory, attention processes, and visuospatial functioning. In the fourth section, recent studies concerning preclinical neurophysiological and neuropsychological changes in Alzheimer's disease (AD) are examined, and their implications for future theory and research methodology in cognitive aging are explored. A final section provides a brief summary and conclusions.

COMPARING NEUROPSYCHOLOGICAL TASK PERFORMANCE IN BRAIN DAMAGE AND NORMAL AGING

Attempting to understand normal psychological functions and processes through observation of their disintegration following brain damage has been a major research strategy throughout the 20th century. Kurt Goldstein (1939) used this strategy in his development of an organismic theory of normal human psychology from clinical observations of soldiers with brain injuries. Ward Halstead (1947) continued this tradition in developing his theory of biological intelligence from psychometric assessment of neurosurgical patients. Ralph Reitan (1955a, 1955c) expanded, modified, and further validated Halstead's psychometric approach, resulting in the development of a standardized clinical neuropsychological test battery (for a review, see Reitan & Wolfson, 1996). Reitan (1955b, 1967; Reed & Reitan, 1963a, 1963b) also directly compared aging-associated performance on the Halstead–Reitan Battery (HRB) to that which follows cerebral damage. On the basis of observed similarities, Reitan concluded that many of the cognitive changes of normal aging are due to age-related impairment in cerebral function.

Reitan's initial observations led other investigators to ask whether the pattern of neuropsychological age group differences was more similar to that of patients with diffuse brain damage or to that of patients with hemispherically lateralized focal damage. Overall and Gorham (1972) administered the Wechsler Adult Intelligence Scale (WAIS; Wechsler, 1958) to a group of 271 adult men, ranging in age from 45 to 84 years, who were free of evidence of neurologic or neuropsychiatric disease. They also administered the WAIS to a group of 299 institutionalized men of the same age range who had diagnoses of chronic and diffuse brain disease. Discriminant function analysis showed that the pattern of subtest performance of the healthy older men did not resemble that of the diffuse brain-damaged patients (two discriminant functions were obtained: one associated with chronic brain disease and the other with age). Taking a similar approach, G. Goldstein and Shelly (1975) administered the HRB to 120 men between the ages of 20 and 62, 60 of whom had diagnoses of diffuse brain damage and 60 of whom had no evidence of brain damage. Multivariate analysis of variance (using four measures derived from a previous factor analysis of the HRB subtests) failed to find a significant Age × Diagnosis interaction, arguing against a similarity between aging and diffuse brain damage.

RIGHT-HEMISPHERE HYPOTHESIS

Schaie and Schaie (1977) compared summary data on WAIS subtest scores of normal elderly people with Wechsler–Bellevue (Wechsler, 1939) subtest scores from Fitzhugh, Fitzhugh, and Reitan's (1962) study of focal and diffuse brain-damaged patients. Schaie and Schaie noted that the "aging pattern" differed from that of both chronic and acute diffuse brain-damage patients but was indistinguishable from that of patients with both chronic and acute right-hemisphere focal damage. On the basis of these comparisons they hypothesized that normal aging might involve greater right than left cerebral hemispheric decline. Klisz (1978) attempted to test this hypothesis through a reanalysis of HRB data reported by Reed and Reitan (1963b). Klisz categorized the HRB tests according to whether they could be considered indicators of right-hemisphere, left-hemisphere, or generalized brain dysfunction and found that the right-hemisphere tests were the best discriminators of middle-aged versus older normal adults.

G. Goldstein and Shelly (1981) designed a test of the right-hemisphere hypothesis, administering a modified HRB to 1,247 neuropsychiatric and general medical patients divided into six age groups (from 20s through 70s). Goldstein and Shelly used the Russell, Neuringer, and Goldstein (1970) localization key (an empirically validated quantitative approach to estimating the probability of hemispherically lateralized brain dysfunction from modified HRB data), with each patient evaluated for number of right- and left-hemisphere localization points. They found an equivalent increase of both right- and left-hemisphere HRB localization points with increasing age, although right-hemisphere points were significantly greater across all age groups. Thus, Goldstein and Shelly's data did not provide clear support for the right-hemisphere hypothesis. Studies that take alternative psychometric approaches to neuropsychological assessment, such as the group of tests developed by Benton and colleagues (Benton, Eslinger, & Damasio, 1981) or the Luria–Nebraska battery (Spitzform, 1982), have also failed to find evidence for a differential relationship of right- versus left-hemisphere dysfunction indices to adult age.

A significant problem with inferring hemispheric lateralization of dysfunction from either WAIS or HRB data is the fact that tests that are sensitive to right-hemisphere damage (e.g., visuospatial tasks) tend to require more complex problem-solving skills than do those that are sensitive to left-hemisphere damage (e.g., verbal information recall or vocabulary definition; Elias & Kinsbourne, 1974). As Mack and Carlson (1978) suggested, the performance of older people may be more affected by such task complexity than that of younger people. Furthermore, tasks that supposedly assess right-hemisphere function may be less familiar or overlearned, requiring more fluid cognitive skills than tasks that supposedly assess left-hemisphere function, which depend on more crystallized abilities (cf. Horn & Cattell, 1967). Finally, psychometric tasks thought to be sensitive to right-hemispheric functioning (e.g., WAIS Performance Scale subtests) more often credit bonus points for rapid problem solution than do tasks thought to be sensitive to left-hemispheric functioning (e.g., WAIS Verbal Scale subtests). Age-related slowing of processing has been demonstrated for both verbal and spatial tasks (for a review, see Salthouse, 1991b), and slowing may be able to account for some, although not all, of the age differences in cognitive task performance (Hertzog, 1989; Troyer, Cullum, Smernoff, & Kozora, 1994). Thus, early efforts at testing the right-hemisphere hypothesis cannot be unambiguously interpreted, because of the use of task performance indices in which putative sensitivity to hemispheric functioning is confounded with differential complexity, difficulty, familiarity, processing speed, or some combination of these.

Because of these problems, several studies have attempted to test the right-hemisphere hypothesis by using tasks that eliminate or minimize one or more confounds. Meudell and Greenhalgh (1987) used tasks that assess both verbal and spatial reasoning (rather than recall of previously learned information), thus minimizing familiarity differences between the two task domains. They found a group of healthy older adults to show greater deficits, relative to healthy younger adults, on the spatial than on the verbal tasks and interpreted these results as consistent with a differential hemispheric aging hypothesis. However, it should be noted that the specific verbal and spatial reasoning tasks used by Meudell and Greenhalgh had not been empirically validated as having differential sensitivity to hemispherically lateralized brain damage. Furthermore, it is unclear whether the verbal and spatial reasoning tasks were of equivalent difficulty.

Mittenberg, Seidenberg, O'Leary, and DiGiulio (1989) attempted to test the right-hemisphere hypothesis with a test battery designed to eliminate systematic familiarity or procedural differences among tests (i.e., overlearned vs. familiar, timed vs. untimed). The selection of such tests was also based on published evidence of hemispheric damage lateralizing and localizing ability. The 12 selected tests were administered to 27 healthy young adults (aged 20–35 years) and 41 older adults (aged 55–75 years). Mittenberg and colleagues found left- and right-hemisphere summary scores to both be significantly correlated with age ($rs = -.52$ and $-.41$, respectively), thus failing to support a differentially lateralized age-related decline in cerebral function.

As Mittenberg et al. (1989) noted, neurobiologic studies have also failed to provide support for differential right-hemispheric degenerative change with increasing age. Neither autopsy counts of neuronal cell density (Brody, 1978; Haug et al., 1983), nor regional cerebral blood flow (Gur, Gur, Obrist, Skolnick, & Reivich, 1987; Lavy, Melamed, Bentin, Cooper, & Rinot, 1978), nor electroencephalographic (EEG) recording (Marsh & Thompson, 1977; Woodruff, 1978) have provided evidence of lateralized hemispheric age group differences.

Despite the lack of support for the right-hemisphere hypothesis from neurobiological studies and the mixed results from psychometric neuropsychological studies, this hypothesis has motivated several experiments in the field of cognitive aging. Several investigators have attempted a more direct test of differential hemispheric aging by making comparisons of younger and older adults performing tasks in which stimuli are tachistoscopically presented to either the left visual field or right visual field. Because each visual half-field is represented by retinal cells with connections to the contralateral visual cortex, it is assumed that stimuli presented to a given visual field will be processed first and more completely by the contralateral hemisphere (see Kosslyn & Koenig, 1992). The tachistoscopic half-field method thus appears to allow more direct inferences about hemispheric functioning, which may be less susceptible than psychometric approaches to confounds created by differential task difficulty, complexity, or familiarity. The results of tachistoscopic visual half-field experiments have generally failed to support differential hemispheric aging (e.g., Cherry, Hellige, & McDowd, 1995; Elias & Kinsbourne, 1974; Nebes, Madden, & Berg, 1983; Obler, Woodward, & Albert, 1984). Studies that have used dichotic presentation (i.e., to both ears, simultaneously) of verbal and nonverbal auditory stimuli have also failed to support the hypothesized greater right-hemisphere decline with aging (Borod & Goodglass, 1980; Nebes et al., 1983).

Recently, different experimental aging research methods have provided evidence that has been interpreted as supporting the right-hemisphere hypothesis. For example, Gehardstein, Peterson, and Rapcsak (1998) had younger and older adult participants view, in either the left or right visual field, a pair of object drawings presented sequentially, with a masked interstimulus interval. The paired objects were shown from the same three-dimensional vantage point or from vantage points that differed by 30° or 60°. The objects in each pair were always from the same category (e.g., both ladders) but were not always the same exemplar (e.g., stepladder and extension ladder). Participants determined whether the two successive objects were the same or a different exemplar (regardless of the viewpoint from which the object was depicted). Gehardstein and colleagues found older participants to be generally less sensitive (hit rate − false alarm rate) than the younger participants, and particularly less sensitive when the stimuli were presented in the left visual field. These results were interpreted as consistent with a hypothesized greater posterior right-hemisphere decline with aging.

In summary, several cognitive aging experiments have failed to support the right-hemisphere hypothesis, arguing against any robust difference between the two hemispheres in susceptibility to age-related decline. However, recent research evidence suggests that particular types of tasks may provide evidence consistent with the right-hemisphere hypothesis. The question of whether certain subsystems within the right cerebral hemisphere manifest greater aging changes than corresponding subsystems within the left hemisphere thus remains unsettled. The more recent results are in need of replication and extension to determine both their reliability and the nature of stimulus dimensions responsible for the apparent Age × Hemispheric Asymmetry interaction. Optimally, such future research would be designed to contrast the predictions of a more limited and sub-system-specific right-hemisphere hypothesis with those of alternative hypotheses.

FRONTAL-SYSTEM HYPOTHESIS

A competing neuropsychological hypothesis, originally proposed to account for some of the same observations that suggested the right-hemisphere hypothesis, was first articulated by Albert and Kaplan (1980). After reviewing a range of available psychometric, psychophysiologic, and cognitive aging studies, Albert and Kaplan concluded that older adults "do not develop adequate techniques for selectively attending to material unless a task is constructed in such a way that this necessity is minimized" (p. 416). They also noted that adequate selective attention and maintenance of attention set are usually thought to require the integrity of the frontal lobes and their subcortical connections (Nauta, 1971). Albert and Kaplan provided several examples of age-related differences in visuospatial task performance strategies. Strategies characteristic of older adults appeared to be similar to those typical of patients with frontal-lobe (particularly right frontal) damage. This led Albert and Kaplan to propose that the frontal brain system (the frontal lobes and their subcortical connections) might be particularly vulnerable to age-related decline.

Several investigations have compared the neuropsychological task performance of healthy younger and older adults and provided support for the frontal-system hypothesis. In these studies, neuropsychologic task performance differences between older and younger adults appeared to be similar to those between healthy persons and patients with structural damage to the frontal lobes. For example, Axelrod and Henry (1992), as well as Daigneault, Braun, and Whitaker (1992), have demonstrated age-associated decline in cross-sectional comparisons of healthy adults performing the Wisconsin Card Sorting Test (WCST), which has been found to be sensitive to frontal-lobe damage (Milner, 1963; Nelson, 1976). Other neuropsychological tasks that have been shown to be sensitive to frontal-lobe damage (for a review, see Lezak, 1995), such as the WAIS–R Similarities subtest (Wechsler, 1981) and the Controlled Oral Word Association Test (Benton & Hamsher, 1978), also show marked differences between healthy younger and older adults (Axelrod & Henry, 1992; Comalli, Wapner, & Werner, 1962; Shimamura & Jurica, 1994; Whelihan & Lesher, 1985).

In addition to neuropsychological studies, there is also neurobiological evidence implicating a particular vulnerability of the frontal lobes to the aging process. Age-related atrophy of the frontal cortex has been documented with both computerized tomography (CT; Sandor, Albert, Stafford, & Kemper, 1990) and magnetic resonance imaging (MRI; Coffey et al., 1992). Coffey et al. (1992) found a disproportionate loss of volume in the frontal lobes compared to other areas, suggesting that the frontal lobes may be particularly vulnerable to age-related change. Jernigan et al. (1991), using MRI, found that the greatest age-related volume decrease among subcortical nuclei occurred in the caudate, a structure that is structurally and functionally associated with the prefrontal cortex. Subcortical white matter changes, termed *leukoencephalopathy* or *leukoariosis* (likely representing microvascular and other pathologic causes), visualized with either CT or T_2-weighted MRI, accumulate with increasing age and are frequently concentrated in the anterior (frontal) periventricular region (George et al., 1986; Kawamura et al., 1993). Frontal leukoencephalopathy potentially disrupts frontal–subcortical connections and has been found to correlate with reduced cortical perfusion (Kawamura et al., 1993), impaired performance on neuropsychological tasks that are sensitive to frontal damage (Junque et al., 1990), and reduced cognitive processing speed and attentiveness (Junque et al., 1990; Ylikoski et al., 1993). In quantitative postmortem analyses, Haug and colleagues (Haug et al., 1983; Haug & Eggers, 1991) found the greatest neuronal cell density decreases with age to occur in the prefrontal area and within the thalamus and basal ganglia, structures with particularly strong connections to the frontal lobes (Damasio, 1985). Although not always consistently observed (see Pietrini & Rapoport, 1994), brain imaging measures of regional cerebral blood flow and metabolism have also suggested selective vulnerability of the prefrontal cortex to age-related decline (Gur et al., 1987; Raz et al., 1997).

Working Memory

Cognitive aging research has provided increasing evidence that the frontal-system hypothesis may account for many observed differences between younger and older adults. Performance of tasks that are believed to assess the cognitive construct of working memory (i.e., "the temporary storage of information that is being processed in any of a range of cognitive tasks," Baddeley, 1986, p. 34) is impaired in patients with damage to the frontal lobes (e.g., Owen, Downes, Sahakian, Polkey, & Robbins, 1990). A number of studies have demonstrated age-related decline in working memory, for both verbal and spatial stimuli. For example, Parkin and Walter (1991) showed an age-related impairment on the Brown–Peterson Task (Brown, 1958; Peterson & Peterson, 1959), a measure of short-term or working memory involving the retention of small amounts of information over brief intervals filled with a distracter task to prevent rehearsal. They also found that this deficit correlated with impairments on tests of word fluency and the WCST (tasks typically performed poorly by patients with frontal-lobe damage). It should also be noted that working memory decline in aging may itself account for a substantial proportion of the age-related variance in longer term or secondary memory, as measured by tasks assessing object memory or spatial memory (Frieske & Park, 1992). Salthouse (1991a) proposed an even more general influence, suggesting that diminished working memory skills, reflecting slower execution of simple processing operations, are the source of many age-related deficits in fluid aspects of cognition.

Frontal Versus Hippocampal System Contributions to Recall and Recognition Memory

Moscovitch and Winocur (1992), after reviewing a range of cognitive aging studies, argued that frontal-system dysfunction makes a significant contribution to impairments in several aspects of the memory performance of older adults. West (1996), who also reviewed relevant cognitive aging research, concluded that a decline in the temporal integration function of the prefrontal cortex (supported by the four specific processes of prospective memory, retrospective memory, interference control, and inhibition of prepotent responses) could account for age-related memory impairment on a variety of tasks. However, West also concluded that the frontal-system hypothesis did not appear to be able to account for age-related declines in item recall and recognition, which he suggested might be due to deterioration in medial temporal-lobe/hippocampal system function. Moscovitch and Winocur similarly noted in their review that the "memory processes common to recognition and recall are those likely to be mediated by the hippocampal system, which is involved in consolidation, retention, and the automatic aspects of retrieval . . . that are triggered by the appropriate cue" (p. 352). They noted, however, that strategic self-initiated retrieval is required by many tests of recall but not most tests of recognition. Moscovitch and Winocur argued that this strategic retrieval aspect of memory is mediated by a frontal system.

In addition to the neurobiologic evidence for an age-related vulnerability of the frontal lobes and their related structures, there is also some neurobiologic evidence for a vulnerability of the hippocampal system. This evidence includes MRI documentation of age-related atrophy of the hippocampal region (Jernigan et al., 1991), which has been found to be correlated with performance on delayed-recall tasks among normally aging individuals (Golomb et al., 1993, 1994). Aspects of spatial memory appear to be particularly affected by age-related changes in the hippocampal system, as demonstrated in rodent studies (Barnes, 1991). Furthermore, substantial human age group differences are observed on spatial memory tasks similar to those most sensitive to experimental hippocampal lesions in rats (e.g., Newman, & Kaszniak, in press; Wilkniss, Jones, Korol, Gold, & Manning, 1997). Moscovitch and Winocur (1992) suggested that the greater age-related deficit commonly observed in recall than in recognition (for a review, see Kaszniak, Poon, & Riege, 1986) is likely to reflect the fact that recall depends more heavily on both hippocampal and frontal systems, which each decline with aging. Recognition, with its reduced demand on strategic self-initiated retrieval, is seen as primarily dependent on the hippocampal system.

Organizational Control Processes in Recall

Recent research has continued to provide support for the frontal-system hypothesis in accounting for age-related decline on recall memory tasks. For example, Stuss, Craik, Sayer, Franchi, and Alexander (1996) compared the word list learning of three groups of healthy adults (young, middle aged, and older) with that of three groups of patients who had documented damage in specific frontal brain regions (unilateral right, unilateral left, and bilateral). Qualitative aspects of recall, particularly those reflecting organizational control process, showed similarity between the healthy older adults and patients with frontal damage, especially those with right frontal damage.

Even more direct evidence for the contribution of frontal-system decline to age-group differences in performance of recall tasks requiring strategic self-initiated processing has been provided by recent positron emission tomography (PET) studies of regional cerebral blood flow (rCBF) during memory task performance. The results of these studies concur in that they show age-related differences in frontal rCBF during memory encoding, retrieval, or both (Cabeza et al., 1997; Grady et al., 1995; Schacter, Savage, Alpert, Rauch, & Albert, 1996).

Temporal Order Memory

Moscovitch and Winocur (1992) hypothesized that frontal-system decline plays an important role in age-related impairment on tasks of temporal order memory, and recent research has continued to provide support for this hypothesis. In neuropsychological studies, human frontal-lobe damage has been shown to result in a deficit in the temporal organization of memory (for a review, see Schacter, 1987), reflected in poor performance on memory tasks requiring recency judgments (e.g., Butters, Kaszniak, Glisky, Eslinger, & Schacter, 1994). Older adults have been found to perform worse than young adults on tasks requiring recall of the order of word lists, pictures, and activities (Kausler, Lichty, & Davis, 1985; Naveh-Benjamin, 1990). In a study of temporal order memory and aging, Parkin, Walter, and Hunkin (1995) evaluated healthy younger and older adults on neuropsychological tests known to be sensitive to frontal-lobe damage (i.e., word and design fluency, WCST) and on tests of recognition memory and memory for temporal and spatial information. The older participants showed impairment, relative to the younger adults, on memory for temporal order. This impairment was significantly correlated with deficits on the fluency tasks.

Source Memory

Cognitive aging studies have also provided support for Moscovitch and Winocur's (1992) hypothesis that frontal-system decline contributes to the difficulty older adults experience in identifying the source of information they have learned. This difficulty is particularly marked in the oldest-old (Erngrund, Mäntylä, & Nilsson, 1996). Studies of persons with amnesic syndromes, due to various neurologic etiologies, have shown them to have difficulty in remembering both facts and the sources from which they learned these facts. When disproportionately severe, this source memory deficit has been referred to as *source amnesia* (for a review, see Schacter, 1987). In a study in which amnesic patients' fact memory was experimentally equated with that of normal control patients (by testing the patients with amnesia at shorter delays after fact exposure), it was found that their source memory deficit was correlated with inferred degree of frontal-system dysfunction (from WCST and verbal fluency performance) and not with severity of their amnesia (Schacter, Harbluk, & McLachlan, 1984). Stronger neuropsychological evidence linking source memory to frontal-system functioning comes from a study by Janowsky, Shimamura, and Squire (1989), who demonstrated source memory impairment in patients with frontal-lobe lesions who did not have amnesia for fact information. In a study of healthy adults, Craik, Morris, Morris, and Loewen (1990) reported the accuracy of source memory in their older participants to be correlated with WCST performance, thus providing suggestive evidence linking source memory and frontal-system functioning in aging.

As pointed out by Schacter, Kihlstrom, Kaszniak, and Valdiserri (1993), interpretation of the Craik et al. (1990) study is problematic, because it is unclear whether the difference between older and younger adults' source memory was greater than the group difference in memory for target items. To remedy this, Schacter, Kaszniak, Kihlstrom, and Valdiserri (1991) examined older and younger adults' memory for novel facts that had been read to them by one of two experimenters (sources). For an experimental condition (blocked-item presentation) in which fact memory was equivalent for the two groups, the older adults showed disproportionate source memory deficits. This finding was confirmed and extended by Schacter and colleagues (Schacter, Osowiecki, Kaszniak, Kihlstrom, & Valdiserri, 1994), who showed age-related source memory deficits across encoding conditions that manipulated the allocation of attention to the source or to the fact. Similar to Craik and colleagues (1990), Schacter, Kaszniak, Kihlstrom, & Valdiserri (1991) found a significant negative correlation between source recall (conditionalized for fact recall) and proportion of perseverative errors on the WCST. The correlation between WCST perseverative errors and fact recall was not significant. Thus, suggestive evidence was again provided for a link between frontal-system functioning and source (but not fact) memory in older adults.

Additional evidence for a relationship between source memory and frontal-system functioning in aging was provided by Glisky, Polster, and Routhieaux (1995), who divided older adult participants into two groups on the basis of their performance on a composite measure of frontal-lobe function (derived from a factor analysis showing consistent association among the WCST, verbal fluency, and mental arithmetic and working memory tasks). The two groups did not differ in a test of sentence (fact) memory, although those with "high-frontal" function performed significantly better than those with "low-frontal" function on a test of memory for the voice (source) in which sentences were spoken. When the same participants were divided according to performance on a composite measure of medial temporal lobe/hippocampal system function (also derived from factor analysis, showing consistent association among several psychometric memory measures), the high-functioning group performed better than the low-functioning group on sentence memory, but the groups were not different on memory for voice. Thus, the observed double dissociation is consistent with the interpretation that fact memory is affected by medial temporal/hippocampal system functioning, and source memory by frontal-system functioning, in older aged people (however, see Dywan, Segalowitz, & Williamson, 1994).

Implicit Versus Explicit Memory

A final domain for which the frontal-system hypothesis has contributed to understanding age-related memory differences concerns the distinction between *implicit* and *explicit* memory, referring to two ways in which memories can be expressed. Schacter and colleagues (1993) provide the following definitions:

> Explicit memory entails conscious intentional recollection of previous experiences, as expressed on recall and recognition tests that require subjects to think back to a specific study episode. Implicit memory entails facilitations of test performance that are attributable to specific previous experiences, but are expressed without conscious recollection, on tasks that do not require subjects to think back to a specific study episode. (pp. 329–330)

The hypothesis that performance on implicit versus explicit memory tasks is under the control of different neural systems has been supported by numerous studies documenting intact implicit but impaired explicit memory in neurologic amnesic syndromes (for a review, see Schacter, Kaszniak, & Kihlstrom, 1991). The location of cerebral damage in people with amnesic syndromes has suggested that explicit memory is dependent on the integrity of the medial temporal lobe/hippocampal system, whereas implicit memory is not. Because dissociations among different kinds of implicit-memory tasks (e.g., word stem completion repetition priming, pursuit-rotor tracking, mirror-reversed reading) have been observed when comparing patients with differing neurologic etiologies (e.g., Bondi & Kaszniak, 1991), it is possible that there may be different implicit memory systems, each dependent on distinct neural architecture.

A large number of studies have compared younger and older adults' performance on various explicit- and implicit-memory tasks. As noted by reviewers of this literature (e.g., Light, 1991; Schacter et al., 1993), results have been variable, with some studies showing evidence (e.g., on various priming tasks) of intact implicit memory in older adults and other studies showing impairment, relative to younger participants. Some of the variability in results may reflect methodological differences among studies (see Schacter et al., 1993), although there is the possibility of differential aging vulnerability of distinct neural systems underlying performance on different implicit-memory tasks (Woodruff-Pak & Finkbiner, 1995). More recent evidence has suggested that age-related differences in performance on at least one type of implicit memory task may be related to frontal-system aging. Winocur, Moscovitch, and Stuss (1996) gave groups of older and younger adults tests of implicit and explicit memory, using word stem and word fragment completion paradigms, and also administered neuropsychological tests that were sensitive to frontal and medial temporal/

hippocampal functioning. Comparisons of explicit and implicit test results with the neuropsychological test scores revealed significant correlations between explicit memory (based on word list recall) and performance on standard clinical memory tests (known to be sensitive to medial temporal/ hippocampal damage) in both age groups. In contrast, implicit-memory scores for the word stem completion task (but not for the word fragment task) of both age groups were correlated with neuropsychological tests thought to be sensitive to frontal damage (i.e., WCST and verbal fluency). Winocur et al. interpreted this evidence of double dissociation to be consistent with the hypothesis that explicit and implicit memory are dependent on different neural systems. They also concluded that their results indicate repetition priming in word stem completion and word fragment completion to involve different mechanisms and that frontal lobe dysfunction is a contributor to reduced word stem completion priming.

Neurobiologic evidence for the differential aging of neural systems subserving implicit versus explicit memory comes from PET research. Bäckman et al. (1997) used PET to record rCBF during implicit (word stem completion repetition priming) and explicit (word list recall) retrieval tasks. Younger adults showed significantly better explicit memory than did older adults, and repetition priming (implicit) performance nominally favored the younger adults, although this difference did not reach statistical significance. PET rCBF measures showed a number of similarities between the younger and older participants, for both the priming and recall conditions (i.e., a decrease in posterior cerebral rCBF during the priming task and left prefrontal/anterior cingulate rCBF increase for the recall task). However, the young participants showed left cerebellar and temporal– parietal area rCBF increases during recall, whereas the older participants did not. The cerebellar activation difference is of interest in the context of the frontal-system hypothesis, given that reciprocal connectivity between the cerebellum and prefrontal cortex has been demonstrated (Middleton & Strick, 1994).

Attention and Visuospatial Ability

Other recent cognitive aging research has provided evidence that the frontal-system hypothesis may also be able to explain age group differences in cognitive task performance that extend beyond memory, into the domains of attention and visuospatial ability. One of the most widely used visual selective attention tasks is the Stroop Color Word Test (SCWT; Stroop, 1935; see also MacLeod, 1991). The classical *Stroop effect* involves a slowing of reading speed in an interference condition wherein the color of ink in which color names are printed is incongruent with the color word (in comparison to noninterference conditions in which color words printed in black ink are read or the color of circles or other forms is identified).

The Stroop effect appears to reflect interference and difficulty in response inhibition during the parallel processing of relevant and irrelevant information (Cohen, Dunbar, & McClelland, 1990) and has been shown to be sensitive to frontal-lobe damage (Perret, 1974). PET studies have shown a number of frontal brain structures (particularly the anterior cingulate cortex) to be activated during Stroop task performance (Bench et al., 1993; Pardo, Pardo, Janer, & Raichle, 1990). Cognitive aging research has consistently demonstrated age group differences in the Stroop interference effect (Cohn, Dustman, & Bradford, 1984; Klein, Ponds, Houx, & Jolles, 1997; Panek, Rush, & Slade, 1984; Spieler, Balota, & Faust, 1996; Uttl & Graf, 1997). The age-related increase in the Stroop effect appears to reflect interference for incongruent color and word, because the degree of reading facilitation when color and word are congruent is similar for older and younger people (Spieler et al., 1996).

Recently, West and Bell (1997) provided neuropsychological evidence that furthers a theoretic understanding of these Stroop aging effects. Their study was motivated by a body of research in cognitive neuroscience that has provided evidence for the existence of at least two attention systems (for a review, see Posner, 1995). A posterior attention system involves the posterior parietal cortex, the pulvinar nucleus of the thalamus, and the superior colliculus and appears to be primarily involved in attention allocation to visual space. An anterior attention system, involving the anterior cingulate and prefrontal cortices, appears to be involved whenever there is the need to selectively attend to one of the multiple streams of cognitive processing. West and Bell noted that cognitive aging research has documented robust age group differences for selective attention tasks that presumably are supported by the anterior attention system (e.g., the SCWT). However, research using spatial cueing tasks, which are known to activate the posterior attention system, has consistently failed to show adult age group differences (e.g., Hartley, Kieley, & Slabach, 1990; Nissen & Corkin, 1985). West and Bell compared healthy younger and older adults in performance on a Stroop task in which color and word could be congruent or incongruent and spatially integrated or separated. During task performance, a continuous EEG was recorded from frontal, parietal, and occipital scalp regions. The magnitude of the Stroop interference effect and task-related EEG activation was found to be greater for older adults than for younger adults when the color and word were integrated. The EEG effect was significant over more anterior, but not posterior, scalp regions. In contrast, the interference effect and EEG activation did not differ significantly for younger and older adults when stimuli were separated. West and Bell interpreted these findings as supporting the hypothesis that the anterior attention system is more sensitive to aging effects than is the posterior attention system.

As already noted, observations of greater age-related decline in visuospatial than in verbal task performance originally led theorists to posit the right-hemisphere hypothesis. Poor performance on visuospatial tasks (e.g., the WAIS–R Block Design subtest) can be due to difficulties in spatial relationship representation and processing (which are more dependent on the right cerebral hemisphere than on the left cerebral hemisphere). However, visuospatial task errors can also occur because of poor task strategy or attention deficits, possibly reflecting frontal-system dysfunction (Milberg, Hebben, & Kaplan, 1996). Motivated by such considerations, Libon et al. (1994) administered both timed and untimed versions of various neuropsychological tests thought to be sensitive to frontal damage (e.g., the WCST, verbal fluency) and several visuospatial tests to groups of young-old (ages 74 and younger) and old-old (ages 75 and older) participants. Some of the visuospatial tests required substantial integrative skill for their completion, whereas the others required little or no integrative skill. Libon and colleagues found the two age groups to differ in performance on the high-integrative-skill visuospatial tests and on many of the frontal tests but not on the nonintegrative-function visuospatial tests. Performance on the high-integrative-function visuospatial tests, but not the non-integrative-function ones, was significantly correlated with performance on the frontal tests. Libon et al. interpreted these results as supporting the proposal that an age-related decline in frontal-system functioning underlies the decline in performance of certain visuospatial tasks.

In summary, it is clear that the frontal-system hypothesis has received substantial support from a range of neuropsychological, neurobiological, and cognitive aging studies. The hypothesis of frontal-system decline with aging appears able to account for a variety of age-related memory effects as well as particular age group differences in attention and visuospatial task performance. The frontal-system hypothesis has motivated a large number of cognitive aging studies, influencing both the kinds of questions that have been asked and the research methodologies that have been used. The major theoretical impact of this hypothesis for the field of cognitive aging studies appears to be its ability to tie together a variety of disparate observations concerning different areas of cognitive function, suggesting that they might all have a common basis in age-related frontal-system decline.

PRECLINICAL CHANGES IN AD AND COGNITIVE AGING RESEARCH

Another example of neuropsychology's impact comes from longitudinal studies of dementia and their implications for future research methodologies in cognitive aging. The research reviewed in the previous three sections of this chapter makes the assumption that task performance and neurobiological differences between younger and older individuals are reflective of normal aging phenomena. Some recent research, however, suggests caution in the acceptance of this assumption. AD is an age-related degenerative disorder of the brain that results in severe progressive impairment in a range of cognitive functions (for reviews, see Bondi, Salmon, & Kaszniak, 1996; Kaszniak, 1986). Longitudinal studies (e.g., Bondi et al., 1994; Linn et al., 1995) have shown that subtle cognitive changes can precede the clinical identification of AD by 7 years or more. Given the high prevalence of AD, particularly among the older-old (Jorm, 1990), it is possible that a substantial number of the participants in studies of presumably normal aging may actually be in the preclinical stages of a dementing illness such as AD.

The extent to which this possibility could affect estimates of normal cognitive functioning in aging is illustrated in a study by Sliwinski, Lipton, Buschke, and Stewart (1996). Using longitudinal data, Sliwinski et al. retrospectively identified persons in the preclinical stages of dementia at baseline on the basis of subsequently meeting criteria for a diagnosis of dementia. Age-adjusted norms were computed, using baseline data for the WAIS and a psychometric memory measure (the Selective Reminding Test), both including and then excluding preclinical cases. Results showed that by failing to exclude preclinical dementia cases, conventional normative studies underestimate the mean, overestimate the variance, and overestimate the effect of age on cognitive measures. Such results raise questions about whether the current body of cognitive aging research can reasonably be considered to describe normal aging or rather some combination of normal aging and the preclinical cognitive changes of dementia. Sliwinski and colleagues (1996) discussed various methods (e.g., screening with sensitive memory tests along with other neuropsychological measures shown to be predictive of dementia) for selecting elderly samples that are relatively free of contamination by preclinical dementia. Should future studies support the validity of one or more of these methods, their incorporation would appear to be an important addition to the procedures of future cognitive aging research.

SUMMARY AND CONCLUSION

Since the 1980s, there has been a dramatic increase in research and theory concerned with neurobiological and neuropsychological aspects of both healthy older age and age-associated neurological illness. In this chapter we examined the ways in which this body of research and theory has influenced cognitive aging research and practice. Comparisons between the patterns of neuropsychological deficits observed following focal brain damage and the patterns of cognitive changes seen in normal aging have led theorists to hypothesize neuropsychological models of cognitive aging. The first of these models, the right-hemisphere hypothesis, although not receiving consistent empirical support, has motivated a number of neuropsychological, neurobiological, and novel experimental cognitive investigations designed to test its implications. An alternative model, the frontal-system hypothesis, has been supported by increasingly consistent evidence. This hypothesis has influenced many of the questions and methods of cognitive aging research and has contributed to a better understanding of neurobiological factors in cognitive aging. The frontal-system hypothesis has been shown to be capable of accounting for a wide variety of age-related cognitive changes. The major theoretical impact of the frontal-system hypothesis for the field of cognitive aging appears to be its ability to tie together various apparently disparate aspects of age-related cognitive change, suggesting a possible common basis in frontal-system decline. Finally, recent studies on preclinical neuropsychological changes in AD have suggested the possibility that previous cognitive aging studies may have overestimated the degree of cognitive decline associated with healthy aging. This has important implications for both the interpretation of prior research and for potential methods to be used in the sample selection of future studies.

REFERENCES

Albert, M. S., & Kaplan, E. (1980). Organic implications of neuropsychological deficits in the elderly. In L. W. Poon, J. L. Fozard, L. S. Cermak, D. Arenberg, & L. W. Thompson (Eds.), *New directions in memory and aging* (pp. 403–432). Hillsdale, NJ: Erlbaum.

Axelrod, B. N., & Henry, R. R. (1992). Age-related performance on the Wisconsin Card Sorting, Similarities and Controlled Oral Word Association Tests. *The Clinical Neuropsychologist, 6,* 16–26.

Bäckman, L., Almkvist, O., Andersson, J., Nordberg, A., Winblad, B., Reineck, R., & Langström, B. (1997). Brain activation in young and older adults during implicit and explicit retrieval. *Journal of Cognitive Neuroscience, 9,* 378–391.

Baddeley, A. (1986). *Working memory.* Oxford, England: Oxford University Press.

Barnes, C. A. (1991). Memory changes with age: Neurobiological correlates. In J. L. Martinez & R. P. Kesner (Eds.), *Learning and memory: A biological view* (2nd ed., pp. 259–296). New York: Academic Press.

Bench, C. J., Frith, C. D., Grasby, P. M., Friston, K. J., Paulesu, E., Frackowick, R. S. J., & Dolan, R. J. (1993). Investigations of the functional anatomy of attention using the Stroop task. *Neuropsychologia, 31,* 907–922.

Benton, A. L., Eslinger, P. J., & Damasio, A. R. (1981). Normative observations on neuropsychological test performance in old age. *Journal of Clinical Neuropsychology, 3,* 33–42.

Benton, A. L., & Hamsher, K. (1978). *Multilingual Aphasia Examination manual.* Iowa City: University of Iowa.

Bondi, M. W., & Kaszniak, A. W. (1991). Implicit and explicit memory in Alzheimer's disease and Parkinson's disease. *Journal of Clinical and Experimental Neuropsychology, 13,* 339–358.

Bondi, M. W., Monsch, A. U., Galasko, D., Butters, N., Salmon, D. P., & Delis, D. C. (1994). Preclinical cognitive markers of dementia of the Alzheimer type. *Neuropsychology, 8,* 374–384.

Bondi, M. W., Salmon, D. P., & Kaszniak, A. W. (1996). The neuropsychology of dementia. In I. Grant & K. M. Adams (Eds.), *Neuropsychological assessment of neuropsychiatric disorders* (2nd ed., pp. 164–199). New York: Oxford University Press.

Borod, J. C., & Goodglass, H. (1980). Lateralization of linguistic and melodic processing with age. *Neuropsychologia, 18,* 79–83.

Brody, H. (1978). Cell counts in cerebral cortex and brainstem. In R. Katzman, R. D. Terry, & K. L. Bick (Eds.), *Alzheimer's disease: Senile dementia and related disorders* (pp. 345–352). New York: Raven Press.

Brown, J. (1958). Some tests of the decay theory of immediate memory. *Quarterly Journal of Experimental Psychology, 10,* 12–21.

Butters, M. A., Kaszniak, A. W., Glisky, E. L., Eslinger, P. J., & Schacter, D. L. (1994). Recency discrimination deficits in frontal lobe patients. *Neuropsychology, 8,* 343–353.

Cabeza, R., Grady, C. L., Nyberg, L., McIntosh, A. R., Tulving, E., Kapur, S., Jennings, J. M., Houle, S., & Craik, F. I. M. (1997). Age-related differences in neural activity during memory encoding and retrieval: A positron emission tomography study. *Journal of Neuroscience, 17,* 391–400.

Cherry, B. J., Hellige, J. B., & McDowd, J. M. (1995). Age differences and similarities in patterns of cerebral asymmetry. *Psychology and Aging, 10,* 191–203.

Coffey, C. E., Wilkinson, W. E., Parashos, L. A., Soady, S. A. R., Sullivan, R. J., Patterson, L. J., Figiel, G. S., Webb, M. C., Spritzer, C. E., & Djang, W. T. (1992). Quantitative cerebral anatomy of the aging human brain. *Neurology, 42,* 527–536.

Cohen, J. D., Dunbar, K., & McClelland, J. L. (1990). On the control of automatic processes: A parallel distributed processing account of the Stroop effect. *Psychological Review, 97,* 332–361.

Cohn, N. B., Dustman, R. E., & Bradford, D. C. (1984). Age-related decrements in Stroop Color Test performance. *Journal of Clinical Psychology, 40,* 1244–1250.

Comalli, P. E., Jr., Wapner, S., & Werner, H. (1962). Interference effects of Stroop Color–Word Test in childhood, adulthood, and aging. *Journal of Genetic Psychology, 100,* 47–53.

Craik, F. I. M., Morris, L. W., Morris, R. G., & Loewen, E. R. (1990). Relations between source amnesia and frontal lobe functioning in older adults. *Psychology and Aging, 5,* 148–151.

Daigneault, S., Braun, C. M., & Whitaker, H. A. (1992). Early effects of normal aging on perseverative and non-perseverative prefrontal measures. *Developmental Neuropsychology, 8,* 99–114.

Damasio, A. R. (1985). The frontal lobes. In K. M. Heilman & E. Valenstein (Eds.), *Clinical neuropsychology* (2nd ed., pp. 339–375). New York: Oxford University Press.

Dywan, J., Segalowitz, S. J., & Williamson, L. (1994). Source monitoring during name recognition in older adults: Psychometric and electrophysiological correlates. *Psychology and Aging, 9,* 568–577.

Elias, M. F., & Kinsbourne, M. (1974). Age and sex differences in the processing of verbal and nonverbal stimuli. *Journal of Gerontology, 29,* 162–171.

Erngrund, K., Mäntylä, T., & Nilsson, L.-G. (1996). Adult age differences in source recall: A population-based study. *Journal of Gerontology: Psychological Sciences, 51B,* P335–P345.

Fitzhugh, K. B., Fitzhugh, L. C., & Reitan, R. M. (1962). Wechsler–Bellevue comparisons in groups with "chronic" and "current" lateralized and diffuse brain lesions. *Journal of Consulting Psychology, 26,* 306–310.

Frieske, D. A., & Park, D. C. (1992, April). *Effects of working memory and organization on age differences in memory for scene information.* Paper presented at the fourth Cognitive Aging Conference, Atlanta, GA.

Gehardstein, P. C., Peterson, M. A., & Rapcsak, S. Z. (1998). Age-dependent changes in hemispheric specialization in an object discrimination task. *Journal of Clinical and Experimental Neuropsychology, 20,* 174–185.

George, A. E., de Leon, M. J., Gentes, C. I., Miller, J., London, E., Budzilovich, G. N., Ferris, S., & Chase, N. (1986). Leukoencephalopathy in normal and pathologic aging: I. CT of brain lucencies. *American Journal of Neuroradiology, 7,* 561–566.

Glisky, E. L., Polster, M. R., & Routhieaux, B. C. (1995). Double dissociation between item and source memory. *Neuropsychology, 9,* 229–235.

Goldstein, G., & Shelly, C. H. (1975). Similarities and differences between psychological deficit in aging and brain damage. *Journal of Gerontology, 30,* 448–455.

Goldstein, G., & Shelly, C. (1981). Does the right hemisphere age more rapidly than the left? *Journal of Clinical Neuropsychology, 3,* 65–78.

Goldstein, K. (1939). The organism: A holistic approach to biology derived from pathological data in man. New York: American Book Company.

Golomb, J., de Leon, M. J., Kluger, A., George, A. E., Tarshish, C., & Ferris, S. H. (1993). Hippocampal atrophy in normal aging: An association with recent memory impairment. *Archives of Neurology, 50,* 967–973.

Golomb, J., Kluger, A., de Leon, M. J., Ferris, S. H., Convit, A., Mittelman, M. S., Cohen, J., Rusinek, H., De Santi, S., & George, A. E. (1994). Hippocampal formation size in normal human aging: A correlate of delayed secondary memory performance. *Learning and Memory, 1,* 45–54.

Grady, C. L., MacIntosh, A. R., Horwitz, B., Maisog, J. M., Ungerleider, L. G.,

Mentis, M. J., Pietrini, P., Schapiro, M. B., & Haxby, J. V. (1995, July). Age-related reductions in human recognition memory due to impaired encoding. *Science, 269,* 218–221.

Gur, R. C., Gur, R. E., Obrist, W. D., Skolnick, B. E., & Reivich, M. (1987). Age and regional cerebral blood flow at rest and during cognitive activity. *Archives of General Psychiatry, 44,* 617–621.

Halstead, W. (1947). *Brain and intelligence: A quantitative study of the frontal lobes* Chicago: University of Chicago Press.

Hartley, A. A., Kieley, J. M., & Slabach, E. H. (1990). Age differences and similarities in the effects of cues and prompts. *Journal of Experimental Psychology: Human Perception and Performance, 16,* 523–537.

Haug, H., Barmwater, U., Eggers, R., Fischer, D., Kuhl, S., & Sass, N. L. (1983). Anatomical changes in aging brain: Morphometric analysis of the human prosencephalon. In J. Cervos-Navarro & H. I. Sarkander (Eds.), *Neuropharmacology: Aging* (Vol. 21, pp. 1–12), New York: Raven Press.

Haug, H., & Eggers, R. (1991). Morphometry of the human cortex cerebri and corpus striatum during aging. *Neurobiology of Aging, 12,* 336–338.

Hertzog, C. (1989). Influences of cognitive slowing on age differences in intelligence. *Developmental Psychology, 25,* 636–651.

Horn, J. L., & Cattell, R. B. (1967). Age differences in fluid and crystallized intelligence. *Acta Psychologia, 26,* 701–719.

Janowsky, J. S., Shimamura, A. P., & Squire, L. R. (1989). Source memory impairment in patients with frontal lobe lesions and amnesic patients. *Psychobiology, 17,* 3–11.

Jernigan, T. L., Archibald, S. L., Berhow, M. T., Sowell, E. R., Foster, D. S., & Hesselink, J. R. (1991). Cerebral structure on MRI, Part I: Localization of age-related changes. *Biological Psychiatry, 29,* 55–67.

Jorm, A. F. (1990). *The epidemiology of Alzheimer's disease and related disorders.* London: Chapman & Hall.

Junque, C., Pujol, J., Vendrell, P., Bruna, O., Jodar, M., Ribas, J. C., Vinas, J., Capdevela, A., & Marti-Vilata, J. L. (1990). Leukoaraiosis on magnetic resonance imaging and speed of mental processing. *Archives of Neurology, 47,* 151–156.

Kaszniak, A. W. (1986). The neuropsychology of dementia. In I. Grant & K. M. Adams (Eds.), *Neuropsychological assessment of neuropsychiatric disorders* (pp. 172–220). New York: Oxford University Press.

Kaszniak, A. W., Poon, L. W., & Riege, W. (1986). Assessing memory deficits: An information processing approach. In L. W. Poon, T. Crook, K. L. Davis, C. Eisdorfer, B. J. Gurland, A. W. Kaszniak, L. W. Thompson. (Eds.), *Handbook for clinical memory assessment of older adults* (pp. 168–188). Washington, DC: American Psychological Association.

Kausler, D. H., Lichty, W., & Davis, T. M. (1985). Temporal memory for performed activities: Intentionality and adult age differences. *Developmental Psychology, 211,* 1132–1138.

Kawamura, J., Terayama, Y., Takashima, S., Obara, K., Pavol, M., Meyer, J., Mortel, K., & Weathers, S. (1993). Leukoaraiosis and cerebral perfusion in normal aging. *Experimental Aging Research, 19*, 225–240.

Klein, M., Ponds, R. W. H. M., Houx, P. J., & Jolles, J. (1997). Effect of test duration on age-related differences in Stroop interference. *Journal of Clinical and Experimental Neuropsychology, 19*, 77–82.

Klisz, D. (1978). Neuropsychological evaluation in older persons. In M. Storandt, I. C. Siegler, & M. F. Elias (Eds.), *The clinical psychology of aging* (pp. 71–95). New York: Plenum.

Kosslyn, S. M., & Koenig, O. (1992). *Wet mind: The new cognitive neuroscience.* New York: Free Press.

Lavy, S., Melamed, M., Bentin, S., Cooper, G., & Rinot, Y. (1978). Bihemispheric decreases of regional cerebral blood flow in dementia: Correlations with age-matched normal controls. *Annals of Neurology, 4*, 445–450.

Lezak, M. D. (1995). *Neuropsychological assessment* (3rd ed.). New York: Oxford University Press.

Libon, D. J., Glosser, G., Malamut, B. L., Kaplan, E., Goldberg, E., Swenson, R., & Sands, L. P. (1994). Age, executive functions, and visuospatial functioning in healthy older adults. *Neuropsychology, 8*, 38–43.

Light, L. L. (1991). Memory and aging: Four hypotheses in search of data. *Annual Review of Psychology, 42*, 333–376.

Linn, R. T., Wolf, P. A., Bachman, D. L., Knoefel, J. E., Cobb, J. L., Belanger, A. J., Kaplan, E. F., & D'Agostino, R. B. (1995). The "preclinical phase" of probable Alzheimer's disease: A 13-year prospective study of the Framingham cohort. *Archives of Neurology, 52*, 485–490.

Mack, J. L., & Carlson, J. (1978). Conceptual deficits and aging: The Category Test. *Perceptual & Motor Skills, 46*, 123–128.

MacLeod, C. M. (1991). Half a century of research on the Stroop effect: An integrative review. *Psychological Bulletin, 109*, 163–203.

Marsh, G. R., & Thompson, L. W. (1977). Psychophysiology of aging. In J. E. Birren & K. W. Schaie (Eds.), *Handbook of the psychology of aging* (pp. 219–248). New York: Van Nostrand Reinhold.

Meudell, P. R., & Greenhalgh, M. (1987). Age-related differences in left and right hand skill and in visuo-spatial performance: Their possible relationships to the hypothesis that the right hemisphere ages more rapidly than the left. *Cortex, 23*, 431–445.

Middleton, F. A., & Strick, P. L. (1994, October). Anatomical evidence for cerebellar and basal ganglia involvement in higher cognitive function. *Science, 266*, 458–461.

Milberg, W. P., Hebben, N., & Kaplan, E. (1996). The Boston process approach to neuropsychological assessment. In I. Grant & K. M. Adams (Eds.), *Neuropsychological assessment of neuropsychiatric disorders* (2nd ed., pp. 58–80). New York: Oxford University Press.

Milner, B. (1963). Effects of different brain lesions on card sorting. *Archives of Neurology, 9,* 90–100.

Mittenberg, W., Seidenberg, M., O'Leary, D. S., & DiGiulio, D. V. (1989). Changes in cerebral functioning associated with normal aging. *Journal of Clinical and Experimental Neuropsychology, 11,* 918–932.

Moscovitch, M., & Winocur, G. (1992). The neuropsychology of memory and aging. In F. I. M. Craik & T. A. Salthouse (Eds.), *The handbook of aging and cognition* (pp. 315–372). Hillsdale, NJ: Erlbaum.

Nauta, W. J. H. (1971). The problem of the frontal lobe: A reinterpretation. *Journal of Psychiatric Research, 8,* 167–187.

Naveh-Benjamin, M. (1990). Coding of temporal order information: An automatic process? *Journal of Experimental Psychology: Learning, Memory, and Cognition, 16,* 117–126.

Nebes, R. D., Madden, D., & Berg, W. D. (1983). The effect of age on hemispheric asymmetry in visual and auditory identification. *Experimental Aging Research, 9,* 87–91.

Nelson, H. E. (1976). A modified card sorting test sensitive to frontal lobe defects. *Cortex, 12,* 313–324.

Newman, M. C., Kaszniak, A. W. (in press). Spatial memory and aging: Performance on a human analog of the Morris water maze. *Aging, Neuropsychology and Cognition.*

Nissen, M. J., & Corkin, S. (1985). Effectiveness of attention cueing in older and younger adults. *Journal of Gerontology, 40,* 185–191.

Nussbaum, P. D. (Ed.). (1997). *Handbook of neuropsychology and aging.* New York: Plenum.

Obler, L. K., Woodward, S., & Albert, M. L. (1984). Changes in cerebral lateralization in aging? *Neuropsychologia, 22,* 235–240.

Overall, J. E., & Gorham, D. R. (1972). Organicity versus old age in objective and projective test performance. *Journal of Consulting and Clinical Psychology, 39,* 98–105.

Owen, A. M., Downes, J. J., Sahakian, B. J., Polkey, C. E., & Robbins, T. W. (1990). Planning and spatial working memory following frontal lobe lesions in man. *Neuropsychologia, 28,* 1021–1034.

Panek, P. E., Rush, M. C., & Slade, L. A. (1984). Locus of the age–Stroop interference relationship. *Journal of Genetic Psychology, 145,* 209–216.

Pardo, J. V., Pardo, P. J., Janer, K. W., & Raichle, M. E. (1990). The anterior cingulate cortex mediates processing selection in the Stroop attention conflict paradigm. *Proceedings of the National Academy of Sciences, 87,* 61–63.

Parkin, A. J., & Walter, B. M. (1991). Aging, short-term memory, and frontal dysfunction. *Psychobiology, 19,* 175–179.

Parkin, A. J., Walter, B. M., & Hunkin, N. M. (1995). Relationships between normal aging, frontal lobe function, and memory for temporal and spatial information. *Neuropsychology, 9,* 304–312.

Perret, E. (1974). The left frontal lobe of man and the suppression of habitual responses in verbal categorical behavior. *Neuropsychologia, 12,* 323–330.

Peterson, L. R., & Peterson, M. J. (1959). Short-term retention of individual items. *Journal of Experimental Psychology, 58,* 193–198.

Pietrini, P., & Rapoport, S. I. (1994). Functional neuroimaging: Positron-emission tomography in the study of cerebral blood flow and glucose metabolism in human subjects at different ages. In C. E. Coffey & J. L. Cummings (Eds.), *Textbook of geriatric neuropsychiatry* (pp. 195–213). Washington, DC: American Psychiatric Press.

Posner, M. I. (1995). Attention in cognitive neuroscience: An overview. In M. S. Gazzaniga (Ed.), *The cognitive neurosciences* (pp. 615–624). Cambridge, MA: MIT Press.

Raz, N., Gunning, F. M., Head, D., Dupuis, J. H., McQuain, J., Briggs, S. D., Loken, W. J., Thornton, A. E., & Acker, J. D. (1997). Selective aging of the human cerebral cortex observed in vivo: Differential vulnerability of the prefrontal gray matter. *Cerebral Cortex, 7,* 268–282.

Reed, H. B. C., Jr., & Reitan, R. M. (1963a). Changes in psychological test performance associated with the normal aging process. *Journal of Gerontology, 18,* 271–274.

Reed, H. B. C., Jr., & Reitan, R. M. (1963b). A comparison of the effects of the normal aging process with the effects of organic brain damage on adaptive abilities. *Journal of Gerontology, 18,* 177–179.

Reitan, R. M. (1955a). Certain differential effects of left and right cerebral lesions in human adults. *Journal of Comparative and Physiological Psychology, 48,* 474–477.

Reitan, R. M. (1955b). The distribution according to age of a psychologic measure dependent upon organic brain functions. *Journal of Gerontology, 10,* 338–340.

Reitan, R. M. (1955c). An investigation of the validity of Halstead's measures of biological intelligence. *Archives of Neurology and Psychiatry, 73,* 28–35.

Reitan, R. M. (1967). Psychologic changes associated with aging and with cerebral damage. *Mayo Clinic Proceedings, 42,* 653–673.

Reitan, R. M., & Wolfson, D. (1996). Theoretical, methodological, and validational bases of the Halstead–Reitan Neuropsychological Test Battery. In I. Grant & K. M. Adams (Eds.), *Neuropsychological assessment of neuropsychiatric disorders* (2nd ed., pp. 3–42). New York: Oxford University Press.

Russell, E. W., Neuringer, C., & Goldstein, G. (1970). *Assessment of brain damage: A neuropsychological key approach.* New York: Wiley-Interscience.

Salthouse, T. A. (1991a). Mediation of adult age differences in cognition by reductions in working memory and speed of processing. *Psychological Science, 2,* 179–183.

Salthouse, T. A. (1991b). *Theoretical perspectives on cognitive aging.* Hillsdale, NJ: Erlbaum.

Sandor, T., Albert, M., Stafford, J., & Kemper, T. (1990). Symmetrical and asymmetrical changes in brain tissue with age as measured on CT scans. *Neurobiology of Aging, 11,* 21–27.

Schacter, D. L. (1987). Memory, amnesia, and frontal lobe dysfunction. *Psychobiology, 15,* 21–36.

Schacter, D. L., Harbluk, J. L., & McLachlan, D. R. (1984). Retrieval without recollection: An experimental analysis of source amnesia. *Journal of Verbal Learning and Verbal Behavior, 23,* 593–611.

Schacter, D. L., Kaszniak, A. W., & Kihlstrom, J. F. (1991). Models of memory and the understanding of memory disorders. In T. Yanigihara & R. Peterson (Eds.), *Memory disorders: Research and clinical practice* (pp. 111–134). New York: Marcel Dekker.

Schacter, D. L., Kaszniak, A. W., Kihlstrom, J. F., & Valdiserri, M. (1991). The relation between source memory and aging. *Psychology and Aging, 6,* 559–568.

Schacter, D. L., Kihlstrom, J. F., Kaszniak, A. W., & Valdiserri, M. (1993). Preserved and impaired memory functions in elderly adults. In J. Cerella, J. Rybash, W. Hoyer, & M. L. Commons (Eds.), *Adult information processing: Limits on loss* (pp. 327–350). San Diego, CA: Academic Press.

Schacter, D. L., Osowiecki, D., Kaszniak, A. W., Kihlstrom, J. F., & Valdiserri, M. (1994). Source memory: Extending the boundaries of age-related deficits. *Psychology and Aging, 9,* 81–89.

Schacter, D. L., Savage, C. R., Alpert, N. M., Rauch, S. L., & Albert, M. S. (1996). The role of hippocampus and frontal cortex in age-related memory changes: A PET study. *NeuroReport, 7,* 1165–1169.

Schaie, K. W., & Schaie, J. P. (1977). Clinical assessment and aging. In J. E. Birren & K. W. Schaie (Eds.), *Handbook of the psychology of aging* (pp. 692–723). New York: Van Nostrand Reinhold.

Shimamura, A. P., & Jurica, P. J. (1994). Memory interference and aging: Findings from a test of frontal lobe function. *Neuropsychology, 8,* 408–412.

Sliwinski, M., Lipton, R. B., Buschke, H., & Stewart, W. (1996). The effects of preclinical dementia on estimates of normal cognitive functioning in aging. *Journal of Gerontology: Psychological Sciences, 51B,* P217–P225.

Spieler, D. H., Balota, D. A., & Faust, M. E. (1996). Stroop performance in healthy younger and older adults and in individuals with dementia of the Alzheimer's type. *Journal of Experimental Psychology: Human Perception and Performance, 22,* 461–479.

Spitzform, M. (1982). Normative data in the elderly on the Luria–Nebraska Neuropsychological Battery. *Clinical Neuropsychology, 4,* 103–105.

Stroop, J. R. (1935). Studies of interference in serial verbal reactions. *Journal of Experimental Psychology, 18,* 643–662.

Stuss, D. T., Craik, F. I. M., Sayer, L., Franchi, D., & Alexander, M. P. (1996). Comparison of older people and patients with frontal lesions: Evidence from word list learning. *Psychology and Aging, 11,* 387–395.

Troyer, A. K., Cullum, C. M., Smernoff, E. N., & Kozora, E. (1994). Age effects on block design: Qualitative performance features and extended-time effects. *Neuropsychology, 8,* 95–99.

Uttl, B., & Graf, P. (1997). Color–word Stroop test performance across the adult life span. *Journal of Clinical and Experimental Neuropsychology, 19,* 405–420.

Wechsler, D. (1939). *The measurement of adult intelligence.* Baltimore: Williams & Wilkins.

Wechsler, D. (1958). *The measurement and appraisal of adult intelligence* (4th ed.). Baltimore: Williams & Wilkins.

Wechsler, D. (1981). *The Wechsler Adult Intelligence Scale—Revised.* New York: Psychological Corporation.

West, R. L. (1996). An application of prefrontal cortex function theory to cognitive aging. *Psychological Bulletin, 120,* 272–292.

West, R., & Bell, M. A. (1997). Stroop color–word interference and electroencephalogram activation: Evidence for age-related decline of the anterior attention system. *Neuropsychology, 11,* 421–427.

Whelihan, W. M., & Lesher, E. L. (1985). Neuropsychological changes in frontal functions with aging. *Developmental Neuropsychology, 1,* 371–380.

Wilkniss, S. M., Jones, M. G., Korol, D. L., Gold, P. E., & Manning, C. A. (1997). Age-related differences in an ecologically based study of route learning. *Psychology and Aging, 12,* 372–375.

Winocur, G., Moscovitch, M., & Stuss, D. T. (1996). Explicit and implicit memory in the elderly: Evidence for double dissociation involving medial temporal- and frontal-lobe functions. *Neuropsychology, 10,* 57–65.

Woodruff, D. S. (1978). Brain activity and development. In P. B. Baltes (Ed.), *Life-span development and behavior* (Vol. 1, pp. 19–29). New York: Academic Press.

Woodruff-Pak, D. S., & Finkbiner, R. G. (1995). Larger nondeclarative than declarative deficits in learning and memory in human aging. *Psychology and Aging, 10,* 416–426.

Ylikoski, R., Ylikoski, A., Erkinjuntti, T., Sulkava, R., Raininko, R., & Tilvis, R. (1993). White matter changes in healthy elderly persons correlate with attention and speed of mental processing. *Archives of Neurology, 50,* 818–824.

II

MEMORY AND AGING

PART II: MEMORY AND AGING

The dialogue evoked by these chapters centers around the causes and consequences of age-related memory loss. Leah L. Light documents the harsh facts: Older adults believe their memory is declining, and it is. Across testing conditions, and even across sensory systems, memory clearly declines with advancing age. The exception appears to be automatic memory, or familiarity, which shows more variable patterns. Two important questions are raised in these chapters: (a) why do most memory functions decline? and (b) under what conditions do the potential cognitive advantages of aging, advanced knowledge stores, compensate for memory decline and other kinds of deterioration in cognitive efficiency?

Light overviews three theories of memory that range from what she notes is an optimistic hypothesis—that older adults simply do not use appropriate strategies for encoding or retrieving material—to more pessimistic views that presume deterioration in more general cognitive-processing mechanisms. After examining the evidence for each hypothesis she concludes that the age-related declines evident in memory functions are likely closely linked to those of broader cognitive processes.

Neil Charness examines how age-related cognitive declines in memory and other domains of cognitive functioning might have less impact than expected because of the increased knowledge accumulated with advanced age. He describes conditions under which knowledge can and cannot compensate for the cognitive limitations that accompany aging.

There is probably no other area of psychology of aging that has witnessed the explosive growth in research as the area of cognition. These chapters raise interesting issues at the edge of current understanding while summarizing broad areas of research.

5

MEMORY CHANGES IN ADULTHOOD

LEAH L. LIGHT

Adults over age 60 report more problems with memory (Cutler & Grams, 1988), experience less perceived control over memory functions (Dixon & Hultsch, 1983) and, in fact, show age-related declines in memory. Older adults score lower on laboratory-based memory tasks such as recall and recognition (for reviews, see Light, 1991, 1996), on batteries of tasks designed to emulate memory in everyday life (Kirasic, Allen, Dobson, & Binder, 1996), and on standardized tests designed for use in neuropsychological assessment (Salthouse, Fristoe, & Rhee, 1996). Their memory is poorer for names and faces of people (Bahrick, 1984; Cohen & Faulkner, 1986), for odors they have recently experienced (Murphy, Nordin, & Acosta, 1997), for actions they have performed (Earles, 1996) or intend to perform (Mäntylä & Nilsson, 1997), and for the circumstances under which they learn of major political events (Cohen, Conway, & Maylor, 1994). The magnitude of these memory changes is revealed in a number of recent meta-analyses. Verhaeghen, Marcoen, and Goossens (1993) reported mean weighted effect sizes of −.38 for Digit Span (combined forward and backward spans), −.81 for working-memory measures, −.99 for

Preparation of this chapter was supported in part by Grant R37 AG02452 from the National Institute on Aging.

list recall, $-.91$ for paired-associate recall, and $-.67$ for prose recall. La Voie and Light (1994) obtained mean weighted effect sizes of $-.50$ for recognition memory and $-.97$ for recall; these numbers are virtually identical to those obtained by Spencer and Raz (1995). (An effect size is computed as the difference between means divided by the pooled standard deviation.) Although negative correlations between age and episodic memory tasks requiring recollection are found in adults younger than age 50 (mean weighted correlation = $-.15$), the rate of change in memory is greater after 50 (mean weighted correlation = $-.23$; Verhaeghen & Salthouse, 1997).

Negative relationships between age and memory cannot be attributed solely to health-related factors. When self-rated health measures are entered first in hierarchical regression analyses, age continues to be a significant predictor of memory in both laboratory measures and on neuropsychological tests (Nilsson et al., 1997; Salthouse et al., 1996), although conclusions about the impact of health on memory in older adults are limited by the fact that those who choose to participate in studies of memory typically rate themselves as being in good health. Memory deterioration is a hallmark of Alzheimer's disease and there is reason to believe that memory changes may be manifest well before a diagnosis can be made. Thus, there is a possibility that age-related differences in memory are found because some proportion of the older adult sample is in a preclinical phase of Alzheimer's disease or some other form of dementia. However, in a longitudinal study of a community-based sample of older adults aged 75–85, age-related changes in memory were seen both in those who were later diagnosed with dementia and those not so diagnosed during the study (Sliwinski, Lipton, Buschke, & Stewart, 1996). It is also possible that age-related memory impairment could be associated with depression; however, it is not clear that the rate of clinical depression increases in old age and, although scores on depression indexes can be associated with memory, partialing scores on depression measures does not eliminate the contribution of age to variability on memory tests (Rabbitt, Donlan, Watson, McInnes, & Bent, 1995).

Most studies of the relationship between memory and age in adulthood involve cross-sectional designs. Thus, it is possible that it is not age per se but some other variable associated with increased age at any given moment that is responsible for observed memory declines. The prime candidate for such a cohort-related account would be education, inasmuch as education level is negatively correlated with age in the general population. However, negative correlations between memory and age remain when the effects of education level are statistically controlled. For instance, in a large population-based study, controlling for education did not have much impact on the effects of age on a memory composite that included free recall of sentences, recall of nouns studied and tested under divided-attention conditions, and name recognition, but did eliminate negative effects of age on a memory factor that included verbal fluency and general knowledge (Nilsson et al., 1997). Also, age differences in memory are found even in highly educated groups engaged in professional activities with high memory demands (Perlmutter, 1978). Finally, longitudinal studies in which the same individuals are followed over time show memory declines with increasing age (see Zelinski & Burnight, 1997, for a review).

As suggested by these introductory paragraphs, age-related changes in memory are thoroughly documented. Explanation of such changes, however, has lagged behind their documentation. This chapter provides a brief overview of current theoretical accounts of memory impairment in old age. Three major hypotheses are considered: (a) failures of strategic processing, (b) problems in the utilization of context, and (c) changes in basic mechanisms presumed to underlie many aspects of cognition. The goal here is not to provide exhaustive coverage but rather to convey a sense of how each approaches the explanatory enterprise.

FAILURES OF STRATEGIC PROCESSING

According to one set of views, memory declines in old age arise from problems with metamemory; that is, poorer memory stems from incorrect beliefs about the nature of memory, failure to use task-appropriate encoding and retrieval strategies, faulty monitoring of encoding or retrieval processes, or poor self-efficacy in the memory domain. Although the evidence suggests that folk beliefs about the nature of memory and memory demands in different situations are age invariant (Loewen, Shaw, & Craik, 1990), three hypotheses predict that older adults should be less likely than young adults to act on these beliefs by engaging in strategies that optimize encoding or retrieval of information.

Disuse

According to the *disuse* perspective, younger adults are typically engaged in lifestyles that involve more demands on memory than those of older adults. With fewer memory demands placed on them, older adults would have fewer opportunities to engage in the kinds of mnemonic strategies that enhance performance in laboratory-based memory tasks. The disuse perspective leads to a number of predictions that are by and large inconsistent with available evidence. First, older adults should report using fewer strategies than younger adults, but in questionnaire studies similar frequencies of use for different kinds of internal memory strategies are found across age, although older adults may rely more on external memory aids, whereas younger adults rely more on internal memory aids (Dixon & Hultsch, 1983; Perlmutter, 1978).

Second, the disuse perspective predicts that expertise should moderate age declines in domain-relevant tasks; that is, older people who continue to practice their expertise in a particular domain should experience the same memory demands as young adults who are experts in the same domain and should therefore show the same level of memory in domain-relevant memory tasks. There is some evidence that this is the case (for a more detailed analysis of this issue, see chap. 6). For instance, Morrow, Leirer, Altieri, and Fitzsimmons (1994) found that age differences were smaller for pilots than for nonpilots in a task that simulated memory for air traffic control messages. Nonetheless, there are counterexamples. For example, in Morrow et al.'s study there was no moderation of age differences by expertise when the same people were asked to memorize an air space map. Similarly, age differences in memory for visually presented melodies are found for both musically experienced and inexperienced participants, although the task demands would seem to be relevant to sight-reading music (Meinz & Salthouse, 1998).

Third, the disuse perspective predicts an attenuation of age effects in memory following extended practice. However, Baltes and Kliegl (1992) reported a larger age difference after 38 sessions of training with the method of loci than at the start of practice.

Fourth, it seems unlikely that the frequency of demands for prospective memory decline with age. For example, medication use increases with age, yet age differences have been found for prospective memory in both event-based tasks (in which an external cue signals that it is time to respond) and in duration-based tasks (in which the participant is asked to respond after a certain period of time has elapsed), especially when background task demands are high (Einstein, Smith, McDaniel, & Shaw, 1997; Park, Hertzog, Kidder, Morrell, & Mayhorn, 1997).

Self-Initiation of Encoding and Retrieval Strategies

Memorial representations of experience are likely to be the by-product of routine encoding operations such as those involved in language comprehension. Thus, any age-related changes in memory structures that represent knowledge about language or general world knowledge or in processes that support language comprehension would be expected to have deleterious effects on memory. However, there is little evidence for changes in semantic organization or in the way that word meanings or general world knowledge is accessed during language comprehension. Young and older adults share the same system of meanings for concepts and pragmatic information, and access to this information appears to be similar in extent and time course across age. Extended discussions of these conclusions (and possible qualifications of them) are available elsewhere (Light, 1991, 1992, 1996; MacKay & Abrams, 1996). A few examples will suffice to illustrate this point here. Knowledge of word meanings as exemplified by performance on vocabulary tests is relatively unaffected by age and is often higher in samples of older adults tested in laboratory studies (see Kausler, 1991, for a review). Older adults may also perform even better than young adults when asked to read words with unusual spelling-to-sound correspondences, suggesting that they have larger vocabularies (Graf & Uttl, 1995). Word associations do not differ in kind or distributional frequency across age (Burke & Peters, 1986). The extent of semantic priming in lexical decision and naming tasks is similar across age (Laver & Burke, 1993). Online construction of inferences based on word meaning occurs as readily in old people as in young (Light, Valencia-Laver, & Zavis, 1991).

Nevertheless, it is possible that postcomprehension strategies for acquisition and retrieval of new information differ across age. A number of mnemonic devices are known to improve memory dramatically, although such strategies are rarely used in everyday life, in part because they require a great deal of effort to use. Still, such strategies may play a role in remembering in laboratory studies of memory. Older adults are slower than young adults, have reduced working-memory capacity, and may also have reduced attentional capacity (see below). Less frequent use of self-initiated encoding and retrieval strategies may arise as an adaptation to reduced processing resources (Craik, 1986). If so, then age differences should be reduced by guiding encoding through orienting tasks and using retention tests that demand less effort.

Some, but not all, components of this explanation have received empirical support. For instance, there has been little empirical investigation of the relationships among individual-difference variables (e.g., speed or working memory), strategy use, and memory. In one noteworthy exception to this generalization, older adults said that they engaged less often in strategies of associating items within a list and rehearsing items or testing themselves; age differences in use of these strategies were mediated by speed and in turn predicted list recall (Verhaeghen & Marcoen, 1994, but see Dunlosky & Hertzog, 1998). Nonetheless, not all studies find age differences in strategy use, and age differences persist even when young and older adults report using the same encoding strategies (Dunlosky & Hertzog, 1998). Experimental manipulations that benefit young adults also tend to benefit older adults. Older adults' mean recall has been well predicted by younger adults' mean recall over a wide range of conditions (Verhaeghen & Marcoen, 1993a). In addition, older adults' scores on individual items in list recall, paired-associate learning, and prose memory have been strongly predicted by younger adults' scores on the same items (Verhaeghen

& Marcoen, 1993b). Thus, age differences in memory are not well explained by strategy-failure accounts.

With respect to retrieval support, the data are mixed. Recognition memory tests afford more retrieval support than do free- and cued-recall tests, and age differences are smaller in such tasks (LaVoie & Light, 1994; Spencer & Raz, 1995). However, it is possible to equate retrieval support while varying the precise requirements of the memory task. This is typically done by manipulating task instructions so that a task either requires deliberate recollection (a direct measure of memory) or does not (an indirect measure). For instance, at test people can be provided with category names and asked either to generate members of the category or to use the category names as retrieval cues for recently studied list members. With the first type of instructions, there is an increase in the likelihood of generating previously studied category members, an effect known as *priming*. Age differences are typically found for category-cued recall but not for priming in exemplar generation (Light & Albertson, 1989). Thus, intent to recollect is an important determinant of age differences on memory tasks when retrieval support is held constant.

Memory Self-Efficacy

There is evidence for small correlations between self-efficacy beliefs and performance on memory tests (Zelinski, Gilewski, & Anthony-Bergstone, 1990). The question is whether age differences in self-efficacy are causally related to age differences in memory. The evidence suggests that they are not. First, it might be predicted that reduced self-efficacy would lead older adults to underestimate how much they can remember. However, older adults are at least as good as young adults in assessing feelings of knowing that are involved in predicting recognition of currently unrecallable information (Butterfield, Nelson, & Peck, 1988). Similarly, there do not seem to be age differences in predicting how much of a list will be remembered when the items are assessed during study or shortly afterward (Connor, Dunlosky, & Hertzog, 1997). Second, in longitudinal studies the relationship between memory self-efficacy and performance has been variable. For instance, Taylor, Miller, and Tinklenberg (1992) found a decrease in recall over 4 years in adults aged 60–85, but estimates of frequency of forgetting in everyday life did not change. Moreover, even when self-assessments of memory and performance both decline across measurement occasions, there are competing explanations for the covariation. Changes in assessments of memory may simply track performance changes. Alternatively, changes in self-assessment could reflect implicit theories of memory change, whereas performance changes reflect "real" memory declines (McDonald-Misczak, Hertzog, & Hultsch, 1995).

IMPAIRED PROCESSING OF CONTEXTUAL INFORMATION

Some contemporary theories posit two processes that subserve both recall and recognition memory. Following Jacoby (1991), these are referred to as *recollection* and *familiarity*, although more recently Jacoby and his colleagues have abandoned the term *familiarity* and simply refer to *automatic retrieval processes*. Both recollection (or controlled aspects of retrieval) and familiarity give rise to the subjective experience that something has been previously encountered. Familiarity processes are believed to be more automatic and to be based on activation or intra-item integration (Mandler, 1980) or on perceptual fluency (Jacoby, 1991). Recollective processes involve conscious remembering of particular aspects of a prior episode, such as perceptual details, spatial or temporal information, the source of information, or thoughts and feelings that accompanied the episode. Single-process theories (e.g., Hintzman, 1988) also acknowledge the crucial role played by contextual information in determining the similarity between current experiences and memories of earlier events. Moreover, reality monitoring—separating fact from fantasy—requires memory for episodic details as well as thoughts and feelings or other cognitive activities carried out as an event is experienced (Johnson, Foley, Suengas, & Raye, 1988).

Several lines of evidence comport well with hypotheses that age-related deficits in recall and recognition stem from reduced efficiency in encoding or retrieval of contextual information, while familiarity-based mechanisms are relatively preserved. Although it is unlikely that any measures of memory are process pure (Jacoby, 1991), it is reasonable to assume that recollective processes that depend on contextual information are most heavily involved in recall, with recognition having a larger familiarity component and indirect measures of memory that do not solicit deliberate recollection having the largest contribution from familiarity. This ordering of classes of memory tasks with respect to recollective processes is consonant with the ordering of their effect sizes (La Voie & Light, 1994). Here I briefly discuss evidence from a variety of paradigms that suggests that memory for contextual information declines in later adulthood, whereas performance on indirect measures of memory is relatively spared.

Memory for Contextual Information

When queried about particulars of earlier experiences, older adults report fewer details than do young adults. Summaries of the literature on this topic may be found elsewhere (Kausler, 1991; Light, 1991, 1996), but a few illustrative examples are offered here. Hashtroudi, Johnson, and Chrosniak (1990) asked young and older adults to carry out some scripted activities (e.g., packing a picnic basket) and to imagine carrying out others that were described to them in detail. The recall protocols of older adults contained fewer mentions of colors, nonvisual sensory information (touch, sounds, and smells), spatial references, and actions, although there were no age differences in number of words, ideas, or mentions of people. When asked about particular details of events, older adults are less apt to remember whether a word appeared in the most recent of a series of lists or in an earlier one (Kliegl & Lindenberger, 1993), whether they already carried out a particular act (Koriat, Ben-Zur, & Sheffer, 1988), or which orienting task they performed for particular items during study (Brigham & Pressley, 1988).

In a meta-analysis, Spencer and Raz (1995) found mean effect sizes of .87 and .58 for content and context, respectively, suggesting that memory for context is disproportionally affected in old age. Such a conclusion must be viewed with some caution, because the studies included in the meta-analysis examined memory for contextual information contingent on memory for content. Even if memory for content and for context were equally affected by aging, we would expect to find larger age differences for context than for content on recognition memory tasks—getting a content item correct by chance requires one guess on a recognition test, but getting both content and context correct by chance takes two guesses. Nonetheless, there are several studies that have systematically equated memory for content in young and older adults (e.g., Chalfonte & Johnson, 1996; Kliegl & Lindenberger, 1993) and still report age differences in context memory.

Other findings are also consistent with impairment of recollection and relative sparing of familiarity-based mechanisms. In the remember–know paradigm participants indicate not only whether they recognize test items as previously presented, but also whether they remember specific details about the circumstances in which they originally encountered list words or just "know" that the words were presented. Remember judgments decrease with age, whereas know judgments remain constant or increase (Parkin & Walter, 1992). Older adults are more influenced by misleading information presented after they have witnessed a series of events (Cohen & Faulkner, 1989). After studying lists of items associated with target concepts, older adults have more false alarms for the target concepts than do young adults, a form of memory illusion (K. A. Norman & Schacter, 1997). Older adults are also more likely to call a previously seen nonfamous name "famous" on seeing it later (Dywan & Jacoby, 1990). Finally, using opposition methodology, in which feelings of familiarity can lead to incorrect responses in the absence of contextual information, Jennings and Jacoby (1993, 1997) have obtained separate estimates of familiarity and recollection within a single paradigm. Estimates of recollection show age differences favoring young people, but estimates of familiarity tend to be age invariant; this result must be viewed cautiously, however, because it holds only if familiarity and recollection are assumed to be independent processes, an assumption that has been challenged (e.g., Curran & Hintzman, 1995).

Indirect Measures of Memory

Graf and Schacter (1985) differentiated between two broad classes of indirect measures of memory: (a) those involving memory for words or objects that have pre-existing memory representations (*item priming*) and (b) those involving memory for new connections or for novel stimuli (*associative priming*). Roediger and his colleagues (e.g., Srinivas & Roediger, 1990) have suggested a further distinction between priming tasks that are largely perceptual in nature and those that are primarily conceptual. The former include tasks such as perceptual identification and word stem or word fragment completion that are not sensitive to variations in levels of processing (semantic vs. nonsemantic orienting tasks) at study but are influenced by changes in the format of presentation (e.g., from auditory to visual) between study and test. The latter include tasks such as category exemplar generation and answering general knowledge questions that are sensitive to levels of processing during encoding but not to changes in format between study and test.

Age differences are usually, although not always, unreliable in studies of both item and associative priming. For example, nonsignificant age differences have been observed for perceptual priming tasks such as word identification (Light & Kennison, 1996) and word fragment completion (Light, Singh, & Capps, 1986) and for conceptual priming tasks such as exemplar generation (Light & Albertson, 1989) and answering general knowledge questions (Small, Hultsch, & Masson, 1995). Although age differences are sometimes obtained on item-priming tasks, such findings are not as consistently obtained as are age differences in recall and recognition, and the effect sizes are on average smaller for priming (La Voie & Light, 1994). Such findings are readily interpretable in terms of two-process models that claim that item priming depends on activation, familiarity, or perceptual fluency. Because older adults have difficulty in forming new connections, it might be anticipated that age differences would be obtained on associative priming even if none were found for item priming. However, in La Voie and Light's (1994) meta-analysis, effect sizes for item and associative priming were not reliably different, although the number of effect sizes in each category was too small for definitive conclusions to be drawn.

The evidence reviewed above generally accords well with the existence of age decrements in processes involving context-dependent deliberate recollection together with relative sparing of activation or familiarity processes. Still, there is empirical evidence that is handled less well by this hypothesis. First, the conclusion that context-dependent mechanisms are less efficient in old age depends in part on results from studies in which participants were asked directly about contextual details. When memory for context is tested indirectly by varying the match between study and test contexts, young and older adults appear to be equally influenced by mismatches (e.g., Schramke & Bauer, 1997), a pattern consistent with a more global age deficit in memory for content and context that is detectable only when memory is measured directly. Second, if age differences in recall and recognition arise solely from defective encoding or retrieval of contextual information, equating young and old on content memory might be expected to eliminate age differences in context but, as noted above, this is not invariably the case. It remains possible, of course, that the contribution of familiarity processes is greater in older adults, so that equating overall performance on memory for content does not result from equal contributions from all processes across age. Third, some activation processes may be impaired in old age. For instance, older adults have increased word-finding problems, such as are shown in greater frequency of tip-of-the-tongue experiences, suggesting a deficit in transmission of activation from concepts to orthographic or phonological representations in memory (Burke, MacKay, Worthley, & Wade, 1991). Fourth, finding a significant effect size for indirect measures of memory is potentially problematic. Although this may signify nothing more than the intrusion of deliberate recollection into what are nominally nonrecollective memory tasks, something likely to benefit young adults more than older adults, it is also consistent with a more global age deficit in memory. In addition to these empirical issues, the assumption that the same familiarity processes participate in recall, recognition, and priming may be flawed, necessitating a reexamination of the bases for hypothesizing a unitary familiarity mechanism that is spared in old age (see, e.g., Wagner, Gabrieli, & Verfaellie, 1997).

GENERAL PROCESSING DEFICIT HYPOTHESES

I have thus far considered age-related changes in memory in isolation. However, it has long been known that many other aspects of cognition show changes in old age as well (see Verhaeghen & Salthouse, 1997, for a meta-analysis). Explanations of age-related changes in memory arguably should also be able to encompass age-related changes in other aspects of cognition. In this section I consider four general processing deficit accounts of cognitive aging as they have been applied to episodic memory: reduced attentional capacity, reduced working memory capacity, inhibition deficit, and cognitive slowing. These accounts are often considered under the rubric of *resource deficit hypotheses*.

Reduced Attention Capacity

The attention and working-memory deficit hypotheses share a set of assumptions, namely, that tasks vary in their attentional or working-memory capacity requirements; that there are stable individual differences in attention or working-memory capacity; and that, on average, older adults have less available capacity. The major prediction from this hypothesis is that when two tasks must be performed concurrently the performance of older adults should suffer more than that of younger adults relative to single-task conditions. Early studies of divided attention using memory tasks reported mixed results. Many studies, however, did not provide an adequate test of the hypothesis that older adults are less well able than young adults to divide attention because they failed to equate young and old under single-task conditions. Age-related differences in dual-task conditions involving short-term or working-memory tasks appear to be much smaller when performance is equated across age on the component tasks (Salthouse, Fristoe, Lineweaver, & Coon, 1995). There have been relatively few studies of divided attention, memory, and aging using long-term recall or recognition. Recall involves less retrieval support than recognition and is therefore generally considered to impose heavier demands on attention or working memory. Moreover, there is a large literature that demonstrates negative effects of dividing attention during encoding on subsequent recall and recognition in young adults (see Craik, Govoni, Naveh-Benjamin, & Anderson, 1996, for a summary). It might, therefore, be expected that dividing attention during either study or retrieval would have disproportionally larger effects in the old. Again, however, the literature has not yielded consistent results, with some studies finding greater divided-attention costs for old adults and others reporting similar effects of similar magnitude across age (see Light, 1996, for a review). Recent evidence does suggest that the burden of dividing attention may be greater in old adults for both encoding and retrieval, but that the effects of concurrent activity will be more pronounced on the secondary task than on the memory task itself, especially when the memory task is recall rather than recognition (Anderson, Craik, & Naveh-Benjamin, 1998). This is consistent with the idea that recognition has a smaller attention component than does recall.

Findings from the remember–know paradigms are in accord with this conclusion. In young adults the probability of remember judgments is reduced by division of attention during study, whereas that of know judgments is not (Gardiner & Parkin, 1990). Similarly, estimates of recollection in the process dissociation paradigm are reduced by divided attention, whereas those of familiarity are not (Jacoby, 1996). The pattern of reduced remember judgments and estimates of recollection in older adults, coupled with constant or increased know judgment frequency and constancy of familiarity estimates, discussed earlier, is consistent with the notion that reduced attentional capacity mediates deliberate recollection but not more automatic aspects of memory.

Reduced Working Memory Capacity

Baddeley and Hitch (1994) described a three-component limited-capacity working-memory model. In this model working memory consists of (a) a phonological loop specialized for storage and manipulation of speech-based information, (b) a visuospatial sketchpad specialized for storage and manipulation of visual and spatial information, and (c) a central executive that functions as an attentional control system. Because it is difficult to imagine cognitive tasks that do not require both storage and manipulation of information, age-related changes in working memory would be expected to reduce performance in such tasks as language comprehension, learning, and verbal and spatial reasoning. For instance, Light, Zelinski, and Moore (1982) argued that working-memory limitations explain why older adults have difficulty integrating information across several premises, even when recognition for these premises does not vary with age. Similarly, Kemper and her colleagues have shown that older adults have more difficulty than do young adults in imitating left-branching sentences and in remembering prose passages containing many left-branching sentences and judging the grammaticality of such sentences (Kemper, 1986; S. Norman, Kemper, & Kynette, 1992). Left-branching sentences are more complex syntactically than are right-branching sentences and are thought to impose a heavier load on working memory.

Task complexity has also been manipulated by varying the number of identical mental operations that need to be carried out or the amount of material that must be stored in working memory to accomplish a task. For example, Salthouse (1992) demonstrated that older adults are differentially affected by such manipulations as increasing the number of premises presented in a verbal reasoning task or the number of folds in a piece of paper that must be tracked before a hole is punched and the appearance of the unfolded paper is assessed. Nonetheless, not all manipulations that would be expected to interact with age have done so. Two examples will suffice here (for further examples, see reviews by Light, 1996, and Stine, 1995). Increasing the propositional density of sentences of a constant length, a manipulation that also increases syntactic complexity, produces effects of the same magnitude on gist recall in young and old adults (Stine, Wingfield, & Poon, 1986). Also, the time to decide if a statement is true or false (*semantic verification latency*) is not differentially slowed in older people by increasing the size of a concurrent memory load (Morris, Gick, & Craik, 1988).

In the past several years, considerable attention has been devoted to determining the extent to which working memory mediates age-related changes in other cognitive domains. Age-related differences have been obtained on a variety of both verbal and visuospatial working-memory tasks (see Salthouse, 1994b, for a review). For instance, Salthouse and Babcock (1991) found that older adults have shorter reading and computation spans. In their reading span task, people read a series of sentences, answered a question about each, and then recalled the last word of each sentence in the set. In the computation span task, people solved a series of arithmetic problems and then reported the last digit in each problem. For both types of spans, younger adults were accurate on longer sets than were older adults. Salthouse and Babcock argued that the age differences they observed were best explained by younger adults' greater ability to carry out operations rapidly (i.e., processing efficiency) rather than by age-related differences in the ability to store information or to monitor and coordinate the activities needed to carry out the tasks.

In studies designed to determine whether working-memory capacity mediates age-related changes in memory, participants are administered one or more measures of working memory along with measures of performance in other domains. The typical finding is that partialling out working-memory measures attenuates age-related differences in tasks as diverse as reading comprehension (S. Norman et al., 1992), memory for prose (Kwong See & Ryan, 1995), memory for actions (Earles, 1996), appropriate use of pronouns in recall (Pratt, Boyes, Robins, & Manchester, 1989), memory in simulated everyday tasks (Kirasic et al. 1996), and verbal reasoning (Gilinsky & Judd, 1994; Salthouse, 1992), although results have been mixed for prospective memory (Kidder, Park, Hertzog, & Morrell, 1997; Park et al., 1997). Generally speaking, however, age differences remain after statistical control of working memory, implicating additional factors.

Inhibition Deficit

Rather than focusing on capacity limitations in working memory, the inhibition-deficit hypothesis postulates that age-related deficits in cognition arise from differences in working-memory contents. According to this view, activation processes (such as those involved in semantic priming tasks) are spared in old age, but older adults are impaired in inhibitory processes that prevent the access of off-target ideas to working memory, the deletion of irrelevant or no-longer-relevant information from working memory, and restraint over prepotent but task-inappropriate responses (Hasher & Zacks, 1988; Zacks & Hasher, 1997). The inhibition-deficit approach has been influential in a number of domains, including attention, language, and memory (for reviews of the first two, see Burke, 1997; McDowd, 1997; and Zacks & Hasher, 1997).

In the domain of memory, several findings have been attributed to deficient inhibitory processing. Thus, in garden path passages, in which a plausible interpretation of events is later shown to be incorrect, older adults are more likely to maintain both correct and incorrect inferences than are young adults (Hamm & Hasher, 1992). When asked to read sentences that have highly probable endings that are not actually presented, older adults are more likely than young adults to subsequently produce these on a sentence completion task (Hartman & Hasher, 1991). In directed-forgetting studies, older adults show smaller differences in memory for to-be-remembered and to-be-forgotten words (Zacks, Radvansky, & Hasher, 1996). These findings are all compatible with older adults failing to suppress information that is no longer relevant. Older adults also show larger fan effects than young adults; that is, they are slower to respond that a sentence belongs to a memorized set if that sentence shares concepts with other memorized sentences (Gerard, Zacks, Hasher, & Radvansky, 1991). This result has been interpreted as evidence that older adults are more susceptible to interference at encoding and retrieval. The presence of extraneous thoughts during encoding leads to storage of more irrelevant associations, and at retrieval these irrelevant associations become activated and add to the search burden for older adults. Finally, as discussed above, older adults have larger memory illusions in which unstudied target words that are associates of lists of studied words are falsely recognized (K. A. Norman & Schacter, 1997).

It is interesting that many of these findings have plausible alternative explanations. Dywan and Murphy (1996) found that although younger adults make fewer "stumbles" involving the incorrect reading of to-be-ignored words interspersed in text than older adults make, they subsequently recognize more of these words, suggesting that young adults were more successful at suppressing the pronunciation of distracting material but not at preventing their initial perception of this material. The fact that older adults are more likely to incorrectly select distractor words or phrases as answers to comprehension questions is interpreted as a failure to retain the source of the information. Similarly, Dywan and Murphy suggested that the results of directed-forgetting studies can be interpreted as due to difficulties that older adults have in correctly attributing the source of familiarity attending both to-be-remembered and to-be-forgotten material. Enhanced fan effects in older adults may also arise from confusion about which facts were presented in the study phase of the experiment. Hartman (1995) reported that older adults were not more likely than young adults to use expected but disconfirmed study words as completions in a later sentence completion task if the to-be-selected words were clearly indicated at study. Also, when the unexpected ending that is to be remembered is followed by a sentence that embeds the to-be-selected target in an elaborated context, age differences in completion rates for no-longer-relevant words are abolished (Hasher, Quig, & May, 1997). Both findings are consonant with the view that older adults have difficulty in maintaining contextual information about which words are to be remembered and which are to be forgotten but that this problem can be ameliorated under some circumstances. As far as memory illusions are concerned, these, too, would seem to be explainable as problems in attributing the source of activation in old age.

Some other predictions of the inhibition-deficit hypothesis also lack strong empirical support. There is little evidence that older adults are more likely to entertain both meanings of semantically ambiguous words (Paul, 1996) or to activate a broader range of attributes of concepts during sentence comprehension (Light et al., 1991). The inhibition-deficit hypothesis predicts that older adults should experience more blockers or persistent alternates coming to mind during tip-of-the-tongue states, but this does not occur (Burke et al., 1991). Older adults also claim to have fewer rather than more task-unrelated thoughts during a vigilance task (Giambra, 1989). Older adults report better memory for thoughts and feelings surrounding an event and sometimes also recall more thoughts and feelings and less perceptual and contextual information than do young adults (Hashtroudi et al., 1990), a pattern consistent with older adults having more off-target thoughts during recall. It is possible, however, that this reflects only a difference in young and older adults' construal of the demand characteristics of the recall task (Hashtroudi, Johnson, Vnek, & Ferguson, 1994). One might also expect that if older adults are less able to inhibit target-irrelevant information, age differences should be smaller for contextual information (that people are not asked to remember) than for target information but, if anything, the opposite seems true (Spencer & Raz, 1995).

Cognitive Slowing

Older adults are slower than young adults on virtually every task in which speed of performance has been assessed. Verhaeghen and Salthouse (1997) reported a mean weighted correlation of $-.50$ between age and perceptual speed for 20 studies. Indeed, it is generally found that the latencies of older adults are longer than the latencies of young adults by a constant proportion, although that proportion may vary across domains (Hale, Lima, & Myerson, 1991; Myerson, Ferraro, Hale, & Lima, 1992) or even across apparently similar tasks within a domain (Salthouse & Coon, 1994). Studies of time–accuracy functions also indicate that older adults need more time than do young adults to achieve the same level of performance, although old–young ratios may vary as a function of the type of operation required within a task domain (Mayr & Kliegl, 1993).

Cognitive slowing has been attributed to increased neural noise (Salthouse & Lichty, 1985), broken or attenuated neural connections (Cerella, 1990), weakened connections between nodes in memory (MacKay & Burke, 1990), and to greater loss of information at each stage of processing (Myerson, Hale, Wagstaff, Poon, & Smith, 1990). Deficits in transmission of activation within a network can explain age-related declines in memory without invoking the concept of attentional capacity. For instance, slower transmission of activation could decrease the number of nodes that are simultaneously active (one definition of working memory). Transmission deficits can also prevent formation of new associations and can cause activation failures in existing connections, leading to retrieval failures such as the ones that occur in the tip-of-the-tongue experience (see MacKay & Abrams, 1996, for a review). Salthouse (1996) suggested two mechanisms by which cognitive slowing constrains performance in old age: the *limited time* and *simultaneity* mechanisms. When external constraints limit available time for processing, the need to spend more time on operations early in a sequence decreases the time available for later ones. In addition, slower execution speed may reduce the availability of the outcomes of earlier steps in processing that are needed for the completion of subsequent steps by means of decay or displacement of information. Note that increasing the amount of time allowed for mental operations cannot, on this account, compensate for cognitive slowing, because the problem lies with the individual's processing rate rather than with external time constraints.

Although results have been mixed, strong evidence for speed mediation of age–memory relationships has often been found (Salthouse, 1996). To give but a few examples, speed mediation of age-related variability has been obtained for free and cued recall (Dunlosky & Salthouse, 1996; Park et al., 1996), paired-associate learning (Salthouse, 1994a), memory for activities (Earles, 1996), spatial memory (Park et al., 1996), and text memory (Sliwinski & Buschke, 1997). It is interesting that, in a study using process dissociation methodology, speed measures were found to account for age-related variability in estimates of recollection (controlled memory) but not in familiarity (automatic processes; Salthouse, Toth, Hancock, & Woodard, 1997). In a number of these and other studies, statistical control of speed has reduced age–memory relationships to the point at which they are no longer significant. Although our focus is on memory, it is important to keep in mind that there is considerable shared variance among many aspects of cognition. For example, Lindenberger, Mayr, and Kliegl (1993) found that factors representing reasoning, memory, fluency, and knowledge all loaded on a common factor, with the age–common relationship fully mediated by a speed factor. Thus, processing speed appears to be predictive of performance in a variety of cognitive domains.

Given the considerable success of speed as a mediator of age–memory relationships, one may ask whether processing speed is the sole source of age-related variability in memory. Measures of processing speed mediate relationships between both age and working memory (Salthouse & Babcock, 1991) and between age and measures thought to be markers of inhibition, such as Stroop interference (Salthouse & Meinz, 1995) and performance on the Wisconsin Card Sorting Test (Fristoe, Salthouse, & Woodard, 1997). However, there is evidence that inhibitory constructs are needed to account for some working-memory phenomena, raising the possibility that individual differences in working memory arise not so much from differences in automatic activation as from differences in attentional resources or central executive function (Engle, 1996). Age–cognition relationships are not always fully explained by speed and, in some instances, both speed and working memory have proven to be important predictors of age-related differences in performance (Kirasic et al., 1996; Park et al., 1996; Salthouse, 1996). In a recent meta-analysis of age–cognition relationships in adulthood, Verhaeghen and Salthouse (1997) found that processing speed, primary working memory, episodic memory, reasoning, and spatial ability all declined with increasing age and that processing speed and primary working memory were important mediators of performance on the remaining abilities. For episodic memory the percentages of age-related variance accounted for by speed alone, primary working memory alone, and both together were 70.5, 45.8, and 76.4, respectively. Thus, some unexplained age-related variability remained. Measures of inhibition were not included in this meta-analysis, so it is unknown how inhibition might have fared as a mediator of episodic memory.

In addition, there is emerging evidence that constructs other than speed and working memory can explain age-related differences in cognition. Both simple measures of sensory and sensorimotor function have also been shown to be capable of mediating age–cognition relationships (Anstey, Lord, & Williams, 1997; Lindenberger & Baltes, 1994). As we have seen, it is easy to develop plausible mechanisms by which processing speed, working memory, or inhibition might mediate age–cognition correlations. It is less easy to generate such mechanisms for measures of vision, hearing, and lower limb strength. Baltes and Lindenberger (1997) espoused a common-cause hypothesis by which such measures are taken as indicators of a general decline in brain function. Salthouse, Hambrick, and McGuthry (1998) suggested that the observed dependencies may arise because of variability shared by all measures with age rather than because age-related changes in noncognitive variables are causally related to changes in cognitive variables. Although the precise meaning of these findings is as yet unclear, what is clear is that investigations of memory changes in old age cannot be carried out in isolation from investigations of changes in other aspects of cognition.

CONCLUSION

In this chapter several contemporary hypotheses about the source of pervasive age-related changes in memory have been considered. These have ranged from more optimistic views that memory-related declines stem from reduced use of appropriate encoding or retrieval strategies that hold out the possibility of remediation by appropriately supportive environments or training programs to much less optimistic views that memory impairments are caused by changes in basic processing mechanisms that underlie many or all aspects of cognition. Relatively little support has been educed for the view that changes in strategy use or semantic encoding are responsible for reduced performance on tasks requiring deliberate recollection. There is good evidence that older adults have poorer recollection of contextual information and that more automatic or familiarity mechanisms are relatively preserved in normal aging. Nonetheless, this distinction cannot provide a unified account for the observed patterns of spared and impaired aspects of memory and cognition. In particular, such an explanation is uninformative about relationships among memory, other aspects of cognition, and aging. Understanding such relationships requires an inquiry into more basic processes that subserve cognition in general, not only memory.

REFERENCES

Anderson, N. D., Craik, F. I. M., & Naveh-Benjamin, M. (1998). The attentional demands of encoding and retrieval in younger and older adults: I. Evidence from divided attention costs. *Psychology and Aging, 13*, 405–423.

Anstey, K. J., Lord, R. S., & Williams, P. (1997). Strength in lower limbs, visual contrast sensitivity, and simple reaction time predict cognition in older women. *Psychology and Aging, 12*, 137–144.

Baddeley, A. D., & Hitch, G. J. (1994). Development of the concept of working memory. *Neuropsychology, 8*, 485–493.

Bahrick, H. P. (1984). Memory for people. In J. E. Harris & P. E. Morris (Eds.), *Everyday memory, actions and absent-mindedness* (pp. 19–34). New York: Academic Press.

Baltes, P. B., & Kliegl, R. (1992). Further testing of limits of cognitive plasticity: Negative age differences in mnemonic skill are robust. *Developmental Psychology, 28*, 121–125.

Baltes, P. B., & Lindenberger, U. (1997). Emergence of a powerful connection between sensory and cognitive functions across the adult life span. *Psychology and Aging, 12*, 12–21.

Brigham, M. C., & Pressley, M. (1988). Cognitive monitoring and strategy choices in younger and older adults. *Psychology and Aging, 3*, 249–257.

Burke, D. M. (1997). Language, aging, and inhibitory deficits: Evaluation of a theory. *Journal of Gerontology: Psychological Sciences, 52B*, P254–P264.

Burke, D. M., MacKay, D. G., Worthley, J. S., & Wade, E. (1991). On the tip of the tongue: What causes word finding failures in young and older adults? *Journal of Memory and Language, 30*, 542–549.

Burke, D. M., & Peters, L. (1986). Word associations in old age: Evidence for consistency of semantic encoding during adulthood. *Psychology and Aging, 1*, 283–292.

Butterfield, E. C., Nelson, T. O., & Peck, V. (1988). Developmental aspects of the feeling of knowing. *Developmental Psychology, 24*, 654–663.

Cerella, J. (1990). Aging and information-processing rate. In J. E. Birren & K. W. Schaie (Eds.), *Handbook of the psychology of aging* (3rd ed., pp. 201–221). New York: Academic Press.

Chalfonte, B. L., & Johnson, M. K. (1996). Feature memory and binding in young and older adults. *Memory & Cognition, 24*, 403–416.

Cohen, G., Conway, M. A., & Maylor, E. A. (1994). Flashbulb memories in older adults. *Psychology and Aging, 9*, 454–463.

Cohen, G., & Faulkner, D. (1986). Memory for proper names: Age differences in retrieval. *British Journal of Developmental Psychology, 4*, 187–197.

Cohen, G., & Faulkner, D. (1989). Age differences in source forgetting: Effects on reality monitoring and on eyewitness testimony. *Psychology and Aging, 4*, 10–17.

Connor, L. T., Dunlosky, J., & Hertzog, C. (1997). Age-related differences in absolute but not relative metamemory accuracy. *Psychology and Aging, 12*, 50–71.

Craik, F. I. M. (1986). A functional account of age differences in memory. In F. Klix & H. Hagendorf (Eds.), *Human memory and cognitive capabilities* (pp. 409–422). Amsterdam, The Netherlands: Elsevier.

Craik, F. I. M., Govoni, R., Naveh-Benjamin, M., & Anderson, N. D. (1996). The effects of divided attention on encoding and retrieval processes in human memory. *Journal of Experimental Psychology: General, 125*, 159–180.

Curran, T., & Hintzman, D. L. (1995). Violations of the independence assumption in process dissociation. *Journal of Experimental Psychology: Learning, Memory, and Cognition, 21*, 531–547.

Cutler, S. J., & Grams, A. E. (1988). Correlates of self-reported everyday memory problems. *Journal of Gerontology: Social Sciences, 43*, S82–S90.

Dixon, R. A., & Hultsch, D. F. (1983). Structure and development of metamemory in adulthood. *Journal of Gerontology, 38*, 682–688.

Dunlosky, J., & Hertzog, C. (1998). Aging and deficits in associative memory: What is the role of strategy production? *Psychology and Aging*, 587–607.

Dunlosky, J., & Salthouse, T. A. (1996). A decomposition of age-related differences in multitrial free recall. *Aging, Neuropsychology, and Cognition, 3*, 2–14.

Dywan, J., & Jacoby, L. (1990). Effects of aging on source monitoring: Differences in susceptibility to false fame. *Psychology and Aging, 5,* 379–387.

Dywan, J., & Murphy, W. E. (1996). Aging and inhibitory control in text comprehension. *Psychology and Aging, 11,* 199–206.

Earles, J. L. (1996). Adult age differences in recall of performed and nonperformed items. *Psychology and Aging, 11,* 638–648.

Einstein, G. O., Smith, R. E., McDaniel, M. A., & Shaw, P. (1997). Aging and prospective memory: The influence of increased task demands at encoding and retrieval. *Psychology and Aging, 12,* 479–488.

Engle, R. W. (1996). Working memory and retrieval: An inhibition-resource approach. In J. T. E. Richardson, R. W. Engle, L. Hasher, R. H. Logie, E. R. Stoltzfuss, & R. T. Zacks (Eds.), *Working memory and human cognition* (pp. 89–119). New York: Oxford University Press.

Fristoe, N. M., Salthouse, T. A., & Woodard, J. L. (1997). Examination of age-related deficits on the Wisconsin Card Sorting Test. *Neuropsychology, 11,* 428–436.

Gardiner, J. M., & Parkin, A. J. (1990). Attention and recollective experience in recognition memory. *Memory & Cognition, 18,* 579–583.

Gerard, L., Zacks, R. T., Hasher, L., & Radvansky, G. A. (1991). Age deficits in retrieval: The fan effect. *Journal of Gerontology: Psychological Sciences, 46,* P131–P136.

Giambra, L. M. (1989). Task-unrelated-thought frequency as a function of age: A laboratory study. *Psychology and Aging, 4,* 136–143.

Gilinsky, A. S., & Judd, B. B. (1994). Working memory and bias in reasoning across the life span. *Psychology and Aging, 9,* 356–371.

Graf, P., & Schacter, D. L. (1985). Implicit and explicit memory for new associations in normal and amnesic subjects. *Journal of Experimental Psychology: Learning, Memory, and Cognition, 11,* 501–518.

Graf, P., & Uttl, B. (1995). Component processes of memory: Changes across the adult lifespan. *Swiss Journal of Psychology, 54,* 113–130.

Hale, S., Lima, S. D., & Myerson, J. (1991). General cognitive slowing in the nonlexical domain: An experimental validation. *Psychology and Aging, 6,* 512–521.

Hamm, V. P., & Hasher, L. (1992). Age and the availability of inferences. *Psychology and Aging, 7,* 56–64.

Hartman, M. (1995). Aging and interference: Evidence from indirect memory tests. *Psychology and Aging, 10,* 659–669.

Hartman, M., & Hasher, L. (1991). Aging and suppression: Memory for previously relevant information. *Psychology and Aging, 6,* 587–594.

Hasher, L., Quig, M. B., & May, C. P. (1997). Inhibitory control over no-longer-relevant information: Adult age differences. *Memory & Cognition, 25,* 286–295.

Hasher, L., & Zacks, R. T. (1988). Working memory, comprehension, and aging:

A review and a new view. In G. H. Bower (Ed.), *The psychology of learning and motivation: Advances in research and theory* (Vol. 22, pp. 193–225). New York: Academic Press.

Hashtroudi, S., Johnson, M. K., & Chrosniak, L. D. (1990). Aging and qualitative characteristics of memories for perceived and imagined complex events. *Psychology and Aging, 5,* 119–126.

Hashtroudi, S., Johnson, M. K., Vnek, N., & Ferguson, S. A. (1994). Aging and the effects of affective and factual focus on source monitoring and recall. *Psychology and Aging, 9,* 160–170.

Hintzman, D. L. (1988). Judgments of frequency and recognition memory in a multiple-trace memory model. *Psychological Review, 95,* 528–551.

Jacoby, L. L. (1991). A process dissociation framework: Separating automatic from intentional uses of memory. *Journal of Memory and Language, 30,* 513–541.

Jacoby, L. L. (1996). Dissociating automatic and consciously controlled effects of study/test compatibility. *Journal of Memory and Language, 35,* 32–52.

Jennings, J. M., & Jacoby, L. L. (1993). Automatic versus intentional uses of memory: Aging, attention, and control. *Psychology and Aging, 8,* 283–293.

Jennings, J. M., & Jacoby, L. L. (1997). An opposition procedure for detecting age-related deficits in recollection: Telling effects of repetition. *Psychology and Aging, 12,* 352–361.

Johnson, M. K., Foley, M. A., Suengas, A. G., & Raye, C. L. (1988). Phenomenal characteristics of memories for perceived and imagined events. *Journal of Experimental Psychology: General, 117,* 371–376.

Kausler, D. H. (1991). *Experimental psychology, cognition, and human aging* (2nd ed.). New York: Springer-Verlag.

Kemper, S. (1986). Imitation of complex syntactic constructions by elderly adults. *Applied Psycholinguistics, 7,* 277–288.

Kidder, D. P., Park, D. C., Hertzog, C., & Morrell, R. W. (1997). Prospective memory and aging: The effects of working memory and prospective memory task load. *Aging, Neuropsychology, and Cognition, 4,* 93–112.

Kirasic, K. C., Allen, G. L., Dobson, S. H., & Binder, K. S. (1996). Aging, cognitive resources, and declarative learning. *Psychology and Aging, 11,* 658–670.

Kliegl, R., & Lindenberger, U. (1993). Modeling intrusions and correct recall in episodic memory: Adult age differences in encoding of list context. *Journal of Experimental Psychology: Learning, Memory, and Cognition, 19,* 617–637.

Koriat, A., Ben-Zur, H., & Sheffer, D. (1988). Telling the same story twice: Output monitoring and age. *Journal of Memory and Language, 27,* 23–39.

Kwong See, S. T., & Ryan, E. B. (1995). Cognitive mediation of adult age differences in language comprehension. *Psychology and Aging, 10,* 458–468.

Laver, G. D., & Burke, D. M. (1993). Why do semantic priming effects increase in old age? A meta-analysis. *Psychology and Aging, 8,* 34–43.

La Voie, D., & Light, L. L. (1994). Adult age differences in repetition priming: A meta-analysis. *Psychology and Aging, 9,* 539–553.

Light, L. L. (1991). Memory and aging: Four hypotheses in search of data. *Annual Review of Psychology, 42,* 333–376.

Light, L. L. (1992). The organization of memory in old age. In F. I. M. Craik & T. A. Salthouse (Eds.), *The handbook of aging and cognition* (pp. 111–165). Hillsdale, NJ: Erlbaum.

Light, L. L. (1996). Memory and aging. In E. L. Bjork & R. A. Bjork (Eds.), *Memory* (pp. 443–490). San Diego, CA: Academic Press.

Light, L. L., & Albertson, S. A. (1989). Direct and indirect tests of memory for category exemplars in young and older adults. *Psychology and Aging, 4,* 487–492.

Light, L. L., & Kennison, R. L. (1996). Guessing strategies, aging, and bias effects in perceptual identification. *Consciousness and Cognition, 5,* 463–499.

Light, L. L., Singh, A., & Capps, J. L. (1986). Dissociation of memory and awareness in young and older adults. *Journal of Clinical and Experimental Neuropsychology, 8,* 62–74.

Light, L. L., Valencia-Laver, D., & Zavis, D. (1991). Instantiation of general terms in young and older adults. *Psychology and Aging, 6,* 337–351.

Light, L. L., Zelinski, E. M., & Moore, M. (1982). Adult age differences in reasoning from new information. *Journal of Experimental Psychology: Learning, Memory, and Cognition, 8,* 435–447.

Lindenberger, U., & Baltes, P. B. (1994). Sensory functioning and intelligence in old age: A strong connection. *Psychology and Aging, 9,* 339–355.

Lindenberger, U., Mayr, U., & Kliegl, R. (1993). Speed and intelligence in old age. *Psychology and Aging, 8,* 207–220.

Loewen, E. R., Shaw, R. J., & Craik, F. I. M. (1990). Age differences in components of metamemory. *Experimental Aging Research, 16,* 43–48.

MacKay, D. G., & Abrams, L. (1996). Language, memory, and aging: Distributed deficits and the structure of new-versus-old connections. In J. E. Birren & K. W. Schaie (Eds.), *Handbook of the psychology of aging* (4th ed., pp. 251–265). San Diego, CA: Academic Press.

MacKay, D. G., & Burke, D. M. (1990). Cognition and aging: A theory of new learning and the use of old connections. In T. M. Hess (Ed.), *Aging and cognition: Knowledge organization and utilization* (pp. 213–264). Amsterdam: North-Holland.

Mandler, G. (1980). Recognizing: The judgment of previous occurrence. *Psychological Review, 87,* 252–271.

Mäntylä, T., & Nilsson, L.-G. (1997). Remembering to remember in adulthood: A population-based study on aging and prospective memory. *Aging, Neuropsychology, and Cognition, 4,* 81–92.

Mayr, U., & Kliegl, R. (1993). Sequential and coordinative complexity: Age-based processing limitations in figural transformations. *Journal of Experimental Psychology: Learning, Memory, and Cognition, 19,* 1297–1320.

McDonald-Misczak, L., Hertzog, C., & Hultsch, D. F. (1995). Stability and accuracy of metamemory in adulthood and aging: A longitudinal analysis. *Psychology and Aging, 10,* 553–564.

McDowd, J. M. (1997). Inhibition in attention and aging. *Journal of Gerontology: Psychological Sciences, 52B,* P265–P273.

Meinz, E. J., & Salthouse, T. A. (1998). The effects of age and experience on memory for visually presented music. *Journal of Gerontology: Psychological Sciences, 53B,* P60–P69.

Morris, R. G., Gick, M. L., & Craik, F. I. M. (1988). Processing resources and age differences in working memory. *Memory & Cognition, 16,* 362–366.

Morrow, D., Leirer, V., Altieri, P., & Fitzsimmons, C. (1994). When expertise reduces age differences in performance. *Psychology and Aging, 9,* 134–148.

Murphy, C., Nordin, S., & Acosta, L. (1997). Odor learning, recall, and recognition memory in young and elderly adults. *Neuropsychology, 11,* 126–137.

Myerson, J., Ferraro, F. R., Hale, S., & Lima, S. D. (1992). General slowing in semantic priming and word recognition. *Psychology and Aging, 7,* 257–270.

Myerson, J., Hale, S., Wagstaff, D., Poon, L. W., & Smith, G. A. (1990). The information-loss model: A mathematical theory of age-related cognitive slowing. *Psychological Review, 97,* 475–487.

Nilsson, L.-G., Bäckman, L., Erngrund, K., Nyberg, L., Adolfsson, R., Bucht, G., Karlsson, S., Widing, M., & Winblad, B. (1997). The Betula prospective cohort study: Memory, health, and aging. *Aging, Neuropsychology, and Cognition, 4,* 1–32.

Norman, K. A., & Schacter, D. L. (1997). False recognition in younger and older adults: Exploring the characteristics of illusory memories. *Memory & Cognition, 25,* 838–848.

Norman, S., Kemper, S., & Kynette, D. (1992). Adults' reading comprehension: Effects of syntactic complexity and working memory. *Journal of Gerontology: Psychological Science, 47,* P258–P265.

Park, D. C., Hertzog, C., Kidder, D. P., Morrell, R. W., & Mayhorn, C. B. (1997). Effect of age on event-based and time-based prospective memory. *Psychology and Aging, 12,* 314–327.

Park, D. C., Smith, A. D., Lautenschlager, G., Earles, J. L., Frieske, D., Zwahr, M., & Gaines, C. L. (1996). Mediators of long-term memory performance across the life span. *Psychology and Aging, 11,* 621–637.

Parkin, A. J., & Walter, B. M. (1992). Recollective experience, normal aging, and frontal dysfunction. *Psychology and Aging, 7,* 290–298.

Paul, S. T. (1996). Search for semantic inhibition failure during sentence comprehension by young and older adults. *Psychology and Aging, 11,* 10–20.

Perlmutter, M. (1978). What is memory aging the aging of? *Developmental Psychology, 14,* 330–345.

Pratt, M. W., Boyes, C., Robins, S., & Manchester, J. (1989). Telling tales: Aging, working memory, and the narrative cohesion of story retellings. *Developmental Psychology, 25,* 628–635.

Rabbitt, P., Donlan, C., Watson, P., McInnes, L., & Bent, N. (1995). Unique and interactive effects of depression, age, socioeconomic advantage, and gender on cognitive performance of normal healthy older people. *Psychology and Aging, 10,* 307–313.

Salthouse, T. A. (1992). Why do adult age differences increase with task complexity? *Developmental Psychology, 28,* 905–918.

Salthouse, T. A. (1994a). Aging associations: Influence of speed on adult age differences in associative learning. *Journal of Experimental Psychology: Learning, Memory, and Cognition, 20,* 1486–1503.

Salthouse, T. A. (1994b). The aging of working memory. *Neuropsychology, 8,* 535–543.

Salthouse, T. A. (1996). The processing-speed theory of adult age differences in cognition. *Psychological Review, 103,* 403–428.

Salthouse, T. A., & Babcock, R. L. (1991). Decomposing adult age differences in working memory. *Developmental Psychology, 27,* 763–776.

Salthouse, T. A., & Coon, V. E. (1994). Interpretation of differential deficits: The case of aging and mental arithmetic. *Journal of Experimental Psychology: Learning, Memory, and Cognition, 20,* 1172–1182.

Salthouse, T. A., Fristoe, N. M., Lineweaver, T. T., & Coon, V. E. (1995). Aging of attention: Does the ability to divide decline? *Memory & Cognition, 23,* 59–71.

Salthouse, T. A., Fristoe, N., & Rhee, S. H. (1996). How localized are age-related effects on neuropsychological measures? *Neuropsychology, 10,* 272–285.

Salthouse, T. A., Hambrick, D. Z., & McGuthry, K. E. (1998). Shared age-related influences on cognitive and non-cognitive variables. *Psychology and Aging, 13,* 486–500.

Salthouse, T. A., & Lichty, W. (1985). Tests of the neural noise hypothesis of age-related cognitive change. *Journal of Gerontology, 40,* 443–450.

Salthouse, T. A., & Meinz, E. J. (1995). Aging, inhibition, working memory, and speed. *Journal of Gerontology: Psychological Sciences, 50B,* P297–P306.

Salthouse, T. A., Toth, J. P., Hancock, H. E., & Woodard, J. L. (1997). Controlled and automatic forms of memory and attention: Process purity and the uniqueness of age-related influences. *Journal of Gerontology: Psychological Sciences, 52B,* P216–P228.

Schramke, C. J., & Bauer, R. M. (1997). State-dependent learning in older and younger adults. *Psychology and Aging, 12,* 255–262.

Sliwinski, M., & Buschke, H. (1997). Processing speed and memory in aging and dementia. *Journal of Gerontology: Psychological Sciences, 52B,* P308–P318.

Sliwinski, M., Lipton, R. B., Buschke, H., & Stewart, W. (1996). The effects of preclinical dementia on estimates of normal cognitive functioning in aging. *Journal of Gerontology: Psychological Science, 51B,* P217–P225.

Small, B. J., Hultsch, D. F., & Masson, M. E. J. (1995). Adult age differences in perceptually based, not conceptually based implicit tests of memory. *Journal of Gerontology: Psychological Sciences, 50B,* P162–P170.

Spencer, W. D., & Raz, N. (1995). Differential effects of aging on memory for content and context: A meta-analysis. *Psychology and Aging, 10,* 527–539.

Srinivas, K., & Roediger, H. L., III. (1990). Classifying implicit memory tests: Category association and anagram solution. *Journal of Memory and Language, 29,* 389–412.

Stine, E. A. L. (1995). Aging and the distribution of resources in working memory. In P. A. Allen & T. R. Bashore (Eds.), *Age differences in word and language processing* (pp. 171–186). Amsterdam: Elsevier.

Stine, E. L., Wingfield, A., & Poon, L. W. (1986). How much and how fast: Rapid processing of spoken language in later adulthood. *Psychology and Aging, 1,* 303–311.

Taylor, J. L., Miller, T. P., & Tinklenberg, J. R. (1992). Correlates of memory decline: A 4-year longitudinal study of older adults with memory complaints. *Psychology and Aging, 7,* 185–193.

Verhaeghen, P., & Marcoen, A. (1993a). Memory aging as a general phenomenon: Episodic recall of older adults is a function of episodic recall of young adults. *Psychology and Aging, 8,* 380–388.

Verhaeghen, P., & Marcoen, A. (1993b). More or less the same? A memorability analysis on episodic memory tasks in young and older adults. *Journal of Gerontology: Psychological Sciences, 48,* P172–P178.

Verhaeghen, P., & Marcoen, A. (1994). Production deficiency hypothesis revisited: Adult age differences in strategy use as a function of processing resources. *Aging and Cognition, 1,* 323–338.

Verhaeghen, P., Marcoen, A., & Goossens, L. (1993). Facts and fiction about memory aging: A quantitative integration of research findings. *Journal of Gerontology: Psychological Sciences, 48,* P157–P171.

Verhaeghen, P., & Salthouse, T. A. (1997). Meta-analyses of age–cognition relations in adulthood: Estimates of linear and nonlinear age effects and structural models. *Psychological Bulletin, 122,* 231–249.

Wagner, A. D., Gabrieli, J. D. E., & Verfaellie, M. (1997). Dissociations between familiarity processes in explicit recognition and implicit perceptual memory. *Journal of Experimental Psychology: Learning, Memory, and Cognition, 23,* 305–323.

Zacks, R., & Hasher, L. (1997). Cognitive gerontology and attentional inhibition: A reply to Burke and McDowd. *Journal of Gerontology: Psychological Sciences, 52B,* P274–P283.

Zacks, R. T., Radvansky, G., & Hasher, L. (1996). Studies of directed forgetting in older adults. *Journal of Experimental Psychology: Learning, Memory, and Cognition, 22,* 143–156.

Zelinski, E. M., & Burnight, K. P. (1997). Sixteen-year longitudinal and time lag changes in memory and cognition in older adults. *Psychology and Aging, 12,* 503–513.

Zelinski, E. M., Gilewski, M. J., & Anthony-Bergstone, C. R. (1990). Memory Functioning Questionnaire: Concurrent validity with memory performance and self-reported memory failures. *Psychology and Aging, 5,* 388–399.

6

CAN ACQUIRED KNOWLEDGE COMPENSATE FOR AGE-RELATED DECLINES IN COGNITIVE EFFICIENCY?

NEIL CHARNESS

Can acquired knowledge compensate for age-related declines in cognitive efficiency? Yes and no. The main goal of this chapter is to outline the conditions under which acquired knowledge can and cannot compensate for age-related declines in cognitive efficiency.

I first sketch why knowledge is important and how knowledge transmission enables humans to circumvent their genetic limitations both as individuals and as a species. I next try to outline ways to define knowledge, discuss its advantages and disadvantages, review age-related decline, and discuss cognitive efficiency in the context of information processing. I provide examples of how knowledge can compensate for less efficient processing. Finally, I conclude with a discussion of the limits to compensation.

This research was supported by a grant from the National Institute of Aging (5R01 AG13969-02) and a grant from the Natural Sciences and Engineering Research Council of Canada (NSERC A0790).

KNOWLEDGE AS A MECHANISM TO CIRCUMVENT GENETIC LIMITATIONS

The easiest way to characterize life span is to talk about individual humans, who have a maximal life span of about 120 years, although in U.S. society the typical life span is about 76 years. However, it is intriguing to consider the life span of the species *homo sapiens*, which is about 1.5–2 million years, although *homo sapiens sapiens* may have been around only a few hundred thousand years (Corballis, 1991). The knowledge and long-term memory necessary to enable the species to survive is in our genetic code and the complex processing chain from DNA to RNA to protein.

Mother Nature seems to make relatively slow changes in the knowledge base called the *gene pool*, because a large change to the program of a given individual genetic assemblage can render that individual unfit for survival and reproduction. Natural selection is an efficient pruning device for helping genetic problem solving to succeed.

One outcome of such pruning was the production of a large and complex human brain that has discovered how to acquire and transmit knowledge over much shorter time spans without the need to change the knowledge base represented by gene sequences. Human knowledge is transmitted through cultural inheritance, although this mode is far more fragile than the genetic route. In particular, the development of language systems led to more efficient transmission of knowledge. Language strings could be passed more easily than flints, cutting tools, and weapons. With the advent of the written alphabet, efficient transmission could take place, as long as the language supporting the alphabet survived.

The ensuing information-transmission skills probably led to successful domestication of plants and animals and the creation of the resource base necessary to build cultures and civilizations that endured longer than the then-puny average human life span of 20–30 years. We might even speculate that our memory systems probably did not evolve to manage memories lasting longer than 40–50 years.

Information transmission through language generated phenomenal changes in the size and complexity of human organizational structures. From what were probably small kin groupings or tribes, we have assembled into organized nations of millions of citizens. Humankind's ability to communicate knowledgeably has moved us from face-to-face speech to worldwide electronic commerce.

It was mainly the acknowledgment of the human's role as information transmission channel that sparked the cognitive revolution in psychology. This revolution involved the formal definition of humans as information-processing systems (IPSs).

INFORMATION-PROCESSING SYSTEM

Newell and Simon (1972) outlined the structure of an IPS in their classic book *Human Problem Solving*. A basic IPS has several components: a memory structure to hold programs and data, a processor to carry out actions on the data structures with the aid of programs, and effectors and receptors to communicate with the environment.

Nature apparently adheres to information-processing principles at many levels, from the genetic code at the micro level to human organizations at the macro level. One goal of information-processing theory is to describe the characteristics of the components and the system as a whole.

LEARNING PARAMETERS: KNOWLEDGE AND BYPASSING LIMITS

Communication ability comes at a price. Humans must acquire our native language and be trained to use other transmission systems to deal with messages that come in alphabetic codes. However, we acquire and store information at a glacierlike pace: 5–10 seconds to store a new chunk when learning in rote fashion (H. A. Simon, 1974). Furthermore, we can store and process only a few chunks at a time, as Miller (1956) pointed out. We think and compute painfully slowly, with the fastest operation being perhaps 40 milliseconds (ms) to compare two internal symbols in a memory search task. A more typical operation is roughly 200 ms to recognize a familiar pattern such as a face. Information-processing parameters such as these were outlined by Card, Moran, and Newell (1983).

These information-processing bottlenecks, coupled with exponential increases over time in information available, have meant that we, as a society, have become highly specialized. We devote our entire childhood and much of our early adult life in formal training organizations (schools) to prepare us to participate fully in our societies. Fortunately, we are at a point in our history when the costs of acquiring knowledge, many years of formal training, are amortized over a relatively long life span: about 73 years for men and 79 years for women in the United States.

It is often difficult to bypass genetic and biological limits, but fortunately there are ways to bypass information-processing limits such as the limited capacity of short-term memory. Long-term memory retrieval structures (Ericsson & Kintsch, 1995) enable experts to encode and permanently store even random patterns rapidly. Digit span experts can recall more than 100 random digits courtesy of such retrieval structures. The catch, though, is that it takes many hours of deliberate practice, sometimes hundreds of hours, to build up the structures necessary to achieve such bypasses.

Humans have apparently evolved two knowledge acquisition mechanisms. I use the term *apparently* because this is still an area of considerable controversy. Nonetheless, the distinction has heuristic value. I aggregate a large set of processes together and call them the *knowledge acquisition system* for the sake of convenience, ignoring distinctions such as retrieval, storage, and encoding.

Cognitive scientists have invented a variety of terms to describe these systems: *implicit* and *explicit memory*, *unconscious* and *conscious processing*, and *automatic* and *effortful learning*. One system acts as a frequency-driven event encoding system that seems to work with minimal attentional resource. Learning happens regardless of whether we like it. We can call this system the *A-system*, one that is more or less automatic, requiring minimal attention to function successfully as long as retrieval does not involve effortful search. Our modern advertising industry depends heavily on this system. The aging process reduces the efficiency of this system rather minimally (e.g., Hasher & Zacks, 1979; Light, 1991; Salthouse, Toth, Hancock, & Woodard, 1997; Vakil & Agmon-Ashkenazi, 1997).

The second learning system appears to demand full attention and involves strategic processing. We can call this system the *D-system*, for the role that deliberate, strategic processing plays. The modern education industry is constantly trying to find more effective ways to engage this system. The aging process is particularly deleterious to the efficient functioning of this system (e.g., Salthouse, 1991). For instance, numerous studies of paired-associate and list learning have shown that older adults need considerably more time than younger adults to reach the same learning criteria. Similarly, when given an algorithm to learn, such as the method of loci for retaining word lists, younger adults show an increasing advantage with practice (Kliegl, Smith, & Baltes, 1989).

So, as we age, although we may be acquiring new information fairly efficiently by means of the A-system, we are hard pressed to keep up with our young counterparts when drawing on the D-system. Nonetheless, older adults can perform exceptionally well when they can draw on knowledge that may let them bypass processes undergoing even greater declines in efficiency, such as effortful computation.

PARADOX: INTACT PROBLEM SOLVING WITH DEGRADED MEMORY EFFICIENCY

I entered the field of aging research about 20 years ago by accident. I had been pursuing work on expert performance, following up on my doctoral dissertation work on the role of memory in chess expertise (Charness, 1976). That work had shown that skilled chess players do not store recently perceived information in a short-term store; rather, it seems to be stored directly in long-term memory, or what has recently been termed *long-term working memory* (Ericsson & Kintsch, 1995). Long-term working memory allows experts to bypass the normal limits on information processing.

In research on the game of bridge I found that older players were rather seriously impaired, relative to younger ones, on memory tasks thought to support problem solving. However, they were relatively unimpaired on bridge problem-solving tasks, such as choosing an opening bid or planning out the play of a bridge hand (Charness, 1979). The paradox of intact problem solving with impaired basic information-processing efficiency has preoccupied my research interests ever since. This phenomenon is not restricted to the laboratory; it also seems to occur in the more crucial arena of job performance.

THE CASE FOR COMPENSATION: NO AGE-RELATED CHANGES IN JOB PERFORMANCE

As a recent review of age and job performance has concluded (Salthouse & Maurer, 1996), there is remarkably little direct relationship between age and job performance (e.g., McEvoy & Cascio, 1989; Waldman & Avolio, 1986), despite moderate negative relations between age and cognitive abilities (e.g., Salthouse, 1991) and moderate to strong positive relationships between cognitive abilities and job performance (e.g., Hunter & Hunter, 1984).

There are a number of important caveats in regard to the meta-analyses that have concluded that there is no relationship between age and job performance. Factors such as lack of power, restriction of age range, assessment quality, and selective attrition may have contributed to the failure to show a relationship (Salthouse & Maurer, 1996). Nonetheless, when it is so easy to show age-related declines in cognitive efficiency in the laboratory it is surprising not to show them in real-life performance.

Deficits in real-life performance are readily apparent when peak performances are tracked longitudinally. Professional athletes are a case in point (e.g., Schulz & Curnow, 1988; Schulz, Musa, Staszewski, & Siegler, 1994). Simonton (1997) made a strong case that, in the aggregate, career trajectories of society's top performers show a rise to a peak, which typically occurs in the decade of the 30s, and then a gradual decline. Figure 6.1 depicts the longitudinal change in chess ratings for top-level players, the Grandmasters, which is based on data collected by Elo (1965). Obviously, the vast majority of older people in the workplace either are not sufficiently challenged by their work environment to demonstrate deficits in performance, or they are bypassing the usual limitations on performance that might be expected to hamper them. Many people have speculated that

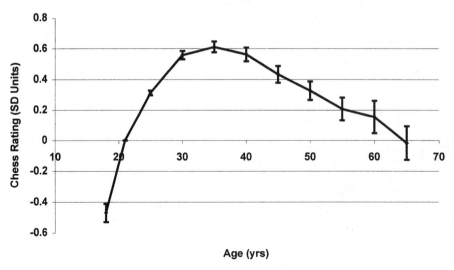

Longitudinal GM Performance

Figure 6.1. Longitudinal performance of chess Grandmasters (GM), derived from data in Elo (1965).

acquired knowledge is the magic potion that allows older workers to avoid declines in performance. How might knowledge compensate for declines in processing efficiency?

THE KNOWLEDGE–COMPUTATION TRADE-OFF

The concise *Oxford Dictionary* gives the following definition of *knowledge*: "knowing, familiarity gained by experience of person, thing, fact); person's range of information" (p. 658). I believe that this definition overlooks something fairly critical, namely, the dimension of time.

IPSs can act effectively in the world when they make correct decisions about their current situation in a timely fashion. They have two ways to do this. First, they can encode the current situation and recognize or know what to do (activating already stored knowledge, both for recognition and for selecting an action). Second, they can encode the current situation, know that they do not know what to do, and use available knowledge and computational ability to search for an appropriate course of action. They can either slowly compute or quickly retrieve an answer.

Knowledge thus has three interrelated features. It consists of acquired information that can be activated in a timely fashion to generate an appropriate response. Also a feature, timely activation, is probably insufficiently appreciated. When one examines problem-solving performance by physics novices and experts, speed of solution is sometimes the major differentiating factor between the two (D. P. Simon & Simon, 1978), given that both groups solve the problem (eventually). It is this feature that will weigh against complete compensation for older adults. They may have as much or more knowledge than do young adults with respect to a given domain. What they may not be able to do is to activate it as efficiently.

It is instructive to consider a conceptualization introduced by Berliner (1981) and elaborated on by Newell (1990) concerning the role of preparation versus deliberation in intelligent behavior. The same outcome can occur when either many patterns are prestored to which appropriate actions have been associated or when the system uses very general computational procedures to search through a problem space to find the best action.

In understanding the impact of aging processes on cognition, there is overwhelming evidence that speed of processing is a critical variable (Salthouse, 1996). Speed is also a critical variable in understanding the role of age in knowledge and long-term memory. Generally, aging is associated with slowing in virtually all processes. Expertise (which is loosely associated with experience and, hence, age) is generally accompanied by increased speed of processing. Of course, expertise is an acquired state, typically taking thousands of hours. What happens when one plays off the two processes against each other? To foreshadow, knowledge can compensate for deficits in information-processing ability by replacing computation (sequences of effortful retrievals) with relatively effortless retrieval.

Ask someone to answer the question "What is 85 × 85?" without benefit of paper and pencil or calculator. Most people will have to struggle for several minutes before coming up with the correct answer, if they do so at all. It is difficult to carry out computations and hold intermediate results because of the limitations of working memory. Now, instruct them with the following "rule": to multiply a 2-digit number ending in 5 by itself, take the left digit and multiply it by 1 more than itself, say that product aloud, and then say "25" aloud. Give them the example of 65 × 65, stepping them through taking 6, multiplying it by 7, generating the product 42, and then saying "42, 25." Now give them 85 × 85. Then 95 × 95. Most people will solve the problems easily and quickly. A little knowledge enabled them to bypass considerable computation. Charness and Campbell (1988) and Campbell and Charness (1990) studied skill acquisition in adulthood for such mental calculation procedures.

The point to the demonstration is that "knowledge is power," something pointed out by computer scientists who had to deal with problemsolving in domains such as chemical analysis (Feigenbaum, 1989). These domains required searching enormous problem spaces. The only way to cut down the search to manageable proportions, and in some cases eliminate it entirely, was to provide the knowledge-poor but relatively fast treesearching programs with knowledge.

Sometimes, however, computational power surpasses knowledge. It is in fact the reason why the best but very slow-computing human chess players, searching at a rate of perhaps 1 node per second (Charness, 1981), can compete on virtually equal terms with computer systems that search 200 million nodes per second. Figure 6.2 depicts that relationship, showing human chess champion Garry Kasparov plotted against Deep Blue 96 and Deep Blue 97 in knowledge versus search space. Man and machine occupy opposite corners in this space. Still, Deep Blue 97 surpassed Kasparov's performance, substituting brute force search capability for Kasparov's slowly and painfully acquired chess knowledge. Humans, although slow, are knowledge sponges, abstracting and storing immense amounts of information about their environments. However, humans are, unfortunately, both slow and often inaccurate at serial computation tasks (e.g., try serial subtraction by 7s starting from 256). People also have fallible memory systems, meaning that they sometimes fail to retrieve relevant information for the situation at hand. This memory fallibility may be an explanation for Kasparov's bad choice of an opening move in the fateful final game of the chess match.

Knowledge vs. Search for Chess Skill

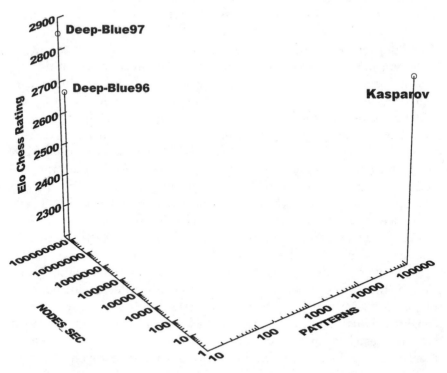

Figure 6.2. Estimates of knowledge (patterns) and search capabilities (nodes examined per second) for world champion Garry Kasparov and Deep Blue.

Although one would think that more knowledge is always better than less, there are some potential problems (Charness & Bieman-Copland, 1992).

Access

Knowledge that cannot be accessed quickly may be useless. Database designers have noted that, generally, the larger the database, the greater the access time. Retrieval time tends to increase as a linear function of the logarithm of number of data records. Some have argued that slowed retrieval in older adults is partially a function of the fact that they have so much knowledge (Lachman & Lachman, 1980). Word-finding difficulties, such as the large age-related increase in frequency of occurrence of the tip-of-the-tongue phenomenon, are consistent with this perspective (Burke, Worthley, & Martin, 1988).

Vocabulary grows extremely quickly in young children, at a rate of perhaps 10–15 new lexical items per day (Landauer & Dumais, 1997). Such learning probably slows as people age at least in part because after common items are learned it becomes increasingly difficult to encounter and learn the rarer ones. Nonetheless, despite having less formal education, aging adults often have larger vocabularies than do young college-age adults, at least into middle age, when tested with Wechsler Adult Intelligence Scale Vocabulary or Primary Mental Abilities (PMA) word-meaning tests (e.g., Salthouse, 1991; Schaie, 1996).

Still, some plausible calculations show that only about 6%–12% slowing in access could be expected on the basis of older adults' presumptive larger vocabularies (Charness & Bieman-Copland, 1992). Assume that lexical access is proportional to the logarithm of number of entries. Assume too that words continue to be added to the vocabulary database at the same rate over the life span (likely an unrealistic assumption). Then the 3:1 ratio for vocabulary size for 60-year-olds compared to 20-year-olds, or the 4:1 ratio for 80-year-olds compared to 20-year-olds, yields estimated vocabulary sizes of 300,000–400,000 for older adults compared to 100,000 for younger ones. Log(300,000)/log(100,000) and log(400,000)/log(100,000) yield predicted slowing factors of 6%–12%. Slowing is typically 30% for older adults in accessing a word name from a definition (e.g., the neutral condition in Bowles & Poon, 1985). General slowing in information processing must be at work, with its 50%+ slowing ratios (Hale & Myerson, 1995). Studies of the fan effect in learning (Anderson, 1974) —that retrieval tends to slow the more information is related to a given item—also point to the costs of increased knowledge for retrieval efficiency.

Acquisition

The phenomenon of *proactive interference* indicates that the more one knows, the more difficult it is to acquire new information in tasks such as learning successive related word lists (Underwood, 1957). Although this effect is powerful, it is also a function of the way in which information is organized and stored. Nonetheless, it is a pervasive finding for the acquisition of episodic information (personally experienced events). As McKay and Abrams (1996) pointed out, older adults seem to have even greater problems than do younger adults in forming new connections for episodic memory tasks, as evidenced by greater susceptibility to repetition blindness. The Elementary Perceiver and Memorizer (EPAM) (e.g., Feigenbaum & Simon, 1984) theory of paired-associate and serial recall provides a plausible interpretation of proactive interference effects. Namely, new items to be memorized that closely resemble old items require the development of more sophisticated tests of difference in the network of nodes and tests sorting items to unique categories (terminal nodes). Fewer tests are required to discriminate the word set of *cat, pet,* and *dog* (a first-letter test will do) than of *cat, tab,* and *cab* (the latter set requiring tests of first- and last-letter positions).

Countering proactive interference, at least theoretically, is the benefit of having some knowledge on acquiring further knowledge. Chunking is one mechanism that helps enormously. Also, one model, Landauer and Dumais's (1997) latent semantic analysis model, depends on the total learning context to boost the acquisition of new vocabulary. New words are both differentiated from all known words that do not appear in the target word's context as well as related to words appearing in the same context. Thus, a version of the model that has already acquired a large vocabulary automatically benefits more when a new word is encountered.

There may be both costs and benefits to having more knowledge. Another important issue for knowledge is its persistence, which also can have positive and negative impacts.

Persistence

One way to represent the activation of knowledge is by means of a cognitive architecture known as a *production system* (Newell & Simon, 1972). A production takes the form of an if–then statement, such as "if the light is green, then cross the street." It has conditions of applicability —the *if* component—and when they match the current situation the action side of the production is triggered, and the action occurs. Unless the *if* components of a set of productions are reasonably flexible, knowledge represented as productions will be applied quite rigidly and can lead to inefficient action. Duncker (1945) and other Gestalt psychologists illustrated how blind application of recently used procedures can cause people to overlook more efficient ones. For instance, even strong chess masters can fall into the trap of using a stereotypic checkmating theme, such as smothered mate, when a more efficient method is available (Saariluoma, 1992). Perhaps such functional fixedness is in part responsible for declines in creativity associated with increasing age as seen with psychometric test materials (Ruth & Birren, 1985) or creative output in a profession (Simonton, 1997).

Related processes are priming and inhibition failure. One's train of thought can be captured all too easily by evoked knowledge. Perhaps this problem is partially responsible for the problem that some older adults have with telling and retelling the same story to a weary listener (Jennings & Jacoby, 1997). Such persistence of knowledge, or perhaps the inability to suppress or inhibit this knowledge (e.g., Hasher, Stolzfus, Zacks, & Rypma, 1991), may also account for increasing rigidity in older adults shown even in longitudinal investigations (e.g., Schaie, Dutta, & Willis, 1991).

AGE-RELATED DECLINES IN COGNITIVE EFFICIENCY

The literature on aging and cognition has provided copious examples of age-related decline in cognitive performance. Excellent surveys have appeared every few years in the venerable *Handbook of the Psychology of Aging*, now in its fourth edition (Birren & Schaie, 1996). Cross-sectional studies have uniformly shown that cognitive functions such as memory, attention, and processing speed all undergo decline, usually from the decade of the 20s. Longitudinal studies provide a somewhat more optimistic view of when decline becomes significant, but the trends seem consistent for age differences and changes. I am oversimplifying slightly, given compelling evidence that some types of memory show little decline (indirect/implicit memory) and some types of processes show less slowing than other types (verbal/semantic compared to nonverbal/spatial). Nonetheless, the weight of evidence favors the conclusion that today's older adults will show inferior performance to young ones on almost any laboratory task that taps unpracticed abilities (a cross-sectional study). Similarly, the logic of basic abilities supporting higher level ones would lead to the conclusion that the more complex problem solving necessary in professional life should also be impaired, unless compensatory mechanisms can be brought into play.

EMPIRICAL CASES OF COMPENSATION

If information-processing efficiency declines with age, then to maintain or improve performance older adults must rely on a compensatory mechanism to accomplish their task. (For a wide-ranging discussion of the concept of compensation, see Dixon & Bäckman, 1995.) They need to substitute an efficient process for the one undergoing decline. In the case of the strong form of compensation they need to substitute a process that is more efficient than that used by young adults if they are to equal young-adult performance.

Few clear-cut cases of compensatory mechanisms have been identified in the literature. The best example is typing, where Salthouse (1984) and Bosman (1993, 1994) have shown that older typists compensate for slowing in psychomotor abilities, such as tapping speed, with increased preview of text, enabling them more time to program the overlapping keystrokes necessary to maintain high typing rates. (Skilled typing is not a reaction time task.) Bosman's (1994) study supplied evidence that some older highly skilled typists may not have to compensate for age-related slowing in basic processes.

Partial compensation has been demonstrated for experienced older pilots repeating air traffic control sequences (Morrow, Leirer, Altieri, & Fitzsimmons, 1994). The issue of whether experience can compensate for observed declines in basic information-processing abilities in pilots is still unresolved (Hardy & Parasuraman, 1997), as is the more important question of the validity of basic abilities as predictors of pilot performance.

One possibility that we may need to entertain is that with the right type of practice—deliberate practice (e.g., Ericsson & Charness, 1994)— little or no age-related decline may occur. Krampe and Ericsson (1996) demonstrated precisely that result for skilled older pianists asked to reproduce complex polyrhythms demanding precise intermanual coordination abilities. Professional musicians who maintained high levels of current deliberate practice performed comparably to equally skilled younger musicians. Older amateur musicians were impaired on this task relative to these two groups and young amateur musicians.

This result runs contrary to the findings for most other laboratory investigations of skilled performers. For basic abilities, even those that appear to be exercised in work settings—such as spatial ability in architects (e.g., Salthouse, Babcock, Skovronek, Mitchell, & Palmon, 1990; Salthouse, Mitchell, & Palmon, 1989) and memory for briefly seen music notation in instrumental performers (Meinz & Salthouse, 1998)—the aphorism seems to be "use it and still lose it."

One way for the study of compensation to make progress, particularly when the compensatory mechanism may involve declarative knowledge, is to find techniques to measure knowledge.

Researchers have used both direct and indirect methods to assess the size of a knowledge base. Some of the earliest work addressed the problem of estimating the size of the lexicon for native English speakers. Oldfield (1963) noted that if one samples items from a large dictionary, asking for definitions, one finds that college undergraduates apparently have English vocabularies of 50,000–100,000 words. More recent investigations tend to use multiple-choice tests asking people to identify synonyms for target words.

Most indirect techniques for estimating knowledge depend on cognitive simulation of individual differences. Mainly for historical reasons, the tasks simulated usually involve recall of briefly presented domain materials. Chase and Simon's (1973) classic work with chess players is a good example. They demonstrated that skilled players were able to recall much more of a briefly presented structured chess position than were less skilled players; however, when randomly arranged chess positions are shown, skilled players are not much different than less skilled players in recall. The theory is that players recognize chess positions in units called *chunks* —familiar arrays of pieces. Skilled players ought to have stored many more chunks in long-term memory than do their less-skilled counterparts. The theory assumes that short-term memory does not differ much between players of different skill levels (they have the same basic hardware limitation). Thus, with limited encoding time, players should use short-term memory processes to encode a position. Skilled players should show a strong recall advantage on structured positions containing many recognizable chunks, but only a weak advantage when recalling random positions, where recognizable chunks show up infrequently.

Simulation studies of chess recall (Gobet, 1993; Gobet & Simon, 1996; H. A. Simon & Gilmartin, 1973) support the conclusion that an EPAM-style network that contains about 50,000–100,000 patterns can adequately simulate master-level recall; that is, the simulation work implies that strong chess players possess a vocabulary of chess patterns that is comparable to the lexical vocabulary that Oldfield (1963) and others have estimated for adult native speakers of English.

Such direct and indirect knowledge-estimation procedures have different strengths and weaknesses. Direct methods may overestimate knowledge by virtue of the procedure of multiplying proportion of correct scores by number of entries in the source. Larger dictionaries lead to larger estimates. Simulations also have problems as sources of estimates. They may not represent knowledge in the same way that people do.

There is a strong need to expand simulation studies to explore how both knowledge extent and speed of processing interact. That way, models can assess potential beneficial effects of age, in terms of opportunity to acquire knowledge, jointly with potential negative effects of age on ability to activate knowledge. The knowledge-versus-activation speed space may prove to be a useful conceptual framework for understanding aging effects.

LIMITS TO COMPENSATION: KNOWLEDGE ACTIVATION

Older adults with more effective knowledge (retrieval based vs. computation based) ought to be able to outperform younger adults with less effective knowledge. However, one is forced to predict that a 20-year-old with the same knowledge as an 80-year-old should outperform the 80-year-old. The older adult should not be able to activate (retrieve or compute) the knowledge as quickly as the young adult, given age-related declines in the efficiency of the hardware for running knowledge-related programs within the human information-processing system.

That said, it is worth noting that the latter hypothetical situation is not easy to obtain; that is, given the very slow rate of acquisition of knowledge by humans it is rarely going to be the case that younger adults will equal older adults in knowledge in most domains where opportunities to acquire knowledge stay the same with age (e.g., vocabulary). An obvious exception arises when considering the specialization that experts pursue. The interesting issue is one of trade-off of activation and possession of knowledge.

In our modern world, particularly in the world of work, obsolescence is an ever-present danger. Knowing keystroke combinations for old versions of WordPerfect will probably not help a person learn Microsoft Word. It might even hurt by providing negative transfer, although finding true negative transfer is a difficult problem (Singley & Anderson, 1989). Finding evidence of disruption may be a fairer test (Kelley, 1996). Obsolescence is probably a function of the exponential explosion of knowledge, coupled with the fact that it really is a case of "use it or lose it" for memory retrieval efficiency. (What is 55×55?)

Older people may have many old facts that may not be retrievable anymore. This situation of sensitivity to recency is probably adaptive, because the old facts may not have current applicability. A good example is fluency of recall for one's current telephone number compared to a prior one.

CONCLUSION

Knowledge can compensate, at least partially, for age-related declines in cognitive efficiency. It does so more successfully when the task is one for which fact retrieval can substitute for computation of answers. A knowledgeable older adult will outperform a computationally swift but less knowledgeable young adult. Rapid changes in the technology of information retrieval may tilt the playing field more to the advantage of the young, however, when they truly can get information at their fingertips. Whether such information always constitutes knowledge is debatable.

Knowledge is also useful for enabling humans to bypass cognitive limitations, such as the limited-capacity short-term memory system by way of long-term working memory. Knowledge acquisition is a slow process, however, and there are definite costs associated with the type of deliberate practice necessary to build up long-term memory-retrieval structures. Knowledge is long term in both the sense of persistence and the sense of time to acquire.

Knowledge can also compensate for our relatively short life spans as organisms, enabling us to transmit knowledge more quickly than Mother Nature can through genetic tinkering. Knowledge transmission within and across generations has permitted incredibly specialized civilizations to rise quickly, compared to evolutionary standards. Successful transmission of knowledge for food production, hygiene, and medicine has also lengthened the life span of the developed countries' citizens just in time to allow them to amortize the cost of acquiring it.

REFERENCES

Anderson, J. R. (1974). Retrieval of propositional information from long-term memory. *Cognitive Psychology, 6,* 451–474.

Berliner, H. J. (1981, October). *Search vs. knowledge: An analysis from the domain of games.* Paper presented at the North Atlantic Treaty Organization symposium on Human and Artificial Intelligence, Lyon, France.

Birren, J. E., & Schaie, K. W. (Eds.). (1996). *Handbook of the psychology of aging* (4th ed.). New York: Academic Press.

Bosman, E. A. (1993). Age-related differences in motoric aspects of transcription typing skill. *Psychology and Aging, 8,* 87–102.

Bosman, E. A. (1994). Age and skill differences in typing related and unrelated reaction time tasks. *Aging and Cognition, 1,* 310–322.

Bowles, N. L., & Poon, L. W. (1985). Aging and retrieval of words in semantic memory. *Journal of Gerontology, 40,* 71–77.

Burke, D., Worthley, J., & Martin, J. (1988). I'll never forget what's-her-name: Aging and tip of the tongue experiences in everyday life. In M. M. Gruneberg, P. E. Morris, & R. N. Sykes (Eds.), *Practical aspects of memory: Current research and issues* (Vol. 2, pp. 113–118). Chichester, England: Wiley.

Campbell, J. I. D., & Charness, N. (1990). Age-related declines in working memory skills: Evidence from a complex calculation task. *Developmental Psychology, 26,* 879–888.

Card, S. K., Moran, T. P., & Newell, A. (1983). *The psychology of human–computer interaction*. Hillsdale, NJ: Erlbaum.

Charness, N. (1976). Memory for chess positions: Resistance to interference. *Journal of Experimental Psychology: Human Learning and Memory, 2*, 641–653.

Charness, N. (1979). Components of skill in bridge. *Canadian Journal of Psychology, 33*, 1–16.

Charness, N. (1981). Search in chess: Age and skill differences. *Journal of Experimental Psychology: Human Perception and Performance, 7*, 467–476.

Charness, N., & Bieman-Copland, S. (1992). The learning perspective: Adulthood. In R. J. Sternberg & C. A. Berg (Eds.), *Intellectual development* (pp. 301–327). New York: Cambridge University Press.

Charness, N., & Campbell, J. I. D. (1988). Acquiring skill at mental calculation in adulthood: A task decomposition. *Journal of Experimental Psychology: General, 117*, 115–129.

Chase, W. G., & Simon, H. A. (1973). Perception in chess. *Cognitive Psychology, 4*, 55–81.

Corballis, M. C. (1991). *The lopsided ape: Evolution of the generative mind*. Oxford, England: Oxford University Press.

Dixon, R. A., & Bäckman, L. (1995). *Compensating for psychological deficits and declines: Managing losses and promoting gains*. Mahwah, NJ: Erlbaum.

Duncker, K. (1945). On problem solving. *Psychological Monographs, 58*(5), ix-113.

Elo, A. E. (1965). Age changes in master chess performances. *Journal of Gerontology, 20*, 289–299.

Ericsson, K. A., & Charness, N. (1994). Expert performance: Its structure and acquisition. *American Psychologist, 49*, 725–747.

Ericsson, K. A., & Kintsch, W. (1995). Long-term working memory. *Psychological Review, 102*, 211–245.

Feigenbaum, E. A. (1989). What hath Simon wrought? In D. Klahr & K. Kotovsky (Eds.), *Complex information processing: The impact of Herbert A. Simon* (pp. 165–182). Hillsdale, NJ: Erlbaum.

Feigenbaum, E. A., & Simon, H. A. (1984). EPAM-like models of recognition and learning. *Cognitive Science, 8*, 305–336.

Gobet, F. (1993). *Les mémoires d'un joueur d'échecs*. [Memories of a chess player]. Saint-Paul Fribourg, Switzerland: Editions Universitaires Fribourg Suisse.

Gobet, F., & Simon, H. A. (1996). Recall of rapidly presented random chess positions is a function of skill. *Psychonomic Bulletin & Review, 3*, 159–163.

Hale, S., & Myerson, J. (1995). Fifty years older, fifty percent slower? Meta-analytic regression models and semantic context effects. *Aging and Cognition, 2*, 132–145.

Hardy, D. J., & Parasuraman, R. (1997). Cognition and flight performance in older pilots. *Journal of Experimental Psychology: Applied, 3*, 313–348.

Hasher, L., Stolzfus, E. R., Zacks, R. T., & Rypma, B. (1991). Age and inhibition.

Journal of Experimental Psychology: Learning, Memory, and Cognition, 17, 163–169.

Hasher, L., & Zacks, R. T. (1979). Automatic and effortful processes in memory. *Journal of Experimental Psychology: General, 108,* 356–388.

Hunter, J. E., & Hunter, R. F. (1984). Validity and utility of alternative predictors of job performance. *Psychological Bulletin, 96,* 72–98.

Jennings, J. M., & Jacoby, L. L. (1997). An opposition procedure for detecting age-related deficits in recollection: Telling effects of repetition. *Psychology and Aging, 12,* 352–361.

Kelley, C. L. (1996). *Age, experience, and transfer across word processors.* Unpublished doctoral dissertation, University of Waterloo, Waterloo, Ontario, Canada.

Kliegl, R., Smith, J., & Baltes, P. B. (1989). Testing-the-limits and the study of adult age differences in cognitive plasticity of a mnemonic skill. *Developmental Psychology, 25,* 247–256.

Krampe, R. T., & Ericsson, K. A. (1996). Maintaining excellence: Deliberate practice and elite performance in young and older pianists. *Journal of Experimental Psychology: General, 125,* 331–359.

Lachman, J. L., & Lachman, R. (1980). Age and the actualization of world knowledge. In L. W. Poon, J. L. Fozard, L. S. Cermak, D. Arenberg, & L. W. Thompson (Eds.), *New directions in memory and aging* (pp. 285–311). Hillsdale, NJ: Erlbaum.

Landauer, T. K., & Dumais, S. T. (1997). A solution to Plato's problem: The latent semantic analysis theory of acquisition, induction, and representation of knowledge. *Psychological Review, 104,* 211–240.

Light, L. L. (1991). Memory and aging: Four hypotheses in search of data. *Annual Review of Psychology, 42,* 333–376.

McEvoy, G. M., & Cascio, W. F. (1989). Cumulative evidence of the relationship between employee age and job performance. *Journal of Applied Psychology, 74,* 11–17.

McKay, D. C., & Abrams, L. (1996). Language, memory, and aging: Distributed deficits and the structure of new-versus-old connections. In J. E. Birren & K. W. Schaie (Eds.), *Handbook of the psychology of aging* (4th ed., pp. 251–265). New York: Academic Press.

Meinz, E. J., & Salthouse, T. A. (1998). The effects of age and experience on memory for visually presented music. *Journal of Gerontology: Psychological Science, 53B,* P60–P69.

Miller, G. A. (1956). The magical number seven, plus or minus two: Some limits on our capacity for processing information. *Psychological Review, 63,* 81–97.

Morrow, D., Leirer, V., Altieri, P., & Fitzsimmons, C. (1994). When expertise reduces age differences in performance. *Psychology and Aging, 9,* 134–148.

Newell, A. (1990). *Unified theories of cognition.* Cambridge, MA: Harvard University Press.

Newell, A., & Simon, H. A. (1972). *Human problem solving.* Englewood Cliffs, NJ: Prentice Hall.

Oldfield, R. C. (1963). Individual vocabulary and semantic currency: A preliminary study. *British Journal of Social and Clinical Psychology, 2,* 122–130.

Ruth, J., & Birren, J. E. (1985). Creativity in adulthood and old age: Relations to intelligence, sex and mode of testing. *International Journal of Behavioral Development, 8,* 99–109.

Saariluoma, P. (1992). Error in chess: The apperception-restructuring view. *Psychological Research, 54,* 17–26.

Salthouse, T. A. (1984). Effects of age and skill in typing. *Journal of Experimental Psychology: General, 13,* 345–371.

Salthouse, T. A. (1991). *Theoretical perspectives on cognitive aging.* Hillsdale, NJ: Erlbaum.

Salthouse, T. A. (1996). The processing-speed theory of adult age differences in cognition. *Psychological Review, 103,* 403–428.

Salthouse, T. A., Babcock, R. L., Skovronek, E., Mitchell, D. R. D., & Palmon, R. (1990). Age and experience effects in spatial visualization. *Developmental Psychology, 26,* 128–136.

Salthouse, T. A., & Maurer, J. J. (1996). Aging, job performance, and career development. In J. E. Birren & K. W. Schaie (Eds.), *Handbook of the psychology of aging* (4th ed., pp. 353–364). New York: Academic Press.

Salthouse, T. A., Mitchell, D. R. D., & Palmon, R. (1989). Memory and age differences in spatial manipulation ability. *Psychology and Aging, 4,* 480–486.

Salthouse, T. A., Toth, J. P., Hancock, H. E., & Woodard, J. L. (1997). Controlled and automatic forms of memory and attention: Process purity and the uniqueness of age-related influences. *Journal of Gerontology: Psychological Sciences, 52B,* P216–P228.

Schaie, K. W. (1996). Intellectual development in adulthood. In J. E. Birren & K. W. Schaie (Eds.), *Handbook of the psychology of aging* (4th ed., pp. 266–286). New York: Academic Press.

Schaie, K. W., Dutta, R., & Willis, S. L. (1991). The relationship between rigidity–flexibility and cognitive abilities in adulthood. *Psychology and Aging, 6,* 371–383.

Schulz, R., & Curnow, C. (1988). Peak performance and age among superathletes: Track and field, swimming, baseball, tennis, and golf. *Journal of Gerontology: Psychological Sciences, 43,* P113–P120.

Schulz, R., Musa, D., Staszewski, J., & Siegler, R. S. (1994). The relationship between age and major league baseball performance: Implications for development. *Psychology and Aging, 9,* 274–286.

Simon, D. P., & Simon, H. A. (1978). Individual differences in solving physics problems. In R. Siegler (Ed.), *Children's thinking: What develops?* (pp. 325–348). Hillsdale, NJ: Erlbaum.

Simon, H. A. (1974, February). How big is a chunk? *Science, 183,* 482–488.

Simon, H. A., & Gilmartin, K. (1973). A simulation of memory for chess positions. *Cognitive Psychology, 5*, 29–46.

Simonton, D. K. (1997). Creative productivity: A predictive and explanatory model of career trajectories and landmarks. *Psychological Review, 104*, 66–89.

Singley, M. K., & Anderson, J. R. (1989). *The transfer of cognitive skill*. Cambridge, MA: Harvard University Press.

Underwood, B. J. (1957). Interference and forgetting. *Psychological Review, 64*, 49–60.

Vakil, E., & Agmon-Ashkenazi, D. (1997). Baseline performance and learning rate of procedural and declarative memory tasks: Younger versus older adults. *Journal of Gerontology: Psychological Sciences, 52B*, P229–P234.

Waldman, D. A., & Avolio, B. J. (1986). A meta-analysis of age differences in job performance. *Journal of Applied Psychology, 71*, 33–38.

III

EMOTION AND AGING

PART III: EMOTION AND AGING

Is there anything different about emotion in older adults as compared to emotion at earlier stages of life? Is there a life-span trajectory of declining emotion that leads from turbulent adolescence to sanguine old age? Furthermore, are age-based changes in emotion biological in nature, that is, based on changes in the nervous system? One might also inquire whether aging offers any developmental strengths in the management of emotion. After all, should we not benefit from the accumulated wisdom that getting older should provide?

In one of the hot fields of geropsychological research, Robert W. Levenson addresses these issues, and more, in the chapter that follows. From a life-span developmental perspective, Levenson points out that human beings do not come fully equipped with a set of complex emotions but that emotions develop as one grows. Thus, emotional control is one example of the development of emotion. As children develop, they become more skilled at emotional regulation.

Age appears to bring advantages in emotion management. Levenson points out that older individuals experience lower rates of psychiatric disorders than do younger individuals. Equally important, he concludes that emotion regulation is one of those areas that is well maintained and even improves as one grows older. Naturally, emotion is an important component of quality of life for older adults; however, emotional development has societal implications as well. As the U.S. population ages, it is important to recognize that age-related emotional development will be increasingly evident in our aging society.

Levenson also addresses a more complex set of questions about how age affects the balance among emotions. He discusses the importance of the balance between emotions in addition to a consideration of the amount of specific emotions during one's life span; he also considers the interpersonal aspect of emotion. As illustration, Levenson describes work on how emotions are regulated interpersonally within marriage.

It is clear that emotion is a vital aspect of human experience, including aging. Some of us tend to separate emotion from cognition, but Levenson encourages us to consider how physiological and psychological processes interact and are interrelated. In a field that has developed rich models in other domains of psychological aging, Levenson offers an intriguing consideration of the role of emotion in the human experience of aging.

7

EXPRESSIVE, PHYSIOLOGICAL, AND SUBJECTIVE CHANGES IN EMOTION ACROSS ADULTHOOD

ROBERT W. LEVENSON

In much of the early writings about the psychology of late life, *loss* was the dominant theme: loss of psychological flexibility, loss of physical strength and endurance, loss of memory and other cognitive abilities, loss of friends and partners, and loss of health. More recent work has managed to separate the impact of age from the impact of illness. Thus, whereas much of the earlier research in gerontology studied the frail elderly population (e.g., residents of nursing homes), recent work has increasingly focused on healthy elders living in community settings. Removing the often profoundly devastating effects of late-life illness has produced a more multifaceted picture of the psychological functioning of elderly people; nonetheless, losses still loom large as a very salient part of old age.

Much of the diminishing of function, strength, adaptability, and

This chapter is based on a presentation given at the 105th Annual Convention of the American Psychological Association, Chicago, August 1997. The research reported in this chapter has been supported by grants from the American Association of Retired Persons Andrus Foundation, the National Institute of Mental Health (MH50841), and the National Institute on Aging (AG07476).

health that occurs with age is directly predictable from the changes that occur at the biological level—encompassing cellular, neural, endocrine, and immunologic systems—as we age. Social changes and losses are similarly predictable by demographic changes that occur as cohorts age and members die. Thus, in these cognitive, social, and health realms, lay opinion and empirical data are consistent with what we know about the biology and sociology of aging.

In contrast, in the realm of emotion, clear predictions about what kinds of age-related changes should occur are not so easy to make. Emotion is subserved by brain areas that are different from those that serve the cognitive processes that are typically studied by psychologists (e.g., explicit memory, association, computation). Accordingly, we know far less about what happens to these emotional processes and their underlying neural substrates as we enter late life. Furthermore, although a significant portion of the human emotional apparatus appears to be hard wired, there is also much about emotion that is learned. In realms such as emotional competency, emotional refinement, and emotional control, learning occurs as we attempt to cope with life's challenges. Many new emotionally relevant challenges appear in late life; thus, there is good reason to expect emotional learning to continue throughout this stage of life as well.

EMOTION: THE "LOSS" THEME

What is known about the nature of emotion in old age? Like so much about aging, there is much opinion, not enough data, and a great deal of disagreement and controversy. Similar to other aspects of aging, early views of emotion and old age were dominated by the theme of *loss*. Old age was seen as a time of dampened, rigid, and flat emotionality, with the lives of old people characterized as having low levels of affective energy, little "enthusiastic zest," and little emotional concern (e.g., Banham, 1951; Jung, 1933; Looft, 1972). According to this view, a central task of old age is disengagement, which includes removing emotional attachments to people, places, and objects in preparation for the end of life. Thus, according to these early depictions, the landscape of emotions in old age is bleak, desolate, and topographically impoverished.

EMOTION: THE "GAIN OR SAME" THEME

Another viewpoint that has been advocated increasingly in recent years regards emotion as a psychological realm that is relatively spared from the losses and ravages of age (e.g., Carstensen & Charles, 1998). According to this view, at the very least, we hold our own emotionally as we age.

What's more, we may even manifest emotional gains as we enter late life, encounter new experiences, and continue the lifelong process of emotional learning with its attendant increases in emotional refinement and competency. For example, in stark contrast to the loss theme, Malatesta and Kalnok (1984) found no evidence of decreasing salience of emotion with age. Similarly, Diener and Suh (1997) found that older individuals show greater life satisfaction than their younger counterparts. According to the gain theme, the landscape of emotion in old age is rich, complex, and topographically variegated.

LOSS OR GAIN?

Which theme best captures the nature of emotion in late life: Loss or gain? Straddling mind and body; occurring in solitary and interpersonal contexts; and encompassing aspects of the human condition as diverse as language, memory, thought, expression, behavior, physiology, subjective experience, and coping, a full accounting of emotion in old age would be a formidable undertaking. As is the case with so many questions involving emotion, the answer at which we arrive may depend in large part on how and where the question is pursued. It is certainly possible that age-related emotional losses will be found in some areas, maintenance of the status quo in others, and emotional gains in yet others.

HOW DOES AGE INFLUENCE EMOTION?

Before reviewing the findings derived from empirical studies of emotion and age that my colleagues and I have conducted, it might be useful to present the model of emotion (Levenson, 1988, 1994) that underlies our research. Using this model, I illustrate some of the ways in which age might exert an influence on emotion, thus making the logic and scope of our research program more clear. In this schematic model (Figure 7.1), emotion is envisioned as having a hard-wired core (the area within the box), which is embedded on both the "input" and "output" side between learned frames.

The Hard-Wired Core

The inner core of emotion consists of a mechanism that continually scans perceptual input from the outside world and mental input from the internal world in search of matches to a small set of templates that represent prototypical situations that are meaningful to the individual's well-being and survival. These prototypical situations are ones that have been

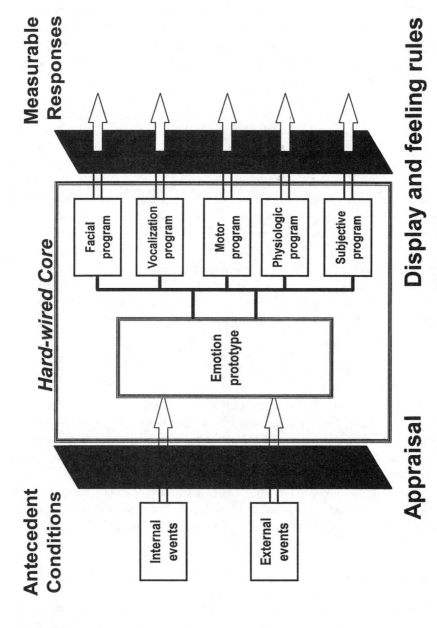

Figure 7.1. The model of emotion.

encountered by the species throughout its history. When a prototype situation is matched, the appropriate emotion is activated. The emotion is composed of the time-tested responses that are most likely to enable the organism to deal successfully with this kind of situation. Thus, prototypical situations involving threat, "taking away what is mine," "loss," or "gain" are detected, and appropriate emotional responses such as fear, anger, sadness, or happiness are activated.

Each emotion activates a set of bodily and psychological adjustments (referred to as *response tendencies* in the model) that act to adjust facial expression, voice tone, posture, autonomic nervous system activity, perceptual focus, and behavioral strategies (e.g., "flee," "fight," "be nurtured," "play") in ways that produce the optimal response for dealing with the prototypical situation. This hard-wired system is rapid, efficient, and does not require much in the way of conscious intervention—it picks the response that is most likely to deal successfully with situations of this type. Of course, this highly generalized response may not be the best response given the nuances of the specific situation, but this hard-wired core emotional system is not about nuances.

Age can affect this core emotional system in a number of ways, most prominently by altering the thresholds that antecedent conditions must reach in order to activate a given emotion and, once an emotion is activated, by altering the strength of the impulses that go out to the various physiological and psychological response systems. These changes are ultimately biological in nature, reflecting age-related changes in the efficiency of neural transmission and in other operating characteristics of the nervous systems.

The Learned Frames

The core emotional system is automatic in operation, requiring little, if any, conscious intervention. However, in humans (and arguably in other species as well), this core hard-wired system is enveloped by control systems, which are shaped by learning and which greatly influence both the final input to the core system and the final output or resultant behaviors and actions.

On the input side, we engage in elaborate processes of appraisal (e.g., Lazarus, 1991; Scherer, 1982) by which we process both perceptions and thoughts in ways that profoundly influence their meaning and thus their capacity to elicit emotion. For example, if we consider the template of "threat," many of the events that we consider to be threatening (as well as many of the things that we consider to be safe) reflect things that we have learned (e.g., beliefs about whether such things as strangers, oceans, or failures are dangerous).

On the output side, the core system produces tendencies to respond in certain ways (e.g., to cry when we are sad), but we can exert a great deal of influence over these tendencies so as to conform to learned emotional display and feeling rules (e.g., rules about when it is appropriate for people of a certain age, gender, and culture to cry). These rules often involve the inhibition of emotional response, but they may also involve the exaggeration or sustaining of emotional responses as well.

Age greatly affects both the input-side and output-side frames. As we age, we appraise the world differently—situations (e.g., social rejection) may be seen as more or less threatening than they did at other times in our lives. With age, things are appraised against a much deeper store of pertinent experiences, which can lend different perspectives on emotionally relevant matters involving such considerations as losses and gains. Also as we age, our inclinations to exert control over our emotional response tendencies may change in significant ways, as may our abilities to impose these controls effectively.

IMPLICATIONS FOR EMPIRICAL STUDIES OF EMOTION AND AGE

In keeping with this model, the empirical work that my colleagues and I have done has searched for age-related changes on both the input and output side of emotion, targeting both appraisal process and measurable emotional responses. Because the antecedents of emotion can originate either outside of the person (e.g., environmental events) or inside the person (e.g., thoughts and memories), we have studied emotions elicited in both ways. The model emphasizes that multiple response systems are involved in emotion; thus, we have attempted to sample broadly from psychological, behavioral, and physiological (primarily autonomic and somatic) systems. Last, because emotional learning and development occur in a cultural context, we have been interested in the impact that culture has on emotion. Cultures differ greatly in their conceptions and dictates concerning emotion. They also differ in the ways they view the aging process, as well as in the public and private roles that are sanctioned and prescribed for the elderly population. For this reason we have recently started to study the ways that culture and age interact in shaping human emotions.

In this chapter I review what my colleagues and I have learned from our research on emotion in late life, using these findings to address the overarching question posed at the start of this chapter, namely, "What best describes the nature of emotion in old age: loss or gain?"

One defining characteristic of our research program is it studies emotion in vivo; that is, our participants are exposed to experimental manipulations or placed into naturalistic situations that maximize the likelihood that emotions will occur. Then we study the psychological, behavioral, and physiological aspects of the emotions that ensue—often measuring emotional response systems continuously, so that we can characterize how patterns of response unfold moment by moment, in real time. Observational research on the nature of emotion in healthy elders has been rare (especially observational research studying emotion in social contexts and involving the measurement of multiple emotional response systems). Thus, much of what we know about normative emotion in old age is based largely on surveys, questionnaires, and demographic data. In our view, questionnaire and observational approaches to the study of emotion each have their own strengths. Questionnaire research is useful for revealing peoples' beliefs and judgments about emotion. Observational research is useful for revealing the magnitude, timing, and coordination of the various aspects of emotion and for elucidating the influence of contextual factors.

It is ironic that in life people spend a great deal of effort trying not to become emotional. To conduct laboratory research on emotion and aging, my colleagues and I have had to spend a great deal of effort finding ways to get people to become emotional—and not just one emotion, but rather a wide range of emotions. Our labors in this area have yielded several emotion elicitors that are useful for producing emotions in the laboratory. We have used four of these eliciting tasks in our studies of aging and emotion: (a) directed facial actions, (b) relived-emotions memories, (c) emotional films, and (d) marital interaction. I briefly describe each task before reviewing the results they have produced.

Directed Facial Actions

In studies involving directed facial actions, participants are given on each trial one of several sequences of simple instructions for moving facial muscles (e.g., "wrinkle your nose," "move your tongue forward in your mouth"). A observer in another room gives corrective feedback as necessary (e.g., "try to wrinkle your nose without raising your eyebrows"). When participants have complied with these instructions to the best of their ability, they are asked to hold the resultant facial configuration for 10 seconds. Although no emotion is ever mentioned to the participant, each sequence of instructions will, if followed correctly, produce a facial configuration that resembles the facial expression associated with a particular emotion (we typically use configurations for anger, disgust, fear, happiness, sadness, and surprise as well as a control configuration that does not have any particular emotional meaning). Physiological responses are measured during the 10-second period when the configuration is held; participants are asked after each trial to rate the intensity of any emotions they experienced, and the facial configuration is coded (Ekman & Friesen, 1978) to determine which facial muscles were actually contracted.

Relived-Emotions Memories

In studies that involve relived emotions, participants are asked on each trial to remember a time in their lives when they experienced a particular emotion very strongly and then to relive that memory. When participants begin to experience the memory, they signal the experimenter, and then continue the experience for 15 seconds. During that 15-second period, physiological responses are measured and facial expressions are coded. After each trial, participants are asked to rate the intensity of the emotions they experienced.

Emotional Films

In studies that include emotional films, participants view short (approximately 3-minute) films that have been selected for their ability to produce particular emotions (Gross & Levenson, 1995). During the film, physiological responses are measured and facial behavior is coded. In some studies participants also indicate their moment-to-moment emotional reactions to the films using a rating dial (Levenson & Gottman, 1983). After each film, participants are asked to rate the intensity of emotions that they experienced.

Marital Interaction

In the marital-interaction task, participants engage in three unrehearsed 15-minute conversations with their spouses, each about a topic related to their marriage (i.e., "events of the day," "marital problem," "pleasant plan"). During the conversations, physiological responses are measured, and emotional behavior is videotaped and coded (Gottman, 1996). After participating in the interactions, spouses view the videotapes and provide moment-to-moment ratings of their emotional experience using a rating dial (Levenson & Gottman, 1983).

EMOTION IN LATE LIFE: LOSS OR GAIN?

To do justice to this important question, my colleagues and I have tried to examine age-related changes in a number of aspects of emotion.

As even a simple model, such as the one presented above, should make abundantly clear, human emotions are complex and multifaceted, and it is possible that the answer to this question may differ as a function of which aspect of emotion is being examined and under what conditions.

Autonomic Differences Among Emotions

In the evolutionary view of emotion that I (e.g., Levenson, 1994) and others hold, autonomically mediated physiological changes exist primarily to support the behavioral adaptations that emotions call forth to deal with prototypical challenges to the organism's well-being and survival. To the extent that different emotions reliably involve different behaviors, and to the extent that these behaviors require different kinds of autonomic support, then autonomic differences among emotions should be expected (e.g., if anger begets fighting behaviors, this will require different kinds of cardiovascular support than would sadness, if sadness begets nuturance-receiving behaviors). Although most people would probably agree that the physiological changes that occur when they are angry appear to be different than those that occur when they are sad, establishing the reliability of autonomic nervous system differences among emotions has proved to be very difficult, and it remains a controversial part of the empirical and theoretical literature on emotion.

In my research on aging, I have addressed the question of whether the same patterns of autonomic activity accompany different emotions when we are young as when we are old. An alternative model would be that autonomic distinctions among emotions are present throughout our prime reproductive years and then become more blurred as we become older.

To attempt to answer this question, my colleagues and I (Levenson, Ekman, & Friesen, 1990) focused on a small set of autonomic differences among negative emotions that we found to be most reliable in a series of studies conducted with young participants and that had been found by other investigators as well (for a review, see Levenson, 1992). These autonomic changes involved three differences in heart rate between negative emotions (faster in anger than in disgust, faster in fear than in disgust, and faster in sadness than in disgust) and one difference in skin temperature (warmer in anger than in fear). We then asked whether these four differences were as likely to be found in older participants (ages 71–83) as they had been in young participants (ages 18–30).

The answer was quite clear: (a) The autonomic differences were found at significantly greater than chance levels in both older and younger participants, and (b) there were no significant differences between older participants and younger participants in how often these autonomic differences were found. It is important that these findings held regardless of whether the emotions were produced using the directed facial action task or the relived-emotions task (Levenson, Carstensen, Friesen, & Ekman, 1991). Thus, it appears that these autonomic differences among emotions are not changed qualitatively by age—in other words, our hearts are just as likely to accelerate when we are angry when we are 75 as when we are 25. The capacity of these emotions to produce these differentiated patterns of autonomic activation appears to be built to last for a lifetime.

Magnitude of Autonomic Response

Whereas the patterning of autonomic responses appears to be unchanged with age, examination of the magnitude of autonomic responses during emotion reveals a different story. Here autonomic responses clearly show diminution with age, particularly in the cardiovascular system (but much less so in the electrodermal system). My colleagues and I have found evidence for this in a number of studies using our full range of emotion-eliciting tasks. In the studies of autonomic differences among emotions mentioned in the preceding section, heart rate changes during negative emotions in the directed facial action task were approximately twice as large for young participants as for old participants, and this difference was even greater in the relived-emotions task (Levenson et al., 1991). In a recent study using emotional films as stimuli (Tsai, Levenson, & Carstensen, 1999), older participants (ages 70–85) had significantly smaller cardiovascular responses (heart rate, vasoconstriction, finger temperature) than younger participants (ages 20–35) to both sad and amusing films, and in studies of interaction in long-term marriages, older couples (ages 60–70) had smaller cardiovascular responses (heart rate, pulse transmission time) than middle-aged couples (ages 40–50) across three 15-minute conversations (Levenson, Carstensen, & Gottman, 1994). Thus, no matter how emotions have been elicited, consistent evidence has been found for diminution in cardiovascular reactivity with age.

These findings raise several issues. First, given that the magnitude of the autonomic response is likely to be proportionate to the magnitude of the emotional response elicited by a given stimulus, it is possible that our manipulations are producing emotions of a smaller magnitude in older participants and thus the autonomic responses merely reflect this. In later sections I present data based on subjective and behavioral responses that suggest that this is not generally the case. More directly to the point, in our marriage research, when my colleagues and I statistically controlled for age-related variation in the intensity of reported emotional experience, the age-related diminution in cardiovascular response still obtained (Levenson et al., 1994). A second issue is the question of whether age-related diminution in cardiovascular reactivity is specific to emotion or rather reflects age-related changes in the general reactivity of the cardiovascular system (e.g., Frolkis, 1977). With currently available data, this question cannot be answered definitively, but my colleagues and I are engaged in collecting additional data that should enable us to determine whether there is age-related diminution in cardiovascular reactivity that is specific to emotion or whether these differences are more general. Regardless, in the cardiovascular realm it is clear that old age brings with it a loss of response magnitude.

Subjective Emotional Experience

In all the studies my colleagues and I have conducted, we have obtained reports of participants' emotional experience in one or more ways. Although early theoretical accounts suggest that we should predominantly find evidence of emotional blunting in the realm of self-reported emotion, this has not been the case. Rather, the picture that has emerged is more complex, with some evidence that emotional experience actually increases in old age, some that it decreases, and some indicating no change.

In Tsai et al.'s (1999) study, in which emotional films were used, my colleagues and I obtained measures of subjective experience in two ways: (a) participants adjusted a rating dial while watching each film to provide continuous online ratings of their emotions (on a *positive–negative–neutral* scale), and (b) participants provided retrospective self-reports using conventional rating scales to rate four positive emotions (amusement, contentment, happiness, pleasant); four negative emotions (anger, disgust, fear, sadness); and one neutral emotion (interest) after watching each film. There were no age differences found for either the sad film or the amusing film on the basis of the continuous online ratings. Similarly, there were no age differences in the retrospective reports following the sad film and no age differences in retrospective reports of negative or neutral emotions following the amusing film. However, there were age-related differences in the retrospective reports of positive emotions following the amusement film: Older participants reported experiencing less amusement, contentment, and happiness.

Levenson et al.'s (1994) study of interaction in long-term marriages revealed that some aspects of emotion might actually increase with age. On the basis of rating-dial data, across all three conversations, we found that older couples reported experiencing more positive affect than middle-aged couples.

There was only one area where my colleagues and I have found clear-cut evidence of a decrease in subjective emotional experience, and that was using the directed facial action task. In this task, young participants reported experiencing the emotion associated with the emotional configuration at greater than chance levels when their facial configurations conformed closely to the prototypical expression for that emotion. For older participants, reports of the associated emotion during the directed facial action task were rare (Levenson et al., 1991). In contrast, when these same participants took part in the relived-emotions task, no age-related differences in the intensity of reported emotional experience were found (Levenson et al., 1991).

Emotional Behavior

Visible emotional behavior provides an important avenue for assessing emotion in old age because it is not as ambiguous in meaning as autonomic nervous system responses (which can reflect any of a number of psychological and biological processes other than emotion) and it is arguably not as amenable to response and presentation biases as is self-report. In all of our studies of emotion and aging, my colleagues and I have measured some aspect of emotional behavior, either facial expressions (in our studies using directed facial actions, relived emotions, and films) or a more global measure that makes use of facial expressions and other expressive behavior (during the marital problem conversation in the study of marital interaction). Each of these has revealed different aspects of age-related changes in emotional behavior.

In the relived-emotions task, participants are not instructed to produce facial expressions, but these occur spontaneously on 15%–20% of trials. Levenson et al. (1991) found no differences in the frequency of occurrence of these expressions between old and young participants.

Facial expressions often occur in response to emotional films. When observing participants viewing a sad film, Tsai et al. (1999) found no differences between old and young individuals in the frequency of facial behavior; when viewing an amusing film, old participants smiled less than young participants.

Levenson et al.'s (1994) study of marital interaction revealed an interesting set of age differences. Controlling for differences in the rated severity of the problem being discussed, we found that older couples showed more affection than middle-aged couples, whereas middle-aged couples showed more interest, humor, and disgust (Levenson et al., 1994).

Levenson et al. (1991) also coded expressive behavior during the directed facial action task, but these data are difficult to interpret. In this task, facial behavior is the manipulated variable, and thus expressive data may not be directly relevant to the overarching question of age-related changes in emotion. Nonetheless, it is worth noting that we found the facial configurations produced by older participants to be of lesser quality (i.e., they did not conform as closely to instructions) than those produced by younger participants (Levenson et al., 1991).

Emotional Appraisals

As indicated earlier, most of the research my colleagues and I have conducted is observational in nature. Nonetheless, we do make use of questionnaires, especially in our studies of marriage. These questionnaires provide a measure of age-related differences in certain emotion-relevant appraisals. Two areas that we regularly assess are how much conflict and pleasure couples perceive in different areas of their relationship. Here our findings consistently indicate that older couples report less conflict and more pleasure than middle-aged couples across a broad range of areas in their marriages, including less conflict about children, recreation, religion, and money and more pleasure with vacations, dreams, things they have done together, and children and grandchildren (Levenson, Carstensen, & Gottman, 1993).

Conclusion: Loss, Gain, or Same?

The empirical studies of emotion and age that my colleagues and I have conducted reveal a complex picture of the nature of emotion in old age, as befits data derived from four different emotion-eliciting tasks and reflecting measurement from the domains of self-report, expressive behavior, and autonomic physiology. The findings from this series of studies (Carstensen, Gottman, & Levenson, 1995; Levenson, Carstensen, Friesen, & Ekman, 1991; Levenson, Carstensen, & Gottman, 1993, 1994; Tsai, Levenson, & Carstensen, 1999) are summarized in highly simplified form in terms of loss, gain, or same, as can been seen in Table 7.1.

TABLE 7.1
Summary of Findings From Studies of the Nature of Emotion
in Old Age

Technique	Self-Report		Behavior	Cardiovascular physiology	
	Retrospective	On-line		Pattern	Magnitude
Directed facial actions	Same	—	Loss	Same	Loss
Relived emotions	Same	—	Same	Same	Loss
Sad film	Same	Same	Same	—	Loss
Amusing film	Loss	Same	Loss	—	Loss
Marital interaction	—	Gain	Gain and Loss	—	Loss
Marital appraisals	Gain	—	—	—	—

Note. Findings in this table are from Carstensen, Gottman, and Levenson, 1995; Levenson, Carstensen, Friesen, and Ekman, 1991; Levenson, Carstensen, and Gottman, 1993, 1994; Tsai, Levenson, and Carstensen, 1999. Please note that dashes indicate data not collected.

As can readily be seen, the kinds of pervasive losses that one sees in other domains of psychological functioning in old age are clearly not present in the realm of emotion. Cardiovascular reactivity during emotion is really the only area in which losses associated with old age have reliably been found and, as I indicated earlier, my colleagues and I do not currently have the data that would enable us to determine whether this diminished reactivity is more, less, or the same as would be expected given well-documented age-related changes in nonemotional cardiovascular reactivity.[1] In contrast, in most of our findings concerning subjective emotional experience and emotional expression (as well as in the noncardiovascular autonomic findings), the predominant theme appears to be one of same or gain in emotional functioning in older individuals.

SAME OR GAIN: OTHER INDICATORS

The findings I have reported so far have focused primarily on the more quantitative aspects of emotion (i.e., how frequent? how large?). Having considered the evidence suggesting that, in many ways, these quantitative aspects of emotion are preserved with age, I now consider briefly some evidence that more qualitative aspects of emotion are also maintained or improve with age.

Emotional Ecology of Relationships

Although the amount of specific emotions at various points in the life span is clearly an important parameter to consider, the balance among emotions is also meaningful. In the course of studying late-life relationships, my colleagues and I have found several indications of actual gains in emotional balance that are associated with age. As indicated earlier, in appraisals concerning marriage, older couples appear to derive more pleasure while experiencing less conflict in their marriages. Handling conflict is arguably one of the most important and most challenging tasks confronting any marriage. Our findings indicate that, when discussing conflictual topics, older couples show a much more favorable balance of two emotions that are very important to perceived marital quality and actual marital stability: They show greater affection and less disgust than middle-aged couples. Affection appears to play an important role in maintaining marital quality, whereas disgust is one of the more corrosive, judgmental emotions associated with marital instability and dysfunction (e.g., Gottman &

---

[1]Transposing the comparison from losses and gains to benefits and costs, one could argue that reduced cardiovascular activation during negative emotions actually is beneficial to older individuals, insofar as excess cardiovascular reactivity is generally viewed as having negative health consequences (e.g., Kaplan, Pettersson, Manuck, & Olsson, 1991).

Levenson, 1992). It is interesting that both of these emotions can be used to de-escalate conflict during marital interaction; however, they have different consequences. Affection is an effective way of backing away from an escalating conflict, providing a soothing action that causes spouses to feel closer to each other and increases their confidence that they can deal with future marital conflict in a constructive manner. Disgust also causes spouses to back away from an escalating conflict, but here the dominant mode of action is withdrawal, with spouses feeling hurt, judged, and abandoned and losing confidence in their ability to work effectively on marital conflicts in the future. Looking at hundreds of hours of videotape of couples dealing with marital conflicts, I have been struck by the virtuoso manner in which many older couples manage their emotions in ways that are constructive rather than destructive.

Emotional Competency, Control, and Refinement

Humans are not born with a complete set of emotions; rather, more complex emotions seem to come online as part of normal social development. For example, self-conscious emotions, such as pride, shame, guilt, and embarrassment, appear later in childhood than emotions such as happiness and distress. Although most of the emphasis on emotional development in the psychological literature has been on childhood, there is good reason to believe that emotional development is a lifelong process, with certain aspects not reaching their apex until late in life. Consistent with this view are findings that emotions becomes increasingly salient with age (Carstensen, 1992; Carstensen & Charles, 1998; Fredrickson & Carstensen, 1990) and that older individuals show increased emotional understanding (Labouvie-Vief & DeVoe, 1991; Labouvie-Vief, DeVoe, & Bulka, 1989; Labouvie-Vief, Hakim-Larson, DeVoe, & Schoeberlein, 1989). Further indication of this increasing level of emotional competence is found in reports that elders actively structure their environments in ways that maximize positive emotion and minimize negative emotion (Carstensen, 1993; Lawton, 1989).

Another area of increasing emotional competency is in the realm of emotional control. Here again, much has been written about early life, especially how infants and children learn to achieve some modicum of skill in emotional regulation and control. But clearly this is an area in which development continues throughout adulthood and into old age, as supported by findings of age-related improvement in the control of emotion (e.g., Gross, Carstensen, Pasupathi, & Tsai, 1997; Lawton, Kleban, Rajagopal, & Dean, 1992). These improvements in emotional competence may contribute to the finding that older people experience lower rates of all psychiatric disorders than do younger people (Lawton et al., 1992).

Finally, I believe it is reasonable to argue that human beings' emotional repertoire becomes more refined with age. There are some emotions, such as poignancy, that are hard to imagine having earlier in life (e.g., imagine a teenager experiencing poignancy). Poignancy may be a quality of our emotional apparatus that takes a lifetime of feeling and experience to develop. Similarly, there are ways of accessing emotional experience, such as reminiscence, that appear to become much more powerful and more effective in eliciting emotion as we move through adulthood and into late life.

SUMMARY AND CONCLUSION

In this chapter I have presented data from my laboratory and from the work of others suggesting that emotion represents one of the few psychological domains in which functioning is well preserved and even improves with age. In considering the larger implications of these findings, having an organism that can remain emotionally competent throughout life has clear advantages both for the individual and for society. For the individual, emotions can continue to serve their essential role in helping us cope with challenges to our well-being and survival. This always-important role may become even more critical as we age and the challenges that confront us increase in number and severity, at the same time as our other physical and psychological resources weaken. For society, there are enormous advantages in having a cohort of emotionally competent elders who can participate in the emotional education of younger people and provide models of successful emotional aging. In cultures such as the United States, where critical social institutions such as marriage are in great crisis, the opportunity to learn from older couples who have weathered the early storms of marriage and have achieved mastery of the emotional aspects represents an extremely valuable and regrettably underutilized resource.

There is a great need for additional research on emotion and aging, especially observational research that examines emotion in the kinds of social contexts where most human emotions occur. Similarly, it will be important not to treat emotion as a monolith but to continue to study the range of human emotions and to include measures of their subjective, behavioral, and physiological aspects (including central nervous, endocrine, and immunologic systems). Much of what is known about emotion and aging at this point in time (including my own work) is based largely on cross-sectional research, with its known vulnerability to cohort, historical, and survival effects. If one takes seriously the notion that emotional development is a lifelong process, then the value of longitudinal research for documenting and understanding that process should be obvious.

REFERENCES

Banham, K. M. (1951). Senescence and the emotions: A genetic study. *Journal of Genetic Psychology, 78*, 175–183.

Carstensen, L. L. (1992). Social and emotional patterns in adulthood: Support for socioemotional selectivity theory. *Psychology and Aging, 7*, 331–338.

Carstensen, L. L. (1993). Motivation for social contact across the life span: A theory of socioemotional selectivity. In J. E. Jacobs (Ed.), *Nebraska Symposium on Motivation* (Vol. 40, pp. 209–254). Lincoln: University of Nebraska Press.

Carstensen, L. L., & Charles, S. T. (1998). Emotion in the second half of life. *Current Directions in Psychological Science, 7*, 144–149.

Carstensen, L. L., Gottman, J. M., & Levenson, R. W. Emotional behavior in long-term marriage. *Psychology & Aging, 10*(1), 140–149.

Diener, E., & Suh, M. E. (1997). Subjective well-being and age: An international analysis. In M. P. Lawton & K. W. Schaie (Eds.), *Annual review of geriatrics and gerontology* (pp. 304–324). New York: Springer.

Ekman, P., & Friesen, W. V. (1978). Facial action coding system. Palo Alto, CA: Consulting Psychologists Press.

Fredrickson, B. L., & Carstensen, L. L. (1990). Choosing social partners: How old age and anticipated endings make people more selective. *Psychology and Aging, 5*, 335–347.

Frolkis, V. V. (1977). Aging of the autonomic nervous system. In J. E. Birren & K. W. Schaie (Eds.), *Handbook of the psychology of aging* (pp. 177–189). New York: Van Nostrand Reinhold.

Gottman, J. M. (1996). *What predicts divorce: The measures.* Hillsdale, NJ: Erlbaum.

Gottman, J. M., & Levenson, R. W. (1992). Marital processes predictive of later dissolution: Behavior, physiology, and health. *Journal of Personality and Social Psychology, 63*, 221–233.

Gross, J. J., Carstensen, L. L., Pasupathi, M., & Tsai, J. (1997). Emotion and aging: Experience, expression, and control. *Psychology and Aging, 12*, 590–599.

Gross, J. J., & Levenson, R. W. (1995). Emotion elicitation using films. *Cognition & Emotion, 9*, 87–108.

Jung, C. G. (1933). *Modern man in search of a soul.* New York: Harcourt, Brace, and World.

Kaplan, J. R., Pettersson, K., Manuck, S. B., & Olsson, G. (1991). Role of sympathoadrenal medullary activation in the initiation and progression of atherosclerosis. *Circulation, 84*, 23–32.

Labouvie-Vief, G., & DeVoe, M. R. (1991). Emotional regulation in adulthood and later life: A developmental view. In K. W. Schaie (Ed.), *Annual review of gerontology and geriatrics* (pp. 172–194). New York: Springer.

Labouvie-Vief, G., DeVoe, M., & Bulka, D. (1989). Speaking about feelings: Conceptions of emotion across the life span. *Psychology and Aging, 4*, 425–437.

Labouvie-Vief, G., Hakim-Larson, J., DeVoe, M., & Schoeberlein, S. (1989). Emotions and self-regulation: A life span view. *Human Development, 32,* 279–299.

Lawton, M. P. (1989). Environmental proactivity in older people. In V. L. Bengtson & K. W. Schaie (Eds.), *The course of later life: Research and reflections* (pp. 15–23). New York: Springer.

Lawton, M. P., Kleban, M. H., Rajagopal, D., & Dean, J. (1992). Dimensions of affective experience in three age groups. *Psychology and Aging, 7,* 171–184.

Lazarus, R. S. (1991). *Emotion and adaptation.* New York: Oxford University Press.

Levenson, R. W. (1988). Emotion and the autonomic nervous system: A prospectus for research on autonomic specificity. In H. L. Wagner (Ed.), *Social psychophysiology and emotion: Theory and clinical applications* (pp. 17–42). Chichester, England: Wiley.

Levenson, R. W. (1992). Autonomic nervous system differences among emotions. *Psychological Science, 3,* 23–27.

Levenson, R. W. (1994). Human emotion: A functional view. In P. Ekman & R. J. Davidson (Eds.), *The nature of emotion: Fundamental questions* (pp. 123–126). New York: Oxford University Press.

Levenson, R. W., Carstensen, L. L., Friesen, W. V., & Ekman, P. (1991). Emotion, physiology, and expression in old age. *Psychology and Aging, 6,* 28–35.

Levenson, R. W., Carstensen, L. L., & Gottman, J. M. (1993). Long-term marriage: Age, gender, and satisfaction. *Psychology and Aging, 8,* 301–313.

Levenson, R. W., Carstensen, L. L., & Gottman, J. M. (1994). Influence of age and gender on affect, physiology, and their interrelations: A study of long-term marriages. *Journal of Personality and Social Psychology, 67,* 56–68.

Levenson, R. W., Ekman, P., & Friesen, W. V. (1990). Voluntary facial action generates emotion-specific autonomic nervous system activity. *Psychophysiology, 27,* 363–384.

Levenson, R. W., & Gottman, J. M. (1983). Marital interaction: Physiological linkage and affective exchange. *Journal of Personality and Social Psychology, 45,* 587–597.

Looft, W. R. (1972). Egocentrism and social interaction across the life span. *Psychological Bulletin, 78,* 73–92.

Malatesta, C. Z., & Kalnok, M. (1984). Emotional experience in younger and older adults. *Journal of Gerontology, 39,* 301–308.

Scherer, K. R. (1982). Emotion as a process: Function, origin and regulation. *Social Science Information, 21,* 555–570.

Tsai, J. L., Levenson, R. W., & Carstensen, L. L. (1999). *Autonomic, expressive, and subjective responses to emotional films in younger and older adults of European American and Chinese descent.* Manuscript submitted for publication.

IV

SOCIAL RELATIONSHIPS IN LATER LIFE

PART IV: SOCIAL RELATIONSHIPS IN LATER LIFE

How do older adults maintain positive well-being in the face of the social losses that are nearly inevitable in later life? The gerontological literature has described in great detail how the social networks of older adults shrink over time and how older adults actually experience fewer social contacts than other adults. An important question is whether and how older adults can continue to maintain well-being in the face of this kind of loss.

The authors of the next two chapters examine social motivation as key to understanding how older adults accommodate social loss. The issue is whether the motivation for social relationships changes across the life span such that loss in size of network and frequency of contact may not be devastating. Richard M. Ryan and Jennifer G. La Guardia present a model of social motivation that identifies three core human needs that must be met relationally to ensure well-being. Karen S. Rook describes another life-span social motivational theory derived from the gerontological literature that suggests how and why network loss may not result in loss of well-being: Carstensen's socioemotional selectivity theory. Examination of the aging period within the context of the life span inevitably raises questions about the extent to which the latest part of the life span is unique. These authors suggest that although the context is unique, the motivational processes are continuous with other life stages.

Although motivational changes across the life span may lead older adults to proactively downsize their networks in ways that are purposeful, the fact still remains that older adults often experience social losses that are not under their control. Thus, the questions of how adults compensate for important social losses (e.g., loss of spouse) and how well such compensatory efforts work are key. The authors in this section push current theoretical frameworks to consider how aging is but one more stage in the life span, but it is a unique one.

The dialogue established in these two chapters illustrates the importance of interaction between geropsychologists and other social psychologists. Ryan and LaGuardia explore new options for investigating the validity and applicability of their theory when they examine the last phase of the life span. The social motivational theories also challenge geropsychologists to look for unifying principles across the life span to explain social behavior in later life. Rook's challenge to consider the impact of involuntary losses on social adjustment and well-being also poses provocative questions for social relationship theories. These chapters represent a meaningful step forward in the effort to integrate developmental processes into theories of social relationships.

8

WHAT IS BEING OPTIMIZED?: SELF-DETERMINATION THEORY AND BASIC PSYCHOLOGICAL NEEDS

RICHARD M. RYAN AND JENNIFER G. LA GUARDIA

Traditionally, development has been conceived as a continuous, progressive process of growth. In this seminal view, individuals are thought to elaborate and synthesize new knowledge and new capacities throughout the life span and, under healthy conditions, move toward wider integrative spans in both cognitive and social–personality functions (Ryan, 1995). The assumed trajectory toward ever more differentiation and higher order integration is even argued by some to differentiate the term *development* from other types of change (Blasi, 1976).

This conceptualization of development is, however, increasingly being questioned. As in the field of evolution, the view that progress or growth best characterizes developmental change is being strongly criticized. Life-span perspectives have specifically added new complexity to traditional views by emphasizing that development brings with it both changing tasks

Preparation of this chapter was facilitated by Grant MH53385 from the National Institute of Mental Health.

and goals, as well as gains and losses in capacities for successfully engaging them (Staudinger, Marsiske, & Baltes, 1995). Thus, according to several life-span views (e.g., P. B. Baltes, 1987; Heckhausen & Schulz, 1995; see also chap. 9, this volume) development is best characterized not as a process of unfolding but rather as a process of optimization of developmental resources in the face of changing goals and capacities. Individuals are viewed as selecting (actively and passively) only certain goals and potentialities, while ignoring or suppressing others, as they maximize adaptive resources.

Life-span psychology therefore recasts development mainly in terms of plasticity and adaptability and thus as a highly domain-, culture-, and age-specific process (P. B. Baltes, Staudinger, & Lindenberger, 1999). There is a de-emphasis on the search for a common core of human nature that might constrain developmental variation and skepticism toward arguments that some goals or trajectories may be better than others to select and "optimize" (M. M. Baltes & Carstensen, 1996). In this respect, life-span perspectives converge with cultural relativists and postmodernists (e.g., Gergen, 1991; Shweder, 1991) by placing on center stage the malleability and flexibility of developmental goals and processes.

The central claim of this chapter is that recent work in self-determination theory (SDT; Deci & Ryan, 1991; Ryan & Deci, 2000) may supply an empirical basis for reconsidering the very "open" ideas of adaptability, optimization, and selection. This claim is a bold one, but if it is at all correct it has major implications for life-span studies. In brief, our claim is that there is a small set of basic psychological needs that must be fulfilled in an ongoing manner across the life span for a person to experience well-being, integrity, and continued growth. These needs are by definition inherent, universal, and relevant to all developmental periods, and their frustration or neglect is predicted to produce both functional losses and decreased eudaemonia, or true well-being (Ryff & Singer, 1998; Waterman, 1993).

By assuming universal needs, however, SDT does not assume universal outcomes. Instead, changing developmental and contextual factors continuously influence the available means and relative efficacy of attempts to meet basic needs, resulting in both group and individual differences in growth, well-being, and integrity. Variations in basic psychological need satisfaction are affected by many factors, including age-related changes in (a) one's inner resources and strategies for meeting needs (including gains and losses in capacity) and (b) the ambient social demands, supports, obstacles, and affordances that surround potentially need-fulfilling activity. Thus, although basic psychological needs remain the same across the life span, their relative salience and the opportunities, resources, and means available for fulfilling them change dramatically. Functional costs and gains are expected to vary according to the extent that the pathways and strategies of adaptation selected by an individual either address or fail to address his or her basic needs.

This view differs in some ways from both traditional "growth" theories and approaches that stress the plasticity of human goals and adaptations. Instead, we seek to integrate concepts of malleability and continuity in a more critical, dialectical view. Specifically, we propose that although growth theories correctly assume that the human psyche is intrinsically oriented toward increased differentiation and integration of capacities and experience, they underemphasize the social–contextual constraints and obstacles that can both delay or fragment development (Edelstein, 1983; Ryan, 1995). On the other hand, although more relativistic life-span views correctly describe the flexibility of human adaptations to changing circumstances, and justifiably emphasize varied cultural scaffoldings for development, they ignore the universal contents of human nature and, as a result, lack the tools to critically analyze the demands and values of social structures with regard to their fit with that nature. The alternative "middle ground" forwarded here is an organismic–dialectical view that highlights the dynamic interaction between the innate orientations of human nature described by the concept of needs and the cultural conditions in which that nature finds itself (Deci & Ryan, 1991; Ryan & Deci, 2000).

DEFINING BASIC PSYCHOLOGICAL NEEDS

Among the fundamental properties that separate living, developing beings from things that are inanimate is the dependence of the former on nurturance. Living things must engage in continual exchanges with their environment from which they draw those necessities that allow them to preserve, maintain, and sometimes enhance their existing structure. Put differently, living things have needs that must be fulfilled if they are to persist and thrive (Jacob, 1973).

The concept of needs is relatively uncontroversial in biology, a field that focuses primarily on the physical structure of the organism, its survival, and its reproduction. There is little doubt that there are empirically specifiable requirements of life, some of which are common across all organisms (e.g., water or hydration). Such essentials are empirically specifiable insofar as any assumption about their necessity is testable. The claim that water is not a "need," for example, could be easily disconfirmed by simply withholding water from an organism and predicting its ensuing deterioration and death. Indeed, the concept of physical needs rests on the idea that deprivation of certain inputs results in degraded forms of growth and impaired functional integrity. Thus, the concept of need informs us about the minimum requirements of a healthy living system. Furthermore, the issue of needs pertains prescriptively to life. If we wish to care for an organism, we must know what it needs and supply those required elements. In turn, the organism must actively assimilate these required materials. If we care for human beings, for example, we would want to ensure that they are afforded food, water, and adequate shelter from hostile elements. Failure to do so is neglect, and the results are disease and death.

Finally, the concept of needs not only supplies criteria for knowing what is essential to life, but it also informs us about the central aims of human life. It describes the telic tendencies or underlying purposes that shape everyday action and give meaning and substance to existence.

Psychological Needs

Although the concept of needs is relatively uncontroversial with regard to the physical development of human organisms, the issue of whether there are definite needs underlying psychological growth is subject to more heated debate. Part of this controversy stems from the way in which prior psychological theorists have used the term *need*.

In perhaps the most common usage, the concept of need is used to denote virtually any motivating force that organizes behavior and experience. For example, Murray (1938) used a definition of need that equated it with nearly any motivating force and thus identified more than 20 psychological needs, including not only obvious ones such as affiliation or autonomy, but also needs to self-abase, to dominate, to defer, and to submit. For Murray, nearly any human goal commonly represented in human ideation could be classified as a need.

Within self-determination theory, however, the term *need* is used more restrictively. For us, a basic psychological need refers not to just any motivating force but rather to nutriments that are essential to psychological growth, integrity, and well-being. Our use of the term also implies that needs are deeply evolved features of human nature (Ryan, Kuhl, & Deci, 1997) that are intrinsic, persistent, and universal. A basic need must be an evident necessity for growth and well-being in all cultures and all developmental periods. It may have different expressions, or vehicles through which it is satisfied, but its core character must be unchanging.

This restrictive definition of basic psychological needs stands in contrast to the broader idea of personal wants or strivings. It is clear that there are many satisfactions and goals whose pursuit is not essential or necessary for growth, integrity, or well-being. In fact, some desires and wants can even interfere with activities that could fulfill basic psychological needs, and thus their pursuit can detract from growth and well-being (Ryan, Sheldon, Kasser, & Deci, 1996).

This is an extremely important point. Much of modern empirical psychology seems to focus on goal efficacy per se, without taking a critical stance concerning efficacy for what (e.g., Bandura, 1989). Yet, from our perspective, many goals, even when efficaciously pursued, supply only fleeting satisfactions and are often merely compensatory or derivative, holding their functional sway only as "stand ins" or symbolic satisfiers of more basic psychological needs. Furthermore, some acquired goals can be harmful to growth and integrity—precisely as a function of the extent to which they distract or compete with the fulfillment of truly basic psychological needs. Put differently, the pursuit of some goals is akin to feeding off of cardboard when one needs bread.

The usage of the term *need* within SDT thus addresses what has historically been the most common criticism of need theories; namely, that there is a potentially infinite list of psychological needs. In our view, there are few psychological nutriments that can be specified as essential for persons to thrive psychologically—that is, to experience growth, mastery, integrity, and well-being.

The Three Basic Needs: Autonomy, Competence, and Relatedness

SDT (Deci & Ryan, 1985, Ryan & Deci, 2000) has from the outset been focused on the motivational dynamics of human development. It has specifically been used to investigate, in both laboratory and field studies, the contextual and personal factors that support versus undermine processes such as intrinsic motivation; the internalization and assimilation of values; and holistic, self-congruent functioning. In identifying the factors whose presence was essential for the success of these processes, the idea of basic psychological needs emerged, because it appeared that such factors could be parsimoniously classified into a short list of needs. Indeed, the list is thus far so short that it reduces to three, namely the needs for autonomy, competence, and relatedness.

Autonomy connotes being an origin or source of one's behavior (deCharms, 1968; Deci & Ryan, 1985). It is experienced whenever a person perceives his or her behavior as congruent and self-endorsed. Thus, phenomenologically, autonomous action stems from one's "true self" (Sheldon, Ryan, Rawsthorne, & Ilardi, 1997), and it has (in attributional terms) an internal perceived locus of causality (deCharms, 1968; Ryan & Connell, 1989). The opposite of autonomy is *heteronomy*, or being regulated by forces felt to be alien to the self.

Autonomy can also be described structurally in terms of the relative integration of a regulation or value into self-organization. Regulations that are not well-assimilated into self-organization, such as those that are compartmentalized or that conflict with other regulations and values, tend to be experienced as less autonomous. By contrast, values and regulations that a person embraces and that have been integrated into one's self-structure are autonomous (Ryan, 1993).

Autonomy is a concept that is often both criticized and confused with other constructs. For instance, autonomy is equated by some with individualism. Yet, in the SDT view a person could be autonomously collectivistic or autonomously individualistic, depending on how well he or she has assimilated these cultural ideals. Indeed, recent research suggests, if anything, a moderately positive correlation between collectivistic attitudes and autonomy within both Eastern and Western samples (Kim, Butzel, & Ryan, 1998), a finding that suggests that individualism may be harder to integrate and endorse than a more collectivistic ideology.

Similarly, SDT makes a strong theoretical distinction between autonomy and the often-associated word *independence*. In our usage, *independence* refers to nonreliance on others (Ryan & Lynch, 1989). From the viewpoint of SDT one can be either autonomously dependent or autonomously independent as a function of specifiable factors in one's social support system (Butzel & Ryan, 1997). Distinguishing between autonomy and independence is critical for developmental studies, as dependencies are clearly ever present across the life course, and the degree to which one can experience autonomy within a relation of dependency is directly related to well-being (Ryan & Solky, 1996). This issue is particularly relevant to those periods of life wherein dependency is highly salient (e.g., early childhood, adolescence, old age).

Competence refers to feeling effective in one's interactions with the social environment and experiencing opportunities to exercise and express one's capacities (Deci, 1975; White, 1963). According to SDT, the feeling of competence attends behaviors that are both self-endorsed and effectively pursued. Thus, efficacy at heteronomous tasks does not typically enhance feelings of competence. This caveat separates our view of competence from those social–cognitive theorists whose definition of competence rests on expectations of success alone (e.g., Bandura, 1989).

Finally, *relatedness* refers to feeling connected, cared for, and a sense of belonging with significant others (Baumeister & Leary, 1995; Carstensen, 1998; Ryan, 1993). Relatedness is an intrinsic need, one manifest from early periods of attachment formation and extending throughout life. The common core of relatedness across the changing forms of social interaction in life is the desire to have others who respond with sensitivity and care to one's experience and who convey that one is significant and loved (Reis, 1994). By contrast, being "contingently" regarded is a substitute gratification and results in an unstable sense of self-worth (Deci & Ryan, 1995).

We hypothesize that when any of these three basic psychological needs is frustrated or neglected in a specific domain or in general, individuals will show motivational and psychological decrements of a specifiable nature, including diminished vitality, volition, integration, and well-being, among other criteria to which we turn shortly. We further believe that this formulation applies as much to the aged as it does to earlier developmental epochs.

By specifying three distinct needs we also suggest that one cannot psychologically thrive by satisfying one need alone, any more than a plant can thrive on soil without sunlight. Social environments that afford, for example, the experience of competence but fail to nurture relatedness conduce an impoverished human condition. Worse yet, contexts that pit one need against another, catalyzing conflicts between basic needs, set up the very foundations of psychopathology (Ryan, Deci, & Grolnick, 1995) and alienation. For example, when a child is asked (implicitly) by parents to give up autonomy in order to feel loved (as when they intrusively control the child with contingent approval), or when competence and achievement can be purchased only by crowding out relationships, then fragmentation and ill-being are likely to be manifest.

This feature separates our theory from previous need theories that place certain needs ahead of others at different points in the life span (e.g., Maslow, 1954). For us, each of the three needs is implicated at every developmental stage, and if any of the basic psychological needs is denied or blocked within a central life domain or in a given period of life, then experiential and functional costs will be evidenced. For example, a career-driven person who forgoes relatedness to stress achievement at a certain point in development would be expected to show specific immediate costs, regardless of how normative, lauded, or "adaptive" this decision may appear within his or her cultural milieu. Although many social environments demand of individuals that they forgo specific need satisfactions, SDT suggests identifiable negative effects whenever this occurs.

Finally, SDT suggests that individuals will gravitate toward domains, activities, and relationships in life wherein basic psychological needs can be potentially fulfilled—and they will tend either to avoid or engage only under duress domains and activities that threaten basic needs. Furthermore, there are costs in terms of motivation, interest, persistence, and performance in domains that are not need fulfilling. On the positive side, the model of need fulfillment explains, in part, why people migrate toward specific interests, vocations, and relationships (and away from others; e.g., Krapp, 1994), and why they function differentially within such domains or relationships as a direct function of how needs are addressed therein (Ryan, 1995). The psychological "gravity" of activities and relationships—their motivational power—is, in this view, a function of the degree to which individuals perceive them as potentially fulfilling the three basic needs.

In sum, our general formulation is that to the degree to which a person is blocked in the fulfillment of one or more of the three basic psychological needs within a domain, activity, or relationship, then to that degree he or she will show signs of impoverished motivation, quality of engagement, productivity, and psychological well-being. This formulation, which seems so simple and parsimonious, will show itself to have many embedded complexities and to operate differently as a function of both individual and social–contextual differences.

DEVELOPMENTAL PROCESSES THAT ARE DEPENDENT ON NEEDS

Basic psychological needs have been argued to subserve development. More specifically, we have extensively examined in our empirical work two developmental processes that are fostered through the fulfillment of the three basic needs and, alternatively, obstructed by conditions that frustrate these needs, namely (a) intrinsically motivated growth and development and (b) the internalization and integration of culturally acquired regulations and values.

Intrinsic Motivation in Growth and Development

Psychological development entails individuals elaborating or extending their capacities while simultaneously striving to maintain cohesion and enhance integration among all aspects of themselves (Blasi, 1976). This proposition assumes that humans are proactive, actively engaging the environment, and attempting to assimilate new knowledge of it into self-organization (Ryan, 1995). It also reflects the view that we are, to a large extent, agents in our own development. By this we mean that development occurs through motivated, purposive behavior. One innate tendency that subserves this proactivity is intrinsic motivation.

Intrinsic motivation refers to behaviors that are motivated by their inherent satisfactions. Prototypes of intrinsically motivated behavior are curious exploration, play, and other self-challenging activities that do not have separable rewards or outcomes as their goal. Intrinsic motivation is clearly evident from birth (Stern, 1985; White, 1963), as infants attempt to contact and affect the world around them for the sheer experience of activity and mastery. It continues to predominate as a motivational form in early childhood, as children energetically engage their surroundings and, in doing so, learn about social and inanimate nature and discover their capacities, interests, and talents. Accordingly, it has been argued that intrinsic motivation is essential to the developmental processes of differentiation and cognitive growth (Elkind, 1971).

The course of intrinsic motivation after early childhood has been less well studied. In the domain of school it appears that intrinsic motivation decreases with age (Harter, 1982; Ryan & La Guardia, 1999). However, the relative contribution of developmental versus contextual factors to this decrease is not known, and there are no systematic cross-sectional or longitudinal studies in other domains to serve as a comparison. Nonetheless, even if intrinsic motivation occurs less frequently with age, the ability to experience intrinsic motivation remains critically important throughout life for both feelings of self-worth (Ryan & Grolnick, 1986) and performance on complex tasks (Amabile, 1983; Utman, 1997). It seems that even in the midst of extrinsic demands people innovatively seek ways to challenge and entertain themselves for intrinsic motives (Sansone, Weir, Harpster, & Morgan, 1992), finding ways to turn work into play. Additionally, outside of the spheres of work and social obligations, people seek out opportunities for intrinsically motivated activities such as sport, hobbies, and mental enrichments (Frederick & Ryan, 1995). Indeed, Sheldon, Ryan, and Reis (1996) recently found that people exhibit enhanced well-being on weekends, largely because of the greater autonomy and competence felt as people pursue more intrinsically motivated activities. Clearly intrinsic motivation is one means through which people renew and revitalize themselves and optimize their experience.

A question that has remained relatively unexplored to date concerns the role and social–contextual dynamics of intrinsic motivation in later life. We are particularly intrigued by the question of the functional role played by intrinsic motivation in the processes by which older people discover new interests and avocations and maintain a sense of vitality, after they have normatively moved beyond many family and work obligations (e.g., after children leave home or during retirement years).

Intrinsically motivated behaviors are highly influenced by interpersonal factors. Social contexts that are conducive to intrinsic motivation are those that support feelings of autonomy and competence. Specifically, experiments and field studies have established that opportunities for competence and autonomy directly enhance the occurrence of intrinsically motivated behaviors, whereas excessive control and nonoptimal challenges decrease the likelihood of its occurrence. Opportunities for choice (Zuckerman, Porac, Lathin, Smith, & Deci, 1978), the use of autonomy-supportive language (Koestner, Ryan, Bernieri, & Holt, 1984), and competence feedback (Vallerand & Reid, 1984) have all been shown to maintain or enhance intrinsic motivation. By contrast, intrinsic motivation is undermined by controlling rewards (Deci, Koestner, & Ryan, 1999), evaluations (Grolnick & Ryan, 1987), controlling language (Ryan, 1982), threats of punishment (Deci & Cascio, 1972), surveillance (Lepper & Greene, 1975; Pittman, Davey, Alafat, Wetherill, & Kramer, 1980), and negative competence feedback (Koestner & McClelland, 1990), among other factors. The implications of this for promoting active engagement and feelings of worth within social settings such as schools, workplaces, and hospitals are manifold and have been extensively reviewed (e.g., Deci & Ryan, 1985; Ryan et al., 1995).

Danner and Lonky (1981) conducted a classic experiment that illustrates both the growth function of intrinsic motivation in development and its vulnerability to being undermined by social factors. Children were classified according to their cognitive skills and then allowed to freely choose learning activities of various levels of difficulty. As predicted by both traditional cognitive-developmental (e.g., Piaget, 1971) and self-determination (Deci & Ryan, 1980) theories, children, when unconstrained, tended to spontaneously choose tasks that were optimally challenging (i.e., just above their established range of ability). However, in the experiment some children were given rewards for problem solving. Rewarded children were more likely than unrewarded children to avoid subsequent challenges, and they showed less interest in the task per se. Theoretically, the use of rewards signified to children an external cause for their activity, thus undermining their sense of autonomy and their intrinsic motivation for this cognitive task.

Internalization and the Development of Self-Regulation

Behaviors that an individual performs for instrumental reasons rather than for inherent satisfaction fall under the category of extrinsic motivation. As individuals mature, acquire more social roles, and face more demands the relative predominance of intrinsic motivation declines and that of extrinsic motivation increases. With age, that is, social environments increasingly place regulations and limits on time and behavior, and individuals increasingly adopt goals that require more and more instrumental actions. Indeed, by adulthood intrinsic motivation for many people can be a relatively rare event. Instead, goals, agendas, and responsibilities take center stage, and for many people these feel alien rather than integral to the self.

However, the increased predominance of extrinsic motivation is not all bad. In fact, from the perspective of SDT, extrinsic motivation is often mischaracterized in the literature as uniformly negative. By contrast, we theorize that there are distinct types of extrinsic motivation that themselves vary in their relative integration to the self. That is, some extrinsically motivated actions represent the willing commitment of a person to a valued goal, and thus are autonomous, whereas other types of extrinsic motivation represent "controlled" motivations in which a person is coerced or seduced into goal pursuits that he or she does not personally value or endorse.

Figure 8.1 illustrates these styles of extrinsic motivation, arranged from left to right in terms of the extent to which the motivation for one's extrinsic behavior has been accepted by and assimilated to the self. Behaviors that are least autonomous are those that are *externally regulated*. Such behaviors are performed either to receive externally administered rewards or to comply with some external force. Individuals typically experience externally regulated behavior as controlling or alienating, and

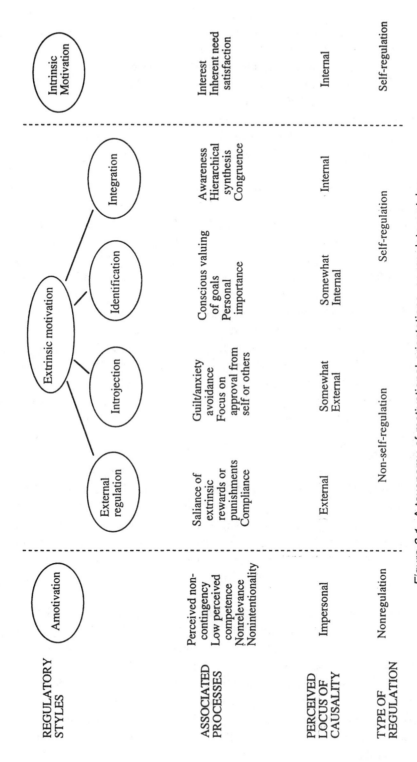

Figure 8.1. A taxonomy of motivational orientations, or regulatory styles.

their actions have an external perceived locus of causality. It is important to point out that external regulation is the only kind of motivation recognized by operant theorists (e.g., Skinner, 1953), and it is external regulations that were typically contrasted with intrinsic motivation in early laboratory and field studies. A second type of extrinsic motivation is labeled *introjection*, an "internally controlling" state (Ryan, 1982) in which one performs an action either to avoid guilt or anxiety or to experience ego-enhancements or pride. Put differently, introjection represents regulation by contingent self-esteem (Deci & Ryan, 1995). Although internally driven, introjected behaviors are not experienced as fully part of the self and still have, in attributional terms, a somewhat external perceived locus of causality. A more autonomous, or self-determined, form of extrinsic motivation is that of *identification*. Behaviors regulated by identifications are ones that are consciously accepted by the person as being worthwhile or valuable. They are typically experienced as volitional and have an internal perceived locus of causality. Finally, the most autonomous form of extrinsic regulation is *integration*, which occurs when regulations and values are fully assimilated to the self, which means they have been evaluated with respect to other values and needs and are fully self-endorsed and congruent.

The movement from left to right in this schematic of extrinsic regulations describes a continuum of *internalization*; that is, the more one internalizes the reasons for acting the more one moves away from external regulation toward integration. With increasing internalization comes the experience of greater autonomy in action. This is not a developmental continuum per se but rather a conceptual one. One does not have to progress through each stage of internalization to achieve integration; indeed, one can begin new regulatory acts at any point along this continuum depending on prior experiences and situational factors (Deci & Ryan, 1991; Ryan, 1995). What is developmental is that the types of regulations and values that can be assimilated to the self increase with greater cognitive and ego development (Loevinger, 1976) and, moreover, there is some evidence of a general or "on average" tendency for the same behaviors to, over time, become more internalized, or truly self-regulated (Chandler & Connell, 1987).

The concept of internalization describes the agentic side of the process of socialization. In socialization, others transmit values and prescriptions for how one is to behave. In most settings socializing agents (e.g., parents, teachers, managers, health care professionals) want to engender not merely passive compliance but rather a willingness to engage in prescribed actions and an inner sense of their value and worth. Internalization concerns the processes by which the socializee more or less assimilates and transforms social demands into a self-organized structure of values and action regulations. The analysis of internalization is thus at the interface of the divergent perspectives of sociology, on the one hand, and organismic psychology on the other.

Although internalization is often treated as a fundamental process in childhood socialization, it is really a life-span issue. Every age, institutional setting, and social circumstance presents a set of regulative prescriptions whose meaning and import will be more or less assimilated by participants. Just as a child faces the task of internalizing the rules of home, neighborhood, and school, so adults must continually adapt to explicit and implicit regulations in work environments, health care settings, and varied social contexts. Thus, internalization processes are pertinent at any point where new goals or behavioral regulations must be adopted.

Greater internalization of ambient social practices has, of course, many adaptive advantages (Ryan et al., 1997). These include greater assimilation of the individual within his or her social group, behavioral effectiveness (due to lessened conflict and greater access to personal resources), and experience of well-being in ongoing actions. Furthermore, more internalized forms of regulation have been associated with greater persistence, higher performance, more satisfaction, and lessened akrasia (lapses of will). Numerous empirical studies have examined the functional benefits resulting from more autonomous forms of internalization (see Grolnick, Deci, & Ryan, 1997; Vallerand, 1997; and Williams, Deci, & Ryan, 1998, for recent reviews.)

The processes through which needs facilitate versus undermine internalization have to some extent been specified, and each of the three needs is centrally implicated. First, internalization occurs in part because people want to emulate and connect with others. They are therefore most likely to internalize the values of those with whom they experience relatedness and to fail to internalize regulations from socializers from whom they feel detached or rejected (Ryan, Stiller, & Lynch, 1994). Cold, rejecting, or uninvolved others may lead the person to seek out other figures to fulfill relatedness needs—and it is their values that will become reference points (Ryan & Lynch, 1989). Second, successful internalization represents an active transformation of what were originally external regulations into regulations that are experienced as one's own. Excessive controls disrupt the experience of autonomy with respect to the goals being internalized, undermining feelings of personal causation (deCharms, 1968), disrupting active assimilation, and often foster reactance rather than volitional adherence. Research supports this view, showing, for example, that children who are exposed to excessive controls show less internalization (e.g., Grolnick & Ryan, 1989). Finally, regulatory demands by socializers must be optimally paced with respect to the existing competencies of the socializee such that one can experience competence by internalizing new behaviors. Attempts to internalize overchallenging standards or overly complex viewpoints lead to frustration, amotivation, and withdrawal. In short, all three needs are implicated in the process of active internalization.

An interesting facet of this relationship between need fulfillment and internalization is that we expect it to yield considerable domain specificity (Ryan, 1995; Vallerand, 1997). People who are willingly responsible in some walks of life or institutional settings may be utterly alienated and unreliable in others. Much of this variability can be explained by the differential presence of supports for the basic psychological needs that subserve the internalization process. Thus, people will be more likely to more fully integrate ambient values in settings that afford support for autonomy, competence, and relatedness, a proposition that has been examined in the domains of work (Baard, Deci, & Ryan, 1998), school (Hayamizu, 1997; Ryan & La Guardia, 1999), religion (Baard, 1994), and health care (Williams, Deci, & Ryan, 1998), among others.

An illustrative study of internalization processes in a specific domain was presented by Williams, Grow, Freedman, Ryan, and Deci (1996), who followed severely obese people through a 6-month weight loss program and a 17-month posttreatment follow-up. They found that more internalized reasons for entering and participating in the program predicted short-term success at weight loss. More important, patients who experienced the treatment staff as high in relational- and autonomy-supportiveness showed not only greater internalization of reasons for participating in the program, but also greater adherence over the follow-up period, evidencing better maintenance of weight loss. The study demonstrates how need-related supports in a social context can facilitate internalization and in turn foster better within-domain adjustment and success.

BASIC PSYCHOLOGICAL NEEDS AND WELL-BEING

In a life-span view, development entails processes of goal selection, optimization, and compensation (P. B. Baltes et al., 1999). However, goal selections can be misdirected, compensations may not fill losses, and sometimes what people emphasize in their "adaptations" may not be at all optimal with regard to their well-being.

According to SDT, for the adaptive maneuverings of individuals to be "optimizing" they must, at minimum, support or enhance fulfillment of basic psychological needs. People may deal with change through varied selections or compensations, but the impact and adequacy of those adaptations is predicted to be largely a function of the extent to which they facilitate the meeting of basic needs, which in turn fosters well-being. In other words, need satisfaction is hypothesized to mediate between resource optimization and well-being. This is expected to be so regardless of the personal salience to the individual of basic needs.

One powerful new way to demonstrate this dynamic relationship be-tween need fulfillment and well-being has been afforded by the application of hierarchical linear modeling techniques to diary studies. These methods allow examination of how fluctuations in basic need satisfaction affect lev-els of well-being on a day-to-day basis, while controlling for individual differences, events from prior days, and other confounding variables. In an initial study, Sheldon et al. (1996) found that daily experiences of auton-omy and competence predicted fluctuations in well-being outcomes such as mood, vitality, physical symptoms, and self-esteem. In another study (Reis, Sheldon, Gable, Roscoe, & Ryan, 2000), fluctuations in all three needs were examined, and each independently predicted changes in well-being. These studies support the view that all three basic psychological needs play a role in optimizing well-being in everyday life.

Another operational route into the question of needs and their re-lations to well-being has evolved from studying the content of life goals and values. Specifically, T. Kasser and Ryan (1993, 1996) argued that some life goals are very closely related to psychological needs, such that their successful pursuit will typically yield basic need fulfillments. Other goals are either unrelated or antithetical to basic needs, such that their pursuit may even detract from need fulfillments. Accordingly, Kasser and Ryan contrasted intrinsic aspirations or life goals (e.g., affiliation, personal growth, or community service) that were assumed to more directly yield need satisfactions with extrinsic aspirations (e.g., money, fame, or image) whose pursuit was assumed to be less need fulfilling. They found that the more one placed relative importance on extrinsic aspirations, the lower one's well-being and life satisfaction, as measured by multiple indicators.

More recent evidence suggests that even the perceived attainment of extrinsic aspirations does not typically enhance well-being. T. Kasser and Ryan (in press) compared participants who rated their attainment of in-trinsic and extrinsic goals. Results showed that attainment of intrinsic as-pirations was the necessary and sufficient condition for predicting well-being, whereas attainment of extrinsic goals did not enhance outcomes. Ryan et al. (1999) replicated this pattern in Russian and American sam-ples, attesting to some generalizability. Finally, Sheldon and Kasser (1998) followed participants pursuing intrinsic and extrinsic goals in a longitudinal design and found that well-being was enhanced only by the attainment of intrinsic goals. Such studies attest to the differential yield of goals, which we theorize to be a function of their relation to basic needs.

Among the important and yet understudied factors affecting goal se-lections are processes of socialization that engender specific conscious goals and values. From the perspective of SDT, the goals, values, and lifestyles fostered by a culture or subculture (e.g., a school, hospital, neighborhood) can be either disabling or enhancing with respect to actually fulfilling basic needs (Ryan et al., 1996). For example, exposure to commercial media can enhance a focus on materialism, which in turn can detract from basic need fulfillments. Furthermore, prior deficits in need fulfillment (e.g., from poor caregiving) can lead individuals to more greatly aspire to extrinsic goals as a substitute or compensatory mechanism. Specifically, aspirations for fame, money, or image all concern "reflected" signs of worth or agency, and we believe that they become more salient and attractive the less secure one feels with regard to relatedness, competence, or autonomy. In accord with this reasoning, T. Kasser, Ryan, Zax, and Sameroff (1995) found that teenagers who had been exposed to cold or controlling maternal care (as assessed by self, maternal, and observer ratings) were more likely to develop strong materialistic orientations in late adolescence than were better nurtured teenagers. Furthermore, the teenagers who embraced materialism evidenced greater maladjustment as indicated by clinical interviews.

In short, developmental and cultural factors dynamically conspire to produce variations in the salience of goals which, when adopted, differentially yield basic need fulfillments and well-being. It follows from this that even a highly efficacious person may attain nonoptimal well-being if he or she is pursuing the "wrong" goals. Furthermore, group differences in well-being would be expected as a function of the capacity of the common goals and values that a community or subcultural group embraces to fulfill basic psychological needs. Thus again, when we consider the issue of what constitutes successful aging, SDT suggests the need to look not only at how efficacious one is at attaining salient goals but also at how adequate the goals one pursues are as vehicles of basic need fulfillment. It also suggests that there is no direct correspondence between a goal's salience and its true functional value over development.

RECENT WORK ON AGING FROM A MOTIVATIONAL PERSPECTIVE

Much of previous work in SDT has focused on intrinsic motivation, internalization, and value adoption during childhood, adolescence, and early to middle adulthood (see Ryan et al., 1995, for an age-related review). Such research has confirmed the functional impact of autonomy, competence, and relatedness supports in these varied life periods. Less well explored, however, has been the role of psychological needs in the later years of life. We now review recent work that bespeaks the relevance of basic needs to an understanding of well-being and motivation in old age.

Autonomy

Autonomy is defined within SDT as volition rather than as nondependence. Accordingly, measurements of autonomy consider the reasons why a person engages in various forms of behavior. When behaviors are controlled by external regulators or introjects, then autonomy is low, whereas when behaviors stem from identifications or intrinsic motivation, autonomy is considered high (Ryan & Connell, 1989). So measured, a growing body of evidence points to the importance of autonomy in later life.

A number of studies have applied the SDT framework to nursing homes, where residents cope in an ongoing manner with an institutional context that "manages" various aspects of their daily lives. For example, Vallerand, O'Connor, and Blais (1989) classified nursing homes into two categories: those high in support of autonomy and those low in support of autonomy. They then compared life-satisfaction ratings of residents of both types of homes as well as of elderly individuals living in low-income housing and private residences. They found that residents in high-autonomy-oriented nursing homes were comparable in their life satisfaction to individuals still living in the community, whereas those residing in low-autonomy-oriented nursing homes evidenced significantly poorer psychological outcomes. In another study, Vallerand and O'Connor (1989) surveyed nursing home residents concerning the degree to which they experienced autonomy with respect to their self-care and religious, interpersonal, and recreational activities. Residents who experienced greater autonomy across these domains reported lower depression and higher self-esteem, life satisfaction, meaning in life, general health, and psychological adjustment. Similarly, V. Kasser and Ryan (1999) showed that greater autonomy for daily activities predicted decreased mortality in residents over a 1-year period. Additionally, perceived autonomy support from staff and family was associated with less depression and greater vitality and life satisfaction.

O'Connor and Vallerand (1994b) extended their earlier work by assessing a number of nursing home samples, finding that greater self-determination in daily life was associated with higher levels of psychological adjustment. In yet another report, O'Connor and Vallerand (1994a) rated 11 nursing homes on the degree to which they supported versus discouraged autonomy. They showed in a path model that observer-rated supports for autonomy predicted greater experienced autonomy in the residents, which in turn was associated with more self-determined activity. These findings point both to the significant effects of individual differences in autonomy on well-being as well as to the effects of nursing home environments in shaping the motivational "climate" of residents. Similar to results with younger participants (e.g., Ryan & Grolnick, 1986), it appears that a more autonomy-supportive climate fosters greater initiative and well-being in old age.

A limitation to these studies is that most were conducted in nursing homes. Only a small percentage of older adults ever reside in nursing homes, suggesting the need to study the significance of autonomy in people who stay in the community throughout life. The opportunities and obstacles to autonomy undoubtedly differ, although we believe that the functional outcomes associated with variations in autonomy would remain.

Relatedness

Individuals at every age appear to function better and be more resilient when they experience others standing behind them with love and affection (Ryan et al., 1994; Sarason et al., 1991). However, as research bespeaking the benefits of relatedness has grown, so have questions concerning the specific nature of its facilitative effects (Ryan & Solky, 1996). In particular, what types of relationships function as true supports? Complicating this question is evidence suggesting that the motives behind social interactions can change over development, becoming more useful for different needs at different times.

Carstensen (1993, 1998) introduced a life-span theory that emphasizes differences in the functions and perceived value of social interactions at different points in development. She labeled her approach *socioemotional selectivity theory* (SST), to emphasize the idea that people are selective in their social interactions and that these selections reflect, in part, changes in the goals and needs faced across the life span. For example, adolescents and young adults may relate to others for both competence and relatedness reasons, as interactions can provide useful information and have instrumental value as well as yield relatedness fulfillments. However, SST proposes that as people age, relationships are less and less needed for gathering "information," but they remain critical for the fulfillment of needs for emotional contact and expression. Thus, in later life relatedness satisfactions per se supply the central motivating focus for social interactions. Thus, according to SST, relationships that afford depth and emotional expression should most benefit the elderly population, whereas more superficial types of contact may yield little benefit and will be less sought.

In a recent study that tested aspects of both SST and SDT, V. Kasser and Ryan (1999) examined the association between the satisfaction of needs for autonomy and relatedness and the well-being, vitality, and perceived health of nursing home residents. They hypothesized that well-being would be facilitated by (a) greater personal autonomy with respect to nursing home living, (b) perceived support for autonomy by both nursing home staff and residents' friends and relatives, and (c) the emotional quality rather than quantity of residents' contacts with friends and family. The results generally supported the hypotheses, showing that both autonomy support and relatedness indices correlated with positive outcomes. Furthermore, whereas quality of relatedness did predict well-being outcomes, quantity of social interactions was less predictive. The study suggests that among nutriments for well-being, autonomy and relatedness supports loom large.

Competence

As with the other psychological needs, competence is clearly a life-long issue. However, as underscored by life-span psychologists, competence is not always an increasing function, and old age in particular commonly brings with it risks for losses in competence.

In the SDT view, however, the need for competence is not a need to be "better than before" but rather a need to feel optimally challenged (Deci, 1975) in the domains of life that one engages and thus able to experience effectiveness and agency. For older people this often requires that they modify existing environments (Lawton, 1988), select out of certain activities that they formerly performed, and rededicate resources to activities that more likely will foster feelings of effectance and meaning. "Choice over challenges" is also an important process issue. For example, when external aids are used to compensate for, or protect against, functional losses, the older adult needs to be involved as much as possible in decisions and choices regarding the change. Thus, a dynamic issue of central import is that of creating a landscape for daily living that involves opportunities for self-selected action that are well matched with existing skills, thereby facilitating both optimal experience (Csikszentmihalyi, 1975) and well-being. However, consideration of this issue brings us to a construct that is uniquely considered from the SDT framework, namely, that of dependence.

Dependence Reconsidered

One of the major theoretical obstacles in the study of basic needs in later life has concerned the confluential treatment of the concepts of in-dependence and autonomy (Ryan & Lynch, 1989). As we argued earlier, autonomy (as defined in SDT) concerns whether one's actions are self-endorsed and congruently valued, versus controlled by forces outside the self. By contrast, SDT defines independence as not relying on others for the provision of goods. These distinct definitions allow us to theoretically and empirically deconfound these concepts so as to consider the dynamic relations between independence and autonomy.

Clearly, dependency is a complex issue, as throughout life people go through cycles of dependence, independence, and (sometimes) renewed dependence regarding the procurement of certain outcomes. The timing of these cycles also differs by content area and culture. However, given the relative salience of functional loss inherent in aging, an increased need to rely on others would appear to be a commonly important theme in late life (M. M. Baltes & Wahl, 1987). The principle focus of SDT regarding this change is not on whether dependence per se is good or bad, but on what factors allow one to be reliant on others without creating threats to the basic psychological needs for autonomy, competence, and relatedness.

Most obviously, dependence can threaten feelings of competence. A person who needs help may feel incompetent or ineffective by virtue of being unable to provide for oneself. Social contexts, however, clearly influence how dependence will be experienced in this respect. Providers can react evaluatively to dependencies, for instance, by emphasizing social comparisons or focusing on inadequate skills. However, they can also focus on one's effective coping with losses and support one's redirecting of resources to new activities. Clearly, the meanings bestowed by a social context will affect the interpretation given to one's dependence, which in turn affects outcomes such as depression, life satisfaction, and self-esteem (Rook, 1984).

Dependencies also bear on feelings of relatedness. A person can feel that his or her dependence is a burden on others and fear a loss of connectedness. Moreover, caregivers often convey to the recipients of their care that providing is a hardship, thus leading the recipient to feel unvalued and "in the way." Such communications, whether implicit or explicit, complicate dependency and make it potentially threatening to a sense of belonging and significance. On the other hand, dependency often brings out a sense of connectedness, as others respond with care and affection. Clearly, then, dependency per se is not a threat to relatedness, but providers and recipients can make it so.

Finally, as we have pointed out, SDT considers dependency and autonomy to be theoretically separate issues. From the SDT view, providers can be either volitional or controlled in their caregiving, and the recipients of care can feel either autonomous or controlled in their position of dependency. It is interesting that we have recently begun to research the question of what allows a person to be experience *volitional reliance*, that is, to be autonomously dependent on others (Ryan & Solky, 1996). Results of these initial studies suggest that people are more able to be volitionally reliant—to willingly turn to an other for help or support—to the extent that the potential provider is not perceived as controlling, and does not use the relation of dependence to undermine feelings of competence or relatedness. That is, when providers are sensitive to basic psychological needs, they are more willingly turned to by a dependent. Furthermore, the more individuals are able to experience volitional reliance on others, the greater their well-being, and the lower their psychological distress (Butzel & Ryan, 1997).

It is clear that the work relating psychological need satisfaction and well-being in later life is still in its infancy. Again, SDT predicts that supports for autonomy, competence, and relatedness will each play a role in fostering well-being, as they do in other age groups and cultures. In addition, it seems that opportunities for engaging in domains and activities that yield satisfaction of basic needs may be critical to maintaining psychological vitality (Ryan & Frederick, 1997). The role of cultural context, social supports, and age-related constraints in both facilitating and forestalling need satisfaction in old age still, however, remains an open area of inquiry.

AMID PLASTICITY ARE COMMON HUMAN NEEDS

Claims against any universality and continuity in development are pervasive in modern psychology (Gergen, 1991; Shweder, 1991). Postmodernists and behaviorists alike claim that psychological variation is due to the specific contingencies of culture and that developmental goals and life aims will thus be as varied as the colors of our global social fabric. They recognize no universal or basic needs of the psyche or goals whose attainment is invariably central or important to human growth and well-being. Life-span psychologists have echoed aspects of these perspectives, questioning whether there are any common tendencies or goals essential to healthy development. They have emphasized plasticity and multiple pathways as characteristic of aging.

Our motivational perspective interfaces with the plasticity issue in several ways. First, motivational studies focus on factors that facilitate versus undermine people's proactivity—specifically, the forces that nurture versus thwart people's active engagement with challenges. We see intrinsic motivation and internalization as important processes subserving development, ones that can be either fostered or undermined by empirically specifiable social–contextual factors. The study of factors that support versus undermine these processes reminds us that the "growth tendencies" that have always been acknowledged within organismic psychologies are not automatic propensities, rather, they depend on specific forms of nurturance and vary greatly in their robustness as a function of contextual factors (Ryan, 1995).

Second, we suggest that underlying the clearly variegated surface of human goals are some common human psychological needs. At all ages, and in all cultures, needs for autonomy, competence, and relatedness both play a role in energizing developmental proactivity and are critical to optimal behavioral functioning and well-being. Although the means through which they are satisfied change as a function of both age- and culture-related factors, these basic needs supply a source of continuity throughout development. They represent psychological nutriments whose optimization continuously occupies the human spirit.

Third, our view suggests that the transmitted goals, values, and regulations of a given social context will be more or less capable of both being integrated into self-organization and of leading to need fulfillment. This is in part due to process factors. Contexts, for example, that are overly controlling, nonoptimally challenging, or relationally unsupportive tend to disrupt the tendency to internalize and integrate social values. It is also due to content factors. Some goals, even those for which one possesses self-efficacy, may simply be contradictory to the fulfillment of basic psychological needs. They are accordingly both more difficult to integrate and less conducive to well-being when adopted and achieved.

Thus, a question worth pondering in life-span studies is that of what outcomes are "optimally optimized" in the flexible course of ontogeny. We believe that the concept of basic needs points us toward satisfactions and goals that, when optimized, actually facilitate essential developmental processes and well-being and those that typically do not. The postulate of basic needs also allows us to look more critically at social practice and the developmental scaffoldings through which individuals are asked to climb. In sum, by separating basic psychological needs from other goals and desires we begin to more directly grapple with the central aspects of human nature that are not so easily compromised, no matter what one's age, culture, or social context.

REFERENCES

Amabile, T. M. (1983). *The social psychology of creativity*. New York: Springer-Verlag.

Baard, P. P. (1994). A motivational model for consulting with not-for-profit organizations: A study of church growth and participation. *Consulting Psychology Journal, 46*, 19–31.

Baard, P. P., Deci, E. L., & Ryan, R. M. (1998). *Intrinsic need satisfaction: A motivational basis of performance and well-being in two work settings*. Unpublished manuscript, Fordham University.

Baltes, M. M., & Carstensen, L. L. (1996). The process of successful ageing. *Ageing and Society, 16*, 397–422.

Baltes, M. M., & Wahl, H. W. (1987). Dependency in aging. In L. L. Carstensen & B. A. Edelstein (Eds.), *Handbook of clinical gerontology* (pp. 204–221). New York: Pergamon.

Baltes, P. B. (1987). Theoretical propositions of life-span developmental psychology: On the dynamics between growth and decline. *Developmental Psychology, 23*, 611–626.

Baltes, P. B., Staudinger, U. M., & Lindenberger, U. (1999). Lifespan psychology: Theory and application to intellectual functioning. *Annual Review of Psychology, 50*, 471–507

Bandura, A. (1989). Human agency in social cognitive theory. *American Psychologist, 44*, 1175–1184.

Baumeister, R., & Leary, M. R. (1995). The need to belong: Desire for interpersonal attachments as a fundamental human motivation. *Psychological Bulletin*, *117*, 497–529.

Blasi, A. (1976). Concept of development in personality theory. In J. Loevinger (Ed.), *Ego development* (pp. 29–53). San Francisco: Jossey-Bass.

Butzel, J. S., & Ryan, R. M. (1997). The dynamics of volitional reliance: A motivational perspective on dependence, independence, and social support. In G. R. Pierce, B. Lakey, I. G. Sarason, & B. R. Sarason (Eds.), *Sourcebook of social support and personality* (pp. 49–67). New York: Plenum.

Carstensen, L. L. (1993). Motivation for social contact across the life span. In J. Jacobs (Ed.), *Nebraska symposium on motivation* (Vol. 40, pp. 209–254). Lincoln: University of Nebraska Press.

Carstensen, L. L. (1998). A life-span approach to social motivation. In J. Heckhausen & C. Dweck (Eds.), *Motivation and self-regulation across the life span* (pp. 341–364). New York: Cambridge University Press.

Chandler, C. L., & Connell, J. P. (1987). Children's intrinsic, extrinsic and internalized motivation: A developmental study of children's reasons for liked and disliked behaviours. *British Journal of Developmental Psychology*, *5*, 357–365.

Csikszentmihalyi, M. (1975). *Beyond boredom and anxiety*. San Francisco: Jossey-Bass.

Danner, F. W., & Lonky, E. (1981). A cognitive–developmental approach to the effects of rewards on intrinsic motivation. *Child Development*, *52*, 1043–1052.

deCharms, R. (1968). *Personal causation: The internal affective determinants of behavior*. New York: Academic Press.

Deci, E. L. (1975). *Intrinsic motivation*. New York: Plenum.

Deci, E. L., & Cascio, W. F. (1972, April). *Changes in intrinsic motivation as a function of negative feedback and threats*. Paper presented at the meeting of the Eastern Psychological Association, Boston.

Deci, E. L., Koestner, R., & Ryan, R. M. (1999). A meta-analytic review of experiments examining the effects of extrinsic rewards on intrinsic motivation. *Psychological Bulletin*, *125*, 627–668.

Deci, E. L., & Ryan, R. M. (1980). The empirical exploration of intrinsic motivational processes. In L. Berkowitz (Ed.), *Advances in experimental social psychology* (Vol. 13, pp. 39–80). New York: Academic Press

Deci, E. L., & Ryan, R. M. (1985). *Intrinsic motivation and self-determination in human behavior*. New York: Plenum.

Deci, E. L., & Ryan, R. M. (1991). A motivational approach to self: Integration in personality. In R. Dienstbier (Ed.), *Nebraska symposium on motivation* (Vol. 38, pp. 237–288). Lincoln: University of Nebraska Press.

Deci, E. L., & Ryan, R. M. (1995). Human autonomy: The basis for true self-esteem. In M. Kernis (Ed.), *Efficacy, agency, and self-esteem* (pp. 31–49). New York: Plenum.

Edelstein, W. (1983). Cultural constraints on development and the vicissitudes of progress. In *Proceedings of the Houston Symposium* (pp. 48–81). Westport, CT: Praeger.

Elkind, D. (1971). Cognitive growth cycles in mental development. In J. K. Cole (Ed.), *Nebraska symposium on motivation* (Vol. 19, pp. 1–31). Lincoln: University of Nebraska Press.

Frederick, C. M., & Ryan, R. M. (1995). Self-determination in sport: A review using cognitive evaluation theory. *International Journal of Sport Psychology, 26,* 5–23.

Gergen, K. J. (1991). *The saturated self: Dilemmas of identity in contemporary life.* New York: Basic Books.

Grolnick, W. S., Deci, E. L., & Ryan, R. M. (1997). Internalization within the family: The self-determination theory perspective. In J. E. Grusec & L. Kuczynski (Eds.), *Parenting and children's internalization of values: A handbook of contemporary theory* (pp. 135–161). New York: Wiley.

Grolnick, W. S., & Ryan, R. M. (1987). Autonomy in children's learning: An experimental and individual difference investigation. *Journal of Personality and Social Psychology, 52,* 890–898.

Grolnick, W. S., & Ryan, R. M. (1989). Parent styles associated with children's self-regulation and competence in school. *Journal of Educational Psychology, 81,* 143–154.

Harter, S. (1982). The perceived competence scale for children. *Child Development, 53,* 87–97.

Hayamizu, T. (1997). Between intrinsic and extrinsic motivation: Examinations of reasons for academic study based on the theory of internalization. *Japanese Psychological Research, 39,* 98–108.

Heckhausen, J., & Schulz, R. (1995). A life-span theory of control. *Psychological Review, 102,* 284–304.

Jacob, F. (1973). *The logic of life: A history of heredity.* New York: Pantheon.

Kasser, T., & Ryan, R. M. (1993). A dark side of the American dream: Correlates of financial success as a central life aspiration. *Journal of Personality and Social Psychology, 65,* 410–422.

Kasser, T., & Ryan, R. M. (1996). Further examining the American dream: Differential correlates of intrinsic and extrinsic goals. *Personality and Social Psychology Bulletin 22,* 80–87.

Kasser, T., & Ryan, R. M. (in press). Be careful what you wish for: Optimal functioning and the relative attainment of intrinsic and extrinsic goals. In P. Schmuck (Ed.), *Life goals and well-being.* Lengerich, Germany: Pabst Science Publishers.

Kasser, T., Ryan, R. M., Zax, M., & Sameroff, A. J. (1995). The relations of maternal and social environments to late adolescents' materialistic and prosocial values. *Developmental Psychology, 31,* 907–914.

Kasser, V. G., & Ryan, R. M. (1999). The relation of psychological needs for autonomy and relatedness to vitality, well-being, and mortality in a nursing home. *Journal of Applied Social Psychology, 29,* 935–954.

Kim, Y., Butzel, J. S., & Ryan, R. M. (1998, June). *Interdependence and well-being:*

A *function of culture and relatedness needs*. Presentation given at meetings of the International Society for the Study of Personal Relationships, Saratoga Springs, NY.

Koestner, R., & McClelland, D. C. (1990). Perspectives on competence motivation. In L. A. Pervin (Ed.), *Handbook of personality: Theory and research* (pp. 527–548). New York: Guilford Press.

Koestner, R., Ryan, R. M., Bernieri, F., & Holt, K. (1984). Setting limits on children's behavior: The differential effects of controlling versus informational styles on intrinsic motivation and creativity. *Journal of Personality, 52,* 233–248.

Krapp, A. (1994). Interest and curiosity: The role of interest in a theory of exploratory action. In H. Keller, K. Schneider, & B. Henderson (Eds.), *Curiosity and exploration* (pp. 79–99). Berlin: Springer-Verlag.

Lawton, M. P. (1988). Behavior-relevant ecological factors. In K. Schaie & C. Schooler (Eds.), *Social structures and aging: Psychological processes* (pp. 57–78). Hillsdale, NJ: Erlbaum.

Lepper, M. R., & Greene, D. (1975). Turning play into work: Effects of adult surveillance and extrinsic rewards on children's intrinsic motivation. *Journal of Personality and Social Psychology, 31,* 479–486.

Loevinger, J. (1976). *Ego development.* San Francisco: Jossey-Bass.

Maslow, A. H. (1954). *Motivation and personality.* New York: Harper & Row.

Murray, H. A. (1938). *Explorations in personality.* New York: Oxford University Press.

O'Connor, B. P., & Vallerand, R. J. (1994a). Motivation, self-determination, and person–environment fit as predictors of psychological adjustment among nursing home residents. *Psychology and Aging, 9,* 189–194.

O'Connor, B. P., & Vallerand, R. J. (1994b). The relative effects of actual and experienced autonomy on motivation in nursing home residents. *Canadian Journal on Aging, 13,* 528–538.

Piaget, J. (1971). *Biology and knowledge.* Chicago: University of Chicago Press.

Pittman, T. S., Davey, M. E., Alafat, K. A., Wetherill, K. V., & Kramer, N. A. (1980). Informational versus controlling verbal rewards. *Personality and Social Psychology Bulletin, 6,* 228–233.

Reis, H. T. (1994). Domains of experience: Investigating relationship processes from three perspectives. In R. Erber & R. Gilmour (Eds.), *Theoretical frameworks for personal relationships* (pp. 87–110). Hillsdale, NJ: Erlbaum.

Reis, H. T., Sheldon, K. M., Gable, S. L., Roscoe, J., & Ryan, R. M. (2000). Daily well-being: The role of autonomy, competence, and relatedness. *Personality and Social Psychology Bulletin, 26,* 419–435.

Rook, K. S. (1984). The negative side of social interaction: Impact on psychological well-being. *Journal of Personality and Social Psychology, 46,* 1097–1108.

Ryan, R. M. (1982). Control and information in the intrapersonal sphere: An extension of cognitive evaluation theory. *Journal of Personality and Social Psychology, 43*, 450–461.

Ryan, R. M. (1993). Agency and organization: Intrinsic motivation, autonomy and the self in psychological development. In J. Jacobs (Ed.), *Nebraska symposium on motivation* (Vol. 40, pp. 1–56). Lincoln: University of Nebraska Press.

Ryan, R. M. (1995). Psychological needs and the facilitation of integrative processes. *Journal of Personality, 63*, 397–427.

Ryan, R. M., Chirkov, V. I., Little, T. D., Sheldon, K. M., Timoshina, E., & Deci, E. L. (1999). The American dream in Russia: Extrinsic aspirations and well-being in two cultures. *Personality and Social Psychology Bulletin, 25*, 1509–1524.

Ryan, R. M., & Connell, J. P. (1989). Perceived locus of causality and internalization: Examining reasons for acting in two domains. *Journal of Personality and Social Psychology, 57*, 749–761.

Ryan, R. M., & Deci, E. L. (2000). Self-determination theory and facilitation of intrinsic motivation, social development, and well-being. *American Psychologist, 55*, 68–78.

Ryan, R. M., Deci, E. L., & Grolnick, W. S. (1995). Autonomy, relatedness, and the self: Their relation to development and psychopathology. In D. Cicchetti & D. J. Cohen (Eds.), *Developmental psychopathology: Vol. 1. Theory and methods* (pp. 618–655). New York: Wiley.

Ryan, R. M., & Frederick, C. M. (1997). On energy, personality, and health: Subjective vitality as a dynamic reflection of well-being. *Journal of Personality, 65*, 529–565.

Ryan, R. M., & Grolnick, W. S. (1986). Origins and pawns in the classroom: Self-report and projective assessments of individual differences in children's perceptions. *Journal of Personality and Social Psychology, 50*, 550–558.

Ryan, R. M., Kuhl, J., & Deci, E. L. (1997). Nature and autonomy: An organizational view of social and neurobiological aspects of self-regulation in behavior and development. *Development and Psychopathology, 9*, 701–728.

Ryan, R. M., & La Guardia, J. G. (1999). Achievement motivation within a pressured society: Intrinsic and extrinsic motivations to learn and the politics of school reform. In T. Urdan (Ed.), *Advances in motivation and achievement: Vol. 11* (pp. 45–85). Greenwich, CT: JAI Press.

Ryan, R. M., & Lynch, J. (1989). Emotional autonomy versus detachment: Revisiting the vicissitudes of adolescence and young adulthood. *Child Development, 60*, 340–356.

Ryan, R. M., Sheldon, K. M., Kasser, T., & Deci, E. L. (1996). All goals are not created equal: An organismic perspective on the nature of goals and their regulation. In P. M. Gollwitzer & J. A. Bargh (Eds.), *The psychology of action: Linking cognition and motivation to behavior* (pp. 7–26). New York: Guilford Press.

Ryan, R. M., & Solky, J. A. (1996). What is supportive about social-support? On the psychological needs for autonomy and relatedness. In G. R. Pierce, B. R. Sarason, & I. G. Sarason (Eds.), *Handbook of social support and the family* (pp. 249–267). New York: Plenum.

Ryan, R. M., Stiller, J., & Lynch, J. H. (1994). Representations of relationships to teachers, parents, and friends as predictors of academic motivation and self-esteem. *Journal of Early Adolescence, 14*, 226–249.

Ryff, C. D., & Singer, B. (1998). The contours of positive human health. *Psychological Inquiry, 9*, 1–28.

Sansone, C., Weir, C., Harpster, L., & Morgan, C. (1992). Once a boring task always a boring task? Interest as a self-regulatory mechanism. *Journal of Personality and Social Psychology, 63*, 379–390.

Sarason, B. R., Pierce, G. R., Shearin, E. N., Sarason, I. G., Waltz, J. A., & Poppe, L. (1991). Perceived social support and working models of self and actual others. *Journal of Personality and Social Psychology, 60*, 273–287.

Sheldon, K. M., & Kasser, T. (1998). Pursuing personal goals: Skills enable progress, but not all progress is beneficial. *Personality and Social Psychology Bulletin, 24*, 1319–1331

Sheldon, K. M., Ryan, R. M., Rawsthorne, L., & Ilardi, B. (1997). Trait self and true self: Cross-role variation in the Big Five traits and its relations with authenticity and subjective well-being. *Journal of Personality and Social Psychology, 73*, 1380–1393.

Sheldon, K. M., Ryan, R. M., & Reis, H. T. (1996). What makes for a good day? Competence and autonomy in the day and in the person. *Personality and Social Psychology Bulletin, 22*, 1270–1279.

Shweder, R. A. (1991). *Thinking through cultures.* Cambridge, MA: Harvard University Press.

Skinner, B. F. (1953). *Science and human behavior.* New York: Macmillan.

Staudinger, U. M., Marsiske, M., & Baltes, P. B. (1995). Resilience and reserve capacity in later adulthood: Potentials and limits of development across the life span. In D. Cicchetti & D. J. Cohen (Eds.), *Developmental psychopathology: Vol. 2. Risk, disorder, and adaptation* (pp. 801–847). New York: Wiley.

Stern, D. N. (1985). *The interpersonal world of the infant.* New York: Basic Books.

Utman, C. H. (1997). Performance effects of motivational state: A meta-analysis. *Personality and Social Psychology Review, 1*, 170–182.

Vallerand, R. J. (1997). Toward a hierarchical model of intrinsic and extrinsic motivation. In M. P. Zanna (Ed.), *Advances in experimental social psychology* (Vol. 29, pp. 271–360). San Diego, CA: Academic Press.

Vallerand, R. J., & O'Conner, B. P. (1989). Motivation in the elderly: A theoretical framework and some promising findings. *Canadian Psychology, 30*, 538–550.

Vallerand, R. J., O'Connor, B. P., & Blais, M. R. (1989). Life satisfaction of elderly individuals in regular community housing, in low-cost community housing, and high and low self-determination nursing homes. *International Journal of Aging and Human Development, 28*, 277–283.

Vallerand, R. J., & Reid, G. (1984). On the causal effects of perceived competence on intrinsic motivation: A test of cognitive evaluation theory. *Journal of Sport Psychology, 6,* 94–102.

Waterman, A. S. (1993). Two conceptions of happiness: Contrasts of personal expressiveness (eudaemonia) and hedonic enjoyment. *Journal of Personality and Social Psychology, 64,* 678–691.

White, R. W. (1963). *Ego and reality in psychoanalytic theory.* New York: International Universities Press.

Williams, G. C., Deci, E. L., & Ryan, R. M. (1998). Building health-care partnerships by supporting autonomy: Promoting maintained behavior change and positive health outcomes. In P. Hinton-Walker, A. L. Suchman, & R. Botelho (Eds.), *Partnerships, power and process: Transforming health care delivery* (pp. 67–88). Rochester, NY: University of Rochester Press.

Williams, G. C., Grow, V. M., Freedman, Z., Ryan, R. M., & Deci, E. L. (1996). Motivational predictors of weight loss and weight-loss maintenance. *Journal of Personality and Social Psychology, 70,* 115–126.

Zuckerman, M., Porac, J., Lathin, D., Smith, R., & Deci, E. L. (1978). On the importance of self-determination for intrinsically motivated behavior. *Personality and Social Psychology Bulletin, 4,* 443–446.

9

THE EVOLUTION OF SOCIAL RELATIONSHIPS IN LATER ADULTHOOD

KAREN S. ROOK

Change and adaptation are central features of life-span development, and this is as true in the area of personal relationships as it is in other life domains. Some changes in the individuals who populate our social worlds and in the ways in which we interact with them result from shifting preferences and needs for social interaction. Other changes result from life events or circumstances that disrupt existing social relationships. This chapter examines how researchers have sought to understand changes in patterns of social interaction that occur as people age. Changes that occur in response to age-related shifts in the underlying motivations for social contact are considered first. This is followed by a discussion of changes that result from the loss or disruption of existing social ties, such as the death of a spouse, and ensuing efforts to compensate for such losses. How such changes in social relationships affect psychological well-being in later life is a central issue, given the robust evidence that links social network involvement to health and well-being across the life course (Baumeister & Leary, 1995; House, Landis, & Umberson, 1988; Ryan, 1991). This chapter emphasizes change, although some dimensions of social involvement exhibit continuity across the life course (Antonucci & Akiyama, 1987; Field & Minkler, 1988). Recognition of these areas of continuity provides a frame of reference for considering the extent and significance of the changes discussed.

CHANGING SOCIAL NEEDS AND MOTIVATIONS: SELECTIVITY

One of the most reliable findings in the life-span literature on social activity is a reduction in social interaction as people age (Carstensen, 1992a). Social networks decrease in size (Lang & Carstensen, 1994; Stoller & Pugliesi, 1988), and contact with social network members becomes less frequent (Carstensen, 1992b).[1] In addition, participation in voluntary organizations declines with age (Morgan, 1988). Findings such as these have emerged since the 1960s (e.g., Cumming & Henry, 1961) and have been replicated in different cohorts of aging adults and in studies that have used diverse measures of social interaction.

Robust evidence of an age-related contraction of social contacts challenged early expectations that social activity would balloon in later life to fill the void left by retirement (Larson, 1978) and, as such, has puzzled and intrigued gerontologists for decades. Efforts to understand this pattern of contracting social activity have focused on two interrelated questions: What causes social activity to decrease as people grow older? How does this decline affect the well-being of aging adults?

Theoretical Perspectives

Early interpretations of these findings emphasized either the older person's disengagement from social roles and involvements (Cumming & Henry, 1961) or societal rejection of the older person (Maddox, 1963, 1964). More recent theoretical perspectives have explained the well-documented reduction in social interaction as the result of selective involvement in relationships that afford the greatest emotional rewards (Carstensen, 1992a).

Disengagement or Societal Rejection

Disengagement theorists reasoned that a major task of later adulthood involves coming to grips with the approaching end of life and that a process of turning inward or disengaging from social roles and preoccupations would facilitate successful resolution of this developmental task (Cumming

---

[1] These differences are most pronounced when the full adult age range is considered; comparisons based on more restricted age ranges sometimes reveal differences (e.g., Lang & Carstensen, 1994) but do not always do so (e.g., Antonucci & Akiyama, 1987).

& Henry, 1961). Such disengagement accordingly was seen as normative and adaptive in later life. Activity theorists, in contrast, interpreted a pattern of declining social activity in later life as evidence of societal rejection or distancing from older people, driven by prevailing ageist attitudes (Maddox, 1963, 1964). Proponents of activity theory believed that maintaining continuity in long-established patterns of social activity was crucial to successful aging. Age-related declines in social activity, therefore, were seen as both involuntary and maladaptive.

Socioemotional Selectivity

An alternative theoretical perspective has emerged in recent years that attributes age-related reductions in social contact to shifts in the underlying motivations for such contact. Socioemotional selectivity theory, developed by Carstensen and her colleagues (see reviews by Carstensen, 1991, 1992a, 1998), posits that social interaction serves three basic psychological goals: (a) the acquisition of information, (b) the development and maintenance of self-concept, and (c) the regulation of emotion.[2] The relative importance of these goals, and their significance in motivating social contact, are believed to change over the life course. As people age, social interaction becomes less important as a means of acquiring information both because a substantial store of information about the world has already been amassed and because other, nonsocial means of acquiring information have been mastered. Similarly, although opportunities for comparison with others through social interaction facilitate the development of the self-concept early in life, they become less important once the self-concept has solidified. Later in life, social interaction becomes more relevant to affirming, rather than elaborating, the self-concept, and such affirmation is most likely to be achieved through selective interaction with close friends and family members. Thus, the role of social interaction in regulating emotion assumes greater motivational prominence in later adulthood.

This reordering of social goals is rooted not only in the declining significance of information acquisition and self-concept development but also in an age-related shift in time perspective (Carstensen, Isaacowitz, & Charles, 1999). As people age, time is perceived as more limited, and goals related to the future, such as knowledge acquisition or social comparison, become less important than proximal goals, such as the enhancement of emotional experiences.

These developmental shifts in the basic motivations for social contact

---

[2]Recent revisions of the theory (e.g., Carstensen, 1998) emphasize two basic social motivations, the acquisition of knowledge and the regulation of emotion, because empirical work has suggested that social goals relevant to the development and maintenance of self-concept tend to be intertwined with the regulation of emotion.

are hypothesized to lead older adults to exhibit a narrower range of preferred interaction partners, with partners who offer the greatest potential to assist in the regulation of affective states preferred over others. The amount of social contact also declines as it becomes focused on fewer partners and fewer categories of interaction (those most relevant to emotional goals).

Socioemotional selectivity theory thus explains the age-related reductions in social involvement that have been documented for decades in the gerontological literature as the result of voluntary, proactive restriction of social contacts to those that are expected to be the most gratifying or meaningful. Continuity of contact is maintained over time with a select subset of the overall social network, and psychological well-being is optimized through involvement with the most emotionally rewarding interaction partners. Opportunities to fulfill the core need of social relatedness (see chap. 8) are thus preserved, but they are expressed within a delimited set of social relationships.

Empirical evidence in support of socioemotional selectivity theory has been growing through an elegant program of research conducted by Carstensen and her colleagues (see reviews by Carstensen, 1992a; Carstensen et al., 1999, in press). This work has revealed that people do indeed appear to frame prospective social interaction in terms of the social goals emphasized by socioemotional selectivity theory (Frederickson & Carstensen, 1990); that the emotional dimensions of social interaction have greater salience to older adults (Frederickson & Carstensen, 1990); and that older adults prefer familiar interaction partners over unfamiliar partners, apparently because interaction with familiar partners is viewed as more emotionally rewarding (Frederickson & Carstensen, 1990). Social networks have been found to decline in size as people age, but the declines appear to be limited to relatively peripheral social ties; neither the number of relationships with close social network members nor the level of satisfaction with social network members exhibit age-related declines (Carstensen, 1992b; Lang & Carstensen, 1994; see also Antonucci & Akiyama, 1987; Field & Minkler, 1988), consistent with the predictions of socioemotional selectivity theory.

The causal role played by time perspective has been demonstrated in a series of studies. In experimental studies, when younger people were induced to have a time perspective similar to that of older adults, their social preferences closely resembled those of older adults; conversely, when the time horizon of older adults was broadened experimentally to resemble that of younger adults, their social preferences changed accordingly and tended to mirror those of younger adults (Frederickson & Carstensen, 1990). In nonexperimental research, younger people whose personal time horizons are eclipsed by terminal illness, such as HIV, have been found to exhibit social preferences very similar to those of older adults (Carstensen & Frederickson, 1998). Other anticipated endings that affect time perceptions also appear to cause social goals and preferences for social partners to resemble those of later adulthood, irrespective of age. Studies conducted in Hong Kong just prior to its political reunification with the People's Republic of China revealed that the social preferences of younger and older adults were similar, presumably because anticipated endings had become salient for the entire population (Fung, Carstensen, & Lutz, 1999). This work thus suggests that is it not age per se that brings about changes in the motivations and preferred partners for social interaction but rather an awareness of constraints on available time that causes fundamental shifts in the priorities for interaction.

Summary

Age-related declines in social network size and in the frequency of social interaction are among the most well-documented findings in social gerontology (Carstensen, 1992a). The work reviewed here suggests that such changes reflect neither disengagement from social roles by older adults nor rejection of older people by society; rather, these changes appear to result from a process of selective investment in the social ties that offer the greatest emotional rewards (Carstensen, 1991, 1992a, 1998). Core social network ties (those that involve close friends and family members) remain stable, whereas more peripheral ties undergo pruning (Antonucci, 1990; Lang & Carstensen, 1994). Older adults' selective engagement in the network relationships that they regard as most meaningful allows social interaction to serve as a means of optimizing their affective states. From this perspective, age-related declines in social activity do not represent threats to well-being; instead, they reflect older adults' exercise of control over their social lives in a manner that preserves emotional health. In this sense, socioemotional selectivity serves basic needs for social relatedness as well as autonomy—needs that have been identified as central to human health and well-being (see chap. 8).

SOCIAL NETWORK LOSSES AND DISRUPTIONS: COMPENSATION

The work discussed thus far has emphasized largely voluntary reductions in social network involvement that reflect selective involvement in preferred social relationships. This view of aging adults as capable of proactively managing their social lives is a valuable antidote to earlier, more negative views that portrayed aging adults either as passive victims of external forces or as intrinsically prone to social withdrawal (Carstensen, 1992a). Yet, without subscribing to such negative views, it would be an oversight to ignore the changing life circumstances in later adulthood that cause losses from personal social networks or that disrupt preferred patterns of social interaction. Such losses and disruptions bring about changes that are more or less involuntary and that, in turn, prompt compensatory responses as a means of preserving well-being.

Widowhood is a common experience in later life, with nearly two thirds of women and one fifth of men likely to be widowed by their mid-70s (U.S. Bureau of the Census, 1993, 1996). Moreover, the experience of widowhood involves not only the loss of the spouse but often the loss of other relationships as well (Allan & Adams, 1989). Contacts with in-laws and couples with whom the widowed person once socialized often dwindle (Brubaker, 1990; Lamme, Dykstra, & Broese Van Groenou, 1996; Lopata, 1973). As people age, deaths of relatives and friends also become increasingly common. For example, 25% of the elderly participants in one recent study reported the death of a friend in the past year (Aldwin, 1990). Such losses are especially common among the very old. In a recent longitudinal study, 59% of men and 42% of women older than age 85 reported that a close friend had died in the preceding year (Johnson & Troll, 1994).

Life events other than the death of friends or family members can also disrupt existing social network ties. Retirement typically reduces contact with former coworkers (e.g., Allan & Adams, 1989; Mutran & Reitzes, 1981; Wright, 1989), and such contact ranks high among the things that retirees say they most miss from their former jobs. In addition, postretirement incomes represent, on average, only about 40%–50% of preretirement incomes (U.S. Bureau of the Census, 1990), and financial limitations can restrict opportunities for social contact if older adults lack discretionary funds for transportation, entertainment, and other costs associated with socializing. Residential relocation, either by the older person or by others, disperses friends geographically, although face-to-face contact is not always required to maintain friendships (Blieszner, 1989; Johnson & Troll, 1994). Moreover, relocation to housing designed specifically for older adults does not necessarily facilitate the formation of new relationships; relationship formation appears to occur most often when the move is to a socially and culturally homogeneous setting (Johnson & Troll, 1994; although see Retsinas & Garrity, 1985).

Chronic disability can erode established patterns of social activity, and deteriorating health has emerged as the strongest predictor of declines in friendship involvement in several longitudinal studies of older adults (e.g., Field & Minkler, 1993; Johnson & Troll, 1994). Physical impairment reduces mobility, hinders interaction (especially if vision and hearing problems or chronic pain are involved), and reduces the ability to reciprocate support provided by others (Johnson & Troll, 1994). In addition, individuals with chronic disabilities may require long-term support from network members, creating conditions for conflict and the resurrection of dormant resentments (Johnson, 1983; Johnson & Catalano, 1983). The potential for conflict increases when more distant family members (e.g., nieces, nephews) are called on to take over the support functions previously performed by others, with the psychological costs of such care sometimes exceeding the benefits (Johnson, 1983). The latter point serves as a reminder that network disruptions can arise from tensions and strains that develop in existing relationships. Such tensions appear to be relatively rare in older adults' relationships, but they detract considerably from well-being when they do occur (Rook, 1990, 1992).

Thus, losses and disruptions of social network relationships in middle and later adulthood may take a variety of forms and may arise from a variety of conditions. Some (perhaps many) of these changes will be significant enough to prompt compensatory responses.

Theoretical Perspectives

Theoretical discussions of such compensatory responses have generally focused on two interrelated questions. First, how do aging adults seek to compensate for social network losses and disruptions? Second, to what extent to do such efforts succeed in preserving their well-being? These questions indicate that two aspects of compensatory processes can be distinguished: those that involve substitution (or the "replacement" of missing network ties) and those that involve actual compensation (or the extent to which such substitute network ties restore well-being; East & Rook, 1992; Rook & Schuster, 1996). Although *compensation* is used here as an umbrella term, it is important to bear in mind that the occurrence of a compensatory response does not in itself guarantee a compensatory outcome; whether such responses bolster or restore well-being is an empirical question (Backman & Dixon, 1992; East & Rook, 1992; Rook & Schuster, 1996).

Compensatory responses to network losses in middle and later adulthood may take several forms. Three forms—the formation of new ties or "rejuvenation" of existing ties, the redefinition of social needs or aspirations, and the development or renewal of nonsocial activities—are discussed below, along with examples of relevant empirical work.

Formation or Rejuvenation of Social Ties

First, and perhaps most obviously, people may respond to social network losses by seeking to develop new social ties or to increase their contact with existing ties. The loss of a close friend, for example, may prompt a person to attempt to establish a new friendship or to seek desired support and companionship from existing friendships. This is not meant to suggest that long-term relationships can be readily replaced (or perhaps ever replaced) by other social ties (Kahn & Antonucci, 1980; Stroebe, Stroebe, Abakoumkin, & Schut, 1996). The shared memories, world views, and finely tuned patterns of interaction that have evolved over decades cannot be replicated. Nonetheless, older adults typically do seek to reorganize their social lives following a network loss (e.g., Bankoff, 1981; Ferraro, Mutran, & Barresi, 1984; Jerome, 1981; Morgan, Carder, & Neal, 1997; Stylianos & Vachon, 1993), and the creation of new social ties or rejuvenation of existing ties may help to enhance well-being (Morgan, 1988). This buttressing of well-being, even if imperfect, can be construed as a form of compensation (Dykstra, 1995).

Most of the empirical work on compensation for social network losses or disruptions in middle and later adulthood has sought to understand the kinds of "substitute" ties that may emerge after a network loss; less work has focused on the effects of such ties (Rook & Schuster, 1996). Cantor's (1979; Cantor & Little, 1985) influential hierarchical-compensatory model of social support proposed that substitution for absent sources of support in later life follows an orderly hierarchy of preferences (with kin typically preferred, for example, over nonkin). Cantor was less concerned with evaluating the impact of such substitute sources of support. The most common empirical approach in this literature, accordingly, has involved comparing the sources and extent of social support received by older adults who have versus have not experienced some form of social network loss, such as those who are widowed versus those who are married. Differences between the groups are interpreted as evidence that substitution has occurred—for example, that new network members have taken over the support-providing role previously performed by other network members.

In a study that illustrates this approach, Connidis and Davies (1992) examined who served as confidants and social companions for widowed versus married older adults. To avoid a possible confound with parental status, participation in the study was limited to individuals who had living children. Friends, other relatives, and children functioned as the primary sources of support and companionship for widowed participants, whereas the spouse performed these roles for the married participants. The researchers construed this pattern as evidence that the widowed participants had established compensatory ties. More detailed analyses of the people to whom participants turned for particular kinds of support led Connidis and Davies (1992) to conclude that widowed individuals substitute certain network members for the former spouse when they wish to confide personal concerns, and they substitute other network members when they desire companionship. Other researchers have applied a similar logic in interpreting group differences in patterns of support provision (see review by Rook & Schuster, 1996).

Few studies have examined whether such group differences reflect intentional efforts on the part of older adults to substitute, or make up for, a particular network deficit. An exception in this regard is a recent study by Lamme et al. (1996), in which elderly individuals who had been widowed 10 years or less were asked: "After the death of your spouse, did you undertake many efforts to obtain, maintain, or intensify contact with your friends and acquaintances?" Participants' current social networks were assessed, with new relationships defined as those with a reported duration shorter than the duration of widowhood. Kin ties, such as those that might have been established with new in-laws or new grandchildren, were excluded from this category. Of the participants who reported having made a deliberate effort to establish new social ties or intensify existing ties after becoming widowed, 44% mentioned new relationships in their enumeration of current network membership, compared to 23% of those who had not made special efforts to kindle new ties. These estimates may have some limitations, given the cross-sectional design of the study and the reliance on retrospective reports covering a period of up to 10 years. Nonetheless, they suggest that older adults' efforts to establish compensatory relationships sometimes, but not always, meet with success; moreover, new social ties sometimes emerge without such efforts.

More generally, inferences about substitution based on cross-sectional studies provide only a snapshot of the changes that may occur following a major social network loss or disruption. In a recent review of research on widowhood and social participation, Stylianos and Vachon (1993) concluded that support from the family (especially from children) is crucial in the initial stages of bereavement but that friends (often new friends) become increasingly important in the long-term adaptation to the role of widowed person. How such compensatory responses unfold and affect well-being over time remains poorly understood, however, for many kinds of network losses or disruptions.

As noted earlier, most of the empirical work on compensation in the interpersonal domain has lacked an outcome measure with which to evaluate the effects of compensatory responses. A few studies, however, have attempted such an evaluation. These studies typically have been cross-sectional and have taken one of two approaches (Rook & Schuster, 1996). Stringent tests of compensation have been based on comparisons of individuals who have sustained a network loss or disruption and who have established a "substitute" network tie with individuals who have not sustained a network loss (e.g., East & Rook, 1992). If the comparison reveals no group differences in well-being, then the substitute tie is assumed to have compensated for the missing tie. Thus, compensation is viewed as having occurred only when people who have sustained a network loss fare as well on an indicator of emotional health as do those who have not sustained a loss. This is akin to the notion of complete buffering in research on the stress-buffering effects of social support (e.g., House, 1981). A less stringent and more common approach has involved analyzing only people who have sustained a network loss. Within this group, if those who have established a replacement tie fare better than those who have not, then compensation is assumed to have occurred. This approach allows for the possibility that, overall, those who have sustained a network loss may continue to exhibit lower well-being than those who have not sustained a loss; a partial degree of compensation can be inferred if the replacement tie boosts the well-being of those in the loss group. This corresponds to the notion of partial buffering in the literature on stress and social support (e.g., House, 1981).

A study that illustrates the latter, more common approach involved an analysis of the links between social support and loneliness in a sample of unmarried (mostly widowed) older adults (Dykstra, 1993). Some of these older unmarried adults had established a new relationship with a cohabiting partner, whereas others had not. Dykstra (1993) reasoned that if the new partners met participants' needs for support, thereby compensating for support deficits they might otherwise have experienced, then additional support from other individuals would have little impact on their well-being. Among those who had not established a compensatory tie with a partner, however, support from other sources was expected to elevate well-being. Consistent with these predictions, receiving support from children and friends was associated with less loneliness among the older adults who lacked a partner, but it was unrelated to loneliness among those who had a partner.

In evaluating the evidence for substitution and compensation in older adults' social networks, it is important to recognize that researchers' strategies for assessing patterns of support provision influence the conclusions that emerge. An emphasis on the source of support, without a corresponding emphasis on quantity or quality, may exaggerate the evidence of substitution. Johnson and Catalano (1983) noted that, unlike spouses and adult children, more distant relatives often provide support that is perfunctory in nature. The perfunctory quality of such support will be missed in measures that assess only the sources of support—that is, who in a social network is willing or able to provide support.

Redefinition of Social Needs or Aspirations

Implicit in the view of compensation discussed thus far is the notion that older adults' social needs remain essentially unchanged following a social network loss or disruption (Rook & Schuster, 1996). Yet it is plausible that some compensatory responses to social network losses take the form of a reassessment (conscious or unconscious) of social needs. For some people, this may entail a psychological redefinition of personal needs for companionship and support. Well-being would be preserved not by creating new social ties or renewing existing ties but rather by modifying one's social aspirations so that the gap between these aspirations and opportunities narrows. This has been referred to in other literatures as an *accommodative strategy of coping* (Brandstadter & Renner, 1990) or a form of *secondary control* (Heckhausen & Schulz, 1995). This process of redefining needs and aspirations may be stimulated in part by lack of success in efforts to change the situation (Brandstadter & Renner, 1990). For example, a lonely older adult who has tried unsuccessfully to find new companions may be compelled at some point to accept more modest aspirations for companionship.

Weiss (1973, 1974) has questioned whether such a psychological redefinition of social needs serves to preserve well-being in the face of a true social network deficit. He suggested that lonely individuals rarely succeed in alleviating the distress of loneliness by attempting to define away their needs for social contact. Other theorists concur, arguing that the need for strong, stable social bonds is universal and essential to human health and well-being, with undesirable consequences stemming from deprivation of this need (Baumeister & Leary, 1995; see also chap. 8, this volume). Denial, or disavowal, of this need is difficult, in their view.

As discussed earlier, however, other theorists believe that shifts in the desire of or motivations for social contact may be relatively common and nonproblematic in later adulthood, leading older adults to restrict their social contacts to those that offer the greatest prospects for emotional rewards (Carstensen, 1991, 1992a). Related work has suggested that the willingness to adjust personal goals as a means of coping with losses and obstacles increases across the life course (Brandstadter & Renner, 1990). Given that such age-related tendencies may exist, it is plausible that some older adults may compensate for network losses by re-evaluating their social needs and desires (Dykstra, 1995; Stevens, 1995).

This possible form of compensation has rarely been investigated. A study by Bearon (1989) provided suggestive evidence, although not specific to the interpersonal domain, that older adults may adjust their personal strivings as a means of maintaining well-being. Bearon coded middle-aged and older adults' open-ended responses to questions about their current sources of life satisfaction and their hopes for the future. Comparison of the responses that reflected future aspirations suggested that older adults more often emphasize preservation of the status quo and prevention of declines (particularly health declines) than the achievement of positive changes in their lives. Such age group differences are consistent with the notion that psychological well-being may be maintained in later life, in part, through cognitive–affective processes that bring aspirations in line with objective conditions (Bearon, 1989; Campbell, Converse, & Rodgers, 1976).

In a study of adaptation to widowhood, Stevens (1995) sought to investigate the association between perceived social needs and loneliness among elderly widowed individuals. The assessed needs were derived from

Weiss's (1974) model of essential social provisions and included intimacy (attachment), social integration (group ties), reassurance of worth, reliable support, advice and guidance, and opportunities to nurture others. The widowed individuals who expressed fewer of these social needs also reported less loneliness. Stevens interpreted this as evidence that older adults who have reduced their needs for intimacy and who are more adept at solving problems independently (without other's help) adjust better to widowhood.

In a related study, Dykstra (1995) investigated friendship support and perceptions of the desirability of being single versus married as predictors of loneliness in sample of unmarried older adults. Dykstra regarded these perceptions as relationship standards against which existing relationships are evaluated. She found that participants who had been widowed longer were more likely to endorse favorable statements about being single and less likely to endorse favorable statements about being married. These findings were suggestive of a shift over time in relationship standards or aspirations, as part of the process of adapting to widowhood. In addition, participants with more favorable views of being single and less favorable views of being married reported less loneliness. Although the cross-sectional design of Dykstra's and Stevens's (1995) studies limit conclusions about causality, the findings are consistent with the idea that some compensatory responses to social network losses in later adulthood may take the form of revised social aspirations.

A related possibility is that basic social aspirations or needs remain largely unchanged but the criteria for relationships change in the wake of a significant social network loss or disruption. Johnson and Troll (1994) found some evidence of this in a sample of adults over the age of 85, some of whom responded to social network deficiencies by applying more inclusive friendship criteria to people with whom they interacted. This allowed casual acquaintances, fellow members of organizations, employees (e.g., home health care aides), and others with whom social exchanges were quite circumscribed to be defined as friends. These elderly individuals thus incorporated into their subjective circle of friends, relationships that (by their own account) were relatively superficial and unlikely to grow more intimate. Moreover, some of the elderly participants had come to define face-to-face contact as no longer essential to maintain friendship. Thus, the elderly participants in this study did not alter their need for social contact but, in a sense, did alter their aspirations for the kind of relationships they could develop to meet this need.

Development or Renewal of Nonsocial Activities

Another kind of compensatory response to social network losses or disruptions might involve establishing new nonsocial interests and hobbies or renewing existing (but presumably dormant) interests. Whether nonsocial activities can compensate for social activities has been debated without much consensus in the literature on loneliness (e.g., Rook & Peplau, 1982; Young, 1982). Nonsocial activities have been found to help elevate mood, however, and have even been incorporated into behaviorally oriented treatments for depression and loneliness (e.g., Lewinsohn & Amenson, 1978; Young, 1982). It is conceivable, therefore, that some older adults might seek to compensate for social network losses by increasing their involvement in gratifying nonsocial activities.

Few studies have examined the possibility that increased participation in nonsocial activities, such as hobbies or leisure pursuits, might represent a compensatory response to the loss of an important social network relationship. In one of the few studies to examine this possibility, Patterson (1996) assessed the leisure activities, anxiety, and adjustment to widowhood of a sample of recently bereaved individuals. Some of the elderly participants indicated that leisure activities had lost their appeal since the death of the spouse, whereas others indicated that such activities provided relief from the pain of bereavement. Analyses of the association between involvement in leisure activities and psychological well-being revealed that greater involvement was related to less anxiety but was unrelated to overall adjustment to widowhood (operationalized as the self-reported ease of transition to the role of widow/widower). Because the measure of leisure participation did not distinguish between social and nonsocial forms of leisure, it is unclear whether the apparent reduction of anxiety should be attributed to the relaxing and absorbing qualities of solitary leisure activities (such as reading or hobbies) or to the support and companionship afforded by social leisure activities (such as being able to confide worries or to getting together with others for visits or shared outings). Nonetheless, some of the most common forms of leisure participation reported by participants involved activities that could be undertaken alone, such as reading, watching television, and gardening. Whether such solitary activities help to preserve well-being in the face of a significant social network loss or disruption requires further empirical investigation.

Summary

This discussion has highlighted three strategies that older adults might use, singly or in combination, to compensate for the loss or disruption of important ties in their social networks. These strategies are not exhaustive, but they illustrate that compensatory activities may take a variety of forms. The use of the term *strategies* is not meant to imply that older adults always pursue these activities in a conscious or planful way, although they may do so at times. Some compensatory responses to social network losses and disruptions may emerge without conscious deliberation or even awareness (cf. Dixon & Backman, 1995; Salthouse, 1995). For example, an elderly woman who has become lonely after a good friend moved away may find herself attempting to extend her contacts with her neighbors in a largely unconscious effort to replace some of the companionship that she misses. Thus, many, but not all, compensatory behaviors may be conscious and planful (Backman & Dixon, 1992).

Moreover, as noted earlier, it should not be assumed that these strategies necessarily yield beneficial outcomes. Compensatory responses are not always successful (Backman & Dixon, 1992; Carstensen, Hanson, & Freund, 1995; Lamme et al., 1996), and the lack of success itself may require an adaptive response (Backman & Dixon, 1992). Compensatory responses and compensatory outcomes represent logically related but nonetheless distinct phenomena (Backman & Dixon, 1992; Rook & Schuster, 1996).

CONCLUSION

This discussion has focused on two broad categories of change in patterns of social interaction that may become increasingly common as people age: (a) change that results from shifts in the underlying motivations or priorities for social contact and (b) change that occurs in response to the loss or disruption of existing social relationships. Research on socioemotional selectivity in later adulthood has been concerned with the first kind of change, whereas research on social compensation in later adulthood has addressed the second kind. These traditions of research complement each other and can be seen as fitting within a broader theoretical framework that emphasizes selection, optimization, and compensation as three fundamental components of adaptation across the life course (Baltes, 1991; Baltes & Baltes, 1990; Freund & Baltes, 1998).

Selection, in the theoretical framework developed by Baltes and Baltes (1990), refers to the increasing restriction of life activities to fewer domains of functioning, reflecting personal priorities or the intersection of environmental demands and personal motivations, behavioral competencies, and biological capacities. Although selection is a lifelong process, it assumes greater prominence in later adulthood as a means of adapting to changing capacities and life circumstances. *Optimization* refers to efforts to preserve and enhance functioning in the chosen domains. Repeated practice of a particular skill relevant to a chosen domain, for example, helps to optimize performance in that domain. *Compensation* refers to the use of behavioral strategies, technological aids, or external supports to maintain adequate functioning when behavioral capacities have declined (or, by extrapolation, when losses of existing supports have occurred). Selective optimization with compensation allows elderly individuals to concentrate on the life goals and tasks that matter the most to them, despite declining biological and psychological reserves and capacities (Baltes & Baltes, 1990).

The work reviewed in this chapter suggests that social relationships and patterns of social interaction evolve in later adulthood in ways that reflect dual themes of selectivity (or selective optimization) and compensation. In the interpersonal domain, both selectivity and compensation appear to operate to preserve well-being, although much remains to be learned about the specific forms that these adaptive strategies take and how they unfold over time. In addition, investigating the individual differences and environmental factors that influence the effectiveness of these strategies represents a formidable challenge but one that warrants our attention in view of the centrality of social relationships to health and well-being at all stages of the life course, including old age.

REFERENCES

Aldwin, C. M. (1990). The elders' life stress inventory. In M. A. P. Stephens, J. H. Crowther, S. E. Hobfoll, & D. L. Tennenbaum (Eds.), *Stress and coping in later life families* (pp. 49–69). Washington, DC: Hemisphere.

Allan, G., & Adams, R. (1989). Aging and the structure of friendship. In R. G. Adams & R. Blieszner (Eds.), *Older adult friendship: Structure and process* (pp. 45–64). Newbury Park, CA: Sage Publications.

Antonucci, T. C. (1990). Social supports and social relationships. In R. H. Binstock & L. K. George (Eds.), *Handbook of aging and the social sciences* (3rd ed., pp. 205–226). New York: Academic Press.

Antonucci, T. C., & Akiyama, H. (1987). Social networks in adult life and a preliminary examination of the convoy model. *Journal of Gerontology, 42,* 519–527.

Backman, L., & Dixon, R. A. (1992). Psychological compensation: A theoretical framework. *Psychological Bulletin, 112,* 259–283.

Baltes, P. B. (1991). The many faces of human ageing: Toward a psychological culture of old age. *Psychological Medicine, 21,* 837–854.

Baltes, P. B., & Baltes, M. (1990). Psychological perspectives on successful aging: The model of selective optimization with compensation. In P. B. Baltes & M. Baltes (Eds.), *Successful aging: Perspectives from the behavioral sciences* (pp. 1–34). New York: Cambridge University Press.

Bankoff, E. A. (1981). Effects of friendship support on the psychological well-being of widows. *Research in the Interweave of Social Roles: Friendship, 2,* 109–139.

Baumeister, R. F., & Leary, M. R. (1995). The need to belong: Desire for interpersonal attachments as a fundamental human motivation. *Psychological Bulletin, 117,* 497–529.

Bearon, L. B. (1989). No great expectations: The underpinnings of life satisfaction for older women. *The Gerontologist, 29,* 772–778.

Blieszner, R. (1989). Developmental processes of friendship. In R. G. Adams &

R. Blieszner (Eds.), *Older adult friendship: Structure and process* (pp. 108–126). Newbury Park, CA: Sage Publications.

Brandstadter, J., & Renner, G. (1990). Tenacious goal pursuit and flexible goal adjustment: Explication and age-related analysis of assimilative and accommodative strategies of coping. *Psychology and Aging, 5,* 58–67.

Brubaker, T. H. (1990). Continuity and change in later life families: Grandparenthood, couple relationships and family caregiving. *Gerontology Review, 3,* 24–40.

Campbell, A., Converse, P. E., & Rodgers, W. L. (1976). *The quality of American life: Perceptions, evaluations, and satisfactions.* New York: Russell Sage Foundation.

Cantor, M. H. (1979). Neighbors and friends: An overlooked resource in the informal support system. *Research on Aging, 1,* 434–463.

Cantor, M. H., & Little, V. (1985). Aging and social care. In R. H. Binstock & E. Shanas (Eds.), *Handbook of aging and the social sciences* (pp. 745–781). New York: Van Nostrand Reinhold.

Carstensen, L. L. (1991). Socioemotional selectivity theory: Social activity in life-span context. *Annual Review of Gerontology and Geriatrics, 11,* 195–217.

Carstensen, L. L. (1992a). Motivation for social contact across the life span: A theory of socioemotional selectivity. *Nebraska Symposium on Motivation* (Vol. 40, pp. 209–254). Lincoln: University of Nebraska Press.

Carstensen, L. L. (1992b). Social and emotional patterns in adulthood: Support for socioemotional selectivity theory. *Psychology and Aging, 7,* 331–338.

Carstensen, L. L. (1998). A life-span approach to social motivation. In J. Heckhausen & C. Dweck (Eds.), *Motivation and self-regulation across the life span* (pp. 341–364). New York: Cambridge University Press.

Carstensen, L. L., & Frederickson, B. L. (1998). Influence of HIV status and age on cognitive representations of others. *Health Psychology, 17,* 494–503.

Carstensen, L. L., Hanson, K. A., & Freund, A. M. (1995). Selection and compensation in adulthood. In R. A. Dixon & L. Backman (Eds.), *Compensating for psychological deficits and declines: Managing losses and promoting gains* (pp. 107–126). Mahwah, NJ: Erlbaum.

Carstensen, L. L., Isaacowitz, D. M., & Charles, S. T. (1999). Taking time seriously: A theory of socioemotional selectivity. *American Psychologist, 54,* 165–181.

Connidis, I. A., & Davies, L. (1992). Confidants and companions: Choices in later life. *Journal of Gerontology: Social Sciences, 47,* S115–S122.

Cumming, E., & Henry, H. W. (1961). *Growing old: The process of disengagement.* New York: Basic Books.

Dixon, R. A., & Backman, L. (1995). Concepts of compensation: Integrated, differentiated, and Janus-faced. In R. A. Dixon & L. Backman (Eds.), *Compensating for psychological deficits and declines: Managing losses and promoting gains* (pp. 3–19). Mahwah, NJ: Erlbaum.

Dykstra, P. A. (1993). The differential availability of relationships and the provision and effectiveness of support to older adults. *Journal of Social and Personal Relationships, 10,* 355–370.

Dykstra, P. A. (1995). Loneliness among the never married and the formerly married: The importance of supportive friendships and a desire for independence. *Journal of Gerontology: Social Sciences, 50,* S321–S329.

East, P. L., & Rook, K. S. (1992). Compensatory patterns of support among children's peer relationships: A test using school friends, nonschool friends, and siblings. *Developmental Psychology, 28,* 163–172.

Ferraro, K. F., Mutran, E., & Barresi, C. M. (1984). Widowhood, health, and friendship support in later life. *Journal of Health and Social Behavior, 25,* 245–259.

Field, D., & Minkler, M. (1988). Continuity and change in social support between young-old and old-old or very-old age. *Journal of Gerontology: Psychological Sciences, 43,* P100–P106.

Field, D., & Minkler, M. (1993). The importance of family in advanced old age: The family is "forever." In P. A. Cowan, D. Field, D. A. Hansen, A. Skolnick, & G. E. Swanson (Eds.), *Family, self, and society: Toward a new agenda for family research* (pp. 331–351). Hillsdale, NJ: Erlbaum.

Frederickson, B. L., & Carstensen, L. L. (1990). Choosing social partners: How old age and anticipated endings make us more selective. *Psychology and Aging, 5,* 335–347.

Freund, A. M., & Baltes, P. B. (1998). Selection, optimization, and compensation as strategies of life management: Correlations with subjective indicators of successful aging. *Psychology and Aging, 13,* 531–543.

Fung, H. H., Carstensen, L. L., & Lutz, A. (1999). Influence of time on social preferences: Implications for life-span development. *Psychology and Aging, 14,* 595–604.

Heckhausen, J., & Schulz, R. (1995). A life-span theory of control. *Psychological Review, 102,* 284–304.

House, J. (1981). *Work stress and social support.* Reading, MA: Addison-Wesley.

House, J. S., Landis, K., & Umberson, D. (1988, July). Social relationships and health. *Science, 241,* 540–545.

Jerome, D. (1981). The significance of friendship for women in later life. *Ageing and Society, 1,* 175–197.

Johnson, C. L. (1983). Dyadic family relations and social support. *The Gerontologist, 23,* 377–383.

Johnson, C. L., & Catalano, D. J. (1983). A longitudinal study of family supports to impaired elderly. *The Gerontologist, 23,* 612–625.

Johnson, C. L., & Troll, L. (1994). Constraints and facilitators to friendships in late late life. *The Gerontologist, 34,* 79–87.

Kahn, R. L., & Antonucci, A. (1980). Convoys over the life course: Attachment, roles, and social support. In P. B. Baltes & O. G. Brim (Eds.), *Life-span development and behavior* (Vol. 3, pp. 253–286). New York: Academic Press.

Lamme, S., Dykstra, P. A., & Broese Van Groenou, M. I. (1996). Rebuilding the network: New relationships in widowhood. *Personal Relationships, 3,* 337–349.

Lang, F. R., & Carstensen, L. L. (1994). Close emotional relationships in late life: Further support for proactive aging in the social domain. *Psychology and Aging, 9,* 315–324.

Larson, R. (1978). Thirty years of research on the subjective well-being of older Americans. *Journal of Gerontology, 33,* 109–125.

Lewinsohn, P. M., & Amenson, C. S. (1978). Some relations between pleasant and unpleasant mood-related events and depression. *Journal of Abnormal Psychology, 87,* 644–654.

Lopata, H. Z. (1973). *Widowhood in an American city.* Cambridge, MA: Schenkman.

Maddox, G. L. (1963). Activity and morale: A longitudinal study of selected elderly subjects. *Social Forces, 42,* 195–204.

Maddox, G. L. (1964). Disengagement theory: A critical evaluation. *The Gerontologist, 4,* 80–82.

Morgan, D. L. (1988). Age differences in social network participation. *Journal of Gerontology: Social Sciences, 55,* S129–S137.

Morgan, D. L., Carder, P., & Neal, M. (1997). Are some relationships more useful than others? The value of similar others in the networks of recent widows. *Journal of Social and Personal Relationships, 14,* 745–759.

Mutran, E., & Reitzes, D. C. (1981). Retirement, identity, and well-being: Realignment of role relationships. *Journal of Gerontology, 36,* 773–781.

Patterson, I. (1996). Participation in leisure activities by older adults after a stressful life event: The loss of a spouse. *International Journal of Aging and Human Development, 42,* 123–142.

Retsinas, J., & Garrity, P. (1985). Nursing home friendships. *The Gerontologist, 25,* 376–381.

Rook, K. S. (1990). Stressful aspects of older adults' social relationships: An overview of current theory and research. In M. A. P. Stephens, J. H. Crowther, S. E. Hobfoll, & D. L. Tennenbaum (Eds.), *Stress and coping in later life families* (pp. 173–192). Washington, DC: Hemisphere.

Rook, K. S. (1992). Detrimental aspects of social relationships: Taking stock of an emerging literature. In H. O. F. Veiel & U. Baumann (Eds.), *The meaning and measurement of social support* (pp. 157–169). New York: Hemisphere.

Rook, K. S., & Peplau, L. A. (1982). Perspectives on helping the lonely. In L. A. Peplau & D. Perlman (Eds.), *Loneliness: A sourcebook of current theory, research and therapy* (pp. 357–378). New York: Wiley.

Rook, K. S., & Schuster, T. L. (1996). Compensatory processes in the social networks of older adults. In G. Pierce, B. R. Sarason, & I. G. Sarason (Eds.), *The handbook of social support and family relationships* (pp. 219–248). New York: Plenum Press.

Ryan, R. M. (1991). The nature of the self in autonomy and relatedness. In J.

Strauss & G. R. Goethals (Eds.), *The self: Interdisciplinary approaches* (pp. 208–238). New York: Springer-Verlag.

Salthouse, T. (1995). Refining the concept of psychological compensation. In R. A. Dixon & L. Backman (Eds.), *Compensating for psychological deficits and declines: Managing losses and promoting gains* (pp. 107–126). Mahwah, NJ: Erlbaum.

Stevens, N. (1995). Gender and adaptation to widowhood in later life. *Ageing and Society, 15*, 37–58.

Stoller, E. P., & Pugliesi, K. L. (1988). Informal networks of community-based elderly: Changes in composition over time. *Research on Aging, 10*, 499–516.

Stroebe, W., Stroebe, M., Abakoumkin, G., & Schut, H. (1996). The role of loneliness and social support in adjustment to loss: A test of attachment versus stress theory. *Journal of Personality and Social Psychology, 70*, 1241–1249.

Stylianos, S. K., & Vachon, M. L. S. (1993). The role of social support in bereavement. In M. S. Stroebe, W. Stroebe, & R. O. Hansson (Eds.), *Handbook of bereavement: Theory, research, and intervention* (pp. 397–410). New York: Cambridge University Press.

U.S. Bureau of the Census. (1990). *Statistical abstracts of the United States* (110th ed.). Washington, DC: U.S. Government Printing Office.

U.S. Bureau of the Census. (1993). *Current population reports: Sixty-five plus in America*. Washington, DC: U.S. Government Printing Office.

U.S. Bureau of the Census. (1996). *Current population reports: Projections of the number of households and families in the United States: 1995 to 2010*. Washington, DC: U.S. Government Printing Office.

Weiss, R. S. (1973). *Loneliness: The experience of emotional and social isolation*. Cambridge, MA: MIT Press.

Weiss, R. S. (1974). The provisions of social relationships. In Z. Rubin (Ed.), *Doing unto others* (pp. 17–26). Englewood Cliffs, NJ: Prentice Hall.

Wright, P. H. (1989). Gender differences in adults' same and cross-gender friendships. In R. G. Adams & R. Blieszner (Eds.), *Older adult friendships: Structure and process* (pp. 197–221). Newbury Park, CA: Sage Publications.

Young, J. E. (1982). Loneliness, depression and cognitive therapy. In L. A. Peplau & D. Perlman (Eds.), *Loneliness: A sourcebook of current theory, research and therapy* (pp. 379–405). New York: Wiley.

V

HEALTH PSYCHOLOGY AND AGING

PART V: HEALTH PSYCHOLOGY AND AGING

How central are health and specific health problems to the study of normal aging? What is the impact of age on typical disease processes, such as diabetes or cardiovascular disease? These questions reflect the intersection of adult development and aging approaches to health psychology and behavioral medicine. To dichotomize the roles of the fields in addressing issues related to health and aging would be a false process; they are inevitably linked. The theories, methods, and findings in the two disciplines are in contant interplay. However, Irene Sigler and Janet Matthews of the next two chapters accepted the challenge of sharpening the differences between them in an effort to engage in dialogue about what each field can and will gain from the other to enhance our understanding of aging.

The two disciplines ask fundamentally different questions. The psychology of adult development and aging examines people who are aging normally, some with and some without specific diseases, to examine how disease influences the aging process. In behavioral medicine the emphasis is on the physiology or pathophysiology of a disease process and how understanding the aging process can contribute to an understanding of that disease and how various behaviors interact with that pathophysiology at different points in the lifecycle.

The organizational and disciplinary structures of the fields also shape their different orientations toward health, disease, and aging. Adult development and aging and health psychology are two subdisciplines of psychology, not only from the point of view of the American Psychological Association, but also in fact. Behavioral medicine is a relatively newly organized multidisciplinary approach to understanding problems in health psychology that interact with the same problems in psychosomatic medicine. The multidisciplinary aspects of studying aging tend to be reserved for the field of gerontology and limited to studying primarily elderly people, whereas the medical aspects of aging are studied as a postgraduate branch of medicine called *geriatrics*.

As readers will see in this set of chapters, the questions one asks about health, behavior and aging, or developmental health psychology have a lot more to do with definitions of disease than with definitions of health. In general, we should probably call the field—or at least the parts of it that are most relevant to the aging process—*disease psychology* of aging rather than *health psychology*. Behavioral medicine approaches the health and aging relationship disease by disease, as illustrated in Elaine A. Blechman and Kelly D. Brownell's (1998) *Behavioral Medicine and Women: A Comprehensive Handbook*, NY: The Guilford Press, which takes a lifecycle approach to health and disease.

Older adults and the people who study or serve them are intensely interested in the impact of health on well-being. The dialogue in these chapters pushes us to think more critically about the various conceptual frameworks and research methods that are available to teach us about how health, disease, and aging are related.

10

A BEHAVIORAL MEDICINE PERSPECTIVE ON AGING AND HEALTH

KAREN A. MATTHEWS

Behavioral medicine is the study of behavioral factors that contribute to understanding the etiology, progression, and recovery from physical illness and applications of those behavioral factors to promoting health and preventing disease. Behavioral medicine research derives from many disciplines, including psychology. Although behavioral medicine research encompasses a broad content area, it is probably best understood as an approach to or perspective on how best to investigate behavioral factors in health and illness. This perspective usually highlights the intersection of psychosocial and biological processes because of two premises: (a) social environments and human behavior modify the effects of biological processes, and (b) studies of health and illness concentrating only on the psychosocial or biological are less than comprehensive at best and inaccurate at worst.

A behavioral medicine approach to aging and health identifies the common or significant health problems of the elderly population that are poorly understood. Then it addresses the following questions from the perspective of psychosocial attributes of the environment and the individual:

First, who becomes sick with the health problem, and why? Second, among those who become ill with the disease, who recovers, and why? Third, how can the illness be prevented, or recovery be promoted, through behavioral interventions?

The remainder of this chapter addresses differences between behavioral medicine and aging approaches. In the first section I review differences in the types of questions asked and study designs used. These differences are illustrated through two studies on the influence of the menopause on women's health: the Pittsburgh Healthy Women Study and the Study of Women's Health Across the Nation (SWAN). In the next section I describe the role that age or aging has in behavioral medicine research and offer suggestions on why aging concepts and perspectives have been relatively neglected in behavioral medicine research. In the final section I highlight several concepts originating in the aging field that I find useful for behavioral medicine research. For the purposes of this chapter, I have exaggerated the distinctions between behavioral medicine and aging to make several key points and facilitate future dialogue between the fields.

DIFFERENCES BETWEEN BEHAVIORAL MEDICINE AND AGING APPROACHES

Researchers in aging obviously have interest in, and knowledge and research pertinent to, who gets sick and why, and who recovers quickly and why. However, the questions themselves are framed in a different way by aging researchers than they would be framed by researchers working from a behavioral medicine orientation. In behavioral medicine the emphasis is on questions regarding the determinants of disease and primary and secondary prevention of disease, whereas aging research emphasizes the determinants of good health and promotion of good health in the elderly population. The behavioral medicine emphasis is due in part to the disciplines of medicine and public health contributing to the multidisciplinary approach and in part to the challenge of defining good health among elderly people (cf. Rowe & Kahn, 1998). Usually, *good health* in elderly people is defined as the absence of clinical disease or of significant disabilities and activity limitations. This definition is less than satisfying, because many elderly people have subclinical disease that adversely affects survival and quality of life, and many with significant disabilities still have a high quality of life. It is important to address whether good health is more than the absence of health problems.

A second difference is that normal aging is emphasized by an aging approach, whereas behavioral medicine does not consider normal aging unless it informs the understanding of the development of, and recovery from, specific disease. This distinction has implications for study design. In behavioral medicine, the emphasis is on understanding behavioral factors in the natural history of disease, usually in individuals without the disease of interest who are approaching the usual age of disease onset, or on behavioral factors in the recovery process. As a consequence, the behavioral medicine approach concentrates on selected subgroups of the general population and does not emphasize the broader context of the aging process. "Pure" participants—who neither have the disease under investigation nor comorbid conditions that complicate an understanding of how the disease of interest develops or how to promote fast recovery—are studied. As a consequence, unique cases of the disease are studied rather than the garden variety diseases that covary in the general population.

This pure approach is partly responsible for many of the early studies of cardiovascular disease concentrating on middle-aged men, because their initial clinical presentation when they did not have comorbid conditions occurs in midlife typically. Women's disease, on the other hand, usually presents after age 65, when women have a number of comorbid conditions. The pure approach is the most reasonable effort to study diseases that appear in midlife or to study the early phase of the disease. It is a less reasonable approach to study aging and health because of the high prevalence of comorbid conditions in the elderly population and the concomitant social and economic changes that elderly people experience as a consequence.

Another important difference between a behavioral medicine approach and an aging approach to health and illness relates to cohort effects. Aging research is uniquely sensitive to the effects of cohorts on patterns of health and disease, and study designs are often stratified in regard to cohort and age. Behavioral medicine researchers are also aware of changing patterns of morbidity and mortality in the population, but their study designs rarely take into account cohort effects.

A final difference is that behavioral medicine models of disease and recovery are specific to the disease in question; in contrast, models on aging are broader and focus on numerous systems and diseases. These general points can be illustrated by differences in approach from two studies on the natural history of the menopause and midlife aging.

The Healthy Women Study in Pittsburgh is funded by the National Heart, Lung, and Blood Institute. Its goals include describing the changes in cardiovascular risk factors, both behavioral and biological, that occur in midlife and attributing those changes to chronological aging versus ovarian aging. Women were ineligible for the study if they were already postmenopausal, taking hormone replacement therapy, or taking medications that were known to affect cardiovascular risk factors. The study represents the pure approach. Of the women interviewed about their interest in and eligibility for the study, 25.8% were excluded because they were hypertensive or on antihypertensive medications; 13.9% because of thyroid medication;

2.7% because of insulin; 1.7% because of psychotropic medications; and 5.7% because of a variety of other drugs, including anticoagulants, lipid-lowering medications, steroids, oral contraceptives, and heart medications (Matthews, Kelsey, Meilahn, Kuller, & Wing, 1989). Thus, the Healthy Women Study participants were unusually healthy middle-aged women with little chronic disease. By design, the study does not investigate "normal" midlife aging. Perhaps a researcher from the perspective of aging and health would conceptualize the study as a one of "successful" midlife aging, although the publications based on the data are not written from that perspective.

The publications based on the Healthy Women Study describe the psychosocial characteristics of women who are likely to get sick and how those characteristics inform the natural history of cardiovascular diseases. For example, my colleagues and I have reported that substantial changes in lipids occur during the perimenopausal transition, above and beyond those accounted for by chronological aging (Matthews, Meilahn, et al., 1989). We have demonstrated that premenopausal and postmenopausal lipid levels predict subsequent subclinical disease in the carotid arteries, that is, extent of intima media thickness and plaque in the carotid arteries (Lassila, Tyrrell, Matthews, Wolfson, & Kuller, 1997; Sutton-Tyrrell et al., 1998). We have evaluated the psychosocial characteristics of those women most likely to have an increasing atherogenic lipid profile. Women who had greater increases in total and low-density lipoprotein cholesterol levels across the first 3 years of the follow-up period reported at study entry more depressive and stress symptoms and anxiety and being less likely to discuss their anger with others. Women who showed greater declines in high-density lipoprotein cholesterol reported feeling angry more frequently and being less likely to express or discuss their anger on standardized tests. Finally, we have demonstrated that women who at study entry reported holding their anger in, having hostile attitudes, and experiencing anger frequently were more likely to have greater intima media thickness in the coronary arteries 10 years later (Matthews, Owens, Kuller, Sutton-Tyrrel, & McWilliams, 1998). None of these publications emphasized normal aging of the cardiovascular system or successful avoidance of subclinical disease in midlife, and the findings were not extrapolated to the general population of middle-aged women. Rather, the publications described changes in cardiovascular function in relationship to ovarian aging and psychosocial characteristics in women whose function was not contaminated by pharmacologic treatment or frank disease.

In contrast to the Healthy Women Study is the multisite Study of Women's Health Across the Nation (SWAN), funded by the National Institutes on Aging (NIA). This study also aims to describe changes in midlife that are due to ovarian and chronological aging on a number of interrelated systems, including cardiovascular, bone, metabolic, psychosocial, and ovarian. A key design feature is that selected minority groups were oversampled at each site to ensure adequate numbers of African Americans, Hispanics, and Asians. Like the Healthy Women Study, SWAN excluded women who were already postmenopausal or using estrogen/progestin therapy. However, SWAN did not exclude women who were already taking pharmacologic treatment for cardiovascular or other diseases. If one applied the same eligibility criteria for the Healthy Women Study participants to SWAN participants from the University of Pittsburgh site, 11.7% would have been excluded for antihypertensive medication; 6.7% for thyroid medication; 3.9% for insulin; 11.9% for psychotropic medication; and almost 8% for other exclusionary medications, for example, lipid lowering medication, anticoagulants, and steroids. Overall, about 30% of SWAN women would have been excluded on the basis of Healthy Women Study criteria.

Because SWAN is a relatively new study, a sufficient number of women have not changed menopausal status to warrant publication of findings. Nonetheless, it is anticipated that findings will be reported in terms of normative change in different systems and their interrelationships, taking into account ethnicity and age. The influence of subclinical and frank disease on changes will influence the pattern of results in addition to ovarian aging and chronological aging.

ROLE OF AGE IN BEHAVIORAL MEDICINE RESEARCH

Given that aging is not the central focus of behavioral medicine research, it is important to consider how age is used in behavioral medicine research in an effort to contrast the perspectives. Often the age of the target group is used to select highly prevalent diseases for behavioral medicine investigation or at least the likely stage of the disease for investigation. Age is often used as a covariate in analyses or as a confounder in investigations. Thus, aging as a process is eliminated statistically from consideration. Occasionally age is viewed as a marker of an underlying psychosocial process. For example, chronological age has been proposed as a marker of a decline in primary control over the environment (Schulz & Heckhausen, 1996) or of an increase in exposure to stressful life events (Rodin, 1986). Perhaps most recently is a consideration that different psychosocial risk factors may be important at different ages (Scheier & Bridges, 1995). Hostility, anger suppression, and cardiovascular reactivity to stress bear stronger associations with cardiovascular disease in younger participants than in older ones (Dembroski, MacDougall, Costa, & Grandits, 1989; Haynes, Feinleib, & Kannel, 1980; Menkes et al., 1989). Similarly, emotional suppression and pessimistic attitudes bear stronger associations with cancer endpoints among younger than older patients (Greer

& Morris, 1975; Schulz, Bookwala, Knapp, Scheier, & Williamson, 1996). Although risk factor effects as modified by age are currently not a strong focus of behavioral medicine research, testing for their presence will improve understanding of the natural history of disease.

The lack of integration of concepts and principles of aging into behavioral medicine research stems from a number of factors. Many investigators in behavioral medicine have specialized in chronic diseases of adults that start in midlife. Researchers interested in aging and health have concentrated on understanding the health problems and disease processes of the elderly population; thus, much less of consequence is known about unique psychosocial issues and processes in midlife.

Some behavioral medicine researchers are trained in personality or trait approaches. *Traits* are defined as characteristics of individuals that are somewhat enduring across times and situations. In consequence, it is assumed that there is no need to study developmental issues, unless one is interested in very early determinants of risk, for example, in adolescence.

Finally, federal funding agencies have promoted studying disease or disease risk factors within specific age groups, so there is little external financial encouragement to model the natural history of disease in light of concepts of aging. For example, the National Heart, Lung, and Blood Institute has funded separate studies on children and adolescence, for example, in the Muscatine Heart Study (Mahoney et al., 1996), the Bogalusa Heart Study (Berenson et al., 1992), young adults initially ages 18–30 in the Coronary Artery Risk Development in Young Adults Study (Liu et al., 1989), middle-aged adults initially ages 45–64 in the Atherosclerosis Risk in Communities Study (Folsom et al., 1994), and elderly people initially age 65 in the Cardiovascular Health Study (Kuller et al., 1995). Several institutes of the National Institutes of Health are focused on specific age groups—for example, the NIA and the National Institute of Child Health and Development—whereas the remainder are disease or system focused. The NIA is not concerned with aging across the full life span.

CONCEPTS OF AGING RELEVANT TO BEHAVIORAL MEDICINE

Several concepts and principles of aging are particularly useful to behavioral medicine research and intervention. First, the view that age is a marker for where one is in the life course is useful for prevention and treatment of disease. Treatment choices and options are very different depending on age. To illustrate, for prostate cancer, recommended treatment options are different for a 50-year-old man and an 80-year-old man, not only because of possible differences in the underlying biology of the cancer at those ages, but also because of implications of the treatment options for quality of life at each life stage.

The distinction between normal aging and disease processes is helpful to understanding health and illness. For example, it used to be thought that hypertension was an inevitable consequence of aging rather than a preventable disease. Although very high blood pressure was recognized as having serious sequelae, it was not recognized that borderline blood pressure could also do structural damage and would also place people at higher risk for cardiovascular morbidity and mortality than those with low normal pressure. With the advent of new technology to measure subclinical disease, people can be classified according to the extent of disease, and processes of disease and normal aging can be distinguished more accurately.

Third, behavioral medicine research has emphasized responses to stress in many of its models of disease. Studies of aging suggest that the ability to deal with stress is adequate among many elderly people but that resilience or ability to recover quickly is compromised. The loss of ability to recover quickly may be due to less reserve for coping with stress. This observation suggests that behavioral medicine researchers should focus also on studying the ability to recover from stress as well as responses to stress exposure.

Finally, the distinction between cohort and aging effects is particularly valuable to behavioral medicine researchers in times of rapid social and economic change. The current generation of elderly people has had a different life course and expectations for well-being and health than the baby boomers have had. Undoubtedly, the psychosocial issues that influence disease and health are at least somewhat different for the current elderly generation and for the baby boomers as they age. Taking into account cohort effects will improve understanding of current patterns of health and illness and their determinants.

CONCLUSION

I have contrasted the perspectives of behavioral medicine and aging research and deliberately chose to exaggerate differences for purposes of this discussion. The differences in the perspectives are matters of emphasis, study design, and objectives. Nonetheless, behavioral medicine and aging research are complementary and in some areas are indistinguishable. Concepts and perspectives originating in understanding aging across the life span are useful to understanding disease processes and outcomes relevant to the role of behavioral factors in the etiology, course, and recovery from disease.

REFERENCES

Berenson, G. S., Wattigney, W. A., Tracy, R. E., Newman, W. P. III, Srinivasan, S. R., Webber, L. S., Dalferes, E. R., Jr., & Strong, J. P. (1992). Atherosclerosis of the aorta and coronary arteries and cardiovascular risk factors in persons aged 5 to 30 years and studied at necropsy (the Bogalusa Heart Study). *American Journal of Cardiology, 70,* 851–858.

Dembroski, T. M., MacDougall, J. M., Costa, P. T., Jr., & Grandits, G. A. (1989). Components of hostility as predictors of sudden death and myocardial infarction in the multiple risk factor intervention trial. *Psychosomatic Medicine, 51,* 514–522.

Folsom, A. R., Eckfeldt, J. H., Weitzman, S., Ma, J., Chambless, L. E., Barnes, R. W., Cram, K. B., & Hutchinson, R. G. (1994). Relation of carotid artery wall thickness to diabetes mellitus, fasting glucose and insulin, body size, and physical activity. *Stroke, 25,* 66–73.

Greer, S., & Morris, T. (1975). Psychological attributes of women who develop breast cancer: A controlled study. *Journal of Psychosomatic Research, 19,* 147–153.

Haynes, S. G., Feinleib, M., & Kannel, W. B. (1980). The relationship of psychosocial factors to coronary heart disease in the Framingham Study. *American Journal of Epidemiology, 111,* 37–58.

Kuller, L. H., Shemanski, L., Psaty, B. M., Borhani, N. O., Gardin, J., Haan, M. N., O'Leary, D. H., Savage, P. J., Tell, G. S., & Tracy, R. (1995). Subclinical disease as an independent risk factor for cardiovascular disease. *Circulation, 92,* 720–726.

Lassila, H. C., Tyrrell, K. S., Matthews, K. A., Wolfson, S. K., & Kuller, L. H. (1997). Prevalence and determinants of carotid atherosclerosis in healthy postmenopausal women. *Stroke, 28,* 513–517.

Liu, K., Ballew, C., Jacobs, D. R., Jr., Sidney, S., Savage, P. J., Dyer, A., Hughes, G., Blanton, M. M., & CARDIA Study Group. (1989). Ethnic differences in blood pressure, pulse rate, and related characteristics in young adults: The CARDIA Study. *Hypertension, 14,* 218–226.

Mahoney, L. T., Burns, T. L., Stanford, W., Thompson, B. H., Witt, J. D., Rost, C. A., & Lauer, R. M. (1996). Coronary risk factors measured in childhood and young adult life are associated with coronary artery calcification in young adults: The Muscatine Study. *Journal of the American College of Cardiology, 27,* 277–284.

Matthews, K. A., Kelsey, S. F., Meilahn, E. N., Kuller, L. H., & Wing, R. R. (1989). Educational attainment and behavioral and biologic risk factors for coronary heart disease in middle-aged women. *American Journal of Epidemiology, 129,* 1132–1144.

Matthews, K. A., Meilahn, E. N., Kuller, L. H., Kelsey, S. F., Caggiula, A. W., & Wing, R. R. (1989). Menopause and coronary heart disease risk factors. *New England Journal of Medicine, 321,* 641–646.

Matthews, K. A., Owens, J. F., Kuller, L. H., Sutton-Tyrrell, K., & McWilliams, L. J. (1998). Are hostility and anxiety associated with carotid atherosclerosis in healthy postmenopausal women? *Psychosomatic Medicine, 60,* 633–638.

Menkes, M. S., Matthews, K. A., Krantz, D. S., Lundberg, U., Mead, L. A., Qaqish,

B., Liang, K.-Y., Thomas, C. B., & Pearson, T. A. (1989). Cardiovascular reactivity to the cold pressor test as a predictor of hypertension. *Hypertension, 14*, 524–530.

Rodin, J. (1986, September). Aging and health: Effects of the sense of control. *Science, 233*, 1271–1276.

Rowe, J. W., & Kahn, R. L. (1998). *Successful aging*. New York: Pantheon Books.

Scheier, M. F., & Bridges, M. W. (1995). Person variables and health: Personality predispositions and acute psychological states as shared determinants for disease. *Psychosomatic Medicine, 57*, 255–268.

Schulz, R., Bookwala, J., Knapp, J. E., Scheier, M., & Williamson, G. M. (1996). Pessimism, age, and cancer mortality. *Psychology and Aging, 11*, 304–309.

Schulz, R., & Heckhausen, J. (1996). A life span model of successful aging. *American Psychologist, 51*, 702–714.

Sutton-Tyrrell, K., Lassila, H. C., Meilahn, E., Bunker, C., Matthews, K. A., & Kuller, L. H. (1998). Carotid atherosclerosis in premenopausal and postmenopausal women and its association with risk factors measured after menopause. *Stroke, 29*, 1116–1121.

11

AGING RESEARCH AND HEALTH: A STATUS REPORT

ILENE C. SIEGLER

This chapter reflects the views that a developmental psychologist brings to health psychology from the experience of approximately 30 years of studying the psychology of adult development and aging and about 10 years of conducting research in behavioral medicine. This chapter reflects the status of research in the psychology of adult development and aging in the study of physical health. The psychology of aging assumes life-span continuities during adult development and aging. These patterns are more discernable as we acquire increasing amounts of data from the full age range of people who now survive. Furthermore, the fact that we are living longer has attracted the attention of policymakers and has made understanding the variation seen with advancing age extremely important.

The aging revolution discussed in the opening chapters of this volume is largely due to the better health status of increasing numbers of older people in society that leads to increased survival. This is a demographic

I thank Paul T. Costa and Karen A. Matthews for comments on an earlier draft of this chapter. This work was supported by Grants R01 AG12458 from the National Institute on Aging and R01 HL55356 from the National Heart, Lung, and Blood Institute and Grants P01 CA72099 from National Cancer Institute to Barbara K. Rimer, P02 HL36587 to Redford B. Williams, R01 HL54807 to John C. Barefoot, and R01 HL45702 to Daniel B. Mark.

revolution that is spread unevenly around the world (Murray & Lopez, 1996; Robine, Vaupel, Jeune, & Allard, 1997), seen in First World countries but, unfortunately, not beyond. Thus understanding the nature and consequences of physical health in later life is critical.

The health status in the United States for individuals up to about age 85 was captured by Rowe and Kahn (1998). Their book, written for the popular press, summarizes the implications of their MacArthur Foundation studies on successful aging. Rowe and Kahn argued that modifications of risky behaviors have had a positive impact on current aging patterns for people whom they deem successful—those who avoid disease, maintain high cognitive and physical functioning, and are engaged in life. Not all elderly people are successful; many who survive do so in worsening health. Cassell, Rudberg, and Olshansky (1992) pointed out the consequences of this for health policy, which may be indeed the "grim side of gerontology" for individuals, their caregivers, and society as a whole.

The "aging revolution" is seen most clearly in studies of centenarians, which have reported both health and frailty in their population samples (Forette, 1997). They also have reported examples of extraordinary adaptation when the studies demand that the respondents be sufficiently healthy to be studied with cognitive tests used across the life span (Poon, Johnson, & Martin, 1997).

Existing statements about aging and health (M. F. Elias, Elias, & Elias, 1990; Siegler, 1989; Siegler & Costa, 1985; Siegler, Nowlin, & Blumenthal, 1980) are still useful and provide the basis for continuing work. The early studies were designed to see if health differentials accounted for the observed age differences.

We now know that health status, in some circumstances, does account for some observed age differences. Since Spieth (1965) presented his data on the cognitive funtioning in airline pilots by their age and their health status (see Figure 11.1), we have known the kind of variance that researchers should expect when looking at age differences in cognition functioning, when stratified by well-defined health and illness conditions. As can be seen in the figure, although there is a trend for speed to decline in older age groups, the fastest performances at ages 55–59 are better than the average performances in the under-34 group. Furthermore, the faster scores at each age range are from individuals without disease; individuals with disease tend to do worse at each age they are tested.

More recently, the effects of diseases on psychological functioning was shown by P. K. Elias et al. (1997) in their analyses of intellectual functioning in the Framingham cohort with particular attention paid to the intellectual performance of people with diabetes and those with hypertension. The authors reported that a diagnosis of diabetes and the duration of diabetes had stronger effects on cognitive performance for people with hypertension than for those without. The picture is really even more complex,

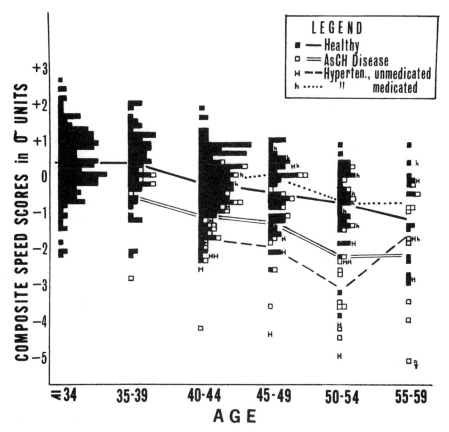

Figure 11.1. Distribution of individual composite speed scores survey by age of healthy participant. From "Slowness of Task Performance and Cardiovascular Diseases" by W. Spieth, in *Behavior Aging and the Nervous System*, A. T. Welford and J. E. Birren (Eds.), p. 371, 1965, Springfield, IL: Charles C Thomas. Copyright 1965 by Charles C Thomas. Reprinted with permission.

as illustrated by data on the specificity of the impact of hypertension on attention processes with age. Madden and Blumenthal (1998) demonstrated that measures of accuracy and speed in reaction time paradigms with age were differentially affected by blood pressure. Specific questions about the role of a disease process (e.g., cardiovascular disease, hypertension, or diabetes) and a particular psychological process under study can be answered only if the disease is measured as specifically as is the age-related phenomenon (e.g., cognition or attention).

Another old question—what is normal aging and how is it different from disease?—now also has an answer. This was the question that drove the initial longitudinal studies of normal aging, such as the Duke Longitudinal Study (Busse et al., 1985). We now know that Nathan Shock's initial observations were essentially correct (see Shock et al., 1984 that is, that some, albeit few, individuals age without the typical declines assumed to accompany advancing age. This was shown by a careful testing of participants in the Baltimore Longitudinal Study of Aging (Shock et al., 1984). These findings suggest that normal aging—when disease is not present—is a relatively benign set of processes (Williams, 1994). This is not to say that older people do not have health problems or that the probability of health problems does not increase with age. However, when they do, they can be attributed to a particular disease process rather than just the passage of time (at least until the 9th or 10th decade). The resulting problems then could be considered the fault of a chronic disease process that is not rapidly fatal but is treated and remains as a companion for the rest of one's life. Thus, it seems unfair to blame aging. This, however, does not explain the fact that age is a prominent risk factor for most diseases (Siegler, Bastian, & Bosworth, 2000). In the area of health care, time of measurement, or period effects—which index changes in medical technology, diagnosis, and treatment—also are critical and may change the meaning of a disease and the likelihood that it will impair functioning or cause disability at any age.

WHERE ARE WE NOW IN THE HEALTH PSYCHOLOGY OF ADULT DEVELOPMENT AND AGING?

To evaluate this, I gathered some general impressions of the Method sections of articles in the journals *Psychology and Aging* and *Health Psychology*. Looking first at *Psychology and Aging* I had to conclude that although, in general, health is not ignored; it is poorly measured. Studies that include individuals with depression and with Alzheimer's disease tend to make better assessments of those conditions than do studies that consider other physical health outcomes.

As a field, we have better measures of disease than we do of health. Researchers who have tried to create an omnibus measure of health, generally a single self-rating, have not been very helpful in understanding the role of physical health in age-related psychological processes. More often than not, the construct of self-rated health is used as a proxy for physical health. The problem with that approach is that self-rated health has important associations with factors other than just physical health; for example, personality, life satisfaction, psychological well-being, and morale. Idler and her colleagues (e.g., Idler, 1993) have begun to explore the meanings of self-rated health in the gerontological literature in a diverse population. My colleagues and I (e.g., Bosworth et al., 1999) have started describing the associations of the categories of self-rated health in a population of patients referred for diagnostic coronary angiography. Table 11.1 shows data for 2,900 people who were enrolled in the Mediators of Social

TABLE 11.1
Associations of Demographic Psychological and Clinical Variables With Self-Rated Health

Variable	Excellent	Very Good	Good	Fair	Poor
General health	86.68	75.70	60.77	40.30	26.24
Hazard score	.90	.89	.88	.83	.75
No. participants	100	452	838	961	549
Age range (years)	39–86	26–89	31–94	28–89	35–87
Mean age (years)	60.3	62.5	61.9	62.8	63.5
% Male	83%	70%	65%	57%	57%
% White	83%	84%	81%	75%	76%
% Married	85%	83%	80%	72%	67%
Education (years)	13.77	12.98	12.16	10.73	10.04
Income	4.10	3.83	3.38	2.53	2.14
Ever smoke (%)	63	68	69	70	71
CES–D	8.93	9.88	12.47	16.78	21.91
% W/depression	0%	1%	4.3%	4.5%	7.0%
% W/hypertension	39%	49%	57%	66%	70%
% W/diabetes	1.6%	2%	3%	7%	16%
% W/arthritis	6.5%	7%	12%	13.5%	15%
% W/myocardial infarction	58%	48%	53%	53%	60%
Mental health	82.67	77.85	74.74	66.47	58.42
Emotional role	89.61	80.02	75.40	60.54	48.67
Physical role	72.80	58.96	47.04	25.31	12.16

Note. Self-rated health is measured as a part of this domain of the Short Form–36 (SF–36). All of the scores from the SF–36 are scaled from 0 to 100, with 100 interpreted as 100% functioning. CES–D = Center for Epidemiologic Studies Depression Scale; *Mental health* = feeling peaceful, happy, and calm versus nervous; *Emotional role* = no problems with work or daily activities as a result of emotional problems versus experiencing problems with work and daily activities as a result of emotional problems; *Physical role* = experiencing no problems with work or daily activities due to physical health versus experiencing problems with work or daily activities due to physical health; *Hazard score* = probability of survival range 0 to 1.0; *Income* = categorized variable from 1 to 6 with 1 = $10,000 or less, 2 = $10,000 to $20,000, 3 = $20,000 to $30,000, 4 = $30,000 to $45,000, 5 = $45,000 to $60,000, and 6 = $60,000 or greater; *CES–D* = ranges 0 to 60 with a score of 16 or greater indicating possible depressive illness.

Support study. This table is based on people who, on the basis of catherization, were found to have significant coronary artery disease and who answered the baseline enrollment question about self-rated health. This question was part of the assessment of health-related quality-of-life domain of "General Health" (see Ware & Associates, 1993), which is shown in the first row. This measure of functional health is a useful indicator of how individuals relate their physical and mental health status to their overall quality of life. Ratings are scaled so that 100% represents the state of being fully functional.

This is not a sample of "normally" aging people. However, the sample includes individuals from a broad range of ages and socioeconomic statuses who are all undergoing the same, significant diagnostic procedure for coronary artery disease. All were admitted to Duke University Medical Center and were well characterized medically. The hazard score shown in Row 2 (Harrell, Lee, Califf, Pryor, & Rosati, 1984) is an overall indicator of prognosis. It reflects primarily age and the variables related to coronary anatomy and physiology. In this particular table, there is no significant association of age with self-rated health.

The remaining rows of the table include standard demographic indicators, risk factors, prevalence of other diseases (in addition to heart disease), and indices of health-related quality of life from the Short Form–36 in the last three rows (Ware & Associates, 1993). All of the rest of the variables listed are significantly correlated with self-rated health at $p < .001$.

The information in Table 11.1 makes clear that, as a single item, self-rated health within a population can provide important information about functional health. In this population, where everyone has heart disease, the single item is not especially useful in telling how sick the individuals are. However, self-rated health is related to depression and psychological well-being as well as reported physical capacity. What cannot be assumed is that everyone who has heart disease will rate their health the same way. Some individuals with disease will rate their health as excellent; others poor, depending on a host of factors beyond the diagnosis. Researchers in the psychology of aging who use self-rated health as an index of health are thus often making assumptions about the disease status of the sample that may not be justified.

In *Health Psychology*, the second journal that I surveyed, many studies controlled for age rather than studied it. Because diseases generally strike within a relatively narrow age range, the age group of the participants who are studied is the result of the disease of interest. This teaches important lessons about health–behavior relationships within restricted ranges. Questions about aging and health are thus secondary research questions. Tests for interaction effects by age are rare. However, the situation is improving. In 1998, we (Siegler & Vitaliano, 1998) edited a special section of *Health Psychology* on aging and health. Three articles were featured.

M. F. Elias, Robbins, Elias, and Streeten (1998) presented findings over 19 years of their longitudinal study of the impact of hypertension on intellectual performance. They contrasted various ways of measuring blood pressure and the ability to understand age-related declines in intellectual functioning. The results show the differences when age is and is not controlled and blood pressure is used as a variable at baseline, averaged over times of measurement as an indicator of hypertensive status. Although both hypertensive status and increased levels of blood pressure predict declines in cognitive performance, increased blood pressure is a stronger predictor of decline. Carstensen and Fredrickson (1998) evaluated the mental representations of social partners. They contrasted older healthy people with younger sick people, as both groups would be expected to have a shortened life expectancies. Their results indicated that the perception of limited time (i.e., distance from death), rather than age, was the critical variable in explaining their findings that potential social partners were chosen for their emotional value. Zelinski, Crimmins, Reynolds, and Seeman (1998) provided an excellent review of the major studies in health, behavior, and aging and then presented new data from the AHEAD (Asset and Health Dynamics Among the Oldest-Old; Soldo, Hurd, Rodgers, & Wallace, 1997) study, a nationally representative study with more than 6,000 respondents. Reporting on the initial cross-section, Zelinski et al. (1998) reported interesting interactions of age with high blood pressure, diabetes, and a general health rating, such that for younger people (ages 70–74) and for some variables up to age 80, individuals without the condition who could be tested had better cognitive performance. The predicted values converged by age 85 and older. There are both strengths and weaknesses with the sampling strategy. Proxy interviews were conducted for older sample members with cognitive impairments and they were thus excluded from the analyses. This may well underestimate the impact of these conditions at the end of life and reflect the difficulties of doing this research in samples representative of the general population.

How Do We Study Individuals Who Have Disease?

Another way to ask some important questions is to ask about the impact of disease on psychological processes. This approach has some design problems that can be solved. First, how do we get assessments from people who are too ill to provide data?

Use of Informant Rating

Costa provided one solution with a rater form of the NEO Personality Inventory (NEO–PI; Costa & McCrae, 1992, 2000a). Informants are asked to rate patients on their personality functioning. We (Siegler et al., 1991) used this technique to try to see if there is consistency in the personality traits that change during development of the disease. We asked caregiver informants (spouses and children) to provide personality ratings of 35 memory-impaired patients. Informants described both premorbid and current personality characteristics using the observer rating version of the original NEO–PI (a version that measured all five factors but specific facets for only the first three). Premorbid personality profiles showed slightly lower than average levels of Openness, but otherwise mean scores were in the normal range. By contrast, current ratings depicted patients as being high in Neuroticism, especially vulnerability to stress; low in Extraversion; and very low in Conscientiousness. These results were clearly replicated in three other studies (Chatterjee, Strauss, Smyth, & Whitehouse, 1992; Siegler, Dawson, & Welsh, 1994; Welleford, Harkins, & Taylor, 1995), with results (expressed as difference between premorbid and current ratings) from all four studies plotted in Figure 11.2 (see also Costa & McCrae, 2000b).

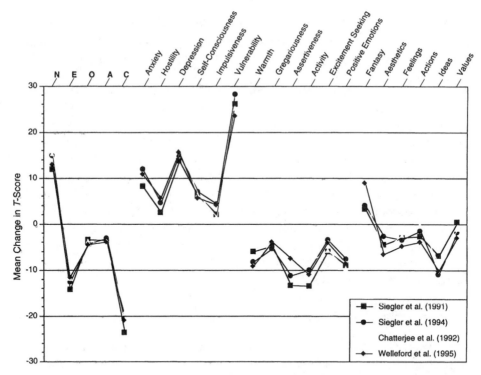

Figure 11.2. Mean changes from premorbid to current personality ratings in four studies of Alzheimer's disease patients. From "Contemporary Personality Psychology" by P. T. Costa, Jr. and R. R. McCrae, 2000b, In *Textbook of Geriatric Neuropsychiatry*, C. E. Coffey and J. L. Cummings (Eds.), pp. 453–462, in press, Washington, DC: American Psychiatric Press. Copyright 2000 by American Psychiatric Press. Reprinted with permission.

Thus, instruments that are developed and standardized as ratings by appropriate observers will open up many new avenues of research. Although this does not give us indexes of cognitive functioning to use in studies, it does allow us to estimate the behavior of people who cannot provide self-report data for their personality functioning.

New analyses of classic epidemiologic studies such as the Framingham Study (see P. K. Elias et al., 1997) provide another source of data for studying health and aging. As epidemiological studies are harnessed to answer important questions and issues in the psychology of aging, the impact on the field should be positive. However, there are a few traditions in epidemiology that are different from those in the psychology of aging that should be pointed out. Psychologists tend to confuse the meaning of the terms *incidence* and *prevalence*. This can be important, because although the number of individuals who have a disease increases with age, an important distinction must be made between individuals who have survived the disease (prevalence) and new cases of the disease developing at a later age (incidence). In epidemiology studies new cases of disease (incidence) are treated differently than the total number of cases of disease present at a single point in time (prevalence). There are some excellent epidemiology primers that will be useful to readers who are unfamiliar with epidemiologic terminology (see Fletcher, Fletcher, & Wagner, 1982). Because the field of epidemiology is often focused on trying to predict a disease when an analysis starts, all persons with the disease at the start of data collection are removed from the analysis. As the cohort gets older and older, that becomes an increasingly difficult proposition and makes the specification of the disease and the time at which is was first noted critical variables to assess accurately.

Measuring Disease

Verification of disease outcomes is not simple. It requires different criteria and strategies, disease by disease. Probstfield, Kumanyika, and Daugherty (1995) provided a continuing annotated bibliography on the assessment of cardiovascular disease according to standard criteria. This is extremely useful because it includes sources that evaluate the literature on verification of heart disease outcomes. An excellent primer for behavioral scientists about cardiovascular disease is Smith and Leon's (1992) *Coronary Heart Disease: A Behavioral Perspective*. An excellent set of strategies for understanding how to assess specific diseases in the elderly is given in the appendix of the Healthy Women Study (see Guralnik, Fried, Simonsick, Kasper, & Lafferty, 1995). The information in these sources in no way solves the problem but should serve to illustrate the types of approaches that need to be adopted in understanding health–behavior relationships in the psychology of adult development and aging. There are no shortcuts that provide quality data. Questions about the best ways to combine multiple diagnoses into useful indexes remain unanswered.

Life-Span Developmental Health Psychology

When thinking about the impact of physical health on psychological functioning, middle age and extreme old age emerge as different. Middle age is organized by gender and Gender × Age interactions. Diseases hit women at different times during midlife than they hit men. Thus it is hard to make conclusions about aging and health during midlife that are "controlled" for gender, that make sense. Very, very old age seems not to be attained by people who have disease. Thus it is not cancer and heart attack survivors who get to be centenarians, but rather those who escape these diseases altogether earlier in the life cycle, suggesting a different relationship between health and aging.

SUMMARY

The psychology of aging and health is in generally good shape. We have a strong research base, and it is now commonplace to ask the right questions about how health and disease status interact with what is defined as normal aging. Future progress in this area is more likely to come from behavioral-medicine approaches that are designed to evaluate the specific pathophysiology of the mechanisms that are responsible for what has traditionally been first observed as an aging change.

REFERENCES

Bosworth, H. B., Siegler, I. C., Brummett, B. H., Barefoot, J. C., Williams, R. B., Vitaliano, P. P., Clapp-Channing, N. E., Lytle, B. L., & Mark, D. B. (1999). The relationship between self-rated health and health status among coronary artery patients. *Journal of Aging and Health, 11*, 565–584.

Busse, E. W., Maddox, G. L., Buckley, C. E., Burger, P. C., George, L. K., Marsh, G. R., Nebes, R. D., Nowlin, J. B., Palmore, E. B., Ramm, D., Siegler, I. C., Vogel, S. F., Wang, S. H., & Woodbury, M. A. (1985). *The Duke Longitudinal Studies of Normal Aging: 1955–1980*. New York: Springer.

Carstensen, L. L., & Fredrickson, B. L. (1998). Socio-emotional selectivity in healthy older people and younger people living with Human Immunodeficiency Virus (HIV): The centrality of emotion when the future is constrained. *Health Psychology, 17*, 494–503.

Cassell, K. C., Rudberg, M. A., & Olshansky, S. J. (1992). The price of success: Health care in an aging society. *Health Affairs, 11*, 87–99.

Chatterjee, A., Strauss, M., Smyth, K. A., & Whitehouse, P. J. (1992). Personality changes in Alzheimer's disease. *Archives of Neurology, 49*, 486–491.

Costa, P. T., & McCrae, R. R. (1992). Normal personality assessment in clinical practice: The NEO Personality Inventory. *Psychological Assessment, 41*, 5–13.

Costa, P. T., Jr., & McCrae, R. R. (2000a). *Revised NEO Personality Inventory (NEO–PI) and NEO Five Factor Inventory (NEO–FFI) professional manual*. Odessa, FL: Psychological Assessment Resources.

Costa, P. T., & McCrae, R. R. (2000b). Contemporary personality psychology: Implications for geriatric neuropsychiatry. In C. E. Coffey & J. L. Cummings (Eds.), *Textbook of geriatric neuropsychiatry* (2nd ed., pp. 453–462). Washington, DC: American Psychiatric Press.

Elias, M. F., Elias, J. W., & Elias, P. K. (1990). Biological and health influences on behavior. In J. E. Birren & K. W. Schaie (Eds.), *Handbook of the psychology of aging* (3rd ed., pp. 79–102). San Diego, CA: Academic Press.

Elias, M. F., Robbins, M. A., Elias, P. K., & Streeten, D. H. P. (1998). A longitudinal study of blood pressure in relation to the performance on the Wechsler Adult Intelligence Scale. *Health Psychology, 17*, 486–493.

Elias, P. K., Elias, M. F., D'Agostino, R. B., Cupples, L. A., Wilson, P. W., Silbershatz, H., & Wolf, P. A. (1997). NIDDM and blood pressure as risk factors for poor cognitive performance. *Diabetes Care, 20,* 1388–1395.

Fletcher, R. H., Fletcher, S. W., & Wagner, E. H. (1982). *Clinical epidemiology— the essentials.* Baltimore: Williams & Wilkins.

Forette, B. (1997). Centenarians: Health and frailty. In J.-M. Robin, J. W. Vanpool, B. Jeanie, & M. Allard (Eds.), *Longevity: To the limits and beyond* (pp. 105–112). New York: Springer-Verlag.

Guralnik, J. M., Fried, L., Simonsick, E. M., Kasper, J. D., & Lafferty, M. E. (Eds.). (1995). *The Women's Health and Aging Study: Health and social characteristics of older women with disability* (NIH Pub. No. 95-4009). Bethesda, MD: National Institute on Aging.

Harrell, F. E., Lee, K. L., Califf, R. M., Pryor, D. B., & Rosati, R. A. (1984). Regression modeling strategies for improved prognostic prediction. *Statistics in Medicine, 3,* 143–152.

Idler, E. L. (1993). Age differences in self-assessment of health: Age changes, cohort differences or survivorship? *Journal of Gerontology: Social Sciences, 48,* S289–S300.

Madden, D. J., & Blumenthal, J. A. (1998). Interaction of hypertension and age in visual selection attention performance. *Health Psychology, 17,* 76–83.

Murray, C. L. G., & Lopez, A. D. (Eds.). (1996). *The global burden of disease.* Washington, DC: World Health Organization.

Poon, L. W., Johnson, M. A., & Martin, P. (1997). Looking into the crystal ball: Will we ever be able to accurately predict individual differences in longevity? In J. M. Robine, J. W. Vaupel, B. Jeune, & M. Allard (Eds.), *Longevity: To the limits and beyond* (pp. 113–119). New York: Springer-Verlag.

Probstfield, J. L., Kumanyika, S., & Daugherty, S. (Eds.). (1995). *CVD endpoint criteria: Cardiovascular disease annotated bibliography* (On-line). Available: http://www.fhcrc.org/-cvdeab

Robine, J.-M., Vaupel, J. W., Jeune, B., & Allard, M. (Eds.). (1997). *Longevity: To the limits and beyond.* New York: Springer-Verlag.

Rowe, J. W., & Kahn, R. L. (1998). *Successful aging.* New York: Pantheon.

Shock, N., Greulich, R. C., Costa, P. T., Jr., Andres, R., Lakatta, E. G., Arenberg, D., & Tobin, J. D. (Eds.). (1984). *Normal human aging: The Baltimore Longitudinal Study of Aging.* Washington, DC: U.S. Department of Health and Human Services, NIH Pub. No. 84-2450.

Siegler, I. C. (1989). Developmental health psychology. In M. Storandt & G. R. Van den Bos (Eds.), *The adult years: Continuity and change* (pp. 119–142). Washington, DC: American Psychological Association.

Siegler, I. C., Bastian, L. A., & Bosworth, H. B. (2000). Health, behavior and aging. In A. Baum, T. A. Revenson, & J. E. Singer (Eds.), *Handbook of health psychology* (pp. 469–476). Mahwah, NJ: Erlbaum.

Siegler, I. C., & Costa, P. T. (1985). Health behavior relationships. In J. E. Birren & K. W. Schaie (Eds.), *Handbook of the psychology of aging* (2nd ed., pp. 144–166). New York: Van Nostrand Reinhold.

Siegler, I. C., Dawson, D. V., & Welsh, K. A. (1994). Caregiver ratings of person-ality change in Alzheimer's disease patients: A replication. *Psychology and Aging, 9,* 464–466.

Siegler, I. C., Nowlin, J. B., & Blumenthal, J. A. (1980). Health and behavior: Methodological considerations for adult development and aging. In L. W. Poon (Ed.), *Aging in the 1980's: Psychological issues* (pp. 559–612). Washing-ton, DC: American Psychological Association.

Siegler, I. C., & Vitaliano, P. P. (1998). In search of a double paradigm. *Health Psychology, 17,* 483–485.

Siegler, I. C., Welsh, K. A., Dawson, D. V., Fillenbaum, G. G., Earl, N. L., Kaplan, E. B., & Clark, C. M. (1991). Ratings of personality change in patients eval-uated for memory disorders. *Alzheimer's Disease and Associated Disorders, 5,* 240–250.

Smith, T. W., & Leon, A. S. (1992). *Coronary heart disease: A behavioral perspective.* Champaign, IL: Research Press.

Soldo, B. J., Hurd, M. D., Rodgers, W. L., & Wallace, R. B. (1997). Asset and health dynamics among the oldest old: An overview of the AHEAD study. *Journals of Gerontology, Series B, 52B,* 1–20.

Spieth, W. (1965). Slowness of task performance and cardiovascular diseases. In A. T. Welford & J. E. Birren (Eds.), *Behavior aging and the nervous system* (pp. 366–400). Springfield, IL: Charles C Thomas.

Ware & Associates. (1993). *SF-36 Health Survey: Manual and interpretation guide.* Boston: The Health Institute, New England Medical Center.

Welleford, E. A., Harkins, S. W., & Taylor, J. R. (1995). Personality change in dementia of the Alzheimer's type: Relations to caregiver personality and bur-den. *Experimental Aging Research, 21,* 295–314.

Williams, M. E. (1994). Clinical management of the elderly patient. In W. R. Hazzard, E. L. Bierman, J. P. Blass, W. H. Ettinger, Jr., & J. B. Halter (Eds.), *Principles of geriatric medicine and gerontology* (3rd ed., pp. 195–201). New York: McGraw-Hill.

Zelinski, E. M., Crimmins, E., Reynolds, S., & Seeman, T. (1998). Do medical conditions affect cognition in older adults? *Health Psychology, 17,* 504–512.

VI

DEPRESSION AND AGING

PART VI: DEPRESSION AND AGING

Depression is commonly, albeit inaccurately, viewed as a normative aspect of aging. The authors of the following two chapters present a brief overview of recent research on the nature, psychological causes, and consequences of depression, with notes on its assessment and treatment. Thomas E. Joiner and Margaret Gatz begin with prevalence data that show fascinating patterns suggestive of a difference between a true developmental trajectory and a cohort pattern. Joiner documents that depression is a growing epidemic that is due to rapidly rising incidence rates in more recent birth cohorts. Thus, the "aging revolution" suggests cause for concern about future high rates in older adults. Gatz focuses on how the very low prevalence of clinical depression and the very high rates of symptom endorsement by current cohorts of older adults suggest a paradox. She further raises the concern that unresolved problems in defining depression are magnified in geropsychology because of the complex biopsychosocial context of aging.

Depression is costly in almost any terms one wishes to use (e.g., costs to the individual's health, suicide risk, and costs of excessive health system utilization); thus, risk factors for depression are an important component of this dialogue. Joiner summarizes portions of the burgeoning literature on psychological risk factors, with an eye toward inquiring about how existing data relate to aging populations. Cognitive factors (e.g., attributional style and dysfunctional thought patterns) and interpersonal factors such as excessive reassurance-seeking and personality factors (e.g., neuroticism and shyness) also place a person at risk for depression. Gatz argues that in older adults risk factors must be examined separately for early- and late-onset depressions, because late-onset depression appears to be associated with brain changes and a family history of dementia. Other factors—such as physical health status, cognitive status, and psychosocial contexts—may also be uniquely relevant to older adults. Both authors conceptualize risk factors within a diathesis–stress model that can predict when specific risk factors should be most likely to produce depression. This model may help organize some of the data available in the mainstream research domain as well as within geropsychology.

Joiner and Gatz converge in their recognition that assessment and treatment of depression in older adults can be presumed to be remarkably similar to that in young adults. The key points appear to be the importance of recognizing depression early, treating it aggressively, and monitoring closely the possibility of suicide.

Taken together, these two chapters lay the groundwork for at least a decade of research on the risk factors for depression that operate uniquely in later life as well as those that are common across age groups.

12

DEPRESSION: CURRENT DEVELOPMENTS AND CONTROVERSIES

THOMAS E. JOINER, JR.

The purpose of this chapter is to provide an overview of recent research on the nature, causes, consequences, assessment, and treatment of depression. Several facts about depression are summarized, including its prevalence, pernicious consequences, and definitional controversies. Psychological risk factors are briefly reviewed, and implications for assessment and therapy are drawn out.

THE INCREASING PREVALENCE OF DEPRESSION

With regard to depression, an enormously important age-related phenomenon has occurred and is still occurring (Seligman, 1998). If, in 1998, a person is about 70 years old, the chance that he or she has experienced depression in his or her lifetime is about 1%–2%. If, in 1998, a person is in his or her 50s, the lifetime chance of depression is approximately 3%–4%. Despite less opportunity (i.e., fewer years) for depression, this younger group is about twice as likely to have experienced depression. This is remarkable enough, but astoundingly, the same pattern continues as younger and younger groups are examined. Those in their 30s in 1998 experience approximately a 6% risk of lifetime depression; teenagers in 1998, despite four times fewer years than their 70-year-old counterparts, experience a risk for lifetime depression approximately 10 times higher. This trend is similar across all industrialized countries examined to date (Cross-National Collaborative Group, 1992).

The upshot of this is a looming (if not current) epidemic of depression. In 2058, when the teenagers of 1998 are in their 70s, their lifetime prevalence of depression may approach 20%. Further, as will be discussed, depression is rarely a once-in-a-lifetime event—someone with a lifetime history of depression is far more likely than others to experience current depression. A cohort with a 20% lifetime rate of depression is thus quite likely to have a high rate of current depression. Accordingly, as younger and more vulnerable cohorts age, geriatric depression looms as a pressing national health problem.

CONSEQUENCES OF A DEPRESSION EPIDEMIC

Depression has been termed "the common cold" of mental disorders. With regard to prevalence, this analogy may be apt: Depression is becoming more and more common. Otherwise, however, the analogy may be unfortunate, because it belies the pernicious quality of a depressive episode. Depression is among the most debilitating and costly of any health problem. In a recent large-scale study of medical outcomes, only heart disease was associated with more bed days, physical symptoms, and social and role impairment than depression. Depression was associated with worse outcomes than all other conditions studied, including chronic lung disease, diabetes, arthritis, gastrointestinal problems, back problems, and hypertension (Stewart et al., 1989; Wells, 1991).

In a 2-year follow-up of more than 1,000 participants in the Medical Outcomes Study, Hays, Wells, Sherbourne, Rogers, and Spritzer (1995) reported that depressed patients were similar to or worse off than all patients with other medical problems, including congestive heart failure and myocardial infarction. It is interesting to note that this result applied to many types of depression, including an acute episode of clinically severe depression (i.e., major depression), subclinical but disruptive depressive symptoms, and persistent but less acute and severe forms (e.g., dysthymia). Thus, as Hays et al. stated, "depressed patients have substantial and long-lasting decrements in multiple domains of functioning and well-being that equal or exceed those of patients with chronic medical illnesses" (p. 11).

When depression goes untreated, the impairment in functioning and well-being is worse still (Coryell et al., 1995).

In addition to its impact on individual suffering and impairment, depression burdens the health care system. Simon, Ormel, VonKorff, and Barlow (1995) found that, among primary care patients, those with clinical depression were twice as costly to treat than were other patients. This finding was not due to increased medical problems among those who are depressed but rather from increased utilization of health care services. Even when improvement in depression had occurred 1 year later, the costs associated with the care of formerly depressed patients had not decreased substantially.

Depression can be fatal. One of its primary features is suicidal thoughts or actions. Of all the people who commit suicide, a majority have experienced some form of diagnosable depression at the time of their death (Hawton, 1992). In a recent study, approximately 70% of young adults who had recently attempted suicide had a diagnosable mood disorder (Rudd et al., 1996). Compared to the general population, depressed people's risk of death by suicide is around 30 times higher (Hawton, 1992). Suicide affects all age ranges. Among adolescents, suicide is the third leading cause of death, accounting for 14% of total deaths in this age group, and the overall suicide rate among this group has increased 312% from 1957 to 1987 (Berman & Jobes, 1991, pp. 12–15). Suicide also affects older people. Indeed, suicide rates for people over age 65 are at least as high, if not higher, than those for other age groups. This is particularly true for White men, whose suicide rate among those 65 and older is at least double that of any other group (U.S. Bureau of the Census, 1993).

All of this would be bad enough, even if depression were an isolated event in the lives of its sufferers. But depression is remarkably persistent and recurrent. The average length of major depressive episodes—the acute and most incapacitating and distressing phase of depression—is approximately 8 months in adults (Shapiro & Keller, 1981) and, incredibly, the mean length of dysthymic episodes (i.e., low-grade but distressing symptoms) may be as much as 30 years in adults (Shelton, Davidson, Yonkers, & Koran, 1997). Two-year relapse rates exceed 50% (Belsher & Costello, 1988). Coryell and Winokur (1992) found that in studies with follow-up intervals of 10 years or more 70% of people with one depressive episode subsequently experienced at least one more. Lee and Murray (1988) reported that 18 years after an initial depressive episode, approximately 20% of patients remained fully incapacitated by depression. Depression is thus persistent within acute episodes and recurrent across substantial portions of people's lives.

Unlike the common cold, then, depression is a human scourge. It is incapacitating, costly, potentially lethal, and chronic. Its prevalence is ominously increasing worldwide.

MOOD DISORDER NOSOLOGY: WHAT *IS* DEPRESSION?

Can one seriously question whether major depressive disorder (MDD), as defined in current classificatory systems (e.g., American Psychiatric Association, 1994), represents a true and valid construct? From diverse perspectives ranging from the genetic (Kendler et al., 1995) to the interpersonal (Coyne, 1976), the construct enjoys considerable support. To take just one example, Kendler and colleagues have shown that "typical depression," similar in composition to MDD, can be discerned as a syndromal class, distinct from nondepression as well as from "atypical depression" (characterized by increased eating and sleep), among a large sample of women from a population-based twin registry (Kendler et al., 1996). These and other results, when added to the actuarial, historical, grant-making, industrial, and conventional momentum enjoyed by the concept of MDD, combine to make it a formidable concept indeed.

Yet even despite all this, there are disquieting strands of evidence and thought. For example, is depression a category, an all-or-none, "either-you-have-it-or-you-don't" phenomenon, similar to heart attack or biological gender? Or is depression a continuum, distributed along a graded dimension, similar to temperature or mass, where a thing can have very little of it, or a little more of it, and so on, up to having very much of it? There are persuasive advocates of both positions (Coyne, 1994; Vredenburg, Flett, & Krames, 1993). As another example, it is well known that MDD is a very heterogeneous category. Two hundred twenty-seven different possible combinations of symptoms all satisfy the current definition of just one form of depression—a bewildering array of manifestations for a supposedly singular entity (whether continuous or dichotomous). Buchwald and Rudick-Davis (1993) found that, of these 227 possible combinations of symptom presentations, 42 were represented among their sample of depressed people, and 26 of these 42 were single occurrences (i.e., a combination of symptoms that occurred in only 1 person in the sample). Of course, resolution of fundamental definitional issues is a virtual prerequisite of real progress in science. A lurking but neglected issue in depression research, then, is the very definition of the syndrome in the population at large, not to mention the possibility that the properties of the syndrome may vary in different subpopulations (e.g., older people).

Also, there is some reason to suspect that depression's properties may be different in older people or at least a subset of older people. Depressions that first occur in later life, as compared to those that first occur in early adulthood, may be about equally common in men and women (whereas "early" depressions are more common in women; Krishnan, Hays, Tupler, & George, 1995); less associated with first-degree relatives' depression risk (Bland, Newman, & Orn, 1986); more related to neurological or medical disease (Alexopoulos, Young, Meyers, & Abrams, 1988); less severe (Burvill, Hall, Stampfer, & Emmerson, 1989); less associated with suicidal and anxious symptoms (Cassano, Akiskal, Savino, & Soriani, 1993); and less related to personality problems, such as excessive dependency and avoidance (Abrams, Rosendahl, Card, & Alexopoulos, 1994).

THE PSYCHOLOGY OF RISK FOR DEPRESSION

The finding that excessive dependency and avoidance are less related to late-onset depression is interesting in light of current theories on the psychological causes of depression, each of which emphasizes variants of one or both of dependency and avoidance. These theories can be grouped into those emphasizing cognitive vulnerability factors, those emphasizing interpersonal vulnerability factors, and those emphasizing personality-based vulnerability factors.

Cognitive Theories of Depression

According to the hopelessness theory of depression (Abramson, Metalsky, & Alloy, 1989), the tendency to attribute negative events to stable and global causes represents a diathesis which, in the presence but not the absence of negative life stress, increases vulnerability to depression. Furthermore, the theory specifies the mechanism by which a negative attributional style (i.e., the tendency to attribute negative events to stable, global causes) leads to depressive symptoms. Specifically, individuals who possess a negative attributional style and who encounter negative life events are predicted to become hopeless and, as a function thereof, become depressed.

Past research on adults has provided support for each of the elements of the hopelessness theory. Several reports have shown that the diathesis–stress component is associated with increases in depression (e.g., Metalsky, Joiner, Hardin, & Abramson, 1993), and some have demonstrated that such increases are mediated, at least in part, by hopelessness (Metalsky & Joiner, 1992).

To date, the most compelling evidence in support of the theory derives from the Temple–Wisconsin Cognitive Vulnerability to Depression project (e.g., Alloy & Abramson, 1998). These researchers selected a group of currently nondepressed young adults—some of whom possessed a negative attributional style and some of whom did not—and followed these participants for more than 2 years to determine who became depressed. At the 2-year follow-up, the rate of current major depression among participants with a negative attributional style was 22%, and the corresponding rate among those with a positive attributional style was 3.4% (difference between rates is significant at the .001 level). In an important supplemental analysis, Alloy and Abramson showed that this same difference emerged when participants with a previous history of depression were excluded; the results were thus not explained by any association between negative attributional style and past history of depression. It is interesting that there were no differences between the negative- versus positive-attributional-style participants with regard to anxiety disorders, consistent with the theory's claim that attributional style is specific to depression, even as compared to closely associated mental disorders.

Like the Temple–Wisconsin study, the majority of research on this topic has been conducted among young adults (see Joiner & Wagner, 1995, however, for a meta-analytic review of research on children and adolescents). Extension to older populations represents an important direction for future research. It will be interesting to determine, for example, the effect (if any) of negative attributional style on depressive symptoms in the context of life events, both positive and negative, that are prominent in the lives of older people (e.g., retirement and attendant freedom or boredom; financial freedom or difficulty; death of friends; health problems). As noted earlier, the distinction between late- and early-onset depressions would be important to address in such research. Of course, physical illness can be a concern for older people, and it is interesting to note that Peterson and his colleagues have documented an association between attributional style and physical health (e.g., Peterson, 1995). Another key issue involves developmental vacillations in attributional style. It is possible that attributional style changes with age, and research is needed on whether, why, and how this is the case.

The other major cognitive model of depression is Beck's (e.g., 1983) theory that dysfunctional attitudes (e.g., "I am nothing if a person I love doesn't love me") represent a vulnerability factor that interacts with negative life events to contribute to the development of depressive symptoms, as a function of the development of stream-of-consciousness-type negative automatic thoughts about the self, the world, and the future (e.g., "There must be something wrong with me," "The future is bleak"; Joiner, Metalsky, Lew, & Klocek, 1999 validated each aspect of this model). Within this line of research, a distinction between sociotropic dysfunctional attitudes (i.e., excessive neediness vis á vis other people) and autonomous dysfunctional attitudes (i.e., perfectionistic expectations regarding achievement) has emerged (Beck, 1983). The validity of this distinction is controversial (Coyne & Whiffen, 1995); to the degree that it is valid, the sociotropic and autonomous dimensions may be fruitful areas for research in older populations, who confront issues that may impinge on both dimensions (see Allen, Ames, Layton, & Bennetts, 1997 article, in which they reported that sociotropy may be the more relevant dimension among older people). The distinction is also interesting in light of the finding that late-onset depression is less related to dependent and avoidant personality dimensions, each of which contains elements of sociotropy.

Interpersonal Theory of Depression

Following Coyne (1976), Joiner, Metalsky, and colleagues (e.g., Joiner, 1994; Joiner, Alfano, & Metalsky, 1992; Joiner & Metalsky, 1995, 1998) have theorized that excessive reassurance-seeking (i.e., the tendency to excessively ask others for reassurance of worth) is an important depression-related variable. Excessive reassurance-seeking may explain, in part, when depressed people will experience interpersonal strife and when they will not (i.e., high reassurance-seekers receive more rejection; Joiner et al., 1992; Joiner & Metalsky, 1995), and when depression will be contagious and when it will not (i.e., contagion occurs more among high reassurance-seekers; Joiner, 1994).

Consistent with previous interpersonal work on depression risk (e.g., Beck, 1983) and stress generation (Hammen, 1991), Joiner and Metalsky (1998) argued that Coyne's (1976) theory has implications for vulnerability. For example, the theory, often characterized as a "depressive spiral" or "vicious cycle," begins with a mildly distressed person who, in response to stress and as a function of excessive reassurance-seeking, generates and then maintains a negative social environment. This negative environment, in turn, leads to more severe depressive symptoms.

In a series of empirical studies, Joiner and Metalsky (1998) validated the view that excessive reassurance-seeking may operate as a vulnerability factor for depression. They found that excessive reassurance-seeking was relatively specific to diagnosed depression among adult VA psychiatric inpatients, clinically diagnosed undergraduates, and youth psychiatric inpatients and that excessive reassurance-seeking predicted future depressive symptoms among stressed college students (Joiner & Schmidt, 1998 and Potthoff, Holahan, & Joiner, 1995, obtained similar findings). Similar to work on the cognitive theories of depression, extension of these findings to older people, as well as research on developmental vacillations of excessive reassurance-seeking, awaits investigation.

It is interesting that there are some reports that aging may be protective vis á vis depression, perhaps as a function of increased interpersonal support (Henderson, 1994). However, depression in a significant other undermines interpersonal support, thus increasing vulnerability to depression for both individuals (cf. "contagious" depression; Joiner, 1994 and Tower & Kasl, 1995, documented the contagion effect among older adults). If older people focus efforts to recruit social support on fewer people (e.g., a spouse; Jorm, 1995), they may particularly benefit from the social support that death of a spouse, or depression in a spouse, is particularly likely to reduce.

Personality-Based Views of Depression

Neuroticism (i.e., the tendency toward emotional distress, self-consciousness, and insecurity) has been proposed as a risk factor for the development of depressive symptoms (Enns & Cox, 1997). It is interesting that Enns and Cox (1997) reported that the self-criticism dimension of neuroticism, which is conceptually similar to Beck's (1983) cognitive autonomy dimension, appears strongly related to depression in adults (somewhat at odds with Allen et al.'s 1997 report on older adults, described earlier). Among a sample of community-dwelling participants ages 73–102, Henderson, Korten, Jacomb, and MacKinnon (1997) found that high neuroticism predicted prospective increases in depressive symptoms over the course of 3 years.

Joiner (1997) proposed a personality-based model of depression in which shyness is viewed as a risk factor for the development of depressive symptoms, in the absence but not in the presence of social support, and as a function of increased experiences of loneliness. This view has not been empirically examined among older adults, but it is interesting to note that Henderson et al. (1997), in their study of older community participants, found that low social support was a significant predictor of depression increases.

The construct of shyness contains aspects of neuroticism as well as of extraversion. It is interesting that there is some evidence that levels of both neuroticism and extroversion (or proxy variables, such as negative and positive emotionality) tend to decrease with age (Eysenck, 1988; Finn, 1986). Older people who, for whatever reason, do not experience muted neuroticism or who experience marked decreases in extraversion may be particularly vulnerable to depression. Factors explaining why some people and not others undergo subtle personality changes in adulthood represent an important area for future research. One—but probably not the only—such factor is neurocognitive changes, which are associated with personality change (Jacomb, Jorm, Christensen, & MacKinnon, 1994). As with the other two areas of vulnerability research (i.e., cognitive and interpersonal models), it would be important to consider the relation of personality (and possible changes in personality) to late- versus early-onset depressions.

SOME NOTES ON CLINICAL APPLICATIONS

Assessment

It is beyond the scope of this chapter to review the considerable literature on the assessment of depressive symptoms in general or in older people specifically. It is worth noting, however, that assessment measures specifically developed for geriatric populations exist (e.g., the Geriatric Depression Scale; Yesavage et al., 1983); there is also evidence that scales such as the Beck Depression Inventory and the Center for Epidemiologic Studies Depression Scale also possess adequate properties in geriatric samples (Lewinsohn, Seeley, Roberts, & Allen, 1997; Olin, Schneider, Eaton, & Zemansky, 1992).

An important development in the assessment of depression is the articulation and empirical validation of the tripartite model of depression and anxiety (Clark & Watson, 1991). The model argues that "pure depression" is characterized by low positive affect and high negative affect. "Pure anxiety," by contrast, is characterized by high physiological hyperarousal and high negative affect. Therefore, pure depression and anxiety have a shared component (negative affect) and specific components (low positive affect and high physiological hyperarousal, respectively). Assessment of each of the three components of the model thus facilitates the sometimes vexing distinction between depressive and anxious syndromes. Empirical support for the model is accruing (Joiner, Catanzaro, & Laurent, 1996; Watson et al., 1995) but has not been examined among older adults.

A final development in the area of depression assessment involves factors of suicidal symptoms. In an investigation of the Modified Scale for Suicidal Ideation (Miller, Norman, Bishop, & Dow, 1986), Joiner, Rudd, and Rajab (1997) found that two factors—Resolved Plans and Preparations and Suicidal Desire and Ideation—best described the instrument's factor space. Furthermore, the Resolved Plans and Preparation factor (intense thoughts, plans, and the courage and capability to commit suicide) was more related to actual suicide attempt than was the Suicidal Desire and Ideation factor (ongoing thoughts or desires about suicide). The Suicidal Desire and Ideation factor was more highly related to depressotypic indicators than was the other factor, suggesting that level of depression, although predictive of ideation, may not be as strong a correlate of preparation. Comparison of depression- and anxiety-related diagnostic groups on these factors revealed little difference, consistent with previous work highlighting the occurrence of suicidality across diagnostic groups. Taken together, these findings highlight the need to emphasize the Resolved Plans and Preparation factor in suicide assessment as well as the fact that, among clinical populations, lack of depression does not indicate low suicide risk. Because suicide is common among older people, particularly White men (U.S. Bureau of the Census, 1993), these findings may be of particular note; however, they have not been replicated among a clinical sample of older adults.

Therapy

In general, with regard to relatively short-term symptom resolution, there are several effective treatments for depression, including psychotherapy and antidepressant medicines. For older adults, however, more research is needed. For example, regarding antidepressant medicines, even the newer, safer agents may produce poorly tolerated side effects and drug interactions in older people (Tourigny-Rivard, 1997). In a study of depressed inpatients ages 60–91 treated with antidepressants, Heeren, Derksen, Heycop ten Ham, and van Gent (1997) reported that, because of fears of side effects and drug interactions, only half of the sample received the full recommended dose of antidepressant medication, and approximately 60% of patients did not recover from depression. Orengo, Kunik, Molinairi, and Workman (1996) presented a brighter picture: Two of their 31 participants stopped taking fluoxetine (Prozac) because of side effects, and the remaining participants experienced symptom improvement.

Of course, psychotherapies do not face the issues of physical side effects and drug interactions and have shown efficacy at least as high, if not higher, than drug therapies. Regarding a variety of brief psychotherapies, Gallagher-Thompson, Hanley-Peterson, and Thompson (1990) reported 2-year relapse rates between 30%–42%; Leung and Orrell (1993), regarding cognitive–behavioral therapy, found a 1-year relapse rate of 30%. It is interesting that when Leung and Orrell focused only on patients with major depression, the 1-year relapse rate was 8%; the relapse rate for other disorders, including more chronic forms of depression, was 50%. Chronic forms of depression may benefit from psychotherapies specifically developed for them (e.g., cognitive–behavior therapy for the chronic depressions; McCullough et al., 1997). Less chronic, depressive stress reactions, even if acute, may respond to psychotherapies targeting interpersonal loss, transition, and conflict (e.g., interpersonal psychotherapy; Klerman, Weissman, Rounsaville, & Chevron, 1984). Early-onset depressions, of course, are more likely to fall within the chronic domain, whereas at late-onset depressions may not.

CONCLUSION

Although depression's definitional boundaries remain unclear, its association with suffering and impairment is obvious. Its increasing prevalence only adds to the urgent need for scientific research on older and other populations. Research on psychological risk factors (i.e., cognitive, interpersonal, and personality-based variables) holds promise in that psychotherapeutic interventions, themselves promising, may be refined as a result.

REFERENCES

Abrams, R. C., Rosendahl, E., Card, C., & Alexopoulos, G. S. (1994). Personality disorder correlates of late and early onset depression. *Journal of the American Geriatrics Society, 42,* 727–731.

Abramson, L. Y., Metalsky, G. I., & Alloy, L. B. (1989). Hopelessness depression: A theory-based subtype of depression. *Psychological Review, 96*, 358–372.

Alexopoulos, G. S., Young, R. C., Meyers, B. S., & Abrams, R. C. (1988). Late-onset depression. *Psychiatric Clinics of North America, 11*, 101–105.

Allen, N. B., Ames, D., Layton, T., & Bennetts, K. (1997). The relationship between sociotropy/autonomy and patterns of symptomatology in the depressed elderly. *British Journal of Clinical Psychology, 36*, 121–132.

Alloy, L. B., & Abramson, L. Y. (1998, February). *Optimistic cognitive styles and invulnerability to depression.* Paper presented at the John F. Templeton Foundation Symposium on Optimism and Hope, Philadelphia.

American Psychiatric Association. (1994). *Diagnostic and statistical manual of mental disorders* (4th ed.). Washington, DC: Author.

Beck, A. T. (1983). Cognitive therapy of depression: New perspectives. In P. Clayton & J. E. Barret (Eds.), *Treatment of depression: Old controversies and new approaches* (pp. 265–290). New York: Raven.

Belsher, G., & Costello, C. G. (1988). Relapse after recovery from unipolar depression: A critical review. *Psychological Bulletin, 104*, 84–96.

Berman, A. L., & Jobes, D. A. (1991). *Adolescent suicide: Assessment and intervention.* Washington, DC: American Psychological Association.

Bland, R. C., Newman, S. C., & Orn, H. (1986). Recurrent and nonrecurrent depression: A family study. *Archives of General Psyhciatry, 43*, 1085–1089.

Buchwald, A. M., & Rudick-Davis, D. (1993). The symptoms of major depression. *Journal of Abnormal Psychology, 102*, 197–205.

Burvill, P. W., Hall, W. D., Stampfer, H. G., & Emmerson, J. P. (1989). A comparison of early-onset and late-onset depressive illness in the elderly. *British Journal of Psychiatry, 155*, 673–679.

Cassano, G. B., Akiskal, H. S., Savino, M., & Soriani, A. (1993). Single episode of major depressive disorder: First episode of recurrent mood disorder or distinct subtype of late-onset depression? *European Archives of Psychiatry and Clinical Neuroscience, 242*, 373–380.

Clark, L. A., & Watson, D. (1991). Tripartate model of anxiety and depression: Psychometric evidence and taxonomic implications. *Journal of Abnormal Psychology, 100*, 316–336.

Coryell, W., Endicott, J., Winokur, G., Akiskal, H., Solomon, D., Leon, A., Mueller, T., & Shea, T. (1995). Characteristics and significance of untreated major depressive disorder. *American Journal of Psychiatry, 152*, 1124–1129.

Coryell, W., & Winokur, G. (1992). Course and outcome. In E. Paykel (Ed.), *Handbook of affective disorders* (pp. 89–108). New York: Guilford Press.

Coyne, J. C. (1976). Toward an interactional description of depression. *Psychiatry, 39*, 28–40.

Coyne, J. C. (1994). Self-reported distress: Analog or ersatz depression? *Psychological Bulletin, 116*, 29–45.

Coyne, J. C., & Whiffen, V. E. (1995). Issues in personality as diathesis for depression: The case of sociotropy/dependency and autonomy/self-criticism. *Psychological Bulletin, 118,* 358–378.

Cross-National Collaborative Group. (1992). The changing rate of major depression: Cross-national comparisons. *Journal of the American Medical Association, 268,* 3098–3105.

Enns, M. W., & Cox, B. J. (1997). Personality dimensions and depression: Review and commentary. *Canadian Journal of Psychiatry, 42,* 274–284.

Eysenck, H. H. (1988). Personality and ageing: An exploratory analysis. *Journal of Social Behavior and Personality, 3,* 11–21.

Finn, S. E. (1986). Stability of personality self-ratings over 30 years: Evidence for an age/cohort interaction. *Journal of Personality and Social Psychology, 50,* 813–818.

Gallagher-Thompson, D., Hanley-Peterson, P., & Thompson, L. W. (1990). Maintenance of gains versus relapse following brief psychotherapy for depression. *Journal of Consulting and Clinical Psychology, 58,* 371–374.

Hammen, C. (1991). Generation of stress in the course of unipolar depression. *Journal of Abnormal Psychology, 100,* 555–561.

Hawton, K. (1992). Suicide and attempted suicide. In E. Paykel (Ed.), *Handbook of affective disorders* (pp. 635–650). New York: Guilford Press.

Hays, R. D., Wells, K. B., Sherbourne, C. D., Rogers, W., & Spritzer, K. (1995). Functioning and well-being outcomes of patients with depression compared with chronic general medical illnesses. *Archives of General Psychiatry, 52,* 11–19.

Heeren, T. J., Derksen, P., Heycop ten Ham, B. F., & van Gent, P. P. (1997). Treatment, outcome and predictors of response in elderly depressed inpatients. *British Journal of Psychiatry, 170,* 436–440.

Henderson, A. S. (1994). Does aging protect against depression? *Social Psychiatry and Psychiatric Epidemiology, 29,* 107–109.

Henderson, A. S., Korten, A. E., Jacomb, P. A., & MacKinnon, A. J. (1997). The course of depression in the elderly: A longitudinal community based study in Australia. *Psychological Medicine, 27,* 119–129.

Jacomb, P., Jorm, A., Christensen, H., & MacKinnon, A. (1994). Personality changes in normal and cognitively impaired elderly: Informant reports in a community sample. *International Journal of Geriatic Psychiatry, 9,* 313–320.

Joiner, T. E., Jr. (1994). Contagious depression: Existence, specificity to depressed symptoms, and the role of reassurance-seeking. *Journal of Personality and Social Psychology, 67,* 287–296.

Joiner, T. E., Jr. (1997). Shyness and low social support as interactive diatheses, and loneliness as mediator: Testing an interpersonal–personality view of depression. *Journal of Abnormal Psychology, 106,* 386–394.

Joiner, T. E., Jr., Alfano, M. S., & Metalsky, G. I. (1992). When depression breeds contempt: Reassurance-seeking, self-esteem, and rejection of depressed college students by their roommates. *Journal of Abnormal Psychology, 101,* 165–173.

Joiner, T. E., Jr., Catanzaro, S., & Laurent, J. (1996). The tripartite structure of positive and negative affect, depression, and anxiety in child and adolescent psychiatric inpatients. *Journal of Abnormal Psychology, 105,* 401–409.

Joiner, T. E., Jr., & Metalsky, G. I. (1995). A prospective test of an integrative interpersonal theory of depression: A naturalistic study of college roommates. *Journal of Personality and Social Psychology, 69,* 778–788.

Joiner, T. E., Jr., & Metalsky, G. I. (1998). Reassurance-seeking: Delineating a risk factor involved in the pathogenesis of depression. Manuscript submitted for publication.

Joiner, T. E., Jr., Metalsky, G. I., Lew, A., & Klocek, J. (1999). Testing the causal mediation component of Beck's theory of depression: Evidence for specific mediation. *Cognitive Therapy and Research, 23,* 401–412.

Joiner, T. E., Jr., Rudd, M. D., & Rajab, M. H. (1997). The Modified Scale for Suicidal Ideation among Suicidal Adults: Factors of suicidality and their relation to clinical and diagnostic indicators. *Journal of Abnormal Psychology, 106,* 260–265.

Joiner, T. E., Jr., & Schmidt, N. B. (1998). Excessive reassurance-seeking predicts depressive but not anxious reactions to acute stress. *Journal of Abnormal Psychology, 107,* 533–537.

Joiner, T. E., Jr., & Wagner, K. D. (1995). Attributional style and depression in children and adolescents: A meta-analytic review. *Clinical Psychology Review, 8,* 777–798.

Jorm, A. F. (1995). The epidemiology of depressive states in the elderly: Implications for recognition, intervention, and prevention. *Social Psychiatry and Psychiatric Epidemiology, 30,* 53–59.

Kendler, K. S., Eaves, L. J., Walters, E. E., Neale, M. C., Heath, A. C., & Kessler, R. C. (1996). The identification and validation of distinct depressive syndromes in a population-based sample of female twins. *Archives of General Psychiatry, 53,* 391–399.

Kendler, K. S., Walters, E. E., Neale, M. C., Kessler, R. C., Heath, A. C., & Eaves, L. J. (1995). The structure of the genetic and environmental risk factors for six major psychiatric disorders in women. *Archives of General Psychiatry, 52,* 374–383.

Klerman, G. L., Weissman, M. M., Rounsaville, B. J., & Chevron, E. S. (1984). *Interpersonal therapy for depression.* New York: Basic Books.

Krishnan, K. R. K., Hays, J. C., Tupler, L. A., & George, L. K. (1995). Clinical and phenomenological comparisons of late-onset and early-onset depression. *American Journal of Psychiatry, 152,* 785–788.

Lee, A. S., & Murray, R. M. (1988). The long-term outcome of Maudsley depressives. *British Journal of Psychiatry, 153,* 741–751.

Leung, S. N., & Orrell, M. W. (1993). A brief cognitive behavioural therapy group for the elderly: Who benefits? *International Journal of Geriatric Psychiatry, 8,* 593–598.

Lewinsohn, P. M., Seeley, J. R., Roberts, R. E., & Allen, N. B. (1997). Center for Epidemiologic Studies Depression Scale (CES–D) as a screening instrument for depression among community-residing older adults. *Psychology and Aging, 12*, 277–287.

McCullough, J., Arnow, B., Blalock, J., Eaves, G., Manber, R., Rothbaum, B., & Vivian, D. (1997, November). *Cognitive behavior therapy for chronic depression.* Workshop presented at the annual convention of the Association for Advancement of Behavior Therapy, Miami, Florida.

Metalsky, G. I., & Joiner, T. E., Jr. (1992). Vulnerability to depressive symptomatology: A prospective test of the diathesis–stress and causal mediation components of the hopelessness theory of depression. *Journal of Personality and Social Psychology, 63*, 667–675.

Metalsky, G. I., Joiner, T. E., Jr., Hardin, T. S., & Abramson, L. Y. (1993). Depressive reactions to failure in a naturalistic setting: A test of the hopelessness and self-esteem theories of depression. *Journal of Abnormal Psychology, 102*, 101–109.

Miller, I. W., Norman, W. H., Bishop, S. B., & Dow, M. G. (1986). The Modified Scale for Suicidal Ideation: Reliability and validity. *Journal of Consulting and Clinical Psychology, 54*, 724–725.

Olin, J. T., Schneider, L. S., Eaton, E. M., & Zemansky, M. F. (1992). The Geriatric Depression Scale and the Beck Depression Inventory as screening instruments in an older adult outpatient population. *Psychological Assessment, 4*, 190–192.

Orengo, C. A., Kunik, M. E., Molinairi, V., & Workman, R. H. (1996). The use and tolerability of fluoxetine in geropsychiatric inpatients. *Journal of Clinical Psychiatry, 57*, 12–16.

Peterson, C. (1995). Explanatory style and health. In G. M. Buchanan & M. E. P. Seligman (Eds.), *Explanatory style* (pp. 233–246). Mahwah, NJ: Erlbaum.

Potthoff, J. G., Holahan, C. J., & Joiner, T. E., Jr. (1995). Reassurance-seeking, stress generation, and depressive symptoms: An integrative model. *Journal of Personality and Social Psychology, 68*, 664–670.

Rudd, M. D., Rajab, M. H., Orman, D. T., Stulman, D. A., Joiner, T. E., Jr., & Dixon, W. (1996). Effectiveness of an outpatient problem-solving intervention targeting suicidal young adults: Preliminary results. *Journal of Consulting and Clinical Psychology, 64*, 179–190.

Seligman, M. E. P. (1998, February). *Reasons and solutions for the increasing prevalence of depression.* Paper presented at the John F. Templeton Foundation Symposium on Optimism and Hope, Philadelphia.

Shapiro, R. W., & Keller, M. B. (1981). Initial 6-month follow-up of patients with major depressive disorder. *Journal of Affective Disorders, 3*, 205–220.

Shelton, R. C., Davidson, J., Yonkers, K. A., & Koran, L. (1997). The undertreatment of dysthymia. *Journal of Clinical Psychiatry, 58*, 59–65.

Simon, G., Ormel, J., VonKorff, M., & Barlow, W. (1995). Health care costs associated with depressive and anxiety disorders. *American Journal of Psychiatry, 152*, 352–357.

Stewart, A., Greenfield, S., Hays, R. D., Wells, K. B., Rogers, W. H., Berry, S. D., McGlynn, E. A., & Ware, J. E. (1989). The functioning and well-being of depressed patients: Results from the medical outcomes study. *Journal of the American Medical Association, 262,* 907–913.

Tourigny-Rivard, M.-F. (1997). Pharmacotherapy of affective disorders in old age. *Canadian Journal of Psychiatry, 42*(Suppl. 1), 10S–18S.

Tower, K. B., & Kasl, S. V. (1995). Depressive symptoms across older spouses and the moderating effect of marital closeness. *Psychology and Aging, 10,* 625–638.

U.S. Bureau of the Census. (1993). *Statistical abstract of the United States: 1993* (113th ed.). Washington, DC: U.S. Government Printing Office.

Vredenburg, K., Flett, G. L., & Krames, L. (1993). Analogue versus clinical depression: A critical appraisal. *Psychological Bulletin, 113,* 327–344.

Watson, D., Clark, L. A., Weber, K., Assenheimer, J. S., Strauss, M. E., & McCormick, R. A. (1995). Testing a tripartite model: II. Exploring the symptom structure of anxiety and depression in student, adult, and patient samples. *Journal of Abnormal Psychology, 104,* 15–25.

Wells, K. B. (1991). Caring and depression in America: Lessons learned from early findings of the Medical Outcomes Study. *Psychiatric Medicine, 9,* 512.

Yesavage, J. A., Brink, T. L., Rose, T. L., Lum, O., Huang, V., Adey, M., & Leirer, V. O. (1983). Development and validation of a geriatric depression scale. *Journal of Psychiatric Research, 17,* 31–49.

13

VARIATIONS ON DEPRESSION IN LATER LIFE

MARGARET GATZ

It is widely believed that depression is rampant in old age. Aging can, in fact, be associated with multiple health-related changes (including chronic illnesses and conditions, sensory and physiological decline, and side effects from medications), cognitive slowing, financial burdens, and social losses (such as death of friends and family members). It is easy to assume that such circumstances would inevitably lead to depression (Jarvik, 1976). Another common view is that depression in older adults tends to express itself in somatic symptoms, sometimes called *masked depression* in the psychiatric literature (Blumenthal, 1980). In this chapter I consider whether older people are more depressed; how depression in later life differs from depression earlier in life; risk factors, correlates, and etiologic mechanisms important in old age; and theoretical perspectives that help to account for the special nature of late life depression. I also mention types of treatments that have been shown to be efficacious, as well as outreach and education strategies.

ARE OLDER PEOPLE MORE DEPRESSED?

Depression in older adults is variously subject to overestimation and to underrecognition. Representing overestimation bias is the assumption

239

that, given the insults associated with aging, it is inevitable to become depressed. For example, in an article intended for general readership, a prominent geriatrician is cited as saying "Depression is a common, normal and predictable consequence of aging" (Nalick, 1998, p. 6). At the same time, geropsychology and geriatric psychiatry advocates are concerned that many general practitioners normalize depression and do not recognize or treat depressive disorder among their older patients (Friedhoff, 1994). Older adults may, similarly, normalize symptoms of depression and therefore not seek professional help.

Available prevalence data suggest that depression is comparatively rare in older adults. Epidemiologic Catchment Area (ECA) survey data on rates of mood disorders indicate that prevalence of clinical depression is lowest among people aged 65 and older compared to other age groups (see Figure 13.1). Using diagnostic criteria from the *Diagnostic and Statistical Manual of Mental Disorders* (3rd ed., *DSM–III*; American Psychiatric Association, 1980; 3rd ed., rev., *DSM–III–R*; American Psychiatric Association, 1987), researchers who conducted the ECA survey in the United States and surveys in several European countries and in Australia found that 1%–2% of older adults has major depressive disorder (e.g., Henderson et al., 1993; Weissman, Bruce, Leaf, Florio, & Holzer, 1991).

In contrast, rates of self-reported depressive symptoms tend to show a curvilinear pattern, with lowest scores in middle adulthood and elevation

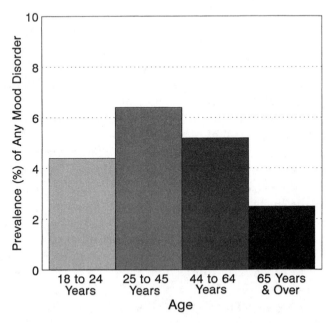

Figure 13.1. One-month prevalence rates of any mood disorder, including major depression, dysthymia, and bipolar disorder, drawn from Regier et al.'s (1988) results.

in very old age (see Figure 13.2). This pattern has been found in a number of cross-sectional and cross-national studies in which the Center for Epidemiological Studies–Depression scale (CES–D) and other self-report scales were used (e.g., Kessler, Foster, Webster, & House, 1992; Newmann, 1989). Thus, the phenomenon of low prevalence of diagnosed disorder and elevated symptoms can be regarded as well established in the geropsychological literature.

A final point with respect to prevalence is that rates of symptoms vary across settings. Rates are elevated within medical populations, progressively more so in settings where more seriously or chronically ill patients are found. On the basis of Blazer's (1994) summary of the literature, the percentage of older adults with clinically significant self-reported depressive symptoms goes from 15% in community samples to 20% among medical outpatients, 33% among hospitalized inpatients, and 40% among nursing home residents.

HOW DOES DEPRESSION IN LATER LIFE DIFFER FROM DEPRESSION EARLIER IN LIFE?

When studying psychopathology in older adults, it is essential to differentiate true late-onset disorder from continuation or recurrence of earlier conditions (see Kahn, 1977). Two studies of successive psychiatric admissions for depression suggest that approximately half of geriatric patients with depression have experienced depression previously, and half have not (Meyers, Greenberg, & Mei-Tal, 1985; Steingart & Herrmann, 1991).

The distinction between late-onset disorder and continuation of earlier conditions is especially relevant because late-onset depression appears likely to be associated with brain changes—for example, deep white matter disease or ventricular dilation—suggesting that the depression has a specific biological etiology (Leuchter, 1994). Clinical research also finds more severe symptoms, especially more frequent psychotic or delusional symptoms, in late-onset cases than in older adults with early-onset recurring depression (Meyers & Greenberg, 1986). The notion that late-onset depression may have special etiological characteristics is further supported by family history studies. It is generally accepted that a family history of depression is more often found with early-onset than with late-onset depression (Baldwin & Tomenson, 1995). A more provocative finding is that older adults with late-onset depression, especially when the depression is accompanied by cognitive decrement, are more likely to have a family history of dementia than to have a family history of depressive disorder (van Ojen et al., 1995).

It is also clinically possible to have a category that falls in between true late onset and continuation of earlier disorder. These cases tend to be

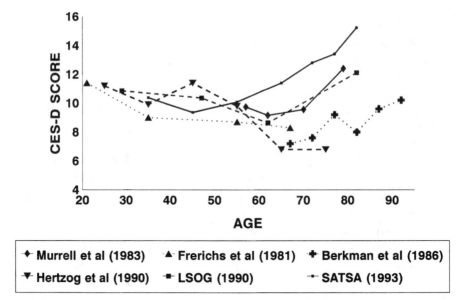

Figure 13.2. Rates of depressive symptoms from various data sources: a representative sample of older adults in Kentucky (Murrell, Himmelfarb, & Wright, 1983); a probability sample of adults from Los Angeles County, California (Frerichs, Aneshensel, & Clark, 1981) a probability sample of older adults from New Haven, Connecticut (Berkman et al., 1986); a recruited life-span sample (Hertzog, Van Alstine, Usala, Hultsch, & Dixon, 1990); the Longitudinal Study of Generations (LSOG; Gatz & Hurwicz, 1990); and the Swedish Adoption/Twin Study of Aging (SATSA; Gatz, Johansson, Berg, Pedersen, & Reynolds, 1993).

clients with a long-standing history of personality disorder insufficient to come to the attention of the mental health system but whose marginal mechanisms of management are sufficiently disrupted by events associated with aging (e.g., retirement, aging of the body) to trigger a depressive reaction (Abrams, Alexopolous, & Young, 1987).

It is common for professionals who see older depressed clients to critique the *DSM* criteria for major depression. In particular, the prerequisite that symptoms cannot be the direct physiological consequence of drugs or general medical conditions requires careful application in older adults, who typically have a number of medical conditions and take several medications. Eliminating somatic symptoms can cause underestimation of depression; interpreting medical symptoms as psychiatric can lead to overdiagnosis. Experiments with modified criteria that place less reliance on somatic symptoms have shown that clinicians may find the modifications easier, although there was not significant gain in diagnostic accuracy over the *DSM–IV* (American Psychiatric Association, 1994; Koenig, Pappas, Holsinger, & Bachar, 1995).

Special subtypes of depression have been suggested as better for characterizing older adults. For example, Newmann, Engel, and Jensen (1991) demonstrated a special symptom constellation that they called a *depletion syndrome*; they contrasted a "depletion syndrome" to a "depression syndrome." Depletion is characterized by loss of interest in things and hopelessness. Dysphoric mood is less prominent; self-deprecating feelings (self-blame and inappropriate guilt) are not present. Depression syndrome is, in addition, characterized by loneliness, enervation, a sense of worthlessness, and sleep disturbance. Analogously, Forsell, Jorm, and Winblad (1994) proposed a "motivational disturbance" and a "mood disturbance," and Mirowsky and Ross (1992) distinguished "malaise" and "mood" components of depression.

Consistent with this differentiation, Gallo, Anthony, and Muthén (1994) used ECA data to show that older adults are less likely to endorse dysphoria. Somewhat similarly, Gatz and Hurwicz's (1990) analyses of the Longitudinal Study of Generations data suggest that older adults may experience a lack of positive feelings rather than active negative feelings. Using CES–D subscales, depressed mood (such as feeling sad) showed no significant age differences, whereas lack of well-being (i.e., not endorsing an item that indicates that one feels happy) was common in the oldest age group.

Finally, it is important to note that symptoms of depression in older adults, even if they do not meet diagnostic criteria, can be consequential. For example, Gallo and his colleagues (Gallo, Rabins, Lyketsos, Tien, & Anthony, 1997) found that nondysphoric depression (similar to the depletion syndrome) predicted increased risk of death, functional impairment, cognitive impairment, and psychological distress at 13-year follow-up of the Baltimore ECA sample.

WHAT ARE THE RISK FACTORS AND CORRELATES OF LATE LIFE DEPRESSION?

The most frequently cited factors relevant to depression in older adults are physical health status, cognitive status, and psychosocial context.

Physical Health Status

Comorbidity between physical health problems and depressive symptoms can represent any one of several processes or more than one of them. On the one hand, physical illness can lead to depression: Poor health is a stressful life experience and therefore can stimulate depression, either directly or through functional limitations or pain (Williamson & Schulz, 1992; Zeiss, Lewinsohn, Rohde, & Seeley, 1996). Furthermore, physical illness (or its treatment by medications) can induce biological changes that trigger depression. For example, depression can appear with stroke, with Parkinson's disease, or with some cardiovascular medications (Frazer, Leicht, & Baker, 1996). On the other hand, the direction of causation can go from depression to physical illness. Depression is associated prospectively with poor health; that is, morbidity and mortality (Burvill & Hall, 1994; Parmelee, Katz, & Lawton, 1992). The mechanism could be psychoneuroimmune or just less effective self-care because of the depression. Finally, both depression and physical illness can be the outcome of some third process, or they can co-occur but represent unrelated medical events.

Physical health status is, of course, a correlate of depression at all ages. However, comorbidity of physical and psychological health assumes greater importance in older adults if only because of the increased prevalence of physical illness and physical impairment in older adults.

Cognitive Impairment

Cognitive deficits can be a consequence of depression, both depression and cognitive losses may be the result of some third process, or cognitive decline and depression may co-occur but represent unrelated etiologies. Specifically, cognitive impairment can lead to depression, insofar as recognizing one's cognitive losses can be depressing (Teri, 1996). Conversely, severe depression may lead to cognitive deficits on effortful tasks (La Rue, Goodman, & Spar, 1992). Finally, depression and dementia often coexist (Reifler, 1994). Depression may also be a prodromal symptom of dementia, with depression a consequence of the same structural or neurotransmitter changes that are leading to the dementia (Kral & Emery, 1989). There is one important clinical implication to be derived from uncertainties with respect to cause-and-effect relationships between depression and dementia: Where differential diagnosis is unclear, one should treat the depression.

Psychosocial Context

According to Murrell and his colleagues (Murrell & Meeks, 1992; Pfifer & Murrell, 1986), the best predictors of depression in older adults are previous depressive symptoms, poor health, loss events, and low social support, with support functioning both additively and interactively. At the same time, life events account for a notoriously small amount of variance in depression at any age (Monroe & Dupue, 1991), and it bears emphasis that the majority of older adults who experience losses do not become depressed. Moreover, loss events that function as risk factors for depression in younger people (e.g., social isolation, bereavement) are not as strongly associated with depression in old age as earlier in life, despite the fact that these events are common occurrences when individuals age (George,

1994). The one stressor that seems to have the most serious consequences with respect to depression in older adults is caring for an impaired family member (Pearlin & Skaff, 1995). Even here, most adults maintain their well-being.

WHAT THEORETICAL PERSPECTIVES ACCOUNT FOR DEPRESSION IN OLDER ADULTS?

Two theoretical perspectives organize existing literature about depression in older adults. The first is a life-span developmental diathesis–stress model (Gatz, Kasl-Godley, & Karel, 1996; Karel, 1997). This model takes the diathesis–stress perspective, which is widespread in adult psychopathology, and adds a developmental component. I suggest that not only the disorder, but also relevant diatheses—stressors—and protective factors all have developmental trajectories. Whether an individual experiences depression depends on a balance among diathesis (e.g., biological dispositions), stress (e.g., life crises), and protective factors (e.g., personal strengths). Because of their distinctive developmental trajectories, each influence takes on differential weight at different ages. On the basis of the review of risk factors and correlates in this chapter, biological diathesis could be seen as increasing in importance with age, whereas the role of stressful life events does not. Protective factors, in the form of coping, adaptation, and maturity, could be said to increase with maturity.

Mirowsky and Ross (1992) tested a similar model empirically, which is shown in Figure 13.3. The solid lines show the well-described curvilinear relationship between age and depressed mood and malaise indexes constructed from the CES–D, with depression symptom scores dropping from young adulthood to middle age, then rising from middle age to old age. The dashed lines show the residual after adjusting for education, gender, indications of diminished social status (loss of marital partner, retirement), reduction in income and financial hardship, physical dysfunction, and lessened personal control. What remains is the residual relationship between depression and age, displaying the inferred benefit of maturity. The analyses depicted in this figure demonstrate that increases in depressive symptoms in old age can be explained by factors such as physiological decline, chronic disease, and other age-related insults. This increase cancels out the decline in depression that would be expected because of greater maturity, practice in living, and integration of the self-concept.

A life-span developmental diathesis–stress model is useful in accounting for the relationship between age and depressive symptoms and in focusing attention on developmental changes in the significance of various risk factors. A second concept, affective reserve, is proposed to address age differences in the quality of depression (Gatz, 1998).

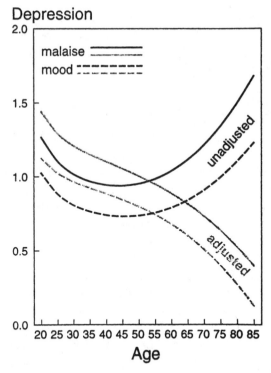

Figure 13.3. Average item response on malaise and mood components of depression. The two age curves are parallel. Black lines represent unadjusted curves, and gray lines represent curves adjusted for all independent variables: minority, female, education, employment, marriage, earnings, income, hardship, control, dysfunction. From "Age and Depression," by J. Mirowsky and C. E. Ross, *Journal of Health and Social Behavior*, 1992, Vol. 33, p. 199. Reprinted with permission.

Reserves are resources on which one can draw at times of stress. Almost all organs show an age-related decline in reserve capacity and in the ability to maintain homeostasis. There are individual differences in the amount of reserve with which people are born and individual differences in rates and reasons for decrease in reserve. Sufficient depletion of reserve leads to a threshold at which chronic disease appears (Fries, 1983). Expanding the model to include the idea of cognitive reserve is fairly well accepted. As the brain ages, there is a loss of neurons and alterations in neurotransmitter availability. With sufficient loss, the individual approaches a critical threshold at which diagnostic criteria for dementia are fulfilled (Mortimer, 1994). Stress forces an individual to dip into his or her reserve. Thus, cognitive losses become most visible when the person is distracted and reserve is less accessible (such as depression), as well as under demanding performance conditions when available reserve is most likely to be taxed or exceeded.

This conceptualization of reserve may be equally applicable to emo-

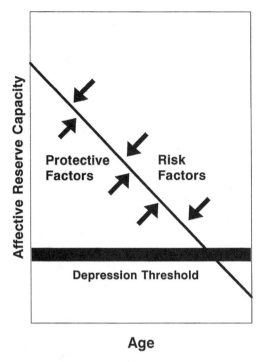

Figure 13.4. Threshold model for late life depression; schematic depiction of age-related decrease in affective reserve, with rate of decrease modified by risk or protective factors. Depressive disorder appears when amount of reserve drops below threshold.

tions, leading to a hypothetical construct of affective reserve. Indeed, affective reserve may have a physiologic basis, reflecting reduced neurotransmitter concentrations, neuroendocrine dysregulation, or a response to medical illness mediated by cytokine systems (Katz, 1998). In very old age, affective reserve may become reduced. Exhausting affective reserve would bring the individual to a threshold for mood disorder. Risk factors such as physical illness or certain medications would drive reserve down; protective factors would preserve reserve (see Figure 13.4). The type of depression that should result from reduced reserve would be characterized by ambiguous features such as fatigue. Thus, the concept of depleted affective reserve helps explain nondysphoric depression, or the depletion syndrome.

WHAT TREATMENTS HAVE BEEN SHOWN TO WORK?

Age is not prognostic of recovery from depression. Much the same array of treatments used with younger adults with depression can be successfully applied to helping older adults with depression. Psychotherapeutic interventions supported by outcome research include (a) cognitive and behavioral therapies and (b) brief psychodynamic, interpersonal, and life review therapies (Scogin & McElreath, 1994; Teri, Curtis, Gallagher-Thompson, & Thompson, 1994). These treatments may be administered individually or in groups.

We do not know enough to say whether there are differences in treatment and outcomes for late-onset versus early-onset depressive disorder; however, we can speculate that individuals who first encounter depression when they are older almost certainly have a reservoir of past successes in managing problems in their lives, and these skills can be brought to bear on dealing with their depression. Cognitive–behavioral strategies, such as increasing pleasant life events and recognizing dysfunctional thoughts in order to replace them with more adaptive self-statements, can effectively be taught to older adults with depression, including those with chronic illness (Rybarczyk et al., 1992) or memory loss (Teri, 1996).

In general, somatic approaches have been overemphasized in the treatment of depression in late life. Although psychopharmacological interventions do appear to be effective for acute treatment, research does not support the conclusion that psychopharmacology should be used with severe depression whereas psychotherapy should be used with mild depression (see Fiske, Kasl-Godley, & Gatz, 1998). Furthermore, Rokke and Scogin (1995) and others have shown that older adults seem to prefer behavioral treatments to other therapies and especially to pharmacotherapy and electroconvulsive therapy.

CAN ACCESS TO MENTAL HEALTH SERVICES BE IMPROVED?

Depression in older adults can frequently go unrecognized until it becomes severe. Because of delays, by the time that treatment is begun, the older adult with depression may more often seem like he or she is in a psychiatric emergency, posing a danger to himself or herself: explicitly by means of creating fears of suicide or implicitly by extreme lack of self-care (e.g., not eating). Concern about suicide is justified. For example, data obtained by Fiske, Gatz, and Brown (2000) for the state of California, in 1997 show that adults aged 65 and older accounted for just over 21.3% of all deaths by suicide, far greater than their proportion in the general population (which was 10.7% that year). Delay in referral for treatment, the sense of psychiatric emergency, and the prominence of somatic symptomatology all may inadvertently lead to greater emphasis on somatic treatments for the depression, once the distress has been recognized. Consequently, outreach and screening are of major importance.

A focus on primary care physicians has multiple rationales. First, there are elevated rates of depression in medical settings; conversely, older adults with mental disorders are more likely to see a general medical provider than a mental health specialist (Burns & Taube, 1990).

Second, it appears that physicians either do not recognize depression or choose not to treat it. In a sample of older individuals of Latino origin in Southern California, Kemp, Staples, and Lopez-Aqueres (1987) found that none of the respondents who scored in the depressed range on a screening instrument reported receiving any treatment for depression. It is notable that 90% had seen a physician within the past year, which could have been an opportunity for screening to occur.

Third, a particularly suggestive finding is the association between suicide and medical visits. Across a couple of studies, it appears that 75% of people who commit suicide have seen their doctor within the month, and 20% have seen their doctor within the past 24 hours (e.g., Conwell, Olsen, Caine, & Flannery, 1991).

The results of one study, conducted by Dorfman et al. (1995), supports the effectiveness of screening. They used a computer-assisted questionnaire with depression items from both the CES–D and another instrument. Among a sample of generally healthy community-dwelling adults aged 65 and older, they found that nearly three quarters of those with major depression were not being treated. However, when these individuals were referred to a mental health professional, two thirds did seek help. The results illustrate both the failure to screen, because these individuals had not heretofore been identified as having depressive disorder, and the fact that screening can be effective in linking older adults with significant distress to professional treatment.

FINAL COMMENT

Depression exists in a social, cultural, and political context. It is vitally important to recognize depression in older adults and to alleviate their misery. At the same time, it is misguided to pathologize older adults for experiencing negative feelings in response to situational factors that are predominantly the fault of society. The full range of preventive interventions must ultimately include changes in the environment and in the political structure.

REFERENCES

Abrams, R. C., Alexopoulos, G. S., & Young, R. C. (1987). Geriatric depression and *DSM–III–R* personality disorder criteria. *Journal of the American Geriatrics Society, 35,* 383–386.

American Psychiatric Association. (1980). *Diagnostic and statistical manual of mental disorders* (3rd ed.). Washington, DC: Author.

American Psychiatric Association. (1987). *Diagnostic and statistical manual of mental disorders* (3rd ed., rev.). Washington, DC: Author.

American Psychiatric Association. (1994). *Diagnostic and statistical manual of mental disorders* (4th ed.). Washington, DC: Author.

Baldwin, R. C., & Tomenson, B. (1995). Depression in later life: A comparison of symptoms and risk factors in early and late onset cases. *British Journal of Psychiatry, 167,* 649–652.

Berkman, L. F., Berkman, C. S., Kasl, S., Freeman, D. H., Leo, L., Ostfeld, A. M., Cornoni-Hunt, J., & Brody, J. A. (1986). Depressive symptoms in relation to physical health and function in the elderly. *American Journal of Epidemiology, 124,* 372–388.

Blazer, D. G. (1994). Epidemiology of late life depression. In L. S. Schneider, C. F. Reynolds III, B. D. Lebowitz, & A. J. Friedhoff (Eds.), *Diagnosis and treatment of depression in late life* (pp. 9–19). Washington, DC: American Psychiatric Press.

Blumenthal, M. D. (1980). Depressive illness in old age: Getting behind the mask. *Geriatrics, 35,* 34–43.

Burns, B. J., & Taube, D. A. (1990). Mental health services in general medical care and in nursing homes. In B. S. Fogel, A. Furino, & G. L. Gottlieb (Eds.), *Mental health policy for older Americans: Protecting minds at risk* (pp. 63–84). Washington, DC: American Psychiatric Press.

Burvill, P. W., & Hall, W. D. (1994). Predictors of increased mortality in elderly depressed patients. *International Journal of Geriatric Psychiatry, 9,* 219–227.

Conwell, Y., Olsen, K., Caine, E. D., & Flannery, C. (1991). Suicide in later life: Psychological autopsy findings. *International Psychogeriatrics, 3,* 59–66.

Dorfman, R. A., Lubben, J. E., Mayer-Oakes, A., Atchison, K., Schweitzer, S. O., DeJong, F. J., & Matthias, R. E. (1995). Screening for depression among a well elderly population. *Social Work, 40,* 295–304.

Fiske, A., Gatz, M., & Brown, E. (2000, April). Suicide in California Counties, 1985–1997. Paper presented at the meeting of the American Association of Suicidology, Los Angeles, California.

Fiske, A., Kasl-Godley, J. E., & Gatz, M. (1998). Mood disorders in late life. In A. S. Bellack & M. Hersen (Eds.), *Comprehensive clinical psychology* (Vol. 7, pp. 193–229). Oxford, England: Elsevier Science.

Forsell, Y., Jorm, A. F., & Winblad, B. (1994). Association of age, sex, cognitive dysfunction, and disability with major depressive symptoms in an elderly sample. *American Journal of Psychiatry, 151,* 1600–1604.

Frazer, D. W., Leicht, M. L., & Baker, M. D. (1996). Psychological manifestations of physical disease in the elderly. In L. L. Carstensen, B. A. Edelstein, & L. Dornbrand (Eds.), *The practical handbook of clinical gerontology* (pp. 217–235). Thousand Oaks, CA: Sage Publications.

Frerichs, R. R., Aneshensel, C. S., & Clark, V. A. (1981). Prevalence of depression in Los Angeles County. *American Journal of Epidemiology, 113,* 691–699.

Friedhoff, A. J. (1994). Consensus panel report. In L. S. Schneider, C. F. Reynolds III, B. D. Lebowitz, & A. J. Friedhoff (Eds.), *Diagnosis and treatment of depression in late life* (pp. 493–511). Washington, DC: American Psychiatric Press.

Fries, J. F. (1983). The compression of morbidity. *The Milbank Quarterly, 61,* 397–419.

Gallo, J. J., Anthony, J. C., & Muthén, B. O. (1994). Age differences in the symptoms of depression: A latent trait analysis. *Journal of Gerontology: Psychological Sciences, 49,* P251–P264.

Gallo, J. J., Rabins, P. V., Lyketsos, C. G., Tien, A. Y., & Anthony, J. C. (1997). Depression without sadness: Functional outcomes of nondysphoric depression in later life. *Journal of the American Geriatrics Society, 45,* 570–578.

Gatz, M. (1998). Towards a developmentally-informed theory of mental disorder in older adults. In J. Lomranz (Ed.), *Handbook of aging and mental health: An integrated approach* (pp. 101–129). New York: Plenum Press.

Gatz, M., & Hurwicz, M.-L. (1990). Are old people more depressed? Cross-sectional data on CES–D factors. *Psychology and Aging, 5,* 284–290.

Gatz, M., Johansson, B., Berg, S., Pedersen, N., & Reynolds, C. (1993). A cross-national self-report measure of depressive symptomatology. *International Psychogeriatrics, 5,* 267–274.

Gatz, M., Kasl-Godley, J. E., & Karel, M. J. (1996). Aging and mental disorders. In J. E. Birren & K. W. Schaie (Eds.), *Handbook of the psychology of aging* (4th ed., pp. 367–382). San Diego, CA: Academic Press.

George, L. K. (1994). Social factors and depression in late life. In L. S. Schneider, C. F. Reynolds, B. D. Lebowitz, & A. J. Friedhoff (Eds.), *Diagnosis and treatment of depression in late life* (pp. 131–154). Washington, DC: American Psychiatric Press.

Henderson, A. S., Jorm, A. F., MacKinnon, A., Christensen, H., Scott, L. R., Korten, A. E., & Doyle, C. (1993). The prevalence of depressive disorders and the distribution of depressive symptoms in later life: A survey using Draft ICD-10 and DSM–III–R. *Psychological Medicine, 23,* 719–729.

Hertzog, C., Van Alstine, J., Usala, P. D., Hultsch, D. F., & Dixon, R. (1990). Measurement properties of the Center for Epidemiology Studies Depression Scale (CES–D) in older populations. *Psychological Assessment, 2,* 64–72.

Jarvik, L. F. (1976). Aging and depression: Some unanswered questions. *Journal of Gerontology, 31,* 324–326.

Kahn, R. L. (1977). Perspectives in the evaluation of psychological mental health problems for the aged. In W. D. Gentry (Ed.), *Geropsychology: A model of training and clinical service* (pp. 9–19). Cambridge, MA: Ballinger.

Karel, M. J. (1997). Aging and depression: Vulnerability and stress across adulthood. *Clinical Psychology Review, 17,* 847–879.

Katz, I. R. (1998). Depression as a pivotal component in secondary aging: Opportunities for research, treatment, and prevention. In J. Lomranz (Ed.), *Hand-*

book of aging and mental health: An integrated approach (pp. 463–482). New York: Plenum.

Kemp, B. J., Staples, F., & Lopez-Aqueres, W. L. (1987). Epidemiology of depression and dysphoria in an elderly Hispanic population: Prevalence and correlates. Journal of the American Geriatrics Society, 35, 920–926.

Kessler, R. C., Foster, C., Webster, P. S., & House, J. S. (1992). The relationship between age and depressive symptoms in two national surveys. Psychology and Aging, 7, 119–126.

Koenig, H. G., Pappas, P., Holsinger, T., & Bachar, J. R. (1995). Assessing diagnostic approaches to depression in medically ill older adults: How reliably can mental health professionals make judgments about the cause of symptoms? Journal of the American Geriatrics Society, 43, 472–478.

Kral, V. A., & Emery, O. A. (1989). Long-term follow-up of depressive pseudodementia of the aged. Canadian Journal of Psychiatry, 34, 445–446.

La Rue, A., Goodman, S., & Spar, J. E. (1992). Risk factors for memory impairment in geriatric depression. Neuropsychiatry, Neuropsychology, and Behavioral Neurology, 5, 178 184.

Leuchter, A. F. (1994). Brain structural and functional correlates of late-life depression. In L. S. Schneider, C. F. Reynolds III, B. D. Lebowitz, & A. J. Friedhoff (Eds.), Diagnosis and treatment of depression in late life (pp. 117–130). Washington, DC: American Psychiatric Press.

Meyers, B. S., & Greenberg, R. (1986). Late-life delusional depression. Journal of Affective Disorders, 11, 133–137.

Meyers, B. S., Greenberg, R., & Mei-Tal, V. (1985). Delusional depression in the elderly. In C. A. Shamoian (Ed.), Treatment of affective disorders in the elderly (pp. 19–28). Washington, DC: American Psychiatric Press.

Mirowsky, J., & Ross, C. E. (1992). Age and depression. Journal of Health and Social Behavior, 33, 187–205.

Monroe, S. M., & Dupue, R. A. (1991). Life stress and depression. In J. Becker & A. Kleinman (Eds.), Psychosocial aspects of depression (pp. 101–130). Hillsdale, NJ: Erlbaum.

Mortimer, J. A. (1994). What are the risk factors for dementia? In F. Huppert, C. Brayne, & D. O'Connor (Eds.), Dementia and normal aging (pp. 208–229). Cambridge, England: Cambridge University Press.

Murrell, S. A., Himmelfarb, S., & Wright, K. (1983). Prevalence of depression and its correlates in older adults. American Journal of Epidemiology, 117, 173–185.

Murrell, S. A., & Meeks, S. (1992). Depressive symptoms in older adults: Predispositions, resources, and life experiences. In K. W. Schaie & M. P. Lawton (Eds.), Annual review of gerontology and geriatrics (Vol. 11, pp. 261–275). New York: Springer.

Nalick, J. (1998, Winter). Go for the golden years. USC Health, 5(3), 4–7.

Newmann, J. P. (1989). Aging and depression. Psychology and Aging, 4, 150–165.

Newmann, J. P., Engel, R. J., & Jensen, J. E. (1991). Changes in depressive-symptom experiences among older women. *Psychology and Aging, 6,* 212–222.

Parmelee, P. A., Katz, I. R., & Lawton, M. P. (1992). Depression and mortality among institutionalized aged. *Journal of Gerontology: Psychological Sciences, 47,* P3–P10.

Pearlin, L. I., & Skaff, M. M. (1995). Stressors and adaptation in late life. In M. Gatz (Ed.), *Emerging issues in mental health and aging* (pp. 97–123). Washington, DC: American Psychological Association.

Pfifer, J. F., & Murrell, S. A. (1986). Etiologic factors in the onset of depressive symptoms in older adults. *Journal of Abnormal Psychology, 95,* 282–291.

Regier, D. A., Boyd, J. H., Burke, J. D., Rae, D. S., Myers, J. K., Kramer, M., Robins, L. N., George, L. K., Karno, M., & Locke, B. Z. (1988). One-month prevalence of mental disorders in the United States. *Archives of General Psychiatry, 45,* 977–986.

Reifler, B. V. (1994). Depression: Diagnosis and comorbidity. In L. S. Schneider, C. F. Reynolds III, B. D. Lebowitz, & A. J. Friedhoff (Eds.), *Diagnosis and treatment of depression in late life* (pp. 55–59). Washington, DC: American Psychiatric Press.

Rokke, P., & Scogin, F. (1995). The credibility of treatments for depression among younger and older adults. *Journal of Clinical Geropsychology, 1,* 243–257.

Rybarczyk, B., Gallagher-Thompson, D., Rodman, J., Zeiss, A., Gantz, F. E., & Yesavage, J. (1992). Applying cognitive–behavioral psychotherapy to the chronically ill elderly: Treatment issues and case illustration. *International Psychogeriatrics, 4,* 127–140.

Scogin, F., & McElreath, L. (1994). Efficacy of psychosocial treatments for geriatric depression: A quantitative review. *Journal of Consulting and Clinical Psychology, 62,* 69–74.

Steingart, A., & Herrmann, N. (1991). Major depressive disorder in the elderly: The relationship between age of onset and cognitive impairment. *International Journal of Geriatric Psychiatry, 6,* 593–598.

Teri, L. (1996). Depression in Alzheimer's disease. In M. Hersen & V. B. Van Hasselt (Eds.), *Psychological treatment of older adults* (pp. 209–222). New York: Plenum Press.

Teri, L., Curtis, J., Gallagher-Thompson, D., & Thompson, L. (1994). Cognitive–behavior therapy with depressed older adults. In L. S. Schneider, C. F. Reynolds, B. D. Lebowitz, & A. J. Friedhoff (Eds.), *Diagnosis and treatment of depression in late life* (pp. 279–291). Washington, DC: American Psychiatric Press.

van Ojen, R., Hooijer, C., Bezemer, D., Jonker, C., Lindeboom, J., & van Tilburg, W. (1995). Late-life depressive disorder in the community: II. The relationship between psychiatric history, MMSE and family history. *British Journal of Psychiatry, 166,* 316–319.

Weissman, M. M., Bruce, M. L., Leaf, P. J., Florio, L. P., & Holzer III, C. (1991).

Affective disorders. In L. N. Robins & D. A. Regier (Eds.), *Psychiatric disorders in America* (pp. 53–80). New York: Free Press.

Williamson, G. M., & Schulz, R. (1992). Physical illness and symptoms of depression among elderly outpatients. *Psychology and Aging, 7,* 343–351.

Zeiss, A. M., Lewinsohn, P. M., Rohde, P., & Seeley, J. R. (1996). Relationship of physical disease and functional impairment to depression in older people. *Psychology and Aging, 11,* 572–581.

VII

PSYCHOTHERAPY
AND AGING

PART VII: PSYCHOTHERAPY AND AGING

In a field rich with competing theories and challenged by funding crises, how is psychotherapy progressing? The authors of the next chapter take a bird's-eye view of current trends in research, policy, and practice that affect the field of psychotherapy, especially with older adults. Consistent with their focus on integration within psychotherapy, John C. Norcross and Bob G. Knight chose to examine the commonalities and uniquenesses of issues within mainstream psychotherapy (with general adult populations) and geropsychology in an integrated chapter. They address four themes in current psychotherapy theory and practice: (a) the industrialization of mental health care, (b) the movement toward empirically validated treatments and treatment manuals, (c) the movement toward self-help, and (d) self-change method. For each theme, the authors describe the key issues in the mainstream of psychotherapy and then examine how that theme is being enacted in work with older adults.

Norcross and Knight start with the most imminent challenge: the industrialization of mental health care. How have older adults fared in the managed care environment? Clearly, most practitioners do not like the impact of managed care on psychotherapy. Although its potential advantages (e.g., multidisciplinary care focused on prevention) seem well suited for older adults, pragmatic realities have undermined the potentials. Indeed, the authors argue that ultimately older adults will experience more, rather than fewer, barriers to receiving appropriate psychological services.

Although partially driven by demands for cost containment, practice guidelines and empirically validated treatments have been popular approaches to demonstrating the validity and efficacy of psychotherapy. This movement has favored time-limited structured therapies, with some bias toward cognitive–behavioral approaches. On the one hand, rigorous, controlled research outcome studies have been critical to survival in this environment because these studies document the efficacy of treatment. Indeed, the field has put considerable effort into establishing practice guidelines that are based on empirically validated treatment approaches. On the other hand, the cases seen by practitioners are often more complex than those accepted into treatment-outcomes studies. Norcross and Knight argue that this may be the case for older adults whose biological and social problems are interwoven with the psychological concerns.

The authors' advocacy for a move toward psychotherapy integration attempts to address the complexity of real cases, moving beyond the safety of established therapy protocols. The seeming paradox of needing empirical validation to justify work to payers and to guide clinicians' efforts, but seeing clients whose circumstances are more complex than the research protocols address is not easily resolved in the current climate of industrialized mental health care. Norcross and Knight examine how these forces are working within the mainstream field and make some predictions about what may lie ahead.

Psychotherapy theory and research on older adults shows patterns that are similar to those evident in the mainstream literature, although the geropsychology literature is much smaller. In controlled research studies, psychotherapy works well. At the same time, most older adult clients have needs that are far more complex (especially medically and socially) than those of young or midlife adults, and thus strict psychotherapy protocols are often too restrictive to meet the full array of needs. For geropsychologists, service delivery patterns often need to be nontraditional (e.g., complex assessments and service delivery outreach are key to effectively addressing the full range of needs within a community). Many of the constraints placed on practitioners by the managed care industry are especially limiting to those working with older adults.

We predict that you will be intrigued as Knight and Norcross boldly label current trends and make future predictions about important contextual, theoretical, and practice themes that will affect psychotherapy as it deals with the aging revolution and the field of geropsychology as it matures into a substantial discipline.

14

PSYCHOTHERAPY AND AGING IN THE 21ST CENTURY: INTEGRATIVE THEMES

JOHN C. NORCROSS AND BOB G. KNIGHT

Mainstream psychotherapy research and psychotherapy integration rarely address aging. Hundreds of meta-analyses have aggregated psychotherapy outcome studies (see Lipsey & Wilson, 1993, and Prochaska & Norcross, 1998, for summaries), but we are aware of only one that examined psychotherapy with elderly people (Scogin & McElreath, 1994). Of the two large handbooks on psychotherapy integration (Norcross & Goldfried, 1992; Stricker & Gold, 1993), only one chapter explicitly addresses an integrative approach to psychotherapy with the elderly population, which is written from an object-relations perspective with some cognitive therapy techniques (Papouchis & Passman, 1993). Casebooks on integrative and eclectic therapies do not fare any better: Individual patients in one casebook averaged 32 years of age, with the oldest being 51 (Norcross, 1987), and 29 years of age in the other, with the oldest being 44 (Saltzman & Norcross, 1990).

On the other side, the smaller literature on psychotherapy with elderly people rarely intersects with the mainstream. For example, a recent volume dedicated to psychotherapy with the aging population is clearly divided into distinct systems of intervention, with little reference to integrative concepts or practice (Zarit & Knight, 1996). The relationship between integrative psychotherapy and the psychology of aging has historically been characterized by a benign neglect.

Our goal in this chapter is to initiate a meaningful dialogue between individual psychotherapy and the aging revolution. Such a dialogue, we believe, can enrich both our understanding of psychotherapy with clients of all ages and our understanding of older adults. We outline four predominant themes in individual psychotherapy during the new millennium and, for each theme, address its relevance for the aging population. Breadth rather than depth will obviously be the route as we review the themes of industrialization of mental health care, emergence of practice guidelines and empirically validated treatments (EVTs), proliferation of self-help and self-change methods, and the ascendancy of psychotherapy integration.

THE INDUSTRIALIZATION OF MENTAL HEALTH CARE

Let us begin this whirlwind tour of individual psychotherapy by addressing the rhinoceros in the living room: managed care. Managed care plans now cover 80% of the Americans who attain their health benefits through their employer. With recent legal and financial inducements to run Medicare through managed care, an even higher percentage of older Americans will soon be under the umbrella of managed care—of, if you prefer, the umbrella of managed costs.

It would be unfair and inaccurate to lump all managed care into a monolithic entity. But for the sake of our presentation, we shall broadly frame the theme as "industrialization" and simply list the common mechanisms of "managing" psychotherapy:

- restricting access to treatment (e.g., only "medically necessary" services for *DSM* Axis I disorders)
- limiting the amount of psychotherapy (e.g., 4–10 sessions)
- using lower cost providers (e.g., master's- and baccalaureate-level therapists)
- implementing utilization review (e.g., after 3 or 4 sessions)
- approving primarily short-term, symptom-focused psychotherapies
- shifting to outpatient care (e.g., hospitalize only if a suicide attempt is made)
- permitting referrals only through the primary care physician "gatekeepers"
- restricting the patient's freedom of choice in regard to providers and treatments.

In HMOs specifically, the dominant mental health services are outpatient care, the use of less expensive providers, limited numbers of visits, and a preference for group and family interventions (Mechanic & Aiken, 1989; Wetle & Mark, 1990). There is also a tendency to emphasize the role of primary care physicians and therefore, perhaps unintentionally, the use of psychotropic drugs as the primary form of intervention. Mental health care in the general health sector (not only HMOs) is primarily prescription of psychotropic medications: The ratio of drugs to psychotherapy is 4:1 for this service sector (Burns & Taube, 1990).

Health care is manifesting two cardinal characteristics of any industrial revolution (Cummings, 1986, 1987). First, the producer—in our case, the psychotherapist—is losing control over the services as this control shifts to business interests. Second, practitioners' incomes are decreasing because industrialization minimizes labor costs. Not surprisingly, income surveys consistently demonstrate that, as a group, practicing psychologists are losing income, when adjusted for inflation. Depending on the survey and the methodology, starting around 1995 psychologists averaged 2%–5% less net income per year and, adjusting for inflation, have lost even more ("Fee, practice, and managed care survey," 1995; Rothbaum, Bernstein, Haller, Phelps, & Kohout, 1998). The length of inpatient psychiatric stays has decreased steadily, while reimbursement per hospitalization episode or per capita has gradually eroded. And the worst has probably not yet arrived financially.

Similar concerns arise for older adult consumers of managed care. The radical changes in health care are leading to a "medical–industrial complex" in which both consumers and providers are losing control of the definition and treatment of health problems (Estes, 1992). Especially with regard to the older population, mental health policy is a footnote to health policy (as Kiesler, 1992, argued in general). Mental health services for older adults suffer from the "last in, first out" rule as well as from demands to do something that has not previously been done while saving money. Managed care is likely to change the focus of mental health services from the traditional client, with depression, anxiety, psychosis, and so forth, to clients with psychological factors affecting medical problems—precisely the group among managed care enrollees most likely to show a cost-offset effect from treatment (Knight & Kaskie, 1995).

A recent study of 487 psychologists in the American Psychological Association's (APA's) Division of Clinical Psychology (Division 12) revealed that 75% accept some managed care patients, and 25% accept none (Norcross, Karg, & Prochaska, 1997). The median percentages of managed care patients in Division 12 psychologists' caseloads in 1993, 1995, and 1997 (anticipated) increased exponentially. The percentage of managed care patients expanded tenfold—from 5% to 50%—over the 4-year period. These are the footprints of a rhinoceros.

How is this affecting psychotherapy, according to psychologists? In a word: negatively. In two words: very negatively. A total of 15,918 psychologists responding to the APA's Practice Directorate (1996) CAPP Practitioner Survey were asked to evaluate the impact of managed care on a 7-point scale. Fully 80% perceived managed care as having a negative impact (26%, high negative; 37%, medium negative; and 17%, low negative impact). When asked to endorse the top practice concerns from a list of 18, the psychologists most frequently nominated concerns related to managed care: managed care changing clinical practice, decreased income due to managed care fee structure, excess precertification and utilization review requirements of managed care panels, and ethical conflicts raised by managed care.

How does this picture compare to the practice rules developed in the geriatric mental health literature? For older psychotherapy clients, the potential strength of HMOs would be the high potential for interdisciplinary, coordinated care within a single managed health system. In principle, mental health and physical health care could be completely integrated, with shared record keeping, a single-source pharmacy for improved medication coordination, and providers united by concern for the patient's long-term health. The tendency to move toward carve-out groups of mental health specialists providing mental health services tends to eliminate this potential advantage. Another potential, although as yet unrealized, strength of the HMO model in application to older adults is the preference for group and family therapy in the delivery of mental health services.

The weaker elements of HMOs in meeting the mental health needs of the elderly population are seen in the failures to provide specialized assessment of mental disorders in older patients, to conduct aggressive outreach, and to provide home visits. Although there is no systematically collected evidence on assessment of mental disorders in older patients in managed care, the complexity of accurate assessment in older adults runs counter to the managed care emphasis on use of nonspecialized service providers. With regard to the length of therapy, the application of time limits derived from research and professional experience with younger adults to the older population is likely to put at a disadvantage older adults who can be expected to need more time in treatment to reach similar goals. This is even more likely to be true of the over-75 patient than of the young-old 60-something patient (Knight, 1988).

Managed care in general, and HMOs in particular, are also not well suited organizationally for active outreach, case finding, and home visits. When a guiding principle of an organization is cost containment, seeking outpatients who are not actively pursuing costly services is typically seen as counterproductive. To the extent that older adults underutilize outpatient services respective to their need and may not even recognize their own need for mental health services, public and private sector approaches that encourage outreach efforts on the part of psychologists are needed (Knight, 1989).

In summary, the angst and disillusionment of practitioners toward managed care are almost palpable. Many speak of the "catastrophe that overshadows our profession" and, after careers dedicated to the profession of psychology, find themselves "reduced to numbers in corporate computers" (Graham, 1995, p. 4). The impact of managed care on organized psychology has become an urgent and contentious matter not only for practitioners but also for faculty and students involved in the training and research enterprises.

We do not subscribe to the Cassandran prophecies of the demise of psychotherapy. At the same time, we fully recognize that in the new millennium psychotherapy will increasingly be performed in the public marketplace by subdoctoral professionals for briefer intervals and following "practice guidelines" and approved lists of empirically validated treatments (EVTs). Control of psychotherapy is shifting from the therapist and the client to the payer, with associated shifts in goals and "approved" or reimbursable treatments. These changes are likely to increase the barriers that prevent older adults from obtaining therapy for psychological problems.

EMERGENCE OF PRACTICE GUIDELINES AND EVTs

Beginning in 1993, APA's Division of Clinical Psychology has endeavored to identify effective psychological interventions and to publicize the existence of these treatments to clinical psychologists, third-party payers, training programs, and the public at large. This work has been cast as a logical extension of the Boulder model of scientist–practitioner training (Chambless, 1999; Task Force on Promotion and Dissemination of Psychological Procedures, 1995).

A succession of task forces appointed by presidents of the Division of Clinical Psychology have constructed and elaborated a list of EVTs or the more recent and accurate term, empirically supported treatments. This work continues to evolve, because not all treatments have yet been reviewed, and new evidence for treatments emerges monthly. The task forces have concentrated on specific treatments for specific psychological problems, mainly in adult populations, and have periodically updated these lists in *The Clinical Psychologist* (Chambless et al., 1996, 1998; Task Force on Promotion and Dissemination of Psychological Procedures, 1995).

The task forces follow a number of decision rules in determining what is sufficient evidence for listing a treatment. Decisions are largely based on randomized controlled studies that must have passed muster for methodological soundness. At minimum, for a designation of *well-established* treatment there must be either two sound studies conducted by independent investigators in which the EVT was demonstrated to be superior to another treatment or to a placebo condition or equivalent in efficacy to another treatment that has already been designated well established, or there must be more than nine single case design experiments demonstrating that the therapy works. A treatment can be designated as *probably efficacious* if the comparison is to a waiting list control, if results are available from only one laboratory, or if there are more than three but fewer than nine single-case-design studies.

The EVT project has been widely lauded and widely condemned. Space does not permit a thorough review of these arguments and counterarguments except to point out that the listing favors cognitive–behavioral and manualized treatments—the latter a requirement for consideration by the task force (Norcross, 1999).

The EVT effort in clinical psychology is akin to movements within American psychiatry and British medicine to foster evidence-based practice by educating clinicians about the research base for practice. The American Psychiatric Association has promulgated eight published practice guidelines, ranging from treatment of schizophrenia to eating disorders to nicotine addiction. Another case in point is the controversial Agency for Health Care Policy and Research's guidelines on depression in primary care (Depression Guideline Panel, 1993). With an obvious biomedical bias, the guidelines suggest that a referral to a mental health professional need not occur until after two unsuccessful antidepressant trials have been conducted by the primary care physician. The devaluation of psychotherapy and the supremacy of medication were in full evidence (for those interested in data rather than polemics, we recommend the measured and scholarly rebuttal by Munoz, Hollon, McGrath, Rehm, & Van den Bos, 1994).

In response to the proliferation of guidelines, APA created a task force to develop a template by which to evaluate and direct guidelines (Task Force on Psychological Intervention Guidelines, 1995). Note that APA did not promulgate treatment guidelines, just a template to judge and direct other guidelines.

With this effort, as in with other trends in mainstream psychotherapy, older adults have been only marginally included. A special section on empirically supported psychological therapies in the *Journal of Consulting and Clinical Psychology* did not include an article on psychotherapy with older adults (Kendall & Chambless, 1998). The separate Task Force on Effective Psychological Interventions: A Life Span Perspective has concentrated much of its efforts on treatment of children and prevention research (Chambless, 1999) and published a special issue on empirically supported psychosocial interventions for children in the *Journal of Clinical Child Psychology* (Lonigan & Elbert, 1998). Where is the older adult in these compilations, discussions, and prescriptions of the empirical outcome data on psychotherapy?

Fortunately, the guidelines for empirically supported psychotherapy have been applied to the literature on psychological interventions with older adults by Gatz et al. (in press) who reported that behavioral and environmental interventions for older adults with dementia meet the standards for well-established empirically supported therapy. Probably efficacious therapies for the older adult include cognitive–behavioral treatment of sleep disorders and psychodynamic, cognitive, and behavioral treatments for clinical depression. For nonsyndromal problems of aging, memory retraining and cognitive training are probably efficacious in slowing cognitive decline. Life review and reminiscence are probably efficacious in improvement of depressive symptoms or in producing higher levels of life satisfaction.

A critical problem in the application of these guidelines to the aged population is that research on psychotherapy with older adults is a young field. The earliest empirical investigation of which we are aware was published in 1971, and that involved behavioral retraining of toileting behavior (Sanavio, 1971). The empirical study of outpatient interventions for depression began in 1981 (Perrotta & Meacham, 1981). By contrast, psychotherapy research with younger adults has roots in the 1920s, and modern research methods are traced to Eysenck's classic 1952 review (Eysenck, 1952; Strupp & Howard, 1992). Thus, the relatively cautious recommendations regarding outcomes with older adults reflect a lack of research rooted in historical causes rather than evidence that older adults do less well than younger ones. A meta-analysis of psychological interventions in the treatment of depression in later life shows an aggregate effect size ($d =$ 0.78; Scogin & McElreath, 1994) roughly equal to that found in another meta-analysis for antidepressant medications ($d = 0.57$; Schneider, 1994) and roughly equal to that found for younger adults in meta-analyses using cognitive–behavioral approaches ($d = 0.73$; Robinson, Berman, & Neimeyer, 1990; although some studies overlap with those analyzed by Scogin & McElreath, 1994).

The point that psychological interventions for elderly people may have fewer empirical studies supporting them because of historical neglect rather than because of absence of benefit is all too likely overlooked. The National Institutes of Health Consensus Development Conference on the Diagnosis and Treatment of Depression in Late Life (Schneider, Reynolds, Lebowitz, & Friedhoff, 1994) strongly recommended that "depressed elderly people should be treated vigorously with sufficient doses of antidepressants and for a sufficient length of time to maximize the likelihood of therapy" (Friedhoff, 1994, p. 509) but cautiously noted that "psychosocial treatments can also play an essential role in the care of elderly patients who have significant life crises, lack social support, or lack coping skills to deal with their life situations" (p. 509). This recommendation was made in spite of an earlier note that "available information from randomized controlled clinical trials in elderly patients is meager compared with that for younger patient groups" (p. 499). The recommendations seem to be drawn from the observation that there are more studies on pharmacological treatment of depression (25 randomized controlled trials cited by Friedhoff, 1994, compared to 17 randomized trials of psychological intervention cited by Scogin & McElreath, 1994) and from the fact that the consensus committee was dominated by physicians.

In summary, practice guidelines, however controversial, are growing in number and influence. Clinical practice in the new millennium will be expected to adhere to them—for better and for worse. Whatever the general effects of the movement are on empirically supported therapies for psychotherapy, the specific impact on older adults will be immense if more resources are not devoted to outcome studies on psychological interventions with elderly people. Against the historical backdrop of benign neglect of older adults by mainstream individual psychotherapy, and considering the current emphasis on the gatekeeper role of the primary care physician in managed care, psychotherapy with older adults could be endangered by the application of policies based on the irrational principle that lack of evidence equals negative evidence.

THE PROLIFERATION OF SELF-HELP AND SELF-CHANGE METHODS

Converging forces have contributed to the proliferation of self-help and self-change movements. One is managed care: Minimal professional treatment means that adjunctive and ancillary methods must be incorporated. A second reason is their widespread availability and lower costs. A third is the small percentage of distressed people receiving professional treatment: Although about 30% of the adult American population has a diagnosable mental disorder in any given year, only one in five of these obtained treatment in the mental health specialty sector in the past year (Kessler et al., 1994). The President's Commission on Mental Health (1978) concluded that only about one fourth of people suffering from a behavioral disorder have ever been in treatment and, when they do seek help, it is typically to non-health professionals—with clergy, physicians, and lawyers leading the way (Veroff, Douvan, & Kulka, 1981). That leaves a lot of people struggling on their own, without formal treatment.

Despite the professional proclivity to devalue these self-change and self-help methods, their success is reasonably well established. Lambert (1976) reviewed the empirical evidence on the rate at which neurotic patients improve without professional treatment over a period of 6 months.

The median percentage of patients who demonstrated improvement was 43%. Several meta-analyses have determined that the effectiveness of self-help programs substantially exceed that of no-treatment control groups (Kurtzweil, Scogin, & Rosen, 1996; Scogin, Bynum, & Calhoon, 1990). Gould and Clum (1993), for example, conducted a meta-analysis on the effectiveness of 40 self-help studies that used no-treatment, waiting-list, or placebo comparisons as control groups. The effect sizes for self-help interventions (.76 at posttreatment and .53 at follow-up) were nearly as large as therapist-assisted interventions within the same studies. Fears, depression, headache, and sleep disturbance were especially amenable to self-help approaches.

For multiple reasons, then, people in their natural environments, and psychologists in their consulting rooms, both recommend self-help and self-change resources. These self-help strategies entail, among other things, support groups, self-help books, self-initiated behavior change, and the inspiration and guidance of autobiographies of others who have conquered a particular disorder.

Support or mutual-aid groups have a long and distinguished history in the behavioral disorders. Unlike peer and nonprofessional services under the supervision of professionals, self-help or support groups are voluntary associations of people who act as both helper and helpee (Humphreys & Rappaport, 1994). Outcome studies on these groups are infrequent and plagued with methodological problems; nonetheless, the nascent research shows positive results. A meta-analysis (Tonigan, Toscoova, & Miller, 1995) summarizing the findings of Alcoholics Anonymous (AA) affiliation and outcome found that most AA studies lacked sufficient statistical power to detect relationships of interest. Nonetheless, AA participation and reduction in drinking were positively related, especially in outpatient populations. Several well-controlled evaluations of 12-step programs for addictive disorders show that they generally perform as effectively as professional treatment, including at follow-up (Morgenstern, Labouvie, McCrady, Kahler, & Frey, 1997; Ouimette, Finney, & Moos, 1997; Project MATCH Research Group, 1997). Similarly, "effectiveness" research, conducted on psychotherapy practiced in naturalistic settings, as opposed to "efficacy" research, based on randomized controlled studies, has generally found that clients rate 12-step groups as helpful as professional psychotherapists (e.g., Seligman, 1995).

Psychologically oriented self-help groups for older adults are rare, if one means by this term groups that are created and run by the members. The American Association of Retired Persons is the prime example of a self-help group, but its focus is advocacy rather than psychological in nature. Caregiving groups have been a major component of the mental health and aging scene for about 20 years (see Toseland & Rossiter, 1989, for a review) and often function like self-help groups. Some degree of professional leadership or sponsorship is common, but this is often the case for self-help groups for younger adults as well (Knight, Wollert, Levy, Frame, & Padgett, 1980). Most evaluations of such caregiver interventions are based on groups organized by the researcher; these evaluations are less encouraging with regard to caregiving groups than is true of the other self-help approaches (d = 0.31 for dysphoric mood; Knight, Lutzky, & Macofsky-Urban, 1993). Self-help groups for widows have also been an important part of mental health and aging for a number of years and are frequently offered by the American Association of Retired Persons, by other community groups, and by some mortuaries. Outcome research has not been reported on these groups.

Bibliotherapy (the use of self-help books with or without formal treatment) and the use of autobiographies as adjuncts to psychotherapy also serve as valuable self-help resources. A recent meta-analysis examined the efficacy of bibliotherapy compared to control groups and therapist-administered treatments (Marrs, 1995). The mean effect size of biblio-therapy was 0.56—a moderately powerful effect and one not different than therapist-administered treatments. Another meta-analysis of the effectiveness of bibliotherapy for unipolar depression (Cuijpers, 1997) delivered essentially the same verdict: The mean effect size was 0.82—a large effect and one not different from the effect sized obtained by individual and group treatment.

Two published reports have appeared on bibliotherapy with older adults. The first (Scogin, Hamblin, & Beutler, 1987) reported an effect size of 0.91 for the use of bibliotherapy versus attention placebo for depression: 1.44 as compared to no treatment. The second (Scogin, Jamison, & Gochnauer, 1989) reported an effect size of 0.70 for the use of Burn's *Feeling Good* versus no treatment and of 1.11 for the use of Lewinsohn, Munoz, Youngren, and Zeiss's (1986) *Control Your Depression* versus no treatment. Neither book is specifically oriented to older adults.

Practicing psychologists have apparently reached similar conclusions on their own, because the vast majority—85% to 88%—prescribe self-help books to supplement their treatment (e.g., Clifford, Norcross, & Sommer, 1998; Marx, Royalty, Gyorky, & Stern, 1992; Norcross, et. al., 2000; Starker, 1988). About one third of practitioners also recommend autobiographies written by mental health clients to their psychotherapy patients (Clifford et al., 1998).

Self-help books and autobiographical accounts promise similar therapeutic benefits as adjuncts to ongoing psychotherapy. Specifically, they can provide phenomenological accounts of behavioral disorders in everyday terms, enhance identification and empathy, generate hope and insight, offer concrete advice and techniques, explain treatment strategies, and summarize research findings (Pardeck & Pardeck, 1992). When done right, the use of autobiographies and self-help materials can complement and accelerate the process of professional treatment.

In an attempt to identify the most useful self-help books, Santrock, Minnett, and Campbell (1994) conducted a national survey of clinical and counseling psychologists and asked them to rate only the books with which they were sufficiently familiar from the list of more than 350 self-help books. To be eligible for the top 25 list, a self-help book had to be rated by a minimum of 75 mental health professionals. Table 14.1 lists the 25 books with the highest average rating in order from highest to lowest in their study. Ten of these 25 volumes concern themselves directly with children; none concern themselves directly with aging or the elderly population.

Yet there are many self-help books that are helpful and specific to older adults. Skinner and Vaughan's *Enjoy Old Age: A Program of Self-Management* (1983), Linkletter's *Old Age Is Not for Sissies: Choices for Senior Americans* (1988), Friedan's *Fountain of Age* (1993), and Gerike's *Old Is Not a Four Letter Word* (1997) all address the aging process as such. Mace and Rabin's *The 36 Hour Day* (1982) and Zarit, Orr, and Zarit's *Hidden Victims: Caregivers Under Stress* (1985) are classics in the caregiving intervention field. The principles of psychotherapy with the elderly population (e.g., Knight, 1996b) could be generalized to the self-help literature as well: The tools of psychotherapy are likely to be specific to the problems of older clients rather than to age itself. This principle would suggest that books on grief will be useful for older adults as will self-help books on adjusting to the specific illnesses to which an older client may be struggling to adapt (Neysmith-Roy & Kleisinger, 1997). The research of Scogin and his associates, cited above (Scogin et al., 1987, 1989), which shows the effectiveness of using self-help books developed for depressed younger adults with depressed older adults, supports the notion that it is the problem and not the age of the client that is most important.

Autobiographies written by recovering or recovered psychiatric patients may also play a curative role in self-help and self-change efforts. A recent attempt to identify the most useful autobiographies (Clifford, Norcross, & Sommer, 1998) ascertained psychologists' recommendations of autobiographies to their patients during psychotherapy. To be eligible for the top 12 list, an autobiography had to be rated by a minimum of 10 psychologists. Table 14.2 presents the dozen autobiographies with the highest average rating, listed in order from highest to lowest (Clifford et al., 1998). Although the authors are obviously adults, none of the books concern disorders that specifically or disproportionately afflict elderly people. The depression described by William Styron (1990) in *Darkness Visible* began when he was about 60 years of age.

Autobiographies exploring the mental disorders of late life, or addressing mental disorders from the perspective of an older author, are un-

TABLE 14.1
Top 25 Rated Self-Help Books

Title	Author(s)	Topic
The Courage to Heal	Ellen Bass and Laura Davis	Abuse and recovery
Feeling Good	David Burns	Depression
Infants and Mothers	T. Berry Brazelton	Child development and parenting
What Every Baby Knows	T. Berry Brazelton	Child development and parenting
Dr. Spock's Baby and Child Care	Benjamin Spock and Michael Rothenberg	Child deveopment and parenting
How to Survive the Loss of a Love	Melba Colgrove, Harold Bloomfield, and Peter McWilliams	Death and grief
To Listen to a Child	T. Berry Brazelton	Child development and parenting
The Boys and Girls Book About Divorce	Richard Gardner	Divorce
The Dance of Anger	Harriet Lerner	Anger
The Feeling Good Handbook	David Burns	Depression
Toddlers and Parents	T. Berry Brazelton	Child development and parenting
Your Perfect Right	Robert Alberti and Michael Emmons	Assertion
Between Parent and Teen-ager	Haim Ginott	Teenagers and parenting
The First Three Years of Life	Burton White	Child development and parenting
What Color Is Your Parachute?	Richard Bolles	Career development
Between Parent and Child	Haim Ginott	Child development and parenting
The Relaxation Response	Herbert Benson	Relaxation
The New Aerobics	Kenneth Cooper	Exercise
Learned Optimism	Martin Seligman	Positive thinking
Man's Searching for Meaning	Victor Frankl	Self-fulfillment
Children: The Challenge	Rudolph Dreikurs	Child development and parenting
You Just Don't Understand	Deborah Tannen	Communication
The Dance of Intimacy	Harriet Lerner	Love and intimacy
Beyond the Relaxation Response	Herbert Benson	Relaxation
The Battered Women	Lenore Walker	Abuse and recovery

Note.   Source: J. W. Santrock, A. M. Minnett, and B. D. Campbell (1994).

common. One reason, no doubt, is that one of the more frequent disorders of later life is dementia, which will often preclude writing about it. There are exceptions, however, such as Diana Friel McGowin's *Living in the Labyrinth* (1993). More common are autobiographies describing the caregiver's experience in watching the dementing process unfold in a loved one. Prominent examples of this genre include Ann Davidson's *A Love Story* (1997),

TABLE 14.2
Top 12 Rated Autobiographies

Title	Author(s)	Topic
An Unquiet Mind	K. R. Jamison	Bipolar disorder
Darkness Visible: A Memoir of Madness	W. Styron	Depression
Girl Interrupted	S. Kaysen	Bipolar disorder
Nobody Nowhere: The Extraordinary Autobiography of an Autistic	D. Williams	Autism
Out of the Depths	A. T. Boisin	Schizophrenia
Welcome Silence: My Triumph Over Schizophrenia	C. L. North	Schizophrenia
Too Much Anger, Too Many Tears	J. Gotkin & P. Gotkin	Schizophrenia
Diary of a Fat Houswife: A True Story of Humor, Heartbreak, and Hope	R. Green	Eating disorder
Undercurrents: A Therapist's Reckoning With Her Own Depression	M. Manning	Depression
A Drinking Life: A Memoir	P. Hamill	Substance abuse
Leaves From Many Seasons	O. H. Mowrer	Depression
The Liar's Club: A Memoir	M. Karr	Family dysfunction
A Brilliant Madness: Living With Manic Depressive Illness	P. Duke	Bipolar disorder

Note. Source: Clifford et al. (1998).

Frank Wall's *Where Did Mary Go?* (1996), and Bob Artley's *Ginny: A Love Remembered* (1993).

The relative lack of self-help groups and resources for older adults raises interesting questions worthy of further exploration. Does this reflect developmental or cohort-based differences in older client populations? Or perhaps a reluctance on the part of professionals to let older clients help themselves? Discussions of psychotherapy ethics with older adults have pointed to the tendency to give beneficence more consideration than autonomy (e.g., Knight, 1996b). Perhaps it is significant that the "indigenous" self-help groups for the elderly emphasize advocacy and power politics over support for emotional distress.

In the 21st century, self-change methods and self-help groups are destined to flourish for all ages. In fact, when 75 experts predicted the future of psychotherapy using Delphi methodology, the fastest growing psychotherapy provider was the self-help group (Norcross, Alford, & DeMichele, 1992). Self-help groups were predicted to increase the most of any psychotherapy provider, as evidenced by the mean rating of 5.21 on a 7-point scale on which 1 = great decrease, 3 = remain the same, and 7 = great increase. Table 14.3 shows that the panel of experts also forecast that psychiatric nurses, social workers, clinical psychologists, counseling psychol-

TABLE 14.3
Composite Predictions of Psychotherapists for the Future, in Ranked Order

Psychotherapist	M	SD
Self-help groups	5.21	0.84
Social workers	4.93	0.98
Psychiatric nurses	4.81	1.04
Clinical psychologists	4.75	0.99
Master's-level counselors	4.37	1.22
Peer counselors	4.32	0.96
Counseling psychologists	4.31	0.89
Paraprofessionals	4.12	1.03
Bachelor's-level therapists	3.43	1.22
Psychiatrists	2.89	0.82

Note. 1 = great decrease, 4 = remain the same, 7 = great increase.
Source: Norcross, Alford, and DeMichele (1992).

ogists, and peer counselors will provide an increasing proportion of mental health services.

THE ASCENDANCY OF PSYCHOTHERAPY INTEGRATION

The experts' composite predictions on the theoretical orientations of the future are presented in Table 14.4 in ranked order according to the same 7-point scale mentioned above. As seen there, theoretical integration and technical eclecticism were presaged to lead the way, with the former

TABLE 14.4
Composite Predictions for Theoretical Orientations of the Future

Orientation	M	SD
Systems/family systems	5.32	1.10
Technical eclecticism	5.23	0.97
Cognitive	5.15	0.93
Theoretical integration	5.01	0.93
Psychobiological	4.96	1.04
Behavioral/social learning	4.70	0.95
Feminist	4.21	1.14
Humanistic	3.53	1.06
Psychodynamic/neo-Freudian	3.47	1.01
Client/person-centered	3.22	0.83
Existential	3.15	0.93
Neurolinguistic programming	2.80	1.15
(Classic) Psychoanalytic	2.68	0.87
Transactional analysis	2.37	0.82

Note. 1 = great decrease, 4 = remain the same, 7 = great increase.
Source: Norcross, Alford, and DeMichele (1992).

attempting to meld disparate theories and the latter synthesizing diverse techniques. Cognitive therapy and systems therapies were also expected to expand. If these are the hot theories, then transactional analysis, classical psychoanalysis, client-centered therapy, and existentialism are definitely "not."

Table 14.4 introduces our fourth and final theme of individual psychotherapy during the next millennium: psychotherapy integration. As the field of psychotherapy has matured, integration has gradually emerged, and the ideological cold war has slowly abated. The unprecedented growth of interest in psychotherapy integration during the past decade has crystallized into a formal "movement" or, more dramatically, a "metamorphosis" in mental health. Psychotherapy integration is characterized by a dissatisfaction with single-school approaches and a concomitant desire to look across and beyond school boundaries to see what can be learned—and how patients can benefit—from other ways of practicing psychotherapy. The ultimate outcome of doing so, which is not yet fully realized, is to enhance the effectiveness and applicability of psychosocial treatment.

Although the notion of integrating various therapeutic approaches has intrigued mental health professionals for some time, integration has developed into a clearly delineated area of interest only within the past 20 years. The recent and rapid increase leads one to inquire "Why now?" and "Why in the future?" At least eight interacting factors have fostered the development of integration (from Norcross & Newman, 1992):

1. The sheer proliferation of diverse schools has been one important reason for the surge of integration. The field of psychotherapy has been staggered by myriad choices and fragmented by future shock. Which of 400+ therapies should be studied, taught, or bought? The hyperinflation of brand-name therapies has produced narcissistic fatigue: "With so many brand names around that no one can recognize, let alone remember, and so many competitors doing psychotherapy, it is becoming too arduous to launch still another new brand" (London, 1988, pp. 5–6).

2. A related and second factor is the growing awareness that no one approach is clinically adequate for all cases. The proliferation of theories is both a cause and symptom of the problem; no single approach is adequate to deal with the complexity of people and disorders.

3. The third factor is a matrix of economic and social pressures: Attacks from outside the mental health professions have started to propel them together. Psychotherapy has experienced mounting pressures from such not easily disregarded

sources as the courts, government policy makers, informed consumers, and insurance companies. There is something to be said for having the different therapies "hang together" rather than "hang separately."

4. A fourth factor is rising interest in short-term, problem-focused psychotherapies. Managed mental health care portends a future that is discontinuous with our expansive past; short-term therapy has become the model. One study of 294 HMO therapists, for instance, discovered that the prevalence of eclecticism/integration as a theoretical orientation nearly doubled as a function of their employment in HMOs favoring brief, problem-focused psychotherapy (Austad & Hoyt, 1992).

5. Another factor in the promotion of psychotherapy integration over the past 20 years has been the increasing opportunities for clinicians of disparate orientations actually to observe and experiment with various treatments. Specialized clinics, treatment manuals, and psychotherapy videotapes have all exposed clinicians to what various therapeutic schools do. In behavioral terms, these developments may have induced an informal version of *theoretical exposure*. Previously feared and unknown therapies were approached gradually, anxiety dissipated, and the previously feared therapies were integrated into the clinical repertoire.

6. Research has revealed few consistent differences in outcome among different therapies. Luborsky, Singer, and Luborsky (1975), borrowing a line from the Dodo bird in *Alice's Adventures in Wonderland*, wryly observed that "everybody has won and all must have prizes." Meta-analytic reviews show charity for all treatments and malice toward none. Although we should be cautious in accepting the null hypothesis, the Dodo bird's verdict likely served as a catalyst for many who began to consider the meta-analyses' integrative implications.

7. At the same time, empirical research has determined some "treatments of choice" for specific pathological conditions. Certain therapeutic marriages—such as cognitive therapy or interpersonal therapy for depression, conjoint treatment for distressed relationships, exposure or cognitive therapy for panic attacks, and behavior therapy for childhood conduct disorders—tend to work better (Lambert & Bergin, 1994). Such matches will lead practitioners to acquire competence in a number of disparate psychotherapy methods, thus facilitating integration within individual practitioners as well as within entire clinics.

8. Last but not least, the development of a professional network has been both a consequence and cause of interest in psychotherapy integration. In 1983 the interdisciplinary Society for the Exploration of Psychotherapy Integration (SEPI) was formed. SEPI provides a newsletter, annual conferences, regional networks, and a quarterly journal, thus simultaneously reflecting and promulgating the integrative spirit throughout the therapeutic community.

There are numerous pathways to the integration of the psychotherapies, of which three predominate at present. *Theoretical integration* combines two or more disparate theories of psychotherapy, such as psychodynamic–behavioral or cognitive–interpersonal hybrids. It entails a commitment to an emergent conceptual creation beyond a technical blend of methods. In *common factors*, therapists attempt to implement the core ingredients that different therapies share in common in order to develop more parsimonious and effective treatments based on those commonalities. In *technical eclecticism* therapists adopt efficacious procedures from various schools of thought without necessarily subscribing to the underlying theories that spawned them. The foundation is actuarial rather than theoretical: Pragmatically use what typically works for this type of disorder and patient. By whatever pathway, integration is destined to be the psychotherapy *Zeitgeist* of the new millennium.

It is curious that psychotherapy with older adults has not embraced the integrative movement earlier or more enthusiastically—at least judging from the published literature. Yet it is a field that practically requires some form of integration. The practice of psychotherapy with an older population necessitates familiarity with health psychology, rehabilitation counseling, grief work, neuropsychology, social gerontology, life span psychology, psychopharmacology, life review methods, and more. Psychotherapy with older adults has been characterized by integration across these domains, by biopsychosocial models of aging, and by interdisciplinary team practice, but rarely by psychotherapy integration per se.

Although practitioners who treat elderly clients may have not yet formally embraced the integration of diverse psychotherapy systems, elderly people themselves come to it quite naturally (Prochaska, Norcross, & DiClemente, 1995). Clinical experience and self-change research suggest that older adults are likely to have an integrative approach to their own therapy: the drive toward reminiscence (Butler, 1963) and to life review (Lewis & Butler, 1974) that calls for psychodynamic explanation of lifespan themes makes it difficult to focus entirely on the present, even in cognitive–behavioral work. Conversely, older adults have multiple problems, many of which are concrete, medically based, or both: The press to solve immediate problems and the role of the environment in shaping or causing the problems of older clients cry out for cognitive–behavioral and social-learning. The more cognitively impaired or the more non-psychologically minded the older client is, the more one is likely to rely on behavioral and cognitive techniques. Grief work, as such, is largely supportive–expressive in technique and principle. Working in age-segregated settings tends to require environmental analysis and intervention in an applied behavior analysis–social learning–community psychology manner. Finally, it is difficult, perhaps impossible, to work with older adults without a family systems perspective.

Knight (1996b) developed a transtheoretical framework for thinking about what changes are needed in psychological interventions with older adults: the *contextual, cohort-based, maturity, specific challenge model* (CCMSC). Like other integrative paradigms, the CCMSC model is not a specific school of therapy but a framework for thinking about the adaptation of any therapy system to work with older adults. The CCMSC model draws on life-span developmental psychology and scientific gerontology to guide the adaptation of psychological interventions to use with older clients. In the model, *context* means that changes in therapy are often related to the social–environmental context of older adults both in the community, and especially within hospital and nursing home settings, rather than to their developmental stage. Cohort differences are based on maturing in a specific historical time period, leading to a focus on generational groups, such as the Depression-era generation, the GI generation, and baby boomers, rather than on age groups. They lead to a need for more explanation of therapy and of rationale for specific change techniques and the use of less psychological jargon in therapy conversation. Developmental maturation leads to relatively minor changes, such as slowing down and the use of simpler language, but also to a greater emotional complexity and a wealth of expertise on which to draw. Specific challenges means that because of the high prevalence of chronic medical problems and neurological disorders, more assessment and therapy are related to these problems; there is also a higher frequency of grief work.

The CCMSC model has been successfully applied to psychodynamic therapy (Knight, 1996a), behavioral interventions and theory (Knight & Fox, in press), cognitive–behavioral therapy (Knight & Satre, in press), and family systems interventions (Knight & McCallum, 1998). In time, the CCMSC model could be a bridge toward developing an integrative therapy theory for older adults.

In the meantime, the integration movement portends substantial changes in psychotherapy research and training for the 21st century. In broad strokes, integration will facilitate more clinically valid approaches to therapy research by fostering a productive collaboration among clinicians and researchers, emphasizing clinical validity (as contrasted to internal validity) in outcome research, investigating heterogeneous problems and dually diagnosed patients, and focusing on optimal matches between psychotherapies and individual clients (Goldfried & Wolfe, 1998; Lazarus, Beutler, & Norcross, 1992; Norcross, 1993; Wolfe & Goldfried, 1988). In narrower strokes, we can expect controlled-outcome research to be conducted on so-called "combined" treatments (Kazdin, 1996) and on leading integrative and eclectic therapies, such as Prochaska and DiClemente's (1992) transtheoretical approach, Lazarus's (1997) multimodal therapy, Wachtel's (1997) integrative psychodynamic–behavioral systems therapy, and Beutler and Clarkin's (1990) systematic treatment selection. Of particular urgency is prospective outcome research that demonstrates the differential effectiveness or efficiency of integrative therapies with diagnostically heterogeneous patients.

Furthermore, the meaning of "matching" or "customizing" psychotherapy to individual patients will be expanded to denote not only technical methods but also therapist relationship stances (Norcross & Beutler, 1997). Analogous to "treatments of choice" in terms of clinical techniques, future research will increasingly identify the "relationships of choice" for particular patients in terms of interpersonal styles. Empirical research in the integrative spirit will actualize our learning, or perhaps our relearning, that psychotherapy is an emotional and interpersonal process involving unique people, not simply an impersonal EVT of disembodied disorders (Norcross, 1997).

In the past, eclectic and integrative practice was driven by the diffuse notion of "different strokes for different folks," but this philosophical pluralism was not concretely translated into empirically driven matches for the purposes of training. In the future, psychotherapy training will be grounded in treatment selection, including the type of therapeutic relationship, which will itself be largely based on indications and contraindications culled from the comparative-outcome research (Norcross, 1997).

The 21st century will herald the establishment and evaluation of psychotherapy training programs that ensure competence in integrative approaches to psychotherapy or in differential referral. Some programs will routinely opt to train their students in a single, "pure form" psychotherapy and subsequent referral of an appreciable portion of clientele to more appropriate treatments based on the treatment selection literature. Other programs will train students to accommodate most of these patients themselves by virtue of the students' competence in a multimethod, multimodality psychotherapy. This shall be accomplished by training students to competence in two or more systems of psychotherapy, in a single integrative system, or some combination thereof. The decision of which path to follow will probably be made by the program faculty on the basis of their own theoretical biases, length of the program, and their ability to coordinate the coursework, practica, and supervision. Although it is an ambitious and arduous process, integrative training represents psychotherapy training well into the new millennium (Lazarus et al., 1992; Norcross, 1997).

CONCLUDING PARABLE

The application of a life course perspective to psychotherapy can move us beyond the conventional dichotomous conceptualizations of therapies as present-centered or past-centered and as insight-oriented or action-oriented. A mature and effective psychotherapy inevitably entails integration of the present, past, and future; of the self and the system; of the psyche and the behavior. Maturity, be it in the development of people or in the evolution of psychotherapy, involves growing up and viewing life as a complicated, cumulative endeavor. Solving current problems, resolving conflicts from earlier life, and planning for future life, for instance, are complementary and synergistic undertakings, although some therapy systems would insist that they are rival and incompatible pursuits.

Consider how an integrated, life course perspective on psychotherapy alters the perceptions and the probable impact of our psychology. The healthy maintenance of family relationships will assume greater importance as one considers the increased number of years that will be spent together and the greater reliance on family predicted by socioemotional selectivity theory (Carstensen, Gross, & Fung, 1998). The individuation conflicts of adolescence and youth will take on different meanings for all participants if the full future life span is considered. The dominance of work in determining self-concept will be cast in a different light when the probable length of postretirement life is considered. Daughters-in-law and sons-in-law will be evaluated differently if one contemplates them as future caregivers. Prevention of health and mental health disorders assumes increased urgency when one thoughtfully calculates the length of the life span and the amount of time one can be disabled or chronically ill. The life-span time frame alters everything about our personal and societal psychology and allows us to synthesize different points of view.

We conclude with a parable that fuses the dual themes of psychotherapy integration and the psychology of aging. In the aging of people and in the maturation of psychotherapists, both develop toward some form of integration. Older people and seasoned psychotherapists look at the world in more complex, relativistic, and pluralistic ways. They grow up, rather than growing down. The parable is adapted from Norton Juster's (1961, pp. 102–108) delightful book, *The Phantom Tollbooth*:

> Milo has just emerged from a deep, dark woods and sees before him a rich green landscape.
> "What a beautiful view," gasped Milo.

"Oh, I don't know," answered a strange voice. "It's all in the way you look at things."

"I beg your pardon?" said Milo, for he didn't see who had spoken.

"I said, it's all in how you look at things," repeated the voice.

Milo turned around and found himself staring at two very neatly polished brown shoes, for standing directly in front of him (if you can use the word *standing* for anyone suspended in midair) was another boy just about his age, whose feet were easily 3 feet off the ground.

"For instance," continued the boy, "if you happened to like deserts, you might not think this was beautiful at all. . . . Or, for instance, from here that looks like a bucket of water," the boy said, pointing to a bucket of water, "but from an ant's point of view it's a vast ocean, from an elephant's just a cool drink, and to a fish, of course, it's home. So, you see, the way you see things depends a great deal on where you look at them from."

"How do you manage to stand up there?" asked Milo, for this was the subject that most interested him.

"Well," said the boy, "in my family everyone is born in the air, with his head at exactly the height it's going to be when he's an adult, and then we all grow toward the ground. When we're fully grown up or, as you can see, grown down, our feet finally touch . . . You certainly must be very old to have reached the ground already."

"Oh, no," said Milo seriously. "In my family we all start on the ground and grow up, and we never know how far until we actually get there."

"What a silly system." The boy laughed. "Then your head keeps changing its height and you always see things in a different way. Why, when you're 15 things don't look at all the way they did when you were 10, and at 20 everything will change again."

"We always see things from the same angle," the boy continued. "It's much less trouble that way."

"Does everyone here grow the way you do?" asked Milo.

"Almost everyone," replied the boy, and then he stopped a moment and thought. "Now and then, though, someone does begin to grow differently. Instead of down, his feet grow up toward the sky. But we do our best to discourage awkward things like that."

"What happens to *them?*" insisted Milo.

"Oddly enough, they often grow ten times the size of everyone else," said the boy thoughtfully, "and I've heard that they walk among the stars." And with that he skipped off once again toward the waiting woods.

REFERENCES

Artley, B. (1993). *Ginny: A love remembered.* Ames: Iowa State University Press.

American Psychological Association Practice Directorate. (1996). *CAPP practitioner survey.* Washington, DC: Author.

Austad, C. S., & Hoyt, M. F. (1992). The managed care movement and the future of psychotherapy. *Psychotherapy, 29,* 109–118.

Beutler, L. E., & Clarkin, J. F. (1990). *Systematic treatment selection.* New York: Brunner/Mazel.

Burns, B. J., & Taube, C. A. (1990). Mental health services in general medical care and in nursing homes. In B. S. Fogel, A. Furino, & G. L. Gottlieb (Eds.), *Mental health policy for older Americans: Protecting minds at risk* (pp. 63–84). Washington, DC: American Psychiatric Press.

Butler, R. N. (1963). The life review: An interpretation of reminiscence in the aged. *Psychiatry, 119,* 721–728.

Carstensen, L. L., Gross, J. J., & Fung, H. H. (1998). The social context of emotional experience. In K. W. Schaie & M. P. Lawton (Eds.), *Annual review of gerontology and geriatrics* (Vol. 17, pp. 325–352). New York: Springer.

Chambless, D. L. (1999). Empirically validated treatments—What now? *Applied Preventive Psychology, 8,* 281–284.

Chambless, D. L., Baker, M. J., Baucom, D. H., Beutler, L. E., Calhoun, K. S., Crits-Christoph, P., Daiuto, A., DeRubeis, R., Detweiler, J., Haaga, D. A. F., Bennett Johnson, S., McCurry, S., Mueser, K. T., Pope, K. S., Sanderson, W. C., Shoham, V., Stickle, T., Williams, D. A., & Woody, S. R. (1998). Update on empirically validated therapies, II. *The Clinical Psychologist, 51,* 3–16.

Chambless, D. L., Sanderson, W. C., Shoham, V., Bennett Johnson, S., Pope, K. S., Crits-Christoph, P., Baker, M., Johnson, B., Woody, S. R., Sue, S., Beutler, L., Williams, D. A., & McCurry, S. (1996). An update on empirically validated therapies. *The Clinical Psychologist, 49,* 5–18.

Clifford, J. S., Norcross, J. C., & Sommer, R. (1998, February). *Autobiographies of mental patients: Psychologists' uses and recommendations.* Poster presented at the 69th annual meeting of the Eastern Psychological Association, Boston.

Cuijpers, P. (1997). Bibliotherapy in unipolar depression: A meta-analysis. *Journal of Behavior Therapy and Experimental Psychiatry, 28,* 139–147.

Cummings, N. (1986). The dismantling of our health system: Strategies for the survival of psychological practice. *American Psychologist, 41,* 426–431.

Cummings, N. (1987). The future of psychotherapy: One psychologist's perspective. *American Journal of Psychotherapy, 61,* 349–360.

Davidson, A. (1997). *Alzheimer's: A love story.* Secaucus, NJ: Birch Lane Press.

Depression Guideline Panel. (1993). *Depression in primary care: Detection, diagnosis, and treatment: Quick reference guide for clinicians* (Clinical Practice Guideline No. 5, AHCPR Pub. No. 93-0552). Rockville, MD: Department of Health and Human Services, Public Health Service, Agency for Health Care Policy and Research.

Estes, C. (1992, November). *The aging enterprise revisited.* The Donald P. Kent Award Lecture, presented at the meeting of the Gerontological Society of America, Washington, DC.

Eysenck, H. (1952). The effects of psychotherapy: An evaluation. *Journal of Consulting Psychology, 16*, 319–324.

Friedan, B. (1993). *Fountain of age.* New York: Simon & Schuster.

Fee, practice and managed care survey. (1995). *Psychotherapy Finances, 21*(1), 1–8.

Friedhoff, A. J. (1994). Consensus Development Conference statement: Diagnosis and treatment of depression in late life. In L. S. Schneider, C. F. Reynolds, B. D. Lebowitz, & A. J. Friedhoff (Eds.), *Diagnosis and treatment of depression in late life: Results of the NIH Consensus Development Conference* (pp. 491–511). Washington, DC: American Psychiatric Press.

Gatz, M., Fiske, A., Fox, L. S., Kaskie, B., Kasl-Godley, J., McCallum, T., & Wetherell, J. (in press). Empirically-validated psychological treatments for older adults. *Journal of Mental Health and Aging.*

Gerike, A. (1997). *Old is not a four letter word.* Watsonville, CA: Papier Mache Press.

Goldfried, M. R., & Wolfe, B. E. (1998). Toward a more clinically valid approach to therapy research. *Journal of Consulting and Clinical Psychology, 66*, 143–150.

Gould, R. A., & Clum, G. A. (1993). A meta-analysis of self-help treatment approaches. *Clinical Psychology Review, 13*, 169–186.

Graham, S. R. (1995). "A modest proposal." *The Psychotherapy Bulletin, 30*, 4–5.

Humphreys, K., & Rappaport, J. (1994). Researching self-help/mutual aid groups and organizations: Many roads, one journey. *Applied and Preventive Psychology, 3*, 217–231.

Juster, N. (1961). *The phantom tollbooth.* New York: Knopf.

Kazdin, A. E. (1996). Combined and multimodal treatments in child and adolescent psychotherapy. *Clinical Psychology: Science and Practice, 3*, 69–100.

Kendall, P. C., & Chambless, D. L. (Eds.). (1998). Empirically supported psychological therapies [Special section]. *Journal of Consulting and Clinical Psychology, 66*, 3–167.

Kessler, R. C., McGonagle, K. A., Zhao, S., Nelson, C. B., Hughes, M., Eshleman, S., Wittchen, H., & Kendler, K. S. (1994). Lifetime and 12-month prevalence of *DSM–III–R* psychiatric disorders in the United States. *Archives of General Psychiatry, 51*, 8–19.

Kiesler, C. A. (1992). U.S. mental health policy: Doomed to fail. *American Psychologist, 47*, 1077–1082.

Knight, B. G. (1988). Factors influencing therapist-rated change in older adults. *Journal of Gerontology, 43*, 111–112.

Knight, B. G. (1989). *Outreach with the elderly: Community education, assessment, and therapy.* New York: New York University Press.

Knight, B. G. (1996a). Psychodynamic therapy with older adults: Lessons from scientific gerontology. In R. Woods (Ed.), *Handbook of clinical psychology and ageing* (pp. 545–560). London: Wiley.

Knight, B. G. (1996b). *Psychotherapy with older adults* (2nd ed.). Thousand Oaks CA: Sage.

Knight, B. G., & Fox, L. S. (in press). Behavior therapy with the elderly: The contextual, cohort-based, maturity/specific challenge model. In M. Ezal & I. Montorio (Eds. and Trans.), *Manual de gerontolgia conductual*. Madrid: Sintesis.

Knight, B. G., & Kaskie, B. (1995). Models for mental health service delivery to older adults: Models for reform. In M. Gatz (Ed.), *Emerging issues in mental health and aging* (pp. 231–255). Washington, DC: American Psychological Association.

Knight, B. G., Lutzky, S. M., & Macofsky-Urban, F. (1993). A meta-analytic review of interventions for caregiver distress: Recommendations for future research. *The Gerontologist, 33,* 240–249.

Knight, B. G., & McCallum, T. J. (1998). Family therapy with older clients: The contextual, cohort-based, maturity/specific challenge model. In I. H. Nordhus, G. Van den Bos, S. Berg, & P. Fromholt (Eds.), *Clinical geropsychology* (pp. 313–328). Washington, DC: American Psychological Association.

Knight, B. G., & Satre, D. (in press). Adapting cognitive behavioral psychotherapy to the elderly client: The contextual, cohort-based, maturity/specific challenge model. In L. Bizzni (Ed. & Trans.), *Psychotherapie cognitive de lat personne agee*. Madrid: Sintesis.

Knight, B. G., Wollert, R. W., Levy, L. H., Frame, C. L., & Padgett, V. P. (1980). Self-help groups: The members' perspectives. *American Journal of Community Psychology, 8,* 53–65.

Kurtzweil, P. L., Scogin, F., & Rosen, G. M. (1996). A test of the fail-safe N for self-help programs. *Professional Psychology: Research and Practice, 27,* 629–630.

Lambert, M. J. (1976). Spontaneous remission in adult neurotic disorders: A revision and summary. *Psychological Bulletin, 83,* 107–119.

Lambert, M. J., & Bergin, A. E. (1994). The effectiveness of psychotherapy. In A. E. Bergin & S. L. Garfield (Eds.), *Handbook of psychotherapy and behavior change* (4th ed., pp. 143–189). New York: Wiley.

Lazarus, A. A. (1997). *Brief but comprehensive psychotherapy: The multimodal way.* New York: Springer.

Lazarus, A. A., Beutler, L. E., & Norcross, J. C. (1992). The future of technical eclecticism. *Psychotherapy, 29,* 11–20.

Lewinsohn, P., Munoz, R., Youngren, M. A., & Zeiss, A. (1986). *Control your depression.* Englewood Cliffs, NJ: Prentice Hall.

Lewis, M. I., & Butler, R. N. (1974). Life review therapy: Putting memories to work in individual and group psychotherapy. *Geriatrics, 29,* 165–172.

Linkletter, A. (1988). *Old age is not for sissies: Choices for senior Americans.* New York: Viking.

Lipsey, M. W., & Wilson, D. B. (1993). The efficacy of psychological, educational, and behavioral treatment. *American Psychologist, 48,* 1181–1209.

London, P. (1988). Metamorphosis in psychotherapy: Slouching toward integration. *Journal of Integrative and Eclectic Psychotherapy, 7,* 3–12.

Lonigan, C., & Elbert, J. (Eds.). (1998). Empirically supported psychosocial interventions for children [Special issue]. *Journal of Clinical Child Psychology, 27*(2), 138–145.

Luborsky, L., Singer, B., & Luborsky, L. (1975). Comparative studies of psychotherapies: Is it true that "everybody has won and all must have prizes?" *Archives of General Psychiatry, 32*, 995–1008.

Mace, N., & Rabins, P. (1982). *The 36 hour day.* Baltimore: Johns Hopkins University Press.

Marrs, R. W. (1995). A meta-analysis of bibliotherapy studies. *American Journal of Community Psychology, 23*, 843–870.

Marx, J. A., Royalty, G. M., Gyorky, Z. K., & Stern, T. E. (1992). Use of self-help books in psychotherapy. *Professional Psychology: Research and Practice, 23*, 300–305.

McGowin, D. F. (1993). *Living in the labyrinth: A personal journey through the maze of Alzheimer's.* San Francisco: Elder Books.

Mechanic, D., & Aiken, L. H. (1989, Fall). Capitation in mental health: Potentials and cautions. *New Directions for Mental Health Services, 43*, 5–18.

Morgenstern, J., Labouvie, E., McCrady, B. S., Kahler, C. W., & Frey, R. M. (1997). Affiliation with Alcoholics Anonymous after treatment: A study of its therapeutic effects and mechanisms of action. *Journal of Consulting and Clinical Psychology, 65*, 768–777.

Munoz, R. F., Hollon, S. D., McGrath, E., Rehm, L. P., & Van den Bos, G. R. (1994). On the AHCPR Depression in Primary Care guidelines: Further considerations for practitioners. *American Psychologist, 49*, 42–61.

Neysmith-Roy, J. M., & Kleisinger, C. L. (1997). Using biographies of adults over 65 years of age to understand life-span developmental psychology. *Teaching of Psychology, 24*, 116–118.

Norcross, J. C. (Ed.). (1987). *Casebook of eclectic psychotherapy.* New York: Brunner/Mazel.

Norcross, J. C. (Ed.). (1993). Research directions for psychotherapy integration: A roundtable [Special issue]. *Journal of Psychotherapy Integration, 3*, 91–131.

Norcross, J. C. (1997). Emerging breakthroughs in psychotherapy integration: Three predictions and one fantasy. *Psychotherapy, 34*, 86–90.

Norcross, J. C. (1999). Collegially validated limitations of empirically validated treatments. *Clinical Psychology: Science and Practice, 6*, 472–476.

Norcross, J. C., Alford, B. A., & DeMichele, J. T. (1992). The future of psychotherapy: Delphi data and concluding observations. *Psychotherapy, 29*, 150–158.

Norcross, J. C., & Beutler, L. E. (1997). Determining the therapeutic relationship of choice in brief therapy. In J. N. Butcher (Ed.), *Personality assessment in managed health care: A practitioner's guide* (pp. 42–60). New York: Oxford University Press.

Norcross, J. C., & Goldfried, M. R. (Eds.). (1992). *Handbook of psychotherapy integration.* New York: Basic Books.

Norcross, J. C., Karg, R., & Prochaska, J. O. (1997). Clinical psychologists and managed care: Some data from the Division 12 membership. *The Clinical Psychologist, 50*(1), 4–8.

Norcross, J. C., & Newman, C. F. (1992). Psychotherapy integration: Setting the context. In J. C. Norcross & M. R. Goldfried (Eds.), *Handbook of psychotherapy integration* (pp. 3–45). New York: Basic Books.

Norcross, J. C., Santrock, J. W., Campbell, L. F., Smith, T. P., Sommer, R., Zuckerman, E. L. (2000). *Authoritative guide to self-help resources in mental health.* New York: Guilford.

Ouimette, P. C., Finney, J. W., & Moos, R. H. (1997). Twelve-step and cognitive–behavioral treatment for substance abuse: A comparison of treatment effectiveness. *Journal of Consulting and Clinical Psychology, 65,* 230–240.

Papouchis, N., & Passman, V. (1993). An integrative approach to psychotherapy of the elderly. In G. Stricker & J. R. Gold (Eds.), *Comprehensive handbook of psychotherapy integration* (pp. 437–452). New York: Plenum Press.

Pardeck, J. T., & Pardeck, J. A. (1992). *Bibliotherapy: A guide to using books in clinical practice.* New York: Haworth.

Perrotta, P., & Meacham, J. A. (1981). Can a reminiscing intervention alter depression and self esteem? *International Journal of Aging and Human Development, 14,* 23–30.

President's Commission on Mental Health. (1978). *Mental health: Nature and scope of the problems* (Task Panel Report to the President's Commission on Mental Health, Vol. 2). Washington, DC: U.S. Government Printing Office.

Prochaska, J. O., & DiClemente, C. C. (1992). The transtheoretical approach. In J. C. Norcross & M. R. Goldfried (Eds.), *Handbook of psychotherapy integration* (pp. 300–344). New York: Basic Books.

Prochaska, J. O., & Norcross, J. C. (1998). *Systems of psychotherapy: A transtheoretical analysis* (4th ed.). Pacific Grove, CA: Brooks/Cole.

Prochaska, J. O., Norcross, J. C., & DiClemente, C. C. (1995). *Changing for good.* New York: Avon.

Project MATCH Research Group. (1997). Matching alcoholism treatments to client heterogeneity: Project MATCH posttreatment drinking outcomes. *Journal of Studies on Alcohol, 58,* 7–29.

Robinson, L. A., Berman, J. S., & Neimeyer, R. A. (1990). Psychotherapy for the treatment of depression: A comprehensive review of controlled outcome research. *Psychological Bulletin, 108,* 30–49.

Rothbaum, P. A., Bernstein, D. M., Haller, O., Phelps, R., & Kohout, J. (1998). New Jersey psychologists' report on managed metal health care. *Professional Psychology, 29,* 37–42.

Saltzman, N., & Norcross, J. C. (Eds.). (1990). *Therapy wars: Contention and convergence in differing clinical approaches.* San Francisco: Jossey-Bass.

Sanavio, E. (1971). Toilet retraining psychogeriatric patients. *Behavior Modification, 5,* 417–427.

Santrock, J. W., Minnett, A. M., & Campbell, B. D. (1994). *The authoritative guide to self-help books.* New York: Guilford Press.

Schneider, L. S. (1994). Meta-analysis from a clinician's perspective. In L. S. Schneider, C. F. Reynolds, B. D. Lebowitz, & A. J. Friedhoff (Eds.), *Diagnosis and treatment of depression in late life: Results of the NIH Consensus Development Conference* (pp. 361–374). Washington, DC: American Psychiatric Press.

Schneider, L. S., Reynolds, C. F., Lebowitz, B. D., & Friedhoff, A. J. (Eds.). (1994). *Diagnosis and treatment of depression in late life: Results of the NIH Consensus Development Conference.* Washington, DC: American Psychiatric Press.

Scogin, F., Bynum, J., & Calhoon, S. (1990). Efficacy of self-administered treatment programs: Meta-analytic review. *Professional Psychology: Research and Practice, 21,* 42–47.

Scogin, F., Hamblin, D., & Beutler, L. (1987). Bibliotherapy for depressed older adults: A self-help alternative. *The Gerontologist, 27,* 383–387.

Scogin, F., Jamison, C., & Gochnauer, K. (1989). The comparative efficacy of cognitive and behavioral bibliotherapy for mildly and moderately depressed older adults. *Journal of Consulting and Clinical Psychology, 57,* 403–407.

Scogin, F., & McElreath, L. (1994). Efficacy of psychosocial treatments for geriatric depression: A quantitative review. *Journal of Consulting and Clinical Psychology, 62,* 69–74.

Seligman, M. E. P. (1995). The effectiveness of psychotherapy. *American Psychologist, 50,* 965–974.

Skinner, B. F., & Vaughan, M. F. (1983). *Enjoy old age: A program of self management.* New York: Norton.

Starker, S. (1988). Psychologists and self-help books: Attitudes and prescriptive practices of clinicians. *American Journal of Psychotherapy, 42,* 448–455.

Stricker, G., & Gold, J. R. (Eds.). (1993). *Comprehensive handbook of psychotherapy integration.* New York: Plenum Press.

Strupp, H. H., & Howard, K. I. (1992). A brief history of psychotherapy research. In D. K. Freedheim (Ed.), *The history of psychotherapy* (pp. 309–334). Washington, DC: American Psychological Association.

Styron, W. (1990). *Darkness visible.* New York: Random House.

Task Force on Promotion and Dissemination of Psychological Procedures. (1995). Training in and dissemination of empirically validated psychological treatments: Report and recommendations. *The Clinical Psychologist, 48,* 3–23.

Task Force on Psychological Intervention Guidelines. (1995). *Template for developing guidelines: Interventions for mental disorders and psychosocial aspects of physical disorders.* Washington, DC: American Psychological Association.

Tonigan, J. S., Toscoova, R., & Miller, W. R. (1995). Meta-analysis of the literature on Alcoholics Anonymous: Sample and study characteristics moderate findings. *Journal of Studies on Alcohol, 57,* 65–72.

Toseland, R. W., & Rossiter, C. M. (1989). Group interventions to support family caregivers: A review and analysis. *The Gerontologist, 29,* 438–448.

Veroff, J., Douvan, E., & Kulka, R. A. (1981). *Mental health in America.* New York: Basic Books.

Wachtel, P. L. (1997). *Psychoanalysis, behavior therapy, and the relational world.* Washington, DC: American Psychological Association.

Wall, F. A. (1996). *Where did Mary go?* Amherst, NY: Prometheus Books.

Wetle, T., & Mark, H. (1990). Managed care. In B. S. Fogel, A. Furino, & G. L. Gottlieb (Eds.), *Mental health policy for older Americans: Protecting minds at risk* (pp. 221–238). Washington, DC: American Psychiatric Press.

Wolfe, B. E., & Goldfried, M. R. (1988). Research on psychotherapy integration: Recommendations and conclusions from an NIMH workshop. *Journal of Consulting and Clinical Psychology, 56,* 446–451.

Zarit, S. H., & Knight, B. G. (Eds.). (1996). *A guide to psychotherapy and aging: Effective clinical interventions in a life-stage context.* Washington, DC: American Psychological Association.

Zarit, S. H., Orr, N., & Zarit, J. (1985). *Hidden victims: Caregivers under stress.* New York: New York University Press.

AUTHOR INDEX

Numbers in italics refer to listings in the reference sections.

Butterfield, E. C., 78, *91*
Butters, M. A., 52, *60*
Butters, N., 34, 35, *38, 40, 42, 60*
Butzel, J. S., 150, 164, *167, 168*
Bynum, J., 267, *285*
Byrd, M., 28, *39*

Cabeza, R., 51, *60*
Caggiula, A. W., *204*
Cai, J., 33, *38*
Caine, E. D., *250*
Calhoon, S., 267, *285*
Calhoun, K. S., *280*
Califf, R. M., 211, *217*
Campbell, A., 183, *188*
Campbell, B. D., 269, *285*
Campbell, J. I. D., 105, *113, 114*
Campbell, L. F., *284*
Cantor, M. H., 180, *188*
Capdevela, A., *62*
Capps, J. L., 81, *94*
Card, C., 227, *232*
Card, S. K., 101, *114*
Carder, P., 180, *190*
Carlson, J., 46, *63*
Caro, F. G., 13, 17, *18*
Carstensen, L. L., 135
Carstensen, L. L., 124, 132, 135, 137,
        139, 140, 146, 150, 162, *166,*
        167, 174, 175, 176, 177, 183,
        186, *188, 189, 190,* 212, *216,*
        278, *280*
Cascio, W. F., 103, *115,* 153, *167*
Cassano, G. B., 227, *233*
Cassell, K. C., 208, *216*
Catalano, D. J., 179, 182, *189*
Catanzaro, S., 231, *234*
Cattell, R. B., 46, *62*
Cerella, J., 88, *91*
Chalfonte, B. L., 80, *91*
Chambless, D. L., 263, 264, *280, 281*
Chambless, L. E., *204*
Chandler, C. L., 156, *167*
Chan-Palay, V., 33, *38*
Charles, S. T., 124, 137, *139,* 175, *188*
Charness, N., 102, 103, 105, 106, 107,
        110, *113, 114*
Chase, N., *61*
Chase, W. G., 111, *114*
Chatterjee, A., 213, *216*
Cherry, B. J., 47, *60*

Chevron, E. S., 232, *235*
Chirkov, V. I., *170*
Chown, M., *41*
Christensen, H., 230, 234, *251*
Chrosniak, L. D., 79, *93*
Clapp-Channing, N. E., *216*
Clark, C. M., *218*
Clark, L. A., 231, 233, *237*
Clark, V. A., 242, *251*
Clarkin, J. F., 277, *280*
Clifford, J. S., 268, 269, *280*
Clum, G. A., 267, *281*
Cobb, J. L., *63*
Coffey, C. E., 49, *60*
Coghill, G. R., 31, *38*
Cohen, G., 5, 8, 73, 80, *91*
Cohen, J., *61*
Cohen, J. D., 56, *60*
Cohen, N., 27, *38*
Cohn, N. B., 56, *60*
Coleman, P., 32, *42*
Colon, E. J., 31, *39*
Comalli, P. E., Jr., 49, *60*
Connell, J. P., 149, 156, 161, *167, 170*
Connidis, I. A., 180, *188*
Connor, L. T., 78, *91*
Converse, P. E., 183, *188*
Convit, A., *61*
Conway, M. A., 73, *91*
Conwell, Y., *250*
Cooley, S., 8
Cools, A., 33, *39*
Coon, V. E., 83, 87, *96*
Cooper, G., 47, *63*
Corballis, M. C., 100, *114*
Corder, L. S., 4, *9*
Cork, L., 38, *41*
Corkin, S., 25, *39, 40,* 56, *64*
Cornoni-Hunt, J., *250*
Coryell, W., 225, *233*
Costa, P. T., 208, 213, 214, *216, 217*
Costa, P. T., Jr., 201, 204, *216, 217*
Costello, C. G., 225, *233*
Cox, B. J., 230, *234*
Coyne, J. C., 226, 228, 229, *233*
Craik, F., 28, *39*
Craik, F. I. M., 28, *39,* 51, 52, 53, *60,*
        66, 75, 77, 83, 84, 90, *91, 94,*
        95
Cram, K. B., *204*
Crimmins, E., 213, *218*
Crits-Christoph, P., *280*

Csikszentmihalyi, M., 163, *167*
Cuijpers, P., 280
Cullum, C. M., 46, 66
Cumming, E., 174, *188*
Cummings, N., 261, *280*
Cupples, L. A., *216*
Curnow, C., 103, *116*
Curran, T., *91*
Curtis, J., 248, *253*
Cutler, S. J., 73, *91*

D'Agostino, R. B., 63, *216*
Daigneault, S., 48, *61*
Daiuto, A., *280*
Dalferes, E. R., Jr., *203*
Damasio, A., 37, *39*
Damasio, A. R., 39, 45, 49, 59, *61*
Danner, F. W., 153, *167*
Daugherty, S., 215, *217*
Davey, M. E., 153, *169*
Davidson, A., *280*
Davidson, J., 225, *236*
Davies, L., 180, *188*
Davis, T. M., 52, *62*
Dawson, D. V., 213, *218*
Dean, J., 137, *140*
deCharms, R., 149, 157, *167*
Deci, E. L., 146, 147, 148, 149, 150, 151,
    153, 154, 156, 157, 158, 163,
    166, 167, 168, 170, 172
Deitch, I. M., 8
DeJong, F. J., *250*
de Leon, M. J., *61*
Delis, D. C., *60*
Dembroski, T. M., 201, *204*
DeMichele, J. T., 271, 272, *283*
Derksen, P., 232, *234*
DeRubeis, R., *280*
De Santi, S., *61*
DeTeresa, R., 31, *42*
Detweiler, J., *280*
DeVoe, M., 137, *139*
DeVoe, M. R., 137, *139, 140*
DiClemente, C. C., 275, 277, *284*
Diener, E., 125, *139*
DiGiulio, D. V., 46, *64*
Dixon, R., 242, *251*
Dixon, R. A., 73, 76, *91*, 110, *114*, 179,
    185, 186, *187, 188*
Dixon, W., *236*
Djang, W. T., *60*

Dobson, S. H., 73, *93*
Dolan, R. J., *59*
Donlan, C., 74, *96*
Dorfman, R. A., *250*
Douvan, E., 266, *286*
Dow, M. G., 231, *236*
Downes, J. J., 50, *64*
Doyle, C., *251*
Duffy, F., 28, *38*
Dumais, S. T., 107, 108, *115*
Dunbar, K., 56, *60*
Duncker, K., 109, *114*
Dunlosky, J., 77, 78, 88, *91*
Dupue, R. A., 244, *252*
Dupuis, J. H., *65*
Dustman, R. E., 56, *60*
Dutta, R., 109, *116*
Dyer, A., *204*
Dykstra, P. A., 178, 180, 182, 183, 184,
    188, 189, 190
Dywan, J., 53, *61*, 80, 86, *92*

Earl, N. L., *218*
Earles, J. L., 73, 85, 88, *92, 95*
East, P. L., 179, 181, *189*
Eaton, E. M., 231, *236*
Eaves, G., *236*
Eaves, L. J., *235*
Eckfeldt, J. H., *204*
Edelstein, W., 147, *167*
Eggers, R., 49, *62*
Einstein, G. O., 76, *92*
Ekman, P., 130, 131, 132, 135, *139, 140*
Elbert, J., 264, *283*
Elias, J. W., 208, *216*
Elias, M. F., 46, 47, *61*, 208, 212, *216*
Elias, P. K., 208, 212, 214, *216*
Elkind, D., 152, *168*
Elo, A. E., 103, *114*
Emery, O. A., 244, *252*
Emmerson, J. P., 227, *233*
Endicott, J., *233*
Engel, R. J., 243, *253*
Engle, R. W., 89, *92*
Enns, M. W., 230, *234*
Ericsson, K. A., 101, 103, 110, *114, 115*
Erkinjuntti, T., *67*
Erngrund, K., 52, *61, 95*
Eshleman, S., *281*
Eslinger, P. J., 45, 52, 59, *60*
Estes, C., 261, *280*

Evans, D., 41
Eysenck, H., 265, 281
Eysenck, H. H., 230, 234

Faulkner, D., 73, 80, 91
Faust, M. E., 56, 66
Feigenbaum, E. A., 105, 108, 114
Feinleib, M., 201, 204
Feldman, L., 13, 19
Femina, J. D., 14, 19
Ferguson, S. A., 87, 93
Ferraro, E. F., 180, 189
Ferraro, F. R., 87, 95
Ferris, S., 61
Ferris, S. H., 61
Field, D., 174, 176, 178, 189
Figiel, G. S., 60
Fillenbaum, G. G., 218
Finch, C., 33, 41
Finkbiner, R. G., 54, 67
Finn, S. E., 230, 234
Finney, J. W., 267, 284
Fischer, D., 62
Fisjke, A., 281
Fiske, A., 248, 250
Fitzhugh, K. B., 45, 61
Fitzhugh, L. C., 45, 61
Fitzsimmons, C., 76, 95, 110, 115
Flannery, C., 250
Fletcher, R. H., 215, 217
Fletcher, S. W., 215, 217
Flett, G. L., 226, 237
Flood, D., 32, 42
Florio, L. P., 240, 253
Flowers, K., 33, 39
Foley, M. A., 79, 93
Folsom, A. R., 202, 204
Foner, A., 12, 19
Forette, B., 208, 217
Forsell, Y., 243, 250
Foster, C., 241, 252
Foster, D. S., 62
Fox, L. S., 276, 281, 282
Fox, P., 33, 42
Frackowick, R. S. J., 59
Frame, C. L., 268, 282
Franchi, D., 51, 66
Frazer, D. W., 244, 250
Frederick, C. M., 153, 165, 168, 170
Frederickson, B. L., 176, 176–177, 188, 189

Fredrickson, B. L., 137, 139, 212, 216
Freedman, Z., 158, 172
Freeman, D. H., 250
Frerichs, R. R., 242, 251
Freund, A. M., 186, 188, 189
Frey, R. M., 267, 283
Fried, L., 215, 217
Friedan, B., 281
Friedhoff, A. J., 240, 251, 265, 281, 285
Fries, J. F., 246, 251
Friesen, W. V., 130, 131, 132, 135, 139, 140
Frieske, D., 95
Frieske, D. A., 50, 61
Fristoe, N. M., 73, 83, 89, 92, 96
Friston, K. J., 59
Frith, C. D., 59
Frolkis, V. V., 133, 139
Fung, H. H., 177, 189, 278, 280
Funkenstein, H., 41

Gable, S. L., 159, 169
Gabrieli, J. D. E., 82, 97
Gaines, C. L., 95
Galasko, D., 60
Gallagher-Thompson, D., 232, 234, 248, 253
Gallo, J. J., 243, 251
Gantz, F. E., 253
Gardin, J., 204
Gardiner, J. M., 83, 92
Garey, L., 31, 40
Garrity, P., 178, 190
Garvey, A., 31, 42
Gatz, M., 242, 243, 245, 248, 250, 251, 265, 281
Gazzaley, A., 33, 39
Gehardstein, P. C., 47, 61
Gentes, C. I., 61
George, A. E., 49, 61
George, L. K., 11, 19, 216, 226, 235, 244, 251, 253
Gerard, L., 86, 92
Gergen, K. J., 146, 165, 168
Gerike, A., 281
Giambra, L. M., 87, 92
Gibson, P., 31, 39
Gick, M. L., 84, 95
Gilewski, M. J., 78, 97
Gilinsky, A. S., 85, 92
Gilmartin, K., 111, 117

Hertzog, C., 46, 62, 76, 77, 78, 85, 91, 93, 94, 95, 242, 251
Hesselink, J. R., 62
Heycop ten Ham, B. F., 232, 234
Heyman, A., 35, 42
Hill, R. D., 33, 42
Himmelfarb, S., 242, 252
Hinrichsen, G., 8
Hintzman, D. L., 79, 91, 93
Hirsh, R., 27, 39
Hitch, G. J., 84, 90
Holahan, C. J., 229, 236
Hollon, S. D., 264, 283
Holsinger, T., 242, 252
Holt, K., 153, 169
Holzer, C., III, 240, 253
Hooijer, C., 253
Horn, J. L., 46, 62
Horstink, M., 33, 39
Horwitz, B., 61
Houle, S., 60
House, J., 181, 182, 189
House, J. S., 173, 189, 241, 252
Houx, P. J., 56, 63
Howard, K. I., 265, 285
Hoyt, M. F., 274, 280
Huang, V., 237
Hubbard, B. M., 31, 38
Hughes, G., 204
Hughes, J., 35, 42
Hughes, M., 281
Hultsch, D. F., 73, 76, 78, 81, 91, 94, 96, 242, 251
Humphreys, K., 267, 281
Hunkin, N. M., 52, 64
Hunter, J. E., 103, 115
Hunter, R. F., 103, 115
Hurd, M. D., 213, 218
Hurwicz, M.-L., 242, 243, 251
Hutchinson, R. G., 204
Hyman, B., 37, 39
Hyman, B. T., 39
Hyman, B., 37

Idler, E. L., 210, 217
Ilardi, B., 149, 171
Isaacowitz, D. M., 175, 188
Ivnik, R., 29, 41

Jacob, F., 147, 168

Jacobs, D. R., Jr., 204
Jacoby, L., 80, 92
Jacoby, L. L., 79, 80, 83, 93, 109, 115
Jacomb, P., 230, 234
Jacomb, P. A., 230, 234
Jamison, C., 268, 285
Janer, K. W., 56, 64
Janowsky, J. S., 52, 62
Jarvik, L. F., 239, 251
Jennings, J. M., 60, 80, 93, 109, 115
Jensen, J. E., 243, 253
Jernigan, T., 31, 42
Jernigan, T. L., 49, 51, 62
Jerome, D., 180, 189
Jeune, B., 208, 217
Jobes, D. A., 225, 233
Jodar, M., 62
Johansson, B., 242, 251
Johnson, B., 280
Johnson, C. L., 178, 179, 182, 184, 189
Johnson, M. A., 208, 217
Johnson, M. K., 79, 80, 87, 91, 93
Joiner, T. E., Jr., 227, 228, 229, 230, 231, 234, 235, 236
Jolesz, F., 39
Jolles, J., 56, 63
Jones, M. G., 51, 67
Jonker, C., 253
Jorm, A., 230, 234
Jorm, A. F., 62, 229, 235, 243, 250, 251
Judd, B. B., 85, 92
Jung, C. G., 124, 139
Junque, C., 49, 62
Jurica, P. J., 49, 66
Juster, N., 278, 281

Kahler, C. W., 267, 283
Kahn, R. L., 12, 17, 19, 180, 189, 198, 205, 208, 217, 241, 251
Kalnok, M., 125, 140
Kannel, W. B., 201, 204
Kaplan, E., 48, 57, 59, 63
Kaplan, E. B., 218
Kaplan, E. F., 63
Kaplan, J. R., 136, 139
Kapur, S., 60
Karel, M. J., 245, 251
Karg, R., 261, 284
Karlsson, S., 95
Karno, M. L, 253
Kaskie, B., 261, 281, 282

Kasl, S., 250
Kasl, S. V., 229, 237
Kasl-Godley, J., 281
Kasl-Godley, J. E., 245, 248, 250, 251
Kasper, J. D., 215, 217
Kasser, T., 148, 159, 160, 168, 170, 171
Kasser, V. G., 161, 162, 168
Kaszniak, A., 33, 42
Kaszniak, A. W., 51, 52, 53, 54, 58, 60,
       62, 64, 66
Katz, I. R., 244, 247, 251, 253
Kausler, D. H., 52, 62, 77, 79, 93
Kawamura, J., 49, 63
Kazdin, A. E, 277, 281
Keller, M. B., 225, 236
Kelley, C. L., 112, 115
Kelsey, S. F., 200, 204
Kemp, B. J., 252
Kemper, S., 84, 93, 95
Kemper, T., 33, 40, 49, 65
Kendall, P. C., 264, 281
Kendler, K. S., 226, 235, 281
Kennison, R. L., 81, 94
Kessler, R. C., 235, 241, 252, 266, 281
Kidder, D. P., 76, 85, 93, 95
Kieley, J. M., 56, 62
Kiesler, C. A., 261, 281
Kihlstrom, J. F., 53, 54, 66
Kikinis, R., 39
Killiany, R., 30, 31, 39, 40, 41
Kim, Y., 150, 168
Kinsbourne, M., 46, 47, 61
Kintsch, W., 101, 103, 114
Kirasic, K. C., 73, 85, 89, 93
Kleban, M. H., 137, 140
Klein, M., 56, 63
Klein, W. C., 169
Kleisinger, C. L., 269, 283
Klerman, G. L., 232, 235
Kliegl, R., 76, 80, 87, 88, 90, 93, 94,
       102, 115
Klisz, D., 45, 63
Klocek, J., 228, 235
Knapp, J. E., 202, 205
Knight, B. G., 260, 261, 262, 263, 268,
       271, 276, 281, 282, 286
Knight, J. A., 18, 19
Knoefel, J. E., 63
Koenig, H. G., 242, 252
Koenig, O., 47, 63
Koestner, R., 153, 167, 169
Kohout, J., 261, 284

Kokmen, E., 29, 41
Koran, L., 225, 236
Kordower, J., 33, 39
Koriat, A., 80, 93
Korol, D. L., 51, 67
Korten, A. E., 230, 234, 251
Kosslyn, S. M., 47, 63
Kozora, E., 46, 66
Krach, C. A., 3, 8
Kral, V. A., 244, 252
Kramer, M., 253
Kramer, N. A., 153, 169
Krames, L., 226, 237
Krampe, R. T., 110, 115
Krantz, D. S., 204
Krapp, A., 151, 169
Krishnan, K. R. K., 226, 235
Kromer, L., 37, 39
Kuhl, J., 148, 170
Kuhl, S., 62
Kulka, R. A., 266, 286
Kuller, L. H., 200, 202, 204, 205
Kumanyika, S., 215, 217
Kunik, M. E., 232, 236
Kurtzweil, P. L., 267, 282
Kwentus, J. A., 35, 39
Kwong See, S. T., 85, 93
Kynette, D., 84, 95

Labouvie, E., 267, 283
Labouvie-Vief, G., 137, 139, 140
Lachman, J. L., 107, 115
Lachman, R., 107, 115
Lafferty, M. E., 215, 217
La Guardia, J. G., 152, 158, 170
Lai, Z., 30, 31, 40, 41
Lakatta, E. G., 217
Lambert, M. J., 266, 274, 282
Lamme, S., 178, 181, 186, 190
Landauer, T. K., 107, 108, 115
Landis, K., 173, 189
Landis, L., 38
Lang, A., 33, 42
Lang, F. R., 174, 176, 177, 190
Langström, B., 59
Larson, R., 174, 190
La Rue, A., 244, 252
Laslett, P., 13, 19
Lassila, H. C., 200, 204, 205
Lathin, D., 153, 172
Lauer, R. M., 204

Morrison, J., 33, *39*
Morrow, D., 76, 95, 110, *115*
Mortel, K., *63*
Mortimer, J. A., 246, *252*
Moscovitch, M., 50, 52, 54, *64*, *67*
Moss, M., 29, 30, 32, 34, 36, *39*, *40*, *41*
Mueller, T., *233*
Mueser, K. T., *280*
Mufson, E., 33, *39*
Munoz, R., 268, *282*
Munoz, R. F., 264, *283*
Murphy, C., 73, *95*
Murphy, W. E., 86, *92*
Murray, C. L. G., 208, *217*
Murray, E., 29, *40*
Murray, H. A., 148, *169*
Murray, R. M., 225, *235*
Murrell, S. A., 242, 244, *252*, *253*
Musa, D., 103, *116*
Muthén, B. O., 243, *251*
Mutran, E., 178, 180, *189*, *190*
Myers, J. K., *253*
Myerson, J., 87, 88, *92*, 95, 107, *114*

Naeser, M., 28, *38*
Naeser, M. H., 31, *42*
Nalick, J., 240, *252*
Nauta, W. J. H., 48, *64*
Naveh-Benjamin, M., 52, *64*, 83, *90*, *91*
Neal, M., 180, *190*
Neale, M. C., *235*
Nebes, R. D., 47, *64*, *216*
Neimeyer, R. A., 265, *284*
Nelson, C. B., *281*
Nelson, H. E., 49, *64*
Nelson, T. O., 78, *91*
Neuringer, C., 45, *65*
Newell, A., 101, 105, 108, *114*, *115*, *116*
Newman, C. F., 273, *284*
Newman, M. C., 51, *64*
Newman, S. C., 226, *233*
Newman, W. P., III, *203*
Newmann, J. P., 241, 243, *252*, *253*
Neysmith-Roy, J. M., 269, *283*
Nilsson, L.-G., 52, *61*, 73, 74, 75, 94, *95*
Nissen, J. M., 56, *64*
Norcross, J. C., 259, 261, 264, 268, 269,
    271, 272, 273, 275, 277, 280,
    282, *283*, *284*
Nordberg, A., *59*
Nordin, S., 73, *95*

Nores, A., 35, *42*
Norman, D., 26, *42*
Norman, K. A., 80, 86, *95*
Norman, S., 84, 85, *95*
Norman, W. H., 231, *236*
Nowlin, J. B., 208, *216*, *218*
Nussbaum, P. D., 43, *64*
Nyberg, L., 60, *95*

Obara, K., *63*
Obler, L. K., 47, *64*
Obrist, W. D., 47, *62*
O'Conner, B. P., 161, *171*
O'Connor, B. P., *169*
Odenheimer, G., 33, *41*
Oldfield, R. C., 111, *116*
O'Leary, D. H., *204*
O'Leary, D. S., 46, *64*
Olin, J. T., 231, *236*
Olsen, K., *250*
Olshansky, S. J., 208, *216*
Olsson, G., 136, *139*
Orengo, C. A., 232, *236*
Orman, D. T., *236*
Ormel, J., 225, *236*
Orn, H., 226, *233*
Orr, N., *286*
Orrell, M. W., 232, *235*
Osowiecki, D., 53, *66*
Ostfeld, A. M., *250*
Ouimette, P. C., 267, *284*
Overall, J. E., 44, *64*
Owen, A. M., 50, *64*
Owens, J. F., 200, *204*

Padgett, V. P., 268, *282*
Palmon, R., 110, *116*
Palmore, E. B., *216*
Panek, P. E., 56, *64*
Papouchis, N., 259, *284*
Pappas, P., 242, *252*
Parashos, L. A., *60*
Parasuraman, R., 110, *114*
Pardeck, J. A., 268, *284*
Pardeck, J. T., 268, *284*
Pardo, J. V., 56, *64*
Pardo, P. J., 56, *64*
Park, D. C., 50, *61*, 76, 85, 88, 89, *93*,
    95

Young, J. E., 185, *191*
Young, R. C., 226, *233, 242, 249*
Youngren, M. A., 268, *282*

Zacks, R., *97*
Zacks, R. T., 85, 86, *92, 97,* 102, 109, *114, 115*
Zarit, J., *286*
Zarit, S. H., 260, *286*
Zatz, L., 31, *42*
Zavis, D., 77, *94*

Zax, M., 160, *168*
Zeiss, A., *253, 282*
Zeiss, A. M., 243, *254*
Zelinski, E. M., 75, 78, 84, *94, 97,* 213, *218*
Zemansky, M. F., 231, *236*
Zhao, S., *281*
Zola-Morgan, S., 29, 37, *40, 42*
Zorzitto, M., 35, *42*
Zuckerman, E. L., *284*
Zuckerman, M., 153, *172*
Zwahr, M., *95*

SUBJECT INDEX

AA. *See* Alcoholics Anonymous

AARP. *See* American Association of Retired Persons

Access (cognitive), 107
  See also Retrieval

Access to mental health services. *See* Mental health services

Accommodative strategy of coping, 183

Acquisition, 108

Activity theory, 175
  See also Social activity reduction

AD. *See* Alzheimer's disease

Advertisers, 14–16

Affective reserve, and depression, 245–247

Age
  choices in treatment of disease and, 202
  diseases related to, and memory, 27
  role in behavioral medicine, 201–202

Agency for Health Care Policy and Research practice guidelines, 264

Aging, 16–17
  behavioral medicine and, 198–203
  disease vs. health psychology of, 195–196
  distinguished from disease, 209–210
  stereotypes of, 13

Aging revolution
  economic costs of, 3–4
  health and, 207–209
  response of field of psychology to, 4–5
  societal benefits of, 4

AHEAD (Asset and Health Dynamics Among the Oldest-Old) study, 213

Alcoholics Anonymous (AA), 267

Alzheimer's disease (AD), 27
  brain structure changes in, 36–37
  memory changes in, 33–36
  preclinical changes in, 57–58

American Association of Retired Persons (AARP), 14, 267, 268

American Psychiatric Association practice guidelines, 264

American Psychological Association (APA), 5
  Division of Clinical Psychology, 261, 263
  Practice Directorate (1996) CAPP Practitioner Survey, 262
  Presidential Task Force on the Assessment of Age-Consistent Memory Decline and Dementia, 5
  Task Force on Effective Psychological Interventions: A Life Span Perspective, 264
  Task Force on Psychological Intervention Guidelines, 1995, 264

A-system, 102

APA. *See* American Psychological Association

Associative priming, 81

Attention
  See also Working memory
  frontal-system hypothesis and, 55–57
  reduced capacity for, 83–84

Attributional style, and depression, 227–228

Autobiographical accounts, 268–271

Automatic retrieval processes. *See* Familiarity

Autonomic responses, and emotion, 131–133

Autonomy
  concept of, 149–150
  depression and, 230
  relevance in old age and, 160–162, 163–165
  vs. independence, 163–165

Baltimore Longitudinal Study of Aging, 209–210

Beck Depression Inventory, 231

Behavioral medicine
  approach to aging and health in, 195, 197–201

305

intrinsic motivation and, 152–154
self-regulation and, 154–158
Diathesis–stress model, 221, 245
Directed facial actions, 129–130
Disease
　age-related, and memory, 27
　aging process and, 195, 209–210
　behavioral medicine and, 198–199
　incidence vs. prevalence distinction
　　and, 214–215
　measurement of, 215
　psychological processes and, 208–209,
　　213–215
　in women, 199–201
Disease psychology of aging, 195–196
Disengagement, 174–175, 177
Disuse, and memory decline, 75–76
DNMS task. *See* Delayed nonmatching to
　sample task
D-system, 102
Dopamine levels, 33
DRST. *See* Delayed recognition span test
Dysfunctional attitudes model of depres-
　sion, 228

ECA. *See* Epidemiologic Catchment Area
Education
　life expectancy and, 12–13
　memory declines and, 74–75
Elementary Perceiver and Memorizer
　(EPAM), 108
Emotion
　autonomic responses and, 131–133
　balance among emotions and, 136–137
　control of, 137–138
　core system in, 125–127
　directed-facial action studies and, 129–
　　130
　elicitation of, 129–130
　film-based studies and, 130
　"gain or same" theme and, 124–125,
　　135–136
　influence of age on, 121, 123–124,
　　125–128
　learned frames and, 127–128
　"loss" theme and, 124, 135–136
　loss vs. gain and, 125, 130–138
　marital interaction tasks and, 130
　model-based research on, 128–138

model of, 125–128
　relived-emotions studies and, 130
　subjective experience of, 133–134
　visible behavior and, 134
Emotional competency, 137–138
Emotional functioning, 6–7
Empirically validated treatments (EVTs),
　263–266
Encoding strategies, and memory decline,
　76–78
EPAM. *See* Elementary Perceiver and
　Memorizer
Epidemiologic Catchment Area (ECA)
　survey, 240, 243
EVTs. *See* Empirically validated treat-
　ments
Explicit memory, 27, 28, 102
Externally regulated behaviors, 154
Extrinsic motivation, 154–156
Extroversion, 230

Familiarity processes, 79–82
Films, and emotion studies, 130
Focal brain damage, aging deficits com-
　pared with, 43, 44–45
Frontal-system hypothesis, 43, 48–57
　attention and, 55–57
　hippocampal system and, 50–51
　implicit vs. explicit memory and, 54–
　　55
　organizational control processes and,
　　51
　source memory and, 52–53
　temporal order memory and, 52
　visuospatial ability and, 55–57
　working memory and, 49–50
Frontotemporal dementia (FTD), 36
FTD. *See* Frontotemporal dementia

"Gain or same" theme, 124–125
Gene pool, 100
　See also Knowledge
General processing deficit hypotheses,
　82–89
Geriatric Depression Scale, 231
Geriatrics, 195

Halstead–Reitan Battery (HRB), 44–45

HD. *See* Huntington's disease
Health, 7
    See also Behavioral medicine; Depression; Disease; Mental health services
    aging revolution and, 207–209
    depression and, 228, 243–244
    diet and, 17
    memory and, 74
    oxidative stress and, 17
    self-rating of, 210–212
    social activity and, 178–179
    well-being and, 183
    women and, 199–201
Health care system, 225, 261
    See also Mental health services
Health psychology (field), 195–196, 210–216
Healthy Women Study in Pittsburgh, 198, 199–200, 201, 215
Heteronomy, 149
Hippocampal system, and memory, 50–51
HMOs. *See* Managed care
Hopelessness theory of depression, 227
HRB. *See* Halstead–Reitan Battery
Huntington's disease (HD), 34–35

Identification, 156
Immediate memory. *See* Primary memory
Implicit memory, 27, 54–55, 102
Independence
    as term, 150
    vs. autonomy, 163–165
Informant rating, 213–215
Information processing system (IPS), 101
    See also Knowledge
Inhibition failure, 109
Inhibition-deficit hypothesis, 85–87
Institutional lag effects, 12, 14
Integration, 156
Internalization
    concept of, 156–157
    need fulfillment and, 157–158
Intrinsic motivation, 152–154, 160–165
Introjection, 156
IPS. *See* Information processing system
Item priming, 81

Job performance, 103–104

Knowledge
    access and, 107
    acquisition and, 108, 112
    activation of, 112
    computation and, 104–109
    genetic limitation and, 100
    information processing theory and, 101
    job performance and, 103–104
    learning parameters and, 101–102
    persistence and, 108–109
    problem solving and, 102–103
Knowledge acquisition system, 102
Knowledge–computation trade-off, 104–109
Korsakoff's syndrome (KS), 34–35
KS. *See* Korsakoff's syndrome

Lag effects, 12, 14
Language processing
    See also Knowledge
    access and, 107
    memory decline and, 76–78, 84
    vocabulary and, 111
Late-life change, patterns of, 16
Latent semantic analysis model, 108
Learning, parameters of, 101–102
    See also Knowledge
Leukoariosis. *See* Leukoencephalopathy
Leukoencephalopathy (leukoariosis), 49
Life expectancy
    diet and, 17
    education and, 12–13
    increase in average lifespan and, 5–6, 11–13
    positive use of old age and, 13–14
Life goals, 159–160
Life-span developmental psychology, 145–146, 207, 215, 221, 245
Loneliness
    See also Depression
    depression and, 230
    perceived social needs and, 183–184
Longitudinal Study of Generations, 243
Long-term working memory, 103
"Loss" theme, 124

Major depressive disorder (MDD), 226–227

Managed care, 261–263
See also Mental health services

Marketing, 14–16

Marriage
See also Relationship loss and disruption; Widowhood
loneliness and, 184
marital interaction and emotion and, 130

Masked depression, 239

Materialism, 160

Mature market, 14–16

MDD. *See* Major depressive disorder

Mediators of Social Support study, 210–212

Medical Outcomes Study, 224

Medication, and treatment of depression, 231–232

Memory
See also entries for specific types of memory
age-related changes in, 28–31, 73–75
age-related diseases and, 27 (*See also* Alzheimer's disease)
changes in early Alzheimer's, 33–36
for contextual information, 79–81
context utilization and, 79–82
frontal-system hypothesis and, 48–55
frontal vs. hippocampal system and, 50–51
general processing deficit hypotheses and, 82–89
indirect measures of, 81–82
monkey studies on, 29–30
relived emotions and, 130
right-hemisphere hypothesis and, 43, 45–48
speed mediation and, 88–89, 111
strategic processing failures and, 75–78

Mental health. *See* Alzheimer's disease; Depression

Mental health services
See also Behavioral medicine; Psychotherapy
improvement in access to, 248–249
industrialization of, 260–263

Modified Scale for Suicidal Ideation, 231

Monkey studies
brain structure changes and, 31–32
memory changes and, 29–30

Musicians, 110

National Heart, Lung, and Blood Institute, 199, 202

National Institutes of Health, 202
Consensus Development Conference on the Diagnosis and Treatment of Depression in Late Life, 265

National Institutes on Aging (NIA), 200, 202

Need, concept of
See also Psychological needs
biological needs and, 147–148
psychological needs and, 148–149

Neuropsychology, 6, 23
age-related changes and, 28–33, 57–58
Alzheimer's-related changes and, 33–37, 57–58
brain structure changes and, 31–33, 36–37
case of H. M., 25–26
frontal-system hypothesis and, 43, 48–57
memory changes and, 28–31, 33–36
right-hemisphere hypothesis and, 43, 45–48
types of memory and, 26–27

Neuroticism, 230

NIA. *See* National Institutes on Aging

Nondysphoric depression, 247

Nonsocial activities, 184–185

Nursing homes, 161

Optimization, 186

Outcome differences among therapists, 274

Parkinson's disease, 33

Persistance, 108–109

Plasticity, 146, 147, 165–166

Practice, deliberate, 110

Practice guidelines, 263–266

Primary (immediate) memory, 26–27

Priming, 78, 81, 109

Proactive interference, 108
Problem-solving, 102–103
Production system, 108–109
Progressive supranuclear palsy (PSP), 36
PSP. *See* Progressive supranuclear palsy
Psychological needs, 146, 147–152
    See also Autonomy; Competence; Relatedness; Relationship loss and disruption
    characterization of, 149–152
    developmental processes dependent on, 152–158
    internalization and, 157–158
    plasticity and, 165–166
    relevance in old age and, 160–165
    well-being and, 158–160
Psychotherapy, 7
    See also Behavioral medicine; Mental health services
    depression and, 231–232
    EVTs and, 263–266
    impact of managed care on, 262–263
    integration of approaches in, 272–278
    practice guidelines and, 263–266
    self-help methods in, 266–272

Reassurance-seeking, 229
Recall memory, 50–51
    See also Recollection processes
Recent memory, 27
Recognition memory, 50–51, 78
    See also Recollection processes
Recollection processes, 79–82
Registration. *See* Sensory memory
Regulatory styles, 155
Relatedness
    See also Relationship loss and disruption; Social relationships
    concept of, 150
    dependency and, 164
    functioning in old age and, 162–163
    socioemotional selectivity and, 176
Relationship loss and disruption, 177–185
    See also Widowhood
    compensatory responses to, 179–185
    depression and, 244–245
    development of social ties and, 179–182

effects of compensatory responses to, 180–182
redefinition of social needs and, 182–184
rejuvenation of old social ties and, 179–182
theoretical perspectives on, 174–175, 179–185
Relived-emotions memories, 130
Reserve, concept of, 245–247
Residential relocation, 178
Resilience, 203
    See also Reserve, concept of
Resource deficit hypotheses. *See* General processing deficit hypotheses
Response tendencies, 127
Retirement, 12, 178
Retrieval strategies, and memory decline, 76–78
    See also Access
Right-hemisphere hypothesis, 43, 45–48

SCWT. *See* Stroop Color Word Test
SDT. *See* Self-determination theory
Secondary control, 183
Secondary memory, 27, 28
Selection, and life activities, 186
Self-determination theory (SDT), 146
    aging and, 160–165
    basic needs identified in, 149–152
    concept of need and, 147–149
    developmental processes dependent on needs and, 152–158
    well-being and, 158–160
Self-efficacy, and memory, 78
Self-help books, 268–271
Self-help groups, 271–272
Self-help methods, 266–272
Self-rating
    depressive symptoms and, 240–241
    of health, 210–212
Self-regulation, 154–158
Semantic verification latency, 84
Sensory memory, 26
SEPI. *See* Society for the Exploration of Psychotherapy Integration
Short-term therapy, 274
Shyness, 230
Social activity reduction

See also Relationship loss and disruption
age-related, 174–177
compensation for loss and relationship disruption and, 177–185
nonsocial interests and, 185–186
time perspective and, 176–177
Social relationships, 7
See also Relatedness; Relationship loss and disruption; Social activity reduction; Social support
emotional ecology of, 136–137
formation of new friendships and, 179–182
relatedness and, 162–163
selectivity and, 162, 174–177
Social support
depression and, 229, 230, 244–245
depression in a spouse and, 229
disability and, 178–179
relationship loss and, 178–179, 181, 182
Societal rejection, 174–175, 177
Society for the Exploration of Psychotherapy Integration (SEPI), 275
Socioemotional selectivity theory (SST), 162, 175–177
Source amnesia, 52
Source memory, 52–53
Speed of processing
age and, 208, 209
knowledge and, 105–106, 111
memory and, 88–89
SST. See Socioemotional selectivity theory
Stereotypes of aging, 13
Strategic processing, 75–78
Stress
resilience and, 203
theories of depression and, 245–247
Stroop Color Word Test (SCWT), 55
Stroop effect, 55–56
Study of Women's Health Across the Nation (SWAN), 198, 200–201
Subjective experience, and emotion, 133–134
Suicide risk, 225, 231, 248–249
SWAN. See Study of Women's Health Across the Nation

Tachistoscopic half-field method, 47

Technical eclecticism, 275
Temple–Wisconsin Cognitive Vulnerability to Depression project, 227–228
Temporal order memory, 52
Theoretical exposure, 274
Theoretical integration, 275
"Third age," 13
Time perspective, and social activity, 176–177
Training programs, 277–278
Traits, defined, 202
"Treatments of choice," 274, 277
Tripartite model of depression and anxiety, 231

Unconscious processing, 102
University of California, Los Angeles, School of Management, 15

Values, 159–160
Visuospatial ability, 55–57

Wechsler Adult Intelligence Scale (WAIS), 44
Well-being
basic psychological needs and, 158–160
depressed patients and, 224–225
social network losses and, 143
Widowhood
See also Relationship loss and disruption
nonsocial activities and, 185
patterns of support provision and, 180–181
perceived social needs and, 183–184
social network disruptions and, 178
Women. See Healthy Women Study in Pittsburgh; Study of Women's Health Across the Nation
Working memory, 27
See also Attention
frontal-system hypothesis and, 49–50
long-term, 103
reduced capacity for, 84–85
speed and, 88–89

ABOUT THE EDITORS

Sara Honn Qualls, PhD, is professor of psychology and director of the Center on Aging at the University of Colorado at Colorado Springs. Dr. Qualls is a licensed psychologist and offers psychotherapy for older individuals and their families. She has developed a geriatric mental health training clinic in the Colorado Springs community, the CU Aging Center. Her research focuses on marital and family development across the life span and family therapy with later life families. She recently coauthored the book *Aging and Mental Health*. When not working, she enjoys her family, cooking, gardening, and reading.

Norman Abeles, PhD, is professor of psychology and director of the Psychological Clinic at Michigan State University. He was the 1997 president of the American Psychological Association (APA), and the focus of his presidency dealt with various aspects of aging. During his presidency a brochure was published by the APA, *What the Practitioner Should Know About Working With Older Adults*. In addition, the governing body of the APA approved guidelines on the assessment of dementia and cognitive decline. Dr. Abeles and his students are active in research dealing with mood and memory and the concerns of older adults and are currently investigating the comorbidity of anxiety and depression in older adults. Professor Abeles loves to travel and enjoys trying out new restaurants.

DEMCO